Contents

IT Practitioners

Compiled from

IT Practitioners

Series Editor Jenny Lawson

IT Practitioners

By Sharon Yull and Howard Anderson

IT Practitioners

By Geoff Knott and Nick Waites

PEARSON

Custom
Publishing

Edexcel Learning
80 The Strand
London
WC2R 0RL

Part of the Pearson group of companies throughout the world

This Edexcel Learning Edition first published 2005

Compiled from

IT Practitioners
Series Editor Jenny Lawson, published by Heinemann Educational Publishers
ISBN 0 435 45669 5
© Jenny Lawson, Alan Jarvis, K Mary Reid, Andrew Smith, Neela Soomary 2003

IT Practitioners
By Sharon Yull and Howard Anderson, published by Newnes
ISBN 0 7506 56840
© Sharon Yull and Howard Anderson 2002

IT Practitioners
By Geoff Knott and Nick Waites, published by Brancepeth Computer Publications Ltd
ISBN 0 9538848 2 1
© Geoff Knott and Nick Waites 2002

ISBN-13 978 1 84479 586 4
ISBN-10 1 84479 586 1

Printed and bound in Great Britain by Ashford Colour Press, Gosport

Preface

This Study Guide for the BTEC National in IT Practitioners has been published to give you a flavour of the resources that are available to support your course.

A good textbook fulfils many roles. If you have forgotten something your tutor told you in class, you can look it up in the book. If there is something you are not quite sure about or don't quite understand, you can get to grips with it at your own pace and in your own time. If you are unfortunate to miss a class then you can probably read about the topic you missed in the textbook.

Texts also have activities and case studies for you to do so you can see how much you have understood. If you realise you need help, you can then go back to your tutor. Activities also give you the opportunity to practise the skills you will need for assessment.

And most texts will take you beyond their covers! They give you useful websites to explore, they will suggest journals and magazines that will widen your researches and they will have lists of other books to read if you want to explore an issue in greater depth. Make the most of all these leads to broaden your horizons. You will enjoy your course more and you are likely to get better grades.

This Study Guide covers only four of the units you may study for your BTEC National but we hope you will find it useful and will want to make further use of the books that are presented here.

More support for students

There are also other books and support available from the publishers featured in this book.

Heinemann publishes a book for each of the three IT Practitioners Diplomas:

BTEC National IT Practitioners – General	0 435 45669 5
BTEC National IT Practitioners – ICT Systems Support	*0 435 45668 7*
BTEC National IT Practitioners – Software Development	0 435 45667 9

To find out more about Heinemann products, or to order them, go to www.heinemann.co.uk

Newnes website: www.bh.com/companions/0750656840 has answers to the numerical problems in its text as well as other support for IT students.

Brancepeth Computer Publications Ltd also trades as ICT Education Online Ltd and produces eTextbooks for BTEC students.

At *etextbooksonline* students can create their own eTextbooks, tailored specifically to their particular study requirements.

There is a wide range of IT subject modules from which to choose, allowing students to tailor their eTextbook to contain the exact modules needed for a particular course. After having chosen modules and paid the subscription, the modules are combined into a fully integrated study text. Students then have 24/7 Web access to their eTextbook for a full year. Each integrated eTextbook has its own customised, user-friendly interface containing an expandable contents list, a comprehensive index, a search facility and much more.

All of the mandatory units, plus a number of the optional units, for the BTEC National Awards for IT Practitioners are available. Visit www.etextbooksonline.co.uk for more information.

THE SMART WAY TO ACHIEVE YOUR BTEC NATIONAL

We all know people who seem to do well almost effortlessly – at work, at college and even when they are just enjoying themselves. Some of them may be clever or talented but not all of them – so what is their secret? And how does this relate to your BTEC National course?

Every year thousands of students enrol on BTEC National courses. Most are successful and obtain the full qualification. A few do not - either because they don't complete the course or because they don't achieve all the units they need. In some cases students who are successful are still disappointed because they don't achieve the grades they wanted. This can have serious consequences if their offers of a university place are based on the achievement of specific final grades.

The difference between students who don't do as well as they had hoped, and those who do well, rarely has anything to do with brain power. After all, they were all accepted as suitable for the course in the first place. The difference is usually because some work efficiently and some do not. In fact, some students seem to go through college continually making life difficult for themselves – and then wonder why they have problems!

Students who work efficiently are **smart**. The strategies they use mean they are more likely to stay on the course (even if they have problems) and they regularly achieve better grades than other students.

So what do *you* need to do to be smart? First: read this guide. Second: follow it! Third: keep it safely and re-read it at regular intervals to refresh your memory.

The smart way to learn to be smart

1

BTEC National Study Guide: IT Practitioners. See page 293 for order details of individual texts

1

In a nutshell

Working in a smart way means you are more likely to stay on your course, even if you have problems. You will also achieve better grades for doing the same amount of work!

Be smart about your course

There may be quite a gap between your interview at college and the date you start on your BTEC National course. In that time you will probably have forgotten a lot about what you were told. So the first thing to do is to refresh your memory and find out *exactly* what your course entails. You can do this by re-reading college information and also by logging onto the Edexcel website at www.edexcel.org.uk.

- There are three types of BTEC National qualifications and each has a different number of units.

  - The BTEC National Award has 6 units
  - The BTEC National Certificate has 12 units
  - The BTEC National Diploma has 18 units

  You should already know which type of BTEC National you are taking and how long your course lasts. It is useful to find out how many units you will study each term and how many units you will complete each year if you are on a two-year course.

- Every BTEC National qualification has a set number of **core units**. These are the compulsory units which every student must complete. There is also a range of **specialist units** from which you may be able to make a choice. These enable you to study particular areas in more depth. You need to check:

  - the title of each core unit and the topics it contains
  - the title of each specialist unit and the area it covers
  - whether you can choose any specialist units you want, or whether your choice is restricted. This may be because of the structure of the qualification or because your college does not offer the full range.

Knowing all about your course means that you are more likely to choose the most appropriate specialist units for your own needs and interests. You will be more mentally prepared and know what to expect. This also enables you to relate your everyday experiences to the topics you will be learning. You can then be alert to information that relates to your studies, whether you are watching television, reading an article, talking to your family or working – even in a part-time job a few hours a week. The more alert you are to these types of opportunities, the more you will benefit.

In a nutshell

Log on to www.edexcel.org.uk and check the exact content of your BTEC National course. Download the *Student's Guide* for your course which describes the course structure and the unit titles and check with your tutor which you will study each term. Check the course specification to find out the exact content of each unit and check the specialist units that are offered at your college before you select your specialist units. Always be alert to all sources of useful information that relate to your course.

Be smart about resources

A resource is anything that helps you to achieve your goal and so, generally speaking, the more you have the better! You will be introduced to many college resources during your induction, such as the library, the learning resource centre(s) and the computer network. However, most students never actually sit down and list all the resources they have. This is worthwhile because you will probably have far more than you realise. The easiest way is to divide up your resources into different categories and make a list under each heading.

BTEC National Study Guide: IT Practitioners. See page 293 for order details of individual texts

2

There are two aspects to resources. Knowing what they are and using them properly! The main types of resources to consider are given below.

- **Course materials**   These include this Student Guide, all the materials on the Edexcel website, all the information given to you during induction, the textbook(s) you use for particular units, the handouts you are given in class and the notes you make in class. They also include resources you are asked to provide yourself, such as lined paper, folders for storing notes, dividers for sub-dividing topics in your folders, pens, pencils, a hole punch, calculator and a good dictionary. These, by the way, are all essential resources – not optional extras you can scrounge from someone else!

  If you are smart then you always have the right resources for each lesson or session because you get organised in advance. You also file handouts and notes *promptly* in the right place in the right folder so that you can find them again quickly. You have clearly labelled dividers and your notes have a clear heading so that you can find information easily. If you are writing up your own notes from research then you will have made a clear note of the source of your information. How to do this is given in the IVA guide *Ten Steps to a Great IVA*.

- **Equipment and facilities**   These include your college library and learning resource centre(s); the college computer network; other college equipment you can use, such as laptop computers and photocopiers; electronic information resources, such as Internet access, electronic journals and CDs; equipment you have at home – such as a computer; specialist equipment and facilities relevant to your particular course.

  Libraries can be baffling if you don't understand the system used to store books: your college computer network is of limited use if you don't know the difference between an Intranet and the Internet or realise that information is stored on CDs as well as in books. Library and resource centre staff are employed to give you help and advice if you need it – so don't hesitate to ask them! You also need to find the recommended way to transfer data between your home computer and college if your options are limited because of IT security. It is also very important that you check the regulations or guidelines on using the Internet and computers in your college so that you make the most of the equipment without falling foul of any of the rules that apply.

- **People**   These include your tutor(s), specialist staff (such as library and resource centre staff), your employer and your colleagues at work, your relatives and friends who have particular skills or who work in the same area you are studying.

Smart students have their own resources

BTEC National Study Guide: IT Practitioners. See page 293 for order details of individual texts

3

Most people will be keen to help you if you are courteous, well prepared and are not trying to get them to do the work for you! Prepare a list of open questions if you want to interview someone. These are questions that can't be answered with a 'yes' or 'no'. Work down your list but aim to get the person talking freely whilst you make notes. Unless they wander far from the topic you will find out more this way. Then do a final check that you have covered all the areas on your list and get a contact number in case you need to speak to them again. Don't forget to say thank you – and try not to overuse one particular person.

One word of warning! Be careful about asking for help from a friend who has already done the same course and *never* be tempted to borrow their assignments. Tutors can soon tell if the work isn't in your own personal style, or if it varies in style. In addition, assignments are normally changed each year and answers are expected to be up-to-date, so an answer from a previous year is unlikely to be of much use.

- **Your own skills and abilities**   Obviously if you have excellent IT skills then you will produce your written assignments more easily. You will also be better at researching online if you know and understand how to use the Internet and have included useful sites in your Favourites list. Other vital skills include being able to recognise and extract key information from a book, being able to summarise and able to type up your work relatively quickly and accurately. As you will see as you work through this Guide being well-organised and using your time wisely are also invaluable skills and can make all the difference to your final grades.

You can assess yourself as you read this Guide by listing those areas in which you are weak and need to improve your skills. Then talk to your tutor about the best way to do this.

In a nutshell

Resources are vital because they help you to succeed. If you list your resources you may find there are more than you think. Then you must use them wisely. This includes storing handouts safely and thanking people who help you. You also need to develop skills and abilities which will help you to work more easily – such as improving your Internet and typing skills.

Be smart about time

Some weeks you may find you have very little to do – so you can manage your workload easily. Then everything changes. In a short period of time you seem to be overwhelmed with work to do. If you are unlucky, this will coincide with a time when you also have family, personal or work commitments as well. So – how do you juggle everything and still stay in control?

There are several skills you need to be able to do this.

- **Record important dates in advance**   Keep a homework diary or (even better) a wall chart and mark all key dates in colour. You can devise your own system but it is useful to enter assignment review dates with your tutor in one colour and final deadline dates in another. Keep your chart up-to-date by adding any new dates promptly every time you are given another task or assignment. This gives you prior warning when important dates are looming and, if nothing else, stops you from planning a heavy social week for the same time!

- **Prioritise your work**   This means doing the most important and urgent task first. This is normally the task or assignment with the nearest deadline. The exception is when you have to allow for the availability of other people or other resources. For example, if you have two assignments to do and one involves interviewing three people, it is sensible to schedule the interviews first. If you need to send off for information it is also sensible to do this promptly, to allow plenty of time for it to arrive. It also means allowing enough time to print out your assignment well before the deadline – unless you are prepared to join the long queues of students who have the same deadline as you and who are all trying to print out their work at the last minute!

- **Plan your work**   This means analysing each task and estimating how long it will take. For example, you may estimate that an assignment will take you one hour to plan, six hours to research, four hours to type up

BTEC National Study Guide: IT Practitioners. See page 293 for order details of individual texts

4

Be smart about time

and one hour to check. In this case you need *at least* twelve hours to do the work. If you are sensible you will allow a little more, in case you encounter any problems or difficulties. It is wise to schedule fixed times to work and then plan to give yourself time off when you have completed a task or are 'between' tasks or assignments.

- **Regularly review your progress**   You need to check regularly that you are on schedule. It is easy to spend much longer than you think on some tasks – either because you get bogged down or because you become too absorbed. This will mean you have to do the rest of the work in a rush and this may affect your grade.

- **Be smart – but be kind to yourself too!**   If you are over-conscientious you may be tempted to burn the midnight oil to keep up-to-date. This isn't wise on a regular basis because no-one does their best work when they are over-tired. In this case remember to *target* your efforts where they will count most – rather than try to have everything perfect. Schedule in some breaks and relaxation time too; you are allowed a treat from time to time! If your problem is just the opposite – and you struggle to stay focused if you're not in the mood for work – then you need to practise a little more self-discipline. One trick is to find an aspect of a task that you will find easy or really enjoy. Then start with this to get yourself going. Aim to complete a fixed amount of work before you give yourself a small reward – such as a fifteen-minute break or a bar of chocolate!

You can find more detailed information on planning your work and reviewing your progress in the IVA Guide *Ten Steps to a Great IVA*.

BTEC National Study Guide: IT Practitioners. See page 293 for order details of individual texts

We all need a treat from time to time

In a nutshell

Your workload may be unpredictable and some weeks will be worse than others. You will cope better if you note down all key dates in advance, prioritise properly, plan realistically the time work will take and regularly review your progress. Target your efforts so that you can take sensible breaks and start with tasks you enjoy to motivate yourself.

Be smart about assignments

Assignments are the main method of assessment on all BTEC National courses. Edexcel specifies the exact **assessment criteria** for each unit in a grid. In plain English, this is the list of skills and knowledge you must demonstrate to achieve a pass, merit or distinction. You will find these in your course specification immediately after the content of each unit.

There are two types of assignments.

- There are those that are **internally set**. In this case the assignments are set and marked by your own tutors. Each assignment will include tasks and activities that enable you to produce evidence directly linked to the assessment criteria for a particular unit. Most units have internally set and assessed assignments.

- Alternatively there are **externally set** assignments. In this case an **Integrated Vocational Assignment (IVA)** is set by Edexcel.

In both cases Edexcel checks that centres are assessing assignments correctly and that all centres have the same standards.

Many people panic at the thought of assignments, but being smart means you are well-prepared and won't break any golden rules!

- Always check the assessment criteria grid for the unit in advance, so that you know what to expect.

- The grid is divided into three main columns which state what you must do to achieve a pass, a merit and a distinction grade. The main word, which tells you what to do, is called a **command word**. You must understand the command word *and obey it* to obtain a specific grade. This is dealt with in more detail in the next section.

- Read the assignment brief *thoroughly* and query anything you do not understand with your tutor.

- Check those tasks which must be all your own work and which (if any) you will complete as a member of a group. If you are asked to do any work as a member of a team then you must always identify your own individual contribution to each task.

BTEC National Study Guide: IT Practitioners. See page 293 for order details of individual texts

6

- *Always* remember that plagiarism (copying someone else's work) is an extremely serious offence and will result in disciplinary action. *Never* be tempted to share your work (or your disks or CDs) with anyone else and don't ask to borrow theirs!

- Check the other rules that apply. These will include
  - whether you can discuss your research or draft answers with your tutor – and when you must do this
  - the college-set deadline date for submission – and the penalties for handing in work late (this might mean your assignment not being assessed)
  - what to do if you are absent when the assignment is due or have a serious personal problem which affects your ability to complete the work on time. There is normally an official procedure for obtaining an extension. This is only when mitigating circumstances apply and can't be used just because you fail to plan properly!

- Make sure you answer every question fully and present your information according to the instructions. You may, for instance, have to provide information in a table or report rather than simply answering questions. You will get a lower grade if you ignore important presentation instructions.

In a nutshell

The assessment criteria grid for each unit states what you must provide evidence against to achieve a pass, merit or distinction grade. It is important that you read and understand this, as well as the assignment brief, and obey all the instructions. Check you know any other rules that apply, such as how to apply for an extension to the deadline if you have a serious personal problem. Then answer the questions fully and present the work as required.

Sadly, over-sleeping doesn't count as a serious personal problem

BTEC National Study Guide: IT Practitioners. See page 293 for order details of individual texts

7

Be smart about command words

Command words are used to specify how a question must be answered, eg 'describe', 'explain' or 'analyse'. These words are often related to the level of answer required. You will therefore find these command words in the assessment grid and you will usually see, for example, that 'describe' will get you a pass grade. However, you would need to do more than give a straightforward description to get a merit or distinction grade.

Many students don't get the grades they should for an assignment because they do not realise the difference between these words. Instead of applying their knowledge (for a merit grade) they simply give a brief explanation or a list. Just listing *more* facts will not improve your grade; you must show you can use your knowledge.

The chart below shows you what is usually required when you see a particular command word. You can use this, and the answers below, to identify the difference between the types of answers required for each grade. Remember these are just *examples* of acceptable answers to help you. The exact response required will often depend upon the way a question is worded so check with your tutor if you are unsure what it is you have to do.

To obtain a pass grade you must prove your knowledge and understanding by giving the relevant facts clearly and concisely.	
If it says:	This means you should:
Describe	Give a clear description that includes all the relevant features. You might want to think of this as 'painting a picture in words'.
Define	Clearly explain what a particular term means and give an example, if appropriate, to show what you mean.
Design*	Create a plan, proposal or outline to illustrate a straightforward concept or idea.
Explain how/why	Set out in detail the meaning of something, with reasons. This is more difficult than 'describing' or 'listing' so it can often help to give an example to show what you mean. Start by introducing the topic and then give the 'how' or 'why'.
Identify	Point out (ie choose the right one) or give a list of the main features.
Illustrate	Include examples or a diagram to show what you mean.
Interpret	Define or explain the meaning of something.
List	Provide the information in a list, rather than in continuous writing.
Outline	Write a clear description but not a detailed one.
Plan	Work out and explain how you would carry out a task or activity.
State	Write a clear and full account.
Summarise	Write down the main points or essential features.

Q   Describe the Apple iPod.

Below is an example answer that would achieve a pass grade.

A   The Apple iPod is a digital player on which music can be stored and played without the need for CDs or tapes. Music is stored on an iPod by transferring MP3 music files that have been downloaded from the Internet or copied from a CD. The Apple iPod with the largest capacity will store up to 10,000 songs and costs about £420. A mini version is much cheaper but stores far fewer – about 1,000 – for about £180. Both have been praised in reviews for their excellent sound quality, ease of use and stylish design.

* You may also find the word 'design' at merit level, as you will see below.

BTEC National Study Guide: IT Practitioners. See page 293 for order details of individual texts

8

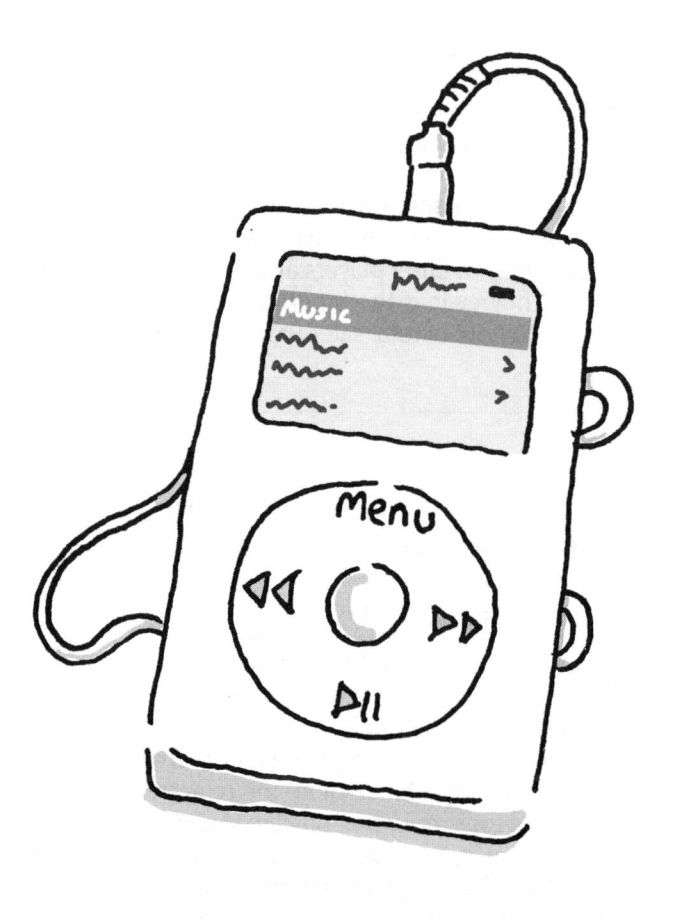

To obtain a merit grade you must prove you can apply your knowledge in a specific way.	
If it says:	This means you should:
Analyse	Identify separate factors, say how they are related and how each one contributes to the topic. This is one step up from the explanation you gave at pass level.
Compare/contrast	Identify the main factors that apply in two or more situations and explain the similarities and differences or advantages and disadvantages.
Demonstrate	Provide several relevant examples or related evidence which clearly support the arguments you are making. If you are doing a practical subject, this might be, e.g. showing your computer or coaching skills.
Design	Create a plan, proposal or outline to illustrate a relatively complex concept or idea.
Assess	Give careful consideration to all the factors or events that apply and identify which are the most important and relevant.
Explain in detail	Provide details and give reasons and/or evidence to clearly support the argument you are making.
how/why Justify	Give reasons or evidence to support your opinion or view to show how you arrived at these conclusions.

Q   Analyse why Apple iPods are so popular.

Below is an example answer that would achieve a merit grade.

A   Apple is one of several brands of MP3 players on the market. Rivals include the iAudio player and the Sony net walkman. Some rivals are cheaper than the iPod, so price is not the main reason for Apple iPod popularity. The iPod took off because its stylish design looked so good and there was some great

BTEC National Study Guide: IT Practitioners. See page 293 for order details of individual texts

9

advertising that turned it into the 'must have' item as early as Christmas 2003. It was also praised more by reviewers than other digital players. The Apple iPod stores music on a moving hard disk whereas some players store it on computer chips. Hard disk players have better sound quality and greater storage capacity. The Apple is also easy to use. Apple then developed the brand by adding accessories and introducing the mini iPod which comes in five different colours. Apple is also popular because it was the first to develop a portable MP3 player and supports its customers with its iTunes music store online. Downloads from the site aren't compatible with other players and so iPod users are tied to the iTunes site. Many people have criticised this. Apple, however, is the brand that is cool to own – so much so that over 10 million Apple iPods were sold in 2004 out of total sales worldwide of between 20 and 25 million portable music players.

To obtain a distinction grade you must prove you can make a reasoned judgement based on evidence.

If it says:	This means you should:
Appraise	Consider the plus and minus points and give a reasoned judgement
Assess	Must make a judgement on the importance of something. It is similar to 'evaluate' (see below).
Comment critically	Give your view after you have considered all the evidence. In particular decide the importance of all the relevant positive *and* negative aspects.
Criticise	Review a topic or issue objectively and weigh up both plus and minus points before making a decision. It is similar to 'comment critically'.
Draw conclusions	Use the evidence you have provided to reach a reasoned judgement.
Evaluate	Review the information and then bring it together to form a conclusion. Give evidence for each of your views or statements.
Evaluate critically	Decide the degree to which a statement is true or the importance or value of something by reviewing the information. Include precise and detailed information and assess possible alternatives, bearing in mind their strengths and weaknesses if they were applied instead.

Q   Evaluate the effect of Apple iPods on the music industry.

An example answer that would achieve a distinction grade:

A   Apple iPods – together with other digital music players – have helped to give the music industry a new lease of life. In the late 1990s music companies were alarmed that the Internet could ruin their business because of illegal file sharing and they forced the Napster website to close down. This site had allowed music fans to log on and exchange songs free of charge. Music companies also took legal action against private individuals. A famous case was of an American girl of 12 whose mother had to pay $2,000 in fines, which frightened other parents. However, the development of portable digital music players has boosted the popularity of legal download sites such as Apple iTunes, MyCokeMusic and the new Napster subscription service, which sell tracks for about 80p each. These enable music fans to select and store only the tracks they want to hear, rather than have to spend money on a CD album that may contain many tracks they don't want. In Britain in 2004, 5.7 million download tracks were sold compared with virtually none in 2003 and sales are predicted to double in 2005. This growth is being fuelled by global sales of portable music players – the most popular of which is the Apple iPod. The music industry is taking advantage of the trend by pre-releasing tracks online and there is now an official download chart. By 2009, experts predict that the digital market could be worth 25% of total music sales, compared to a mere 1.5% in late 2004. There is no doubt that the Apple iPod, and other portable digital music players, have been a major factor in this huge growth rate.

BTEC National Study Guide: IT Practitioners. See page 293 for order details of individual texts

10

In a nutshell

The assessment criteria grid for each unit states what you must know to get a pass, merit or distinction grade. It is vital that you understand the command words used and obey them or you will not achieve the best grade possible.

Be smart about your grades

On the Edexcel website you can download a form called *Recording Your Achievement*. This enables you to record the grade for each unit you complete. The form also tells you how many points you achieve for gaining a Pass, Merit or Distinction for each unit and how these are added together to obtain your final grade(s). You obtain *one* final grade if you are taking a BTEC National Award, *two* final grades if you are taking a BTEC National Certificate and *three* final grades if you are taking a BTEC National Diploma.

This is very important information, because it helps you to plan where to target your efforts, particularly later in the course.

- Remember that you will obtain more overall points if you divide up your time so that you put the most effort and work into areas where you are weak, rather than spending the most time on assignments you enjoy or find easy! Although it is tempting to keep working on something you like doing, even when you have already done a good job, the danger is that you then don't do so well in other assignments that you have neglected or where you have cut corners. The secret is to put in the right amount of effort in *every* assignment to get the grade you need. For topics you find easy, this may mean you need to spend less time on the assignment than for work you find difficult – despite the fact that you may be tempted to do exactly the opposite! If you do consistently well in all your assignments you will find that this results in higher overall grades than if you do very well in some but poorly in others.

- Keeping your grade profile up-to-date and discussing it with your tutor at regular intervals is an excellent way of keeping yourself on track throughout the course.

In a nutshell

If you are smart you will plan to manage your grades and your overall profile. Do this by recording your grades, spending more time on important or difficult assessments and discussing your profile, as you go, with your tutor.

Be smart at work or on work experience

On some BTEC National courses there is a vocational element and you will need evidence from work or work experience to prove your skills and abilities. In this case your tutor will give you a logbook to keep. On other courses, workplace evidence is not essential but the knowledge and practical experience you gain is still extremely useful, if not invaluable. This only applies, of course, if you are smart enough to recognise the opportunities that occur. Relevant events are likely to include:

- your induction and any subsequent training courses you are asked to attend – even if these are only very short, work-based sessions

- any performance reviews or appraisals you have with your supervisor or boss

- your dealings with customers of the organisation – particularly if you had to respond to a difficult enquiry or solve a problem.

BTEC National Study Guide: IT Practitioners. See page 293 for order details of individual texts

11

Your tutor will tell you how to get a witness statement

- the rules, regulations or guidelines that you must follow. You should think about why these have been put in place as well as the consequences of not abiding by them
- your own duties and specific areas of responsibility
- your relationships with your colleagues and how you resolve any problems or difficulties that occur
- skills you have learned or developed by being at work – from time keeping to achieving targets.

If you have to provide formal evidence then one method is to ask your manager, supervisor or colleagues for a **witness statement.** This is a formal document that confirms something you have done and when you did it. Your tutor will give you a form for this. It is also useful to keep your own work diary and to jot down important things that happen that you could use as evidence in current or future assignments to support your arguments for a merit or distinction grade question.

In a nutshell

Work experience may be an essential part of your BTEC National course. Even if it is not, you will gain many useful skills at work that can help you to achieve your award. Make a note of all key events and activities you are involved in. If you need formal evidence, ask your boss for a witness statement.

BTEC National Study Guide: IT Practitioners. See page 293 for order details of individual texts

12

Be smart about key skills

Key skills are so-called because they are considered invaluable to everyone at work. Most BTEC National students study for a key skills award and in this case the majority of key skills will often be integrated into your main programme of study. This not only helps you to improve your skills, it also means you have the potential to achieve additional points when you submit your UCAS application. Unfortunately not all students complete their key skills awards and so fail to achieve their maximum points score. This is less likely to happen if you are smart and get key skills to work for you, and don't simply see them as more work to do!

- Always check the tracking sheet you are given with your assignments to see which key skills are covered by that particular piece of work.

- Take advantage of any specific classes for key skills, particularly Application of Number, unless you have passed a GCSE Maths examination that exempts you. Otherwise use the classes to improve your abilities.

- There are dozens of benefits if you can communicate effectively and there are almost endless opportunities for practice. You communicate every day – with your friends, family, tutor, boss and colleagues at work – in a variety of different ways. You spend time writing notes in class and writing up researched information. You prepare written documents for your assignments. You work with your classmates when you are doing role-plays or preparing a presentation. If you communicate effectively you will be able to make better presentations, ask the right questions when you are interviewing and write clearer answers to your assignments. You will then gain better grades for your BTEC National as well as your key skills award!

- Information technology is a crucial tool for completing work related tasks. If you develop your word processing skills and your Internet research skills you will produce better, more professional assignments more quickly and more easily. If you intend to continue studying you will find that good IT skills are invaluable at university. If you hope to start working in business when you leave your course then you can expect your future employer to take a keen interest in your IT abilities.

Make key skills work for you

BTEC National Study Guide: IT Practitioners. See page 293 for order details of individual texts

13

- The 'wider' key skills are Improving own learning and performance, Working with others and Problem solving. These are likely to be required in many of your assignments. You will also demonstrate these skills if you go to work or are on work experience. Talk to your tutor about how you can use evidence from the workplace to help you to achieve your key skills award.

In a nutshell

There are many advantages to developing your key skills and achieving your key skills award. You will find this easier if you take advantage of all the opportunities you can to develop your key skills and use naturally occurring situations to provide much of the evidence.

Be smart if you have a problem

Many students have personal problems when they are studying. Knowing what to do in this situation makes all the difference. It also means you have one less thing to worry about when life is going wrong.

- Check your college induction information carefully. This should give you detailed information about the people you can talk to if you have a problem. Normally your personal tutor will be the first person on your list but there will be other people available, too, in case your tutor is absent or if you would prefer to talk to someone else in confidence.
- If you cannot find the information you want, ask a tutor you like and trust for advice – or visit the central student support area instead and ask there.
- All colleges have sets of procedures to cover different events. These include the following.
  - **The appeals procedure**   This tells you what to do if you feel that an assignment has been unfairly marked. The obvious first step in this situation is to ask your tutor to explain the grade you have been given, and how this links with the assessment grid. Do this before you think of taking formal action. If you are unhappy with the tutor's explanation then talk to your personal tutor. If you are still unhappy then you have the right to make a formal appeal.
  - **Student complaint procedures**   This is normally the 'last resort' for a student and is only used when a major worry or concern can't be resolved informally. You therefore have the right to make an official complaint but should only do so when you have exhausted all the other avenues open to you. It is not normally used for trivial matters.
  - **Student disciplinary procedures**   This tells you what to expect if you are disciplined for any reason. Although it is wise to avoid trouble, if you do break a rule then it is sensible to read these procedures carefully. Always remember that an honest confession and an apology will normally count in your favour, so if you do have this type of problem, don't be tempted to make matters worse by being devious.
- All colleges will arrange confidential counselling for you if you have a serious personal problem. The counsellor is a trained expert, not a member of the teaching staff. Without giving away any personal details, your counsellor can ensure that you receive the additional support you need from the teaching team – such as more time for an assignment or time off for personal commitments.
- *Never* be tempted to keep a serious worry or problem to yourself. In this situation your concentration is affected, your time is more precious and allowance must be made for this. Being smart about the way you handle problems will enable you to stay on the course and means the problems will have far less impact on your final grades.

In a nutshell

All colleges have a wide range of support mechanisms and procedures in place that are invoked when problems occur. Take advantage of all the help you can get if you have serious personal difficulties. This can be used to support you on the course until the problem passes and your life is nearer to normal again.

BTEC National Study Guide: IT Practitioners. See page 293 for order details of individual texts

14

BTEC National Study Guide: IT Practitioners. See page 293 for order details of individual texts

15

Most computers in the marketplace are binary. There are analogue machines that are quite different, and these will not be considered here.

Binary machines use logic circuits, and the purpose of this unit is to introduce binary logic, simple binary circuits and their assembly into devices. It is not the intention to look at the practical or economic issues involved in designing digital circuits.

2.1 Binary logic

Logic works with the idea of a **proposition**. A proposition is a statement that is either **true** or **false**; it can have no other value. The statement or proposition 'You are sitting down' may or may not be true as you read this book, so it has the value **true** or **false**. Notice it is not a question; it is not 'Are you sitting down?', which could have a range of answers such as yes, no, I will in a moment etc. For the purposes of logic, the proposition 'You are sitting down' is either true or it is not, there are no other possibilities.

It is usual to represent the value **true** as a '1' and the value **false** as a '0'. In an electronic circuit, this may mean 'on' or 'off', or it may mean 3 volts for true and 0 volts for false etc.

To save writing long statements to represent a proposition, it is normal to use the letters A, B, C etc. For example, the proposition 'You are sitting down' could therefore be represented as A, and the proposition 'You feel warm' by B. Both A and B could be true, which would mean you are sitting down and feeling warm. There are four possible combinations of true and false in this case:

1. You are not sitting down   AND   you are not feeling warm
2. You are not sitting down   AND   you are feeling warm
3. You are sitting down   AND   you are not feeling warm
4. You are sitting down   AND   You are feeling warm.

A more normal representation would be to write:

A = the proposition 'You are sitting down'
B = the proposition 'You are feeling warm'

and then to put them in a **truth table**:

BTEC National Study Guide: IT Practitioners. See page 293 for order details of individual texts

16

A	B	R
0	0	0
0	1	0
1	0	0
1	1	1

where 1 = true, 0 = false. This table represents the same logic values as the list above. It is the truth table for the **logical AND function**, so named because the question being asked is: 'is A true AND is B true'. The column marked R is the resultant, i.e. the result of the logic. As you can see, only one line shows a 1, when A = 1 AND B = 1.

In more formal terms, the truth table here shows the AND logic function. As there are two propositions, there are $2^2 = 4$ lines in the truth table. If there were three propositions, there would be $2^3 = 8$ lines. The following table shows the resultants for the proposition 'A = true AND B = true AND C = true'; a three-input AND function:

A	B	C	R
0	0	0	0
0	0	1	0
0	1	0	0
0	1	1	0
1	0	0	0
1	0	1	0
1	1	0	0
1	1	1	1

This shows all the possible combinations of the propositions, A, B and C, and shows R = 1 only when all three propositions (A, B and C) are true.

Some of the assembly language files in this section can be downloaded from http://www.bh.com/companions/0750656840.

Other logic functions

We could ask some different questions, for example: Is A true OR is B true?

This is represented in the truth table of the **logical OR function**:

Question 2.1

How many lines would be in a truth table with eight propositions?

Answer

There would be $2^8 = 256$ lines, a fact that will be used a little later on.

BTEC National Study Guide: IT Practitioners. See page 293 for order details of individual texts

17

A	B	R
0	0	0
0	1	1
1	0	1
1	1	1

This shows true when A = true OR B = true, or when they are both true.

Sometimes it is necessary to reverse or invert logic. In this case we could say NOT A – so if A = 1, NOT A will = 0, and vice versa. This is written as $\overline{A}$. The bar over the A means 'invert the value of A', and this is usually described as NOT A.

Table 2.1 shows a truth table with all the possible resultants of logical functions using two propositions. As there are four lines in the truth table, there are $2^4 = 16$ possible combinations. Some of these combinations have names such as AND or Exclusive OR. Notice that if you rotate the table 90° anticlockwise, the resultants appear to show binary numbers from the bottom, starting at 0000.

Table 2.1   *Truth table for two propositions*

A	B	NOT A $\overline{A}$	NOT B $\overline{B}$	A AND B $A \bullet B$				A XOR B $A \oplus B$	A OR B $A + B$	A NOR B $\overline{A+B}$						A NAND B $\overline{A \bullet B}$	
0	0	1	1	0	0	0 0 0 0		0	0	1	1 1 1 1 1					1	1
0	1	1	0	0	0	0 0 1 1		1	1	0	0 0 0 1 1					1	1
1	0	0	1	0	0	1 1 0 0		1	1	0	0 1 1 0 0					1	1
1	1	0	0	0	1	0 1 0 1		0	1	0	1 0 1 0 1					0	1

The actual functions in logic have some strange symbols. The OR function is often written as A + B (but the + sign does not mean addition!):

A + B is called A OR B
A $\bullet$ B is called A AND B

A $\oplus$ B is called A XOR B, which is short for A Exclusive OR B. This function is nearly the same as A OR B; it differs only when A = 1 and B = 1.

$\overline{A + B}$ is called NOR, short for NOT OR
$\overline{A \bullet B}$ is called NAND, short for NOT AND

Other columns can be generated using a combination of logic functions. For instance, one row shows the function A $\bullet$ $\overline{B}$; it is only true when A = 1 and $\overline{B}$ = 1. The row headed A NOR B can be generated from inverting the previous row, giving $\overline{A + B}$ or NOT(A OR B).

BTEC National Study Guide: IT Practitioners. See page 293 for order details of individual texts

18

Care must be taken with NOT functions! You may have heard the London slang phrase 'I ain't done nothing', meaning 'I ain't done anything'. Since 'I ain't done nothing' contains a NOT function (ain't), the phrase actually means 'I have done **something**'. In logic terms, this is like writing NOT NOT A, which in fact is just A, $\overline{\overline{A}} = A$.

In a similar way, you can show that $A \bullet B = \overline{\overline{A} + \overline{B}}$, something that is called **DeMorgan's Law** which forms part of **Boolean algebra**. A detailed treatment of Boolean algebra is outside the requirements of this course.

George Boole

George Boole was the son of a shoemaker and was born in Lincoln, England, on 2 November 1815. He published *The Mathematical Analysis of Logic* in 1847, which introduced his early ideas on symbolic logic. In 1849 he was appointed Professor of Mathematics at Queen's College in Cork, Ireland, where he remained for the rest of his life. Boole published *An Investigation of the Laws of Thought, on Which Are Founded the Mathematical Theories of Logic and Probabilities* in 1854, which extended his previous work and contained much of what is now called Boolean Algebra.

2.2 Logic gates

Truth tables and Boolean algebra are mathematical descriptions of logic. To make a physical device that performs these logical functions, semiconductors are used to make logic gates. In computers these work on a low voltage, usually in the range of about 3–5 volts, and will perform at high speed with a low power consumption.

Circuits are then made using large numbers of logic gates to make useful devices. The next section will show in principle how this is done whilst ignoring some practical electronic details; it is not the intention of this book to provide practical electronic data.

In order to draw circuits, use is made of symbols to represent each gate. As is often the case in computing, there are several different 'standard' symbols. Table 2.2 shows the British Standard symbols to BS3939 and the more common American ones.

Using the more common American symbols, we can represent the function $A \bullet B$ (Figure 2.1). R is the resultant.

Useful devices can be made from several logic gates and the behaviour of the whole circuit described using a truth table. For example, Figure 2.2 shows a simple three-gate circuit.

Here we have three inputs, labelled A, B and C. To make filling in the truth table easier, the intermediate parts are labelled D and E.

To construct the truth table, first calculate the number of lines required. As there are three inputs, there will be $2^3 = 8$ lines. Now fill in all the possible combinations of A, B and C. The order from top to bottom is not important, but it is common to set them out counting in binary from the top as shown here:

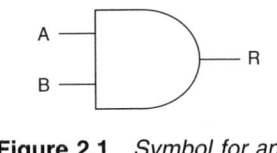

Figure 2.1 *Symbol for an AND gate*

BTEC National Study Guide: IT Practitioners. See page 293 for order details of individual texts

19

A	B	C	D	E	R
0	0	0			
0	0	1			
0	1	0			
0	1	1			
1	0	0			
1	0	1			
1	1	0			
1	1	1			

Table 2.2   *British and US logic symbols*

Logic function	Truth table			Circuit symbols to BS3939	Circuit symbols (US)
NOT	A	R			
	0	1		1	
	1	0			
OR	A	B	R		
	0	0	0	1	
	0	1	1		
	1	0	1		
	1	1	1		
NOR	A	B	R		
	0	0	1	1	
	0	1	0		
	1	0	0		
	1	1	0		
AND	A	B	R		
	0	0	0	&	
	0	1	0		
	1	0	0		
	1	1	1		
NAND	A	B	R		
	0	0	1	&	
	0	1	0		
	1	0	0		
	1	1	0		
XOR	A	B	R		
	0	0	0	=1	
	0	1	1		
	1	0	1		
	1	1	0		

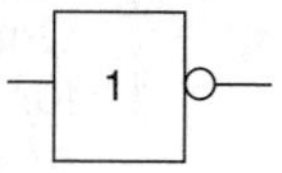

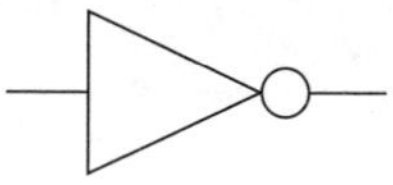

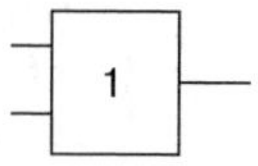

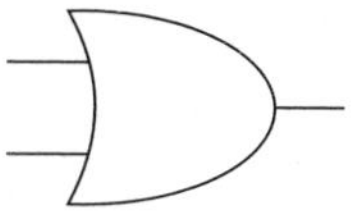

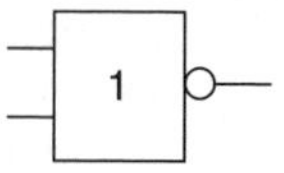

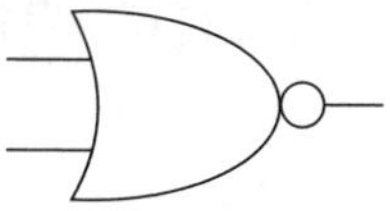

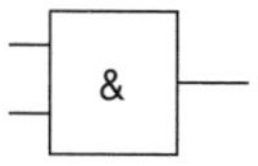

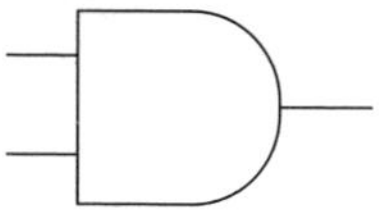

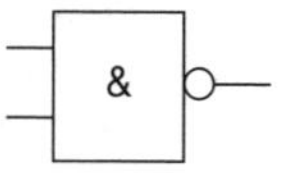

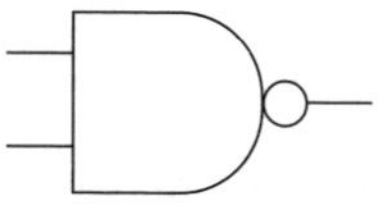

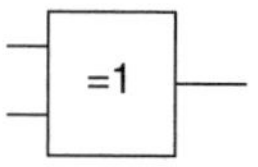

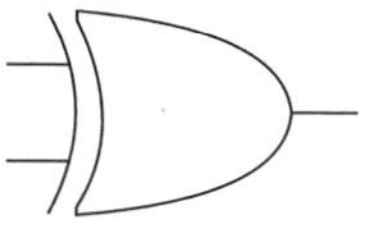

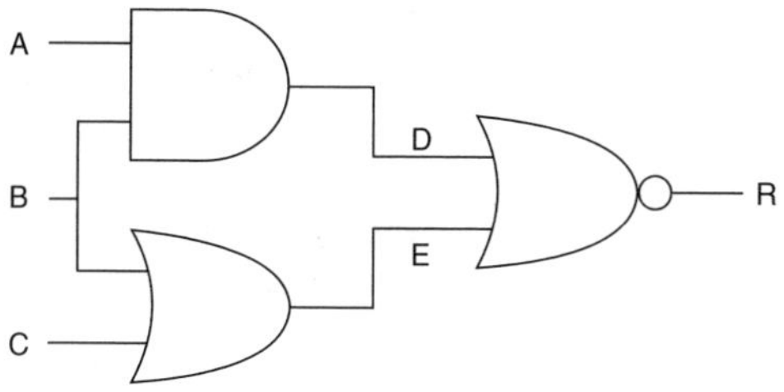

Figure 2.2   *Simple three-gate circuit (a)*

BTEC National Study Guide: IT Practitioners. See page 293 for order details of individual texts

20

Next, fill the column for proposition D, which is given by A • B, i.e. there will only be a 1 when both A AND B are 1. At this stage, you need only to consider the AND gate with inputs A and B:

A	B	C	D	E	R
0	0	0	0		
0	0	1	0		
0	1	0	0		
0	1	1	0		
1	0	0	0		
1	0	1	0		
1	1	0	1		
1	1	1	1		

Now fill in the column for proposition E, which is given by B + C; again, you need only consider the OR gate with inputs B and C:

A	B	C	D	E	R
0	0	0	0	0	
0	0	1	0	1	
0	1	0	0	1	
0	1	1	0	1	
1	0	0	0	0	
1	0	1	0	1	
1	1	0	1	1	
1	1	1	1	1	

Finally, fill in the column for the resultant, given by D NOR E:

A	B	C	D	E	R
0	0	0	0	0	1
0	0	1	0	1	0
0	1	0	0	1	0
0	1	1	0	1	0
1	0	0	0	0	1
1	0	1	0	1	0
1	1	0	1	1	0
1	1	1	1	1	0

The resultant column, R, shows that when A = 1, B = 0 and C = 0, the circuit will output a 1 etc. We could now write the logic function for this circuit:

BTEC National Study Guide: IT Practitioners. See page 293 for order details of individual texts

21

1. First, write down the logic for the 2 gates on the left: (A • B) (B + C)
2. Now connect them together with the NOR function, the gate on the right: (A • B) NOR (B + C) written as $\overline{(A \bullet B) + (B + C)}$

Notice that neither D nor E appear in the completed function; their use was simply to make the truth table easier to write.

Figure 2.3 provides a further example.

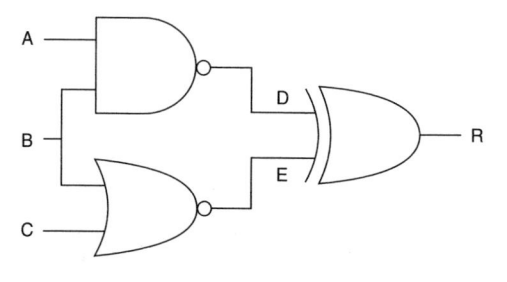

Figure 2.3   *Simple three-gate circuit (b)*

Write out the truth table and logic function for the circuit.

Now, construct the truth table in the same manner as above, column by column, to give:

A	B	C	D	E	R
0	0	0	1	1	0
0	0	1	1	0	1
0	1	0	0	0	0
0	1	1	0	0	0
1	0	0	0	1	1
1	0	1	0	0	0
1	1	0	0	0	0
1	1	1	0	0	0

The logic function = (A NAND B) XOR (B NOR C), written as $\overline{(A \bullet B)} \oplus \overline{(B + C)}$.

Exercise 2.1

Write the truth table and logic function for the circuits below. Remember, if a circuit has four inputs it will have $2^4 = 16$ lines in the table. The three-input OR gate gives an output of 1 if any of the three inputs are 1; otherwise it will output a 0 just like a two-input OR gate. The answers are in Appendix A to this unit.

BTEC National Study Guide: IT Practitioners. See page 293 for order details of individual texts

22

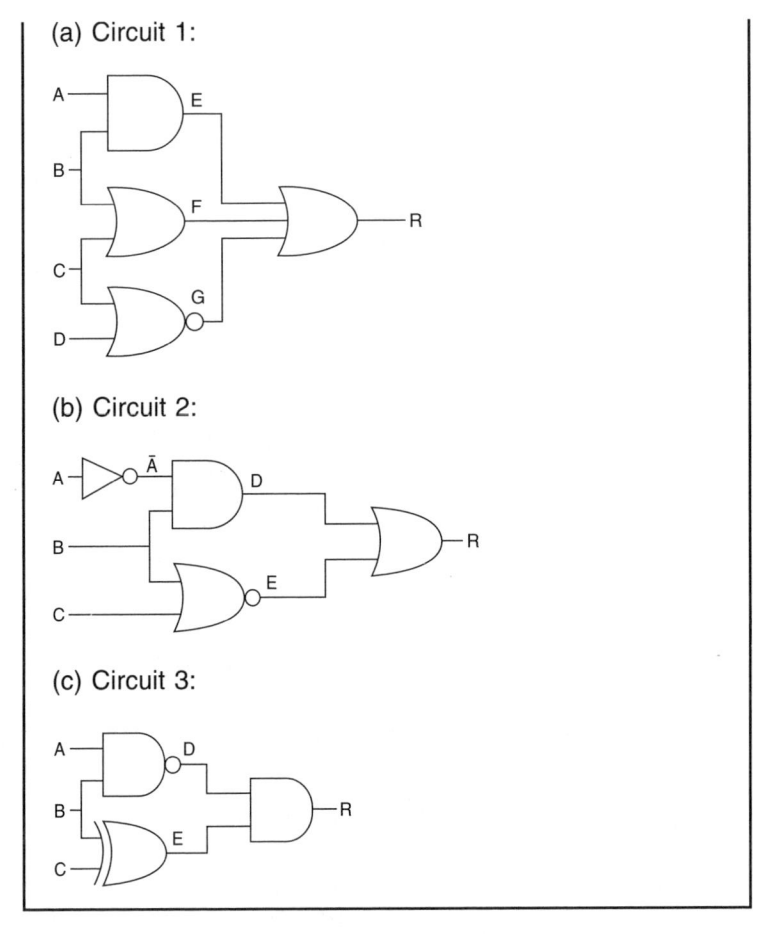

(a) Circuit 1:

(b) Circuit 2:

(c) Circuit 3:

2.3 Circuits with memory

The circuits shown above all work almost instantaneously – i.e. when a logic 1 is applied to the input, the output appears a very, very short time afterwards. Once the input is removed, the output changes as well; there is no 'memory'. Computers clearly need the ability to store values over time. This section will show some simple circuits that demonstrate this behaviour.

SR flip flop

Figure 2.4 shows a circuit that uses the output from one NAND gate to supply the input to the other one and vice versa; they 'keep

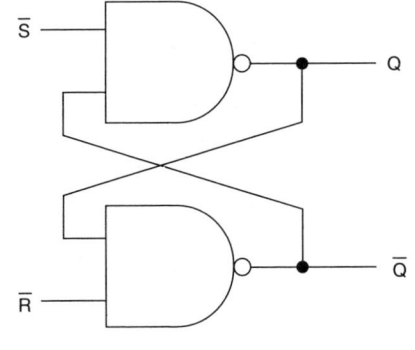

Figure 2.4 *SR flip flop*

BTEC National Study Guide: IT Practitioners. See page 293 for order details of individual texts

23

each other going'. It is called a **Set–Reset Flip Flop** because it flips from one state to another.

The behaviour of the SR flip flop is shown on the **transition table** (Table 2.3) below (it is not really accurate to describe it as a truth table). When S = 1 and R = 0, the output Q goes to 0. When R = 1 and S = 0, the output Q changes to a 1. The interesting behaviour of this circuit is that when S and R both = 0, it remains in whatever state it was before; i.e. it has 'memory'. The S input is called **Set** and the R input is called **Reset** after their main purposes.

Table 2.3   *Transition table for SR flip flop*

S	R	Q	$\overline{Q}$	Q_{n+1}	$\overline{Q}_{n+1}$	Comments
0	0	0	1	0	1	No change in outputs
0	0	1	0	1	0	
1	0	0	1	1	0	SET action when S = 1 and R = 0
1	0	1	0	1	0	
0	1	0	1	0	1	RESET action when R = 1 and S = 0
0	1	1	0	0	1	
1	1	0	1	?	?	Outputs are indeterminate
1	1	1	0	?	?	

The state where S = 1 and R = 1 may cause a **race condition**. In effect, this is where slight timing differences between the two NAND gates cause one gate to react sooner than the other so they 'race'. The result is an indeterminate output.

The circuit in Figure 2.5 has two extra gates on the left of the SR flip flop, and the input 'Clock' is used to control whether the circuit is to be changed or not. When Clock = 0, the inputs S and R have no effect (they can even have S = 1 and R = 1). Such a circuit is used to ensure changes occur at a certain time, the changeover being controlled by a **clock pulse**. This new circuit is called a **Clocked SR flip flop**.

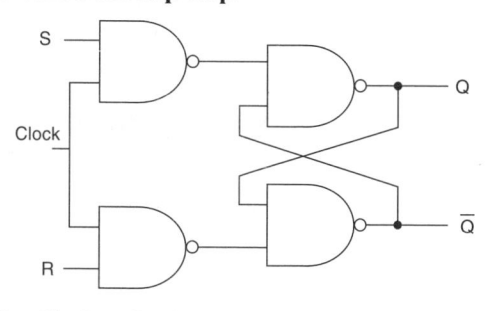

Figure 2.5   *Clocked SR flip flop*

You should note that **clock** has no relation to the timepiece on the wall! In electronic terms a clock is a **pulse** that goes 010 or 101, i.e. changes state from 0 to 1 then back to 0 (or the other way round); see Figure 2.6.

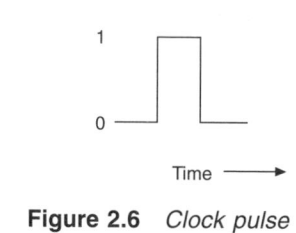

Figure 2.6   *Clock pulse*

D-type flip flop

The SR flip flop may not have S = 1 and R = 1, to avoid a race condition. The simplest way to avoid this is to place a NOT gate

BTEC National Study Guide: IT Practitioners. See page 293 for order details of individual texts

24

(also called an inverter) between S and R as shown in Figure 2.7, and to remove the external connection to the R input. When S = 0 R must = 1, and when S = 1, R must = 0. The outputs will only change when clock = 1, so this forms a very simple unit of **memory**.

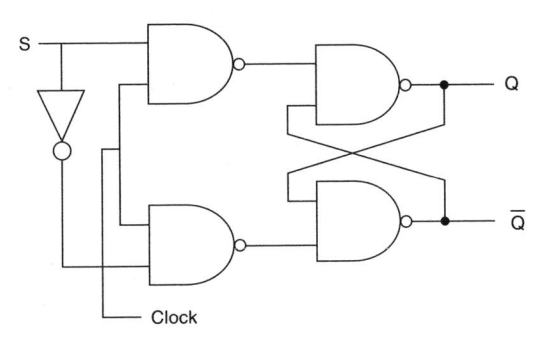

Figure 2.7 *D-type flip flop*

Later in this unit a group of D-type flip flops will be used, and the symbol shown in Figure 2.8 will be used. Remember that a D-type flip flop is a clocked SR flip flop with an inverter, in this case represented by a simple rectangle. A D type has a very useful property; when the clock = 0 it 'remembers', and when the clock = 1 it takes on whatever value line S has.

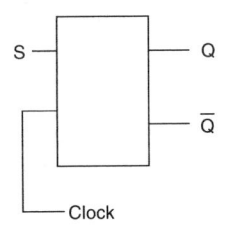

Figure 2.8 *Symbol for D-type flip flop*

Array of eight D-type flip flops

A byte is just eight binary bits. If eight D-type flip flops are arranged in parallel with a common clock signal, a circuit is created that will 'remember' a whole byte of information at once. Such an arrangement is shown in Figure 2.9. The eight wires connected to each of the eight D-type flip flops is called a **bus**.

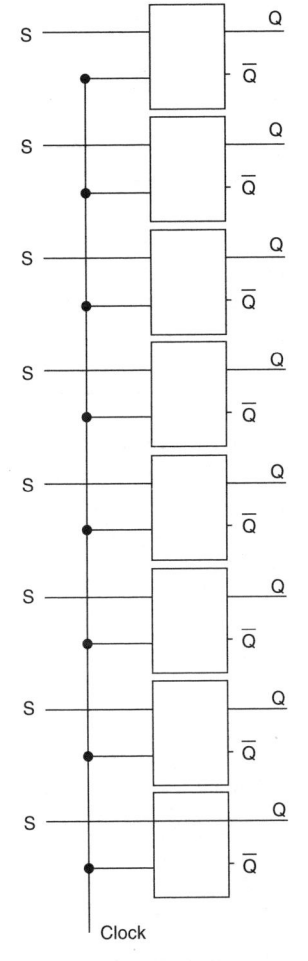

Figure 2.9 *Array of eight D-type flip flops*

2.4 Tri-state devices

It would be most useful if several of these devices could be connected together on a bus to store multiple bytes of information. A problem is caused when the inputs of two such devices are connected together, as the same logic level will be applied to both. To make a useful machine, some way must be found to isolate each device until is it needed – i.e. to 'disconnect it' until required. The arrangement in Figure 2.10 shows the problem.

If the left-hand array of D-type flip flops were all outputting a 1 and the right-hand array was outputting a 0, the state of the bus would be indeterminate because applying a 1 and a 0 would not give a satisfactory logic level.

BTEC National Study Guide: IT Practitioners. See page 293 for order details of individual texts

25

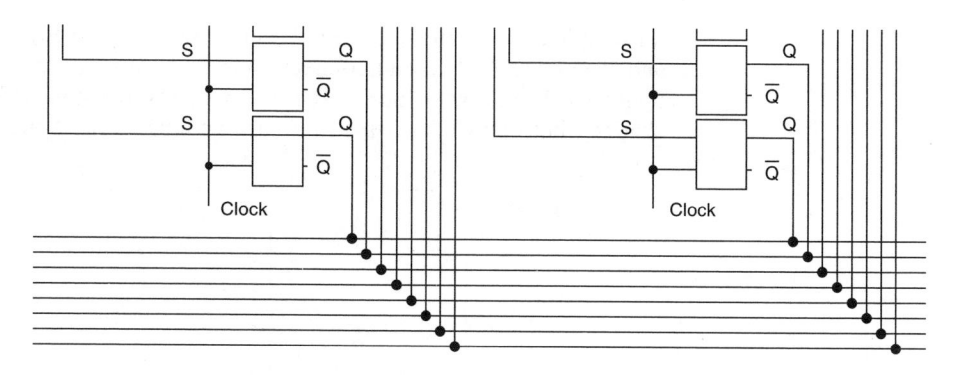

Figure 2.10 *Part of an impractical bus connection*

In a circuit, a logic level of 1 could be, say, 3.3 volts. In practical terms, this means that if the voltage is between about 3.0 and 3.5 volts a logic level of 1 exists, and if the voltage is between 0 and 0.5 volts there is a logic level of 0. If the voltage is some middle value like 1.6 volts, no clear logic level exists.

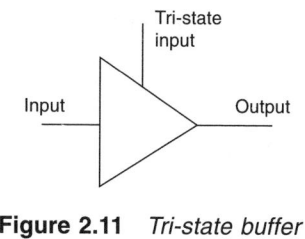

Figure 2.11 *Tri-state buffer symbol*

The solution to the problem is to use a **tri-state buffer**. This seems to go against the idea that computers are binary devices – i.e. their circuits have one of two states. A tri-state buffer has three states! These states are 0, 1, and high impedance. In place of the term 'high impedance' think 'disconnected', even though it is not quite true. When the tri-state buffer (Figure 2.11) is in its high impedance state, it really means that no logic level 0 or 1 exists on its output, and it is effectively disconnected from the circuit. This is summarized on the truth table, Table 2.4.

Table 2.4	*Truth table, tri-state buffer*	
Input	*Tri-state input (T)*	*Output*
0	0	Not connected
1	0	Not connected
0	1	0, i.e. same as input
1	1	1, i.e. same as input

Use of tri-state buffers to make a useful byte storage – a register

If the array of D-type flip flops is connected to the bus via tri-state buffers, as shown in Figure 2.12, many such arrays can be connected to the same bus and the T line can be used to control which array of flip flops is in use. If the controlling circuits are arranged so that only one array of flip flops can output at a time, then the bus can be used to transmit data to other devices. As before, a symbol is used to represent the circuit (Figure 2.13). Notice that to make drawings clearer, the individual wires in a bus are not drawn.

This circuit, made of an array of D-type flip flops connected to a bus via tri-state buffers, is one way to implement a **register**.

BTEC National Study Guide: IT Practitioners. See page 293 for order details of individual texts

26

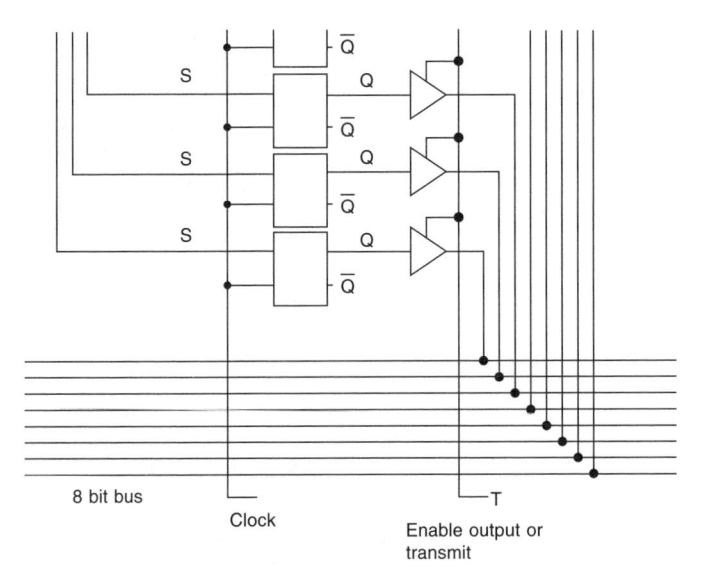

8 bit bus

Clock

—T

Enable output or
transmit

Figure 2.12 *Array of D-types connected via tri-state buffers*

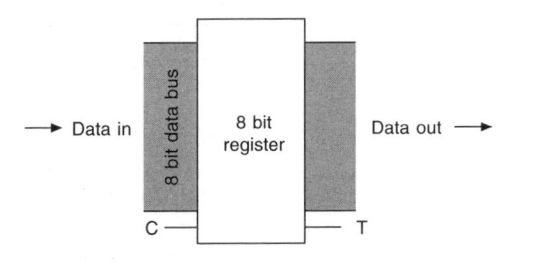

Figure 2.13 *Symbol for a register*

Registers are used in many different components in a computer as a temporary store for data. Their properties are shown in Table 2.5.

Table 2.5 *Properties of a register*		
Clock C	Input (T)	Output
0	0	Not connected
0	1	Stored value output to bus
1	0	Value on input bus 'written' to the register
1	1	Value on input bus written to the register and transmitted to the output bus at the same time

Array of registers

Several of these registers can now be used to build an array to store useful amounts of data. Figure 2.14 shows such an array. Note the following points:

1. The registers are numbered 0–3.
2. The control lines connected to each clock and T input are gathered together to form another bus called the **control bus**.
3. The data bus, 8 bits wide in this case, is connected to both

BTEC National Study Guide: IT Practitioners. See page 293 for order details of individual texts

27

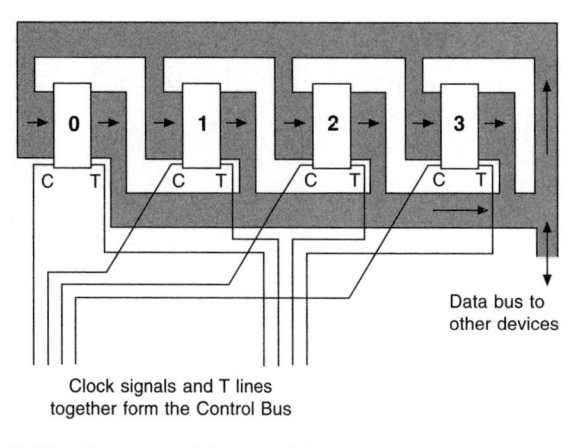

Data bus to
other devices

Clock signals and T lines
together form the Control Bus

Figure 2.14 *An array of four registers*

input and output sides of the registers. A common term to describe this is a **bi-directional bus**, implying that data 'travel' both ways, although this is not really the case.

Bi-directional bus

A bi-directional bus is both a source of data for a device and a way for the device to transmit that data elsewhere. The term 'bi-directional' is unfortunate, as it implies that data 'travel' along the wire when in fact they do no such thing. Imagine you are in Room 2 in a school or college, one of a set of four rooms connected via a straight corridor. Unusually, the rooms are numbered 0 to 3. It is one of those rather noisy buildings, and all the room doors are open. Someone in Room 3 shouts a message, and everyone in all the rooms can hear the message. Which direction did the **data** travel in as distinct from the sound waves? In fact, the data existed everywhere in the corridor (the bus) and the four rooms (the registers). The point is that when we consider a bi-directional bus, data move according to signals on the control lines; they are controlled in **time** rather than **direction**. A better term than bi-directional bus would be **common bus**, as the bus is common to the input and output sides of devices connected to it. Unfortunately, there are many parts of computers that have odd names!

Addressing an array of registers

Once an array of registers is connected via a common bus, a means must be provided to control them – i.e. to turn them on and off as required.

In the array, shown in Figure 2.14, it is not desirable to have more than one register 'on' at a time, so the control circuit must arrange for 0s on all the control lines except the one to be used addressing the register.

Table 2.6 is a truth table of this behaviour.

The truth table for all the variations of A • B is as follows:

BTEC National Study Guide: IT Practitioners. See page 293 for order details of individual texts

28

Table 2.6 *Truth table for addressing an array of register*

T line to register 0	T line to register 1	T line to register 2	T line to register 3
0	0	0	1
0	0	1	0
0	1	0	0
1	0	0	0

A	B	$\overline{A}$	$\overline{B}$	$A \bullet B$	$A \bullet \overline{B}$	$\overline{A} \bullet B$	$\overline{A} \bullet \overline{B}$
0	0	1	1	0	0	0	1
0	1	1	0	0	0	1	0
1	0	0	1	0	1	0	0
1	1	0	0	1	0	0	0

The pattern of 1s in the right-hand four columns is the same as the pattern in Table 2.6, which shows that the functions $A \bullet B$ etc. can be used to make the required circuit. A circuit that has this behaviour is shown in Figure 2.15.

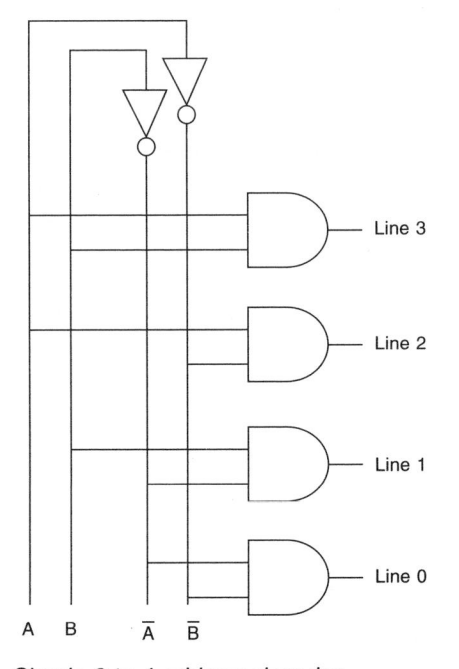

Figure 2.15 *Simple 2 to 4 address decoder*

Referring to the truth table above, the binary value of A and B combined corresponds to the register being 'turned on', so when A = 1 and B = 0, this 'turns on' register number 2, the binary value 10 = 2. In a similar way, when A = 1 and B = 1, register 3 is turned on as binary 11 = 3.

BTEC National Study Guide: IT Practitioners. See page 293 for order details of individual texts

29

This is a very important idea in binary circuits, as the value applied to A and B is called an **address**, so when binary 11 or decimal 3 is applied to the inputs A and B it is said that register 3 is being **addressed**. If the idea is extended to eight inputs instead of two, the circuit could contain $2^8 = 256$ registers; if there were 24 input lines, there could be $2^{24} = 16.7$ million registers etc.

Extending this idea further, if the lines A and B are together considered as a bus, it is called the address bus. We now have three types of bus; the **data bus**, **control bus** and **address bus**. Remember, a **bus** is simply a collection of wires. If the data bus is eight wires (or 8 bits) wide, whole bytes can be transmitted at once, if it is 16 bits wide, 2 bytes can be transmitted at once. If the address bus is 16 bits wide, then $2^{16} = 65536$ addresses or storage locations can be addressed. Table 2.7 shows typical values for address bus width.

Table 2.7 *Typical address bus widths*

Address bus width	2^N	Number	Abbreviation
2	2^2	4	
8	2^8	256	
16	2^{16}	65536	64K
18	2^{18}	262144	256K
20	2^{20}	1048576	1M
24	2^{24}	16777216	16M
28	2^{28}	268435456	256M
30	2^{30}	1073741824	1G
32	2^{32}	4294967296	4G

Memory
Although logic circuits are shown here that have a 'memory' property, it should be noted that the main memory of a modern computer does not use these circuits because they would be too expensive to implement. Many different electronic effects are used to implement memory; all that is required is two stable states that can be modelled using a 1 or a 0. A common type of memory uses capacitance, i.e. tiny components that can be charged or not-charged are used to store 1s and 0s. For more information, look at http://xtronics.com/memory/how_memory-works.htm.

2.5 A simple microprocessor

In the last section, an array of registers was built up from simple binary logic. In this section, other components will be built into a simple microprocessor.

How to add

One of the functions that a microprocessor has to perform is addition. The easiest way to understand how to make a circuit that adds, an 'adder', is first to look at the arithmetic.

BTEC National Study Guide: IT Practitioners. See page 293 for order details of individual texts

30

Consider an addition; in decimal, $1 + 1 = 2$, but in binary, $1 + 1 = 10$. If we set out this in columns we get

	1
+	1
1	0

where the 1 on the left is **carried** over to the next column. This is the notation normally used for addition etc.

If we were to write all the possible additions of two binary digits, we would get:

	1
+	1
1	0

	1
+	0
0	1

	0
+	1
0	1

	0
+	0
0	0

These can be summarized on a truth table like this:

Numbers to be added		Outputs	
A	B	Sum	Carry
0	0	0	0
0	1	1	0
1	0	1	0
1	1	0	1

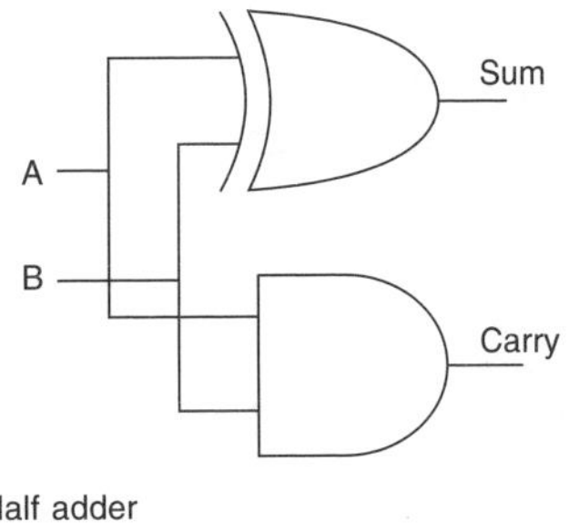

Half adder

Figure 2.16 *Half adder*

As we are using binary numbers they can be treated as logical propositions, as they can only have values of 1 or 0. You should be able to see that the Sum output has the same truth table as the XOR function and the Carry output has the same truth table as the AND function. This means that we can draw a circuit that will add two binary digits and output the result, i.e. the sum and carry. The resulting circuit is called a **half adder** (Figure 2.16), and the outputs from this circuit will be those represented in the truth table.

BTEC National Study Guide: IT Practitioners. See page 293 for order details of individual texts

31

This circuit is fine if all we need to add is two binary digits, but if we need to add, say, 2 bytes together, we need a circuit that will cope with a carry from the previous column.

Consider the addition of 01 and 11:

1	1
0	1
Carry 1	
	0

The sum in the right-hand column is 1 + 1 = 0, but we will need to **carry** 1 over to the next column. If we want a circuit that will add the next column, it will require **three** inputs, i.e. to add the 1 and 0 and the 1 carried over from the previous column. This can be done by using two half adders joined together as shown below. The result is called a **full adder** (Figure 2.17).

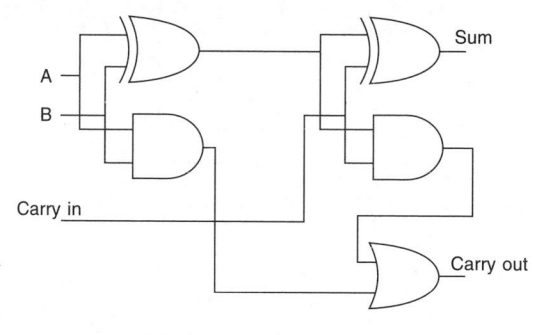

Figure 2.17   *Full adder*

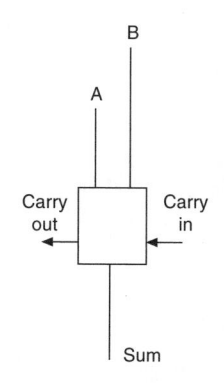

Figure 2.18   *Full adder symbol*

We now have a circuit that takes three inputs (the two binary digits to be added and a previous carry) then outs the sum and the carry ready for the next column in the addition of a multiple bit binary number.

We can now use seven full adders and one half adder to add to 8 bit bytes to give an 8 bit result with a carry. In Figure 2.18, each full or half adder is shown as a square symbol:

These are connected as shown in Figure 2.19.

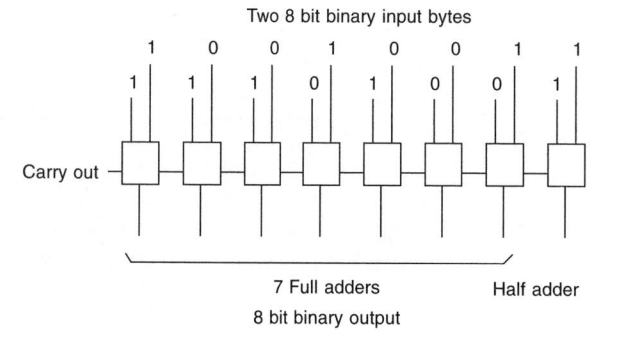

Figure 2.19   *8 bit adder (a)*

BTEC National Study Guide: IT Practitioners. See page 293 for order details of individual texts

32

If we supply the values 147 and 235 as binary values 10010011 and 11101001, we should get the result 382. Eight bits will not hold the value 382, so the result will be 256 (represented as the carry bit) and 126 as the binary pattern 01111110. The carry out from each addition is connected to the carry in of the next adder. This is shown in Figure 2.20.

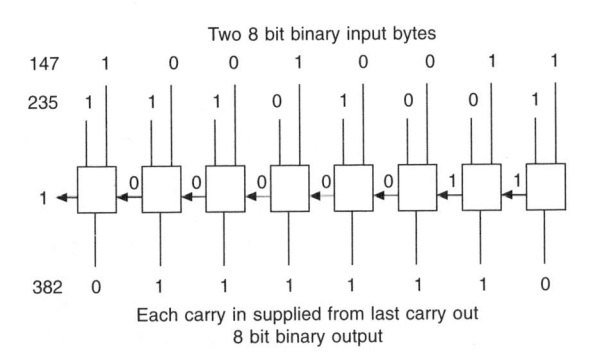

Figure 2.20 *8-bit adder (b)*

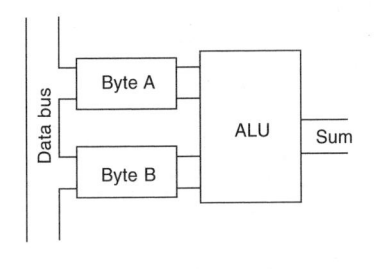

Figure 2.21 *Symbol for the arithmetic and logic unit*

This array of full adders can be incorporated into a more complex circuit that will perform subtraction, logic etc. This is represented as a symbol (Figure 2.21) ready to show in the diagram of a microprocessor. In this case it is called the Arithmetic and Logic Unit (ALU), its function is simply to add, subtract and perform AND, OR functions etc. on whole bytes of data.

A simple microprocessor (also called a CPU, or Central Processing Unit) is shown in Figure 2.22. It consists of simple parts.

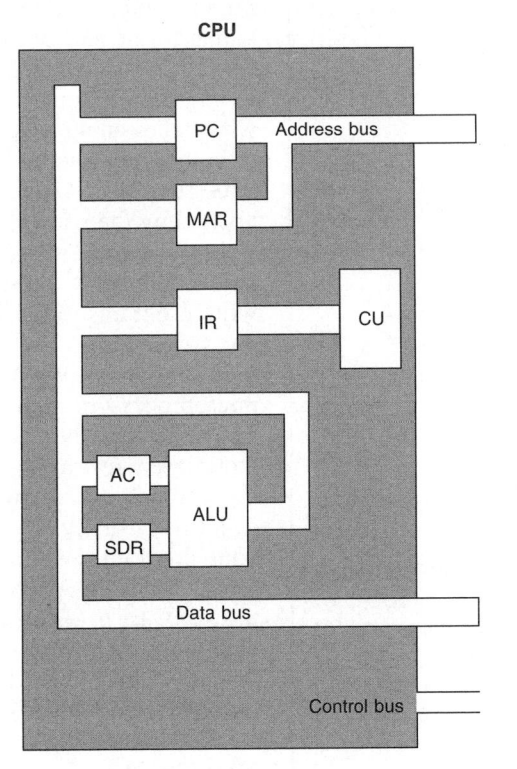

Figure 2.22 *Diagram of a simplified CPU*

BTEC National Study Guide: IT Practitioners. See page 293 for order details of individual texts

33

The CPU

This is not a **real** microprocessor. It is a simplified version of the original microprocessors, and is presented to demonstrate the way that these devices work. Real microprocessors are more complex but share the same basic way of working.

Registers

The CPU contains **registers**. These are circuits that can remember individual numbers for a short time.

1. The AC register is traditionally known as the **Accumulator**; it is the register where the results of calculations are held.
2. The SDR register is called the **Store Data Register**, and is used to hold data ready for and instruction.
3. The IR is the **Instruction Register**, and is used to hold the latest instruction fetched from RAM.
4. The MAR is the **Memory Address Register**, and is used to hold addresses.
5. The PC is the **Program Counter**, and is used to store the location or address of the next instruction to be fetched.

Buses

The components of the CPU and those outside the CPU are connected together using **buses**. A bus is simply a collection of wires, so an 8-bit bus is just eight wires each carrying 1s or 0s. Remember that a byte is 8 bits, so an 8-bit bus could carry a single byte of information. For example, the information at one moment **could** be the letter G, which forms part of the data being processed by the CPU. ASCII for G is 64 + its position in the alphabet = 71 decimal or 47 hex. If you convert this to binary, you get 01000111. If each of the wires takes on the value 1 or 0 in this pattern, the bus could be said to be holding a letter G. There is no way of telling if the pattern 01000111 is a 'G' or not; the 'value' of a piece of data is only applied by the software that is using it.

In this simple microprocessor, the data bus is 8 bits wide so the largest number it can store is $2^8 - 1 = 255$. If it is required, you can write programs to handle larger numbers by breaking them down into 8-bit values. The older 8-bit microprocessors did this, which is one reason why they were much slower than modern microprocessors – arithmetic was laborious.

The address bus is also just 8 bits wide. This causes a much more severe restriction on operations than an 8-bit data bus, because you can only have 256 addresses. If some of the instructions need data (they usually do), you may have as few as 100 instructions in your program. When you consider that the main executable of Microsoft Word 97 comprises more than 5 **million** bytes and that this software needs even more support files to make it work, a 256-byte memory is very small!

The width of the data bus and the address bus are important considerations when specifying a microprocessor. The Pentium microprocessor has a 32-bit address bus and a 64-bit data bus. As $2^{32} = 4294967296$, a 32-bit address will allow 4 294 967 296 different addresses, or 4000 Mb or 4 Gb.

Question 2.2

(a) If a microprocessor has a 20-bit address bus, what is the maximum size of RAM this can address?

Answer

As 2^{20} = 1048576, or 1 Mb, a 20-bit address bus will address 1 Mb of RAM.

(b) How many address lines are required to address 64 Mb of RAM?

Answer

2^N = 64 Mb. You could use a spreadsheet to find that 2^{26} = 67108864, or 64 Mb, so it will need 26 address lines to address 64 Mb. Remember that 1 M = 1024 × 1024 = 1048576, not 1000 × 1000 = 1000000.

BTEC National Study Guide: IT Practitioners. See page 293 for order details of individual texts

34

Control unit

The control unit is the 'heart' of the CPU. When fed with an instruction from the IR, the microprocessor responds with the correct action – i.e. the right registers are used and, if required, the ALU is brought into use.

Arithmetic and Logic Unit

The ALU is the **Arithmetic and Logic Unit** and, as its name suggests, is where the microprocessor actually performs additions and subtraction and logical operations such as AND and OR instructions.

What is a microprocessor?

A microprocessor is a complex circuit built from a large number of simple circuits that is made to perform logical instructions in **sequence** and thus make **decisions**.

The instructions to carry these out (the program) are separately stored outside the circuit in **memory** (Figure 2.23). The decisions or instructions are very modest in human terms; they usually take the form of something like: 'if number A is bigger than number B then execute instruction K else execute instruction X', or 'add 6 to number A'. The logical instructions are executed in sequence by the microprocessor; each is fetched from memory then executed, one at a time. (Complex modern microprocessors can execute several instructions at once.) No **single instruction** does anything really complex like 'move paragraph to the bottom of the document'; they all do relatively simple tasks. Complex tasks are built from hundreds or thousands of these simple tasks; just as a town is built from thousands of bricks, the town is complex, the bricks are simple.

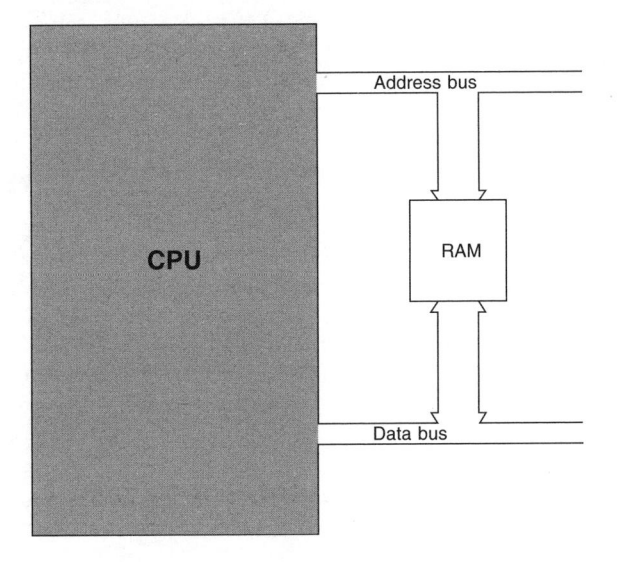

Figure 2.23 *The memory or RAM is outside of the CPU*

All the operations of the microprocessor are controlled by a **clock**, which means that a constant number of pulses or 1s and 0s

BTEC National Study Guide: IT Practitioners. See page 293 for order details of individual texts

35

are fed to the circuit and each instruction is executed on each pulse. A clock in this sense has nothing to do with telling the time! When you see that a Pentium processor has a clock speed of 600 MHz, it means that 600 000 000 clock pulses are supplied to the circuit per second. A quick thought is, if things are happening that fast, why is it that certain operations take some time to execute? The answer is simple; complex tasks are made from a large number of very simple tasks, and the simple tasks get executed at a speed hard to relate to human experience but there are **so** many to execute!

In Figure 2.23 there are two components, the CPU and the RAM. All the instructions are stored in the RAM and must be loaded one by one into the CPU. After a single instruction has been loaded, the CPU decides what it means, i.e. it **decodes** it, then **executes** the instruction. This is called the **Fetch–Execute cycle**. There is a clock input to the CPU, which supplies a series of timed 1s and 0s as a square wave.

In this example, the CPU will fetch an instruction on one pulse of the clock, decode it right away, and execute the instruction on 1, 2 or 3 of the next clock pulses. The reason it might use 1 or 2 or 3 clock pulses is because some instructions are a little more involved than others. The instructions are held in the RAM in a sequence of numbered locations, each of which is called an address. A possible sequence of instructions is shown in Table 2.8 below.

Table 2.8 *Program for the single CPU*

Address in RAM (numbered location)	Code for instruction or data held in RAM	Meaning
161	3A	Load the data at the next address into the AC register
162	23	Number to load, i.e. data not an instruction
163	3D	Load the data at the next address into the SDR register
164	12	Number to load, i.e. data not an instruction
165	8C	Add the numbers in the AC and SDR registers and store the result in the AC register
166	3E	Store the value in the AC register at the RAM address held at the next two addresses, low byte first
167	6E	Low byte of address
168	01	High byte of address
169	3A	Load the data at the next address into the AC register
16A	45	Number to load, i.e. data not an instruction

Fetch-execute cycle

Look carefully at Figure 2.24. You will see that the PC contains the value 161. The other registers have values that do not matter. Leaving

BTEC National Study Guide: IT Practitioners. See page 293 for order details of individual texts

36

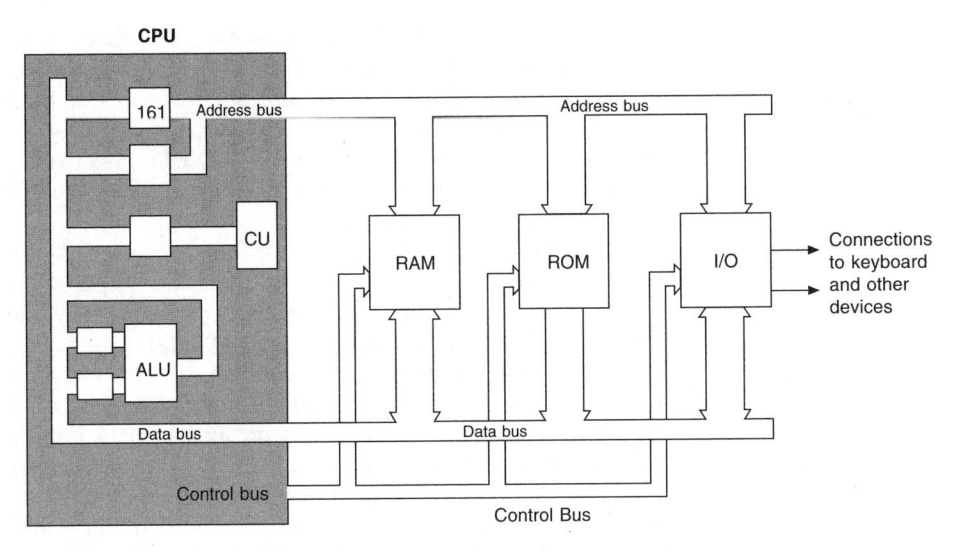

Figure 2.24 *The assembled microcomputer*

out quite a lot of detail, the fetch–execute sequence will proceed as follows.

In the fetch part of the fetch–execute sequence:

1. Instruct the RAM to give the contents of address 161 and place the number found there (3A) into the IR. This is done by putting the value 161 on the address bus and instructing the RAM to read; the value 3A will then appear on the data bus. The Control Unit provides all the signals for this to happen.
2. Allow the IR to feed its value into the Control Unit.
3. The Control Unit reacts by 'decoding' the instruction 3A, which in turn has the effect of putting 162 into the MAR, i.e. the address of the next address where the data is held. The microprocessor is now ready to execute the newly fetched instruction.

Once this is complete, the instruction **Load the data at the next address into the AC register** will be in the CPU, and so is the value of the next address, but note that it has **not** been executed – i.e. the AC register has not been loaded with the data.

In the execute part of the fetch–execute sequence:

1. Allow the contents of the MAR onto the address bus and instruct the RAM to read. This will result in the value 23 appearing on the data bus.
2. Load the contents of the data bus into the AC register.
3. Add 1 to the PC ready for the next fetch sequence.

The fetch–execute sequence is now complete and the next cycle can begin. Remembering this is not a real processor, we can safely ignore some practical details; in this example the fetch sequence took two 'ticks' of the CPU clock and the execute sequence took three ticks. If the clock was running at 1 MHz, i.e. 1 000 000 ticks per second (or, better, 1 000 000 1s and 0s), this would have taken 5/1 000 000 seconds, or 5-millionths of a second. This is quick in human terms, but all that has happened is that a number has been loaded into a register!

The next instruction in the program is **Load the data at the**

BTEC National Study Guide: IT Practitioners. See page 293 for order details of individual texts

37

next address into the SDR register, and this is fetched and executed in a similar way. The next instruction after this is **Add the numbers in the AC and SDR registers and store the result in the AC register**. You should note that this instruction does not have any data associated with it. This means it will take fewer ticks of the clock, so will fetch and execute quicker because it does not have to read the RAM a second time.

In general, instructions will take the form of 'what to do' followed by the 'data to do it with' – or, more formally, **Operation Code** followed by **Operand**. Other instructions will only have the Operation Code (often shortened to **Op Code**).

The actual program code and data are of course in binary, but we humans do not like to see lists of binary numbers or, for that matter, hex numbers. The consequence is that these programs are written down using **mnemonics** for Op Codes, so the instruction **Load the AC register with the contents of address 14** could be written as the mnemonic **LDA, 14** and the instruction **add 21 to the contents of the AC register** would be written as the mnemonic **ADD, #21**. The mnemonic **STA, 25** would mean **Store the contents of AC register at address 25**.

A program fragment containing these instructions is:

LDA, 14
ADD, #21
STA, 25

This means:

load whatever data is at address 14 into the AC register
add the value 21
store the result at address 25.

When a program is written in the form of

LDA, 14
ADD, #21
STA, 25

it is called assembly language.

Machine code

The program and data in RAM would in reality be just a set of numbers. If you write them down as numbers (in hex, decimal or binary, numbers are just numbers!), the resulting code is called **machine code**. This is what is actually run in the microprocessor using the fetch–execute sequence. Everything the CPU executes is machine code; when running Windows, the .EXE or .DLL files are machine code.

Assembly code

If you write down the same program using mnemonics, the resulting program code is called **assembly code**. The reason is that the mnemonics must be converted or 'assembled' into machine code with another program called an 'Assembler'. Writing a program using an assembler is much easier than writing directly in machine code. The sequence is to use a text editor to type the assembly code, then use the assembler to generate the machine code. This is

BTEC National Study Guide: IT Practitioners. See page 293 for order details of individual texts

38

then loaded into the RAM and the program run. With luck, it will do what you want it to!

If the assembly language

LDA, 14
ADD, #21
STA, 25

is converted to machine code with an assembler, it might give something like:

Address	Machine code
234	3A
235	14
236	8C
237	21
238	3E
239	25

What would be stored is just the machine code, i.e. 3A, 14, 8C, 21, 3E, 25. As you can see, machine code is not easy to read.

Actually writing commercial programs using assembly code (often just called assembler) is difficult, but one or two applications in computing are still written this way. Examples include very small but speed-critical parts of an **operating system**, or special high-speed animation sections of a game. Most programs are written using high-level languages such as C++ or Visual Basic, but eventually, after all the compiling and processing of these languages, everything the CPU executes is machine code. **Absolutely** everything!

2.6 Assembly language on real processors

Table 2.9 *Intel 8086 general purpose registers*

AH	AL
BH	BL
CH	CL
DH	DL
SP	
BP	
DI	
SI	

The Intel 8086

It may seem odd to use a microprocessor first introduced in 1978 in a book written in 2002, but it has been done for simplicity. The 8086 has more registers than the simple microprocessor shown above. In place of the AC and SDR registers there are eight 16-bit registers, four of these being 'splitable' into two 8-bit registers as shown in Table 2.9. The register AH can be combined with the register AL to make AX, and so on for BX, CX and DX. AH can be taken as A High, and AL as A Low.

The layout or architecture of the 8086 is also more complex (Figure 2.25). It is not necessary to remember this layout, but the names and behaviour of the registers are important. The registers are connected via buses and the whole microprocessor is controlled via signals over the control bus, most of which has been left out for clarity. One important point to note is that the 8086 has an **instruction queue**, i.e. it can be executing an instruction whilst fetching another. This is one of the ways that microprocessors can yield an increase in execution speed. The 8086 is old enough not to have any floating point hardware. Modern microprocessors have integral floating point units that do floating point arithmetic such as 2.3×4.556

BTEC National Study Guide: IT Practitioners. See page 293 for order details of individual texts

39

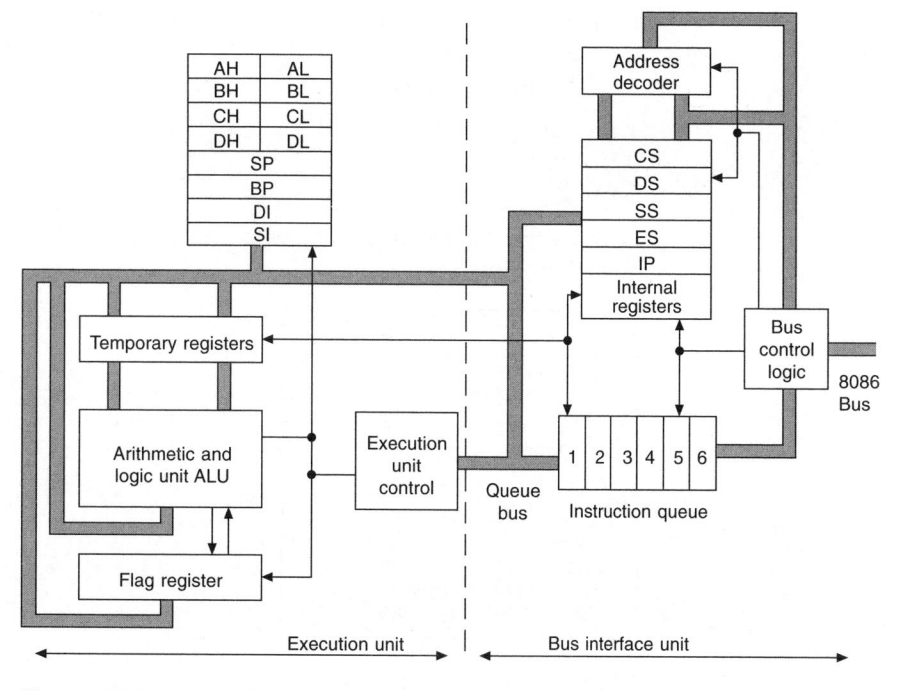

Figure 2.25 *8086 microprocessor architecture*

directly in one instruction; the 8086 would have to execute hundreds of instructions to achieve the same result. (An add-on chip was available, the 8057, that performed these operations.) The assembly code that follows will run on the modern microprocessors, as they are 'backwards compatible'.

An assembler

For the following exercises you will need an assembler. This is a piece of software that converts your program or **assembly code** to **machine code**.

There are several commercial assemblers available for the PC, but the shareware version called A86 is the cheapest and easiest to use. The author, Eric Isaacson, also claims it is the best! You can download A86 directly from his site at http://eji.com/a86/. Please read the legal notices that come with the package. From these you will see that to use the software for evaluation purposes is free, but that a small charge is made if you wish to keep and continue to use the software.

The 8086 instruction set

An **instruction set** is just a list of all the instructions that a microprocessor can execute.

If you have downloaded Eric Isaacson's A86 software (http://eji.com/a86/), you will find that it comes with the complete listing of the Intel microprocessor's instruction set. For the purposes of your course and this book this instruction set is rather too complex, so what is presented in Table 2.10 is an extract from that complete instruction set.

When writing assembly language programs, it is important to realize that almost no services are provided to the programmer. For

BTEC National Study Guide: IT Practitioners. See page 293 for order details of individual texts

40

Table 2.10 *Subset of 8086 instruction set*

Op code	Example	Comment
ADD	ADD AX,12	Add 12 to what is in AX
AND	AND DH, 10011011b	Logical AND with DH and binary value 10011011
CALL	CALL 2000	Call routine at address 2000; it will end with a RET instruction
CMP	CMP SI,12	Compare SI register with value 12. Result sets flag in flag register
DEC	DEC AL	Subtract 1 from AL register
DIV	DIV DL	Divide AX by what is in DL. Answer, AL = Quotient, AH = Remainder
INC	INC SI	Add 1 to what is in SI register
INT	INT 021	Call DOS interrupt 21 (21 hex)
JA	JA 2000	Jump if above to address 2000
JAE	JAE 2100	Jump if above or equal to address 2100
JB	JB 3000	Jump if below to address 3000
JBE	JBE 1000	Jump if below or equal to address 1000
JC	JC 1000	Jump if carry flag set to address 1000
JMP	JMP 2300	Jump unconditionally to address 2300
JNZ	JNZ 2000	Jump is not zero to address 2000
MOV	MOV AX,23	Move 23 into AX register
MUL	MUL CL	Multiply AX register by what is in CL, answer in AX
OR	OR DI, 00110001b	Logical OR DI register with binary value 00110001
POP	POP AX	Take value from stack, put into AX, decrement stack pointer
PUSH	PUSH AX	Take value from AX, place on stack, increment stack pointer
RET	RET	Return from subroutine
SHL	SHL AX,3	Shift the value in AX 3 times to the left
SHR	SHR AX,3	Shift the value in AX 3 times to the right
SUB	SUB AX,8	Subtract 8 from value in AX register
XOR	XOR AL, AL	Logical eXclusive OR of AL with itself (sets AL to zero)

instance, if you wish to write a single character to the screen, you have several choices:

1. You could investigate the precise hardware details of your computer and get your assembly language programme to write directly to that hardware. This would involve knowledge of how the computer controls the screen hardware.
2. You could use somebody else's piece of code that outputs to the screen. Eric Issacson supplies such routines.
3. You could use the Basic Input Output System (BIOS) of your computer.
4. You could ask the operating system of your computer to output to the screen.

BTEC National Study Guide: IT Practitioners. See page 293 for order details of individual texts

41

There is no instruction to print directly to the screen; this is a 'complex' task that involves many instructions. The instructions in assembly language are all very simple, such as ADD, STORE etc. Even an IF statement uses two lines of code.

Example program 1, P1.ASM

The programme below simply adds two numbers, and will not display the result.

```
MOV AX, [5210]
ADD AX,12
MOV [2007],AX
```

The first instruction, MOV AX, [5210], simply places the value stored at address 5210 into the AX 16-bit general purpose register. As AX is a 16 register, it will accept numbers up to one less than 2^{16}, or 65535, no larger. Eight-bit registers can accept up to one less than 2^8, or 255.

The second instruction adds 12 to the number in AX, and the result, 46, remains in the AX register.

The third instruction 'moves' the value in AX to the address 2007 in RAM. This is another example of a silly name in computing; the instruction **stores** the value, it does not **move** it.

In the instruction MOV AX,34, the MOV part is called the **Op Code**, short for Operation code (i.e. **what** to do). The AX,34 part is called the **Operand**, i.e. what the Op Code must **operate on**.

Comments

It is considered to be very bad programming practice to write code without some comments to tell you and others what pieces of code are supposed to do. It is tempting to get on with the interesting job of writing code and to leave the comments out, but in a short while it is easy to forget what you intended. If someone else has to work on your code, it is usually very difficult for them to find out your intentions. In the A86 assembler, comments are added after a ; character, so the code above may look like this:

```
MOV AX, [5210]   ;Get horizontal co-ordinate
ADD AX,12        ;Add offset
MOV [2007],AX    ;Store in frame buffer
```

Notice that comments are related to **why** the op codes are used and not to **what** they are doing. What follows is an example of silly comments!

```
MOV AX, [5210]   ;Get value at address 5210
ADD AX,12        ;Add 12
MOV [2007],AX    ;store in address 2007
```

They are silly because knowledge of the op codes themselves show what is happening; the comments should show **why**.

BTEC National Study Guide: IT Practitioners. See page 293 for order details of individual texts

42

When a program is **assembled**, it produces an **executable file** that contains the **machine code** as shown in Table 2.11.

Table 2.11 *Assembly code and resulting machine code*	
Assembly code	*The resulting machine code*

MOV AX, [5210]
ADD AX,12
MOV [2007],AX
	A1 54 14 05 0C 00 A3 D7 07

As you can see, even the rather obscure looking assembly code is easier to read than machine code! The processor uses machine code for everything, **absolutely everything** – Windows, Word, the whole thing is produced by the processor running machine code. You can see that the simple act of taking two numbers, adding them and storing the answer in RAM has generated three instructions that occupy 9 bytes of machine code. The Windows directory on the machine being used to prepare this book contains over 1 200 000 000 bytes; this is a very large collection of very simple operations and data that make up a complex operating system.

Table 2.12 illustrates how to use A86 to assemble a program.

Table 2.12 *How to use A86 to assemble a program*		
Step 1	Edit	Use any editor that will save simple ASCII files. These files are also known as text files. One of the very best is called UltraEdit, available from www.ultraedit.com, but you can use Microsoft Notepad etc. Save your file with the extension .ASM
Step 2	Assembly	Assuming you save your file as P1.ASM, at the DOS or Command prompt, type A86 P1.ASM and press enter. If everything has worked, this will result in the executable file called P1.COM and a symbol file called P1.SYM being in your directory. For the moment, ignore the symbol file
Step 3	Execute	At the DOS prompt, type P1 and press enter. With luck your program will work! If not, go back to step 1, edit the error and proceed to steps 2 and 3

What happens if it goes wrong

You will rapidly find out that there are almost no error messages! If you have some experience of high-level languages that produce executable code, this lack of error messages can be very frustrating. Often it looks as though it should work but simply refuses to do so. This is one of the reasons that high-level languages were designed! Reasons include the following.

1. The operating system hangs. Some errors will 'hang' the machine, i.e. stop it from running. This is because it is possible for your program to wander around in memory almost without restraint, overwriting important data. If this happens you will have to re-boot and start again at step 1.

BTEC National Study Guide: IT Practitioners. See page 293 for order details of individual texts

43

2. You may have an error in a **symbolic address**, probably due to differences in spelling. In this case, A86 outputs the errors in a file with a .ERR extension. If your original file was p1.asm, the file will be called p1.err.

3. You may have some incorrect op-codes in your program, in which case A86 will output some error messages.

As an example, this program

```
MOV AX, [5210]
ADD AX,12
MOV [2007],AX
```

was modified to

```
MOVE AX, [5210]
ADD AX,12
MOV [2007],AX
```

and saved as **p1.asm**. The first MOV instruction has been changed to the incorrect spelling of MOVE. When assembled, A86 output the message

```
C:\>a86 p1.asm
A86 macro assembler, V4.05 Copyright 2000 Eric Isaacson
Source:
p1.asm
Error messages inserted into p1.asm
Original source renamed as p1.OLD
```

It is clear that your original file is now called p1.OLD and that p1.asm contains the error messages as shown below. If you correct the errors but leave the top two lines in place, A86 will remove the error messages next time you assemble the file.

```
~^
#ERROR messages will be removed if you leave these
first two lines in @@@@#
MOVE AX, [5210]
~ ^
#ERROR 01: Unknown Mnemonic
@@@@#
ADD AX,12
MOV [2007],AX
```

You can see that the incorrect spelling has been detected. To correct this, edit p1.asm, correct **only** the fault, then go back to step 2 – i.e. re-assemble the file.

Example program 2, P2.ASM

This program simply outputs the letter 'A' to the screen. Remember that ASCII 'A' is 65 in decimal, 41 in hex, or 01000001 in binary.

```
MOV DL, 65    ;ASCII A ready for DOS output routine
MOV AH, 2     ;DOS output routine number 2
INT 021       ;Call DOS routine number 2; it outputs whatever
                 is in DL
INT 020       ;Call DOS to terminate program.
```

BTEC National Study Guide: IT Practitioners. See page 293 for order details of individual texts

44

If you use the steps above to edit, assemble and test the program, you should get a single A character output at the DOS prompt when the program is executed.

Points to note about P2.ASM

The first line MOV DL, 65 could have been written in any of these ways:

MOV DL, 65
MOV DL, "A"
MOV DL, 'A'
MOV DL, 01000001b
MOV DL, 041

All the above lines are the same; the assembler simply converts the code to the correct value and inserts it into the executable file. It is easy to forget that all the code in a computer is binary, you may hear that it works on 'hex code' or the like, but in fact hex, decimal, ASCII etc. are only for humans, and the computer is pure binary. In this case, A86 uses the text format 65 as decimal, the quoted formats, "A" or 'A' as ASCII, and 041 (with a leading zero) as hex. Binary is taken as ending in b. **Whatever format you use, the output will be the same.**

As stated above, there is no single instruction in assembler to output to the screen. In this example, use has been made of a service provided by DOS. These DOS services or interrupts are called by number. The service used here is called DOS interrupt 21 (hex, so A86 uses 021), and, as this provides many simple functions, we have to use function number 2. For this to work, DOS expects the function number in the AH register and the letter to be output in the DL register. DOS interrupts are sometimes called system calls; although this is not completely accurate, is it useful to think of them this way – i.e. to ask the 'system' for a service. In effect, this calls a routine written by someone else to do what you need. A full list of these DOS interrupts is available on the Internet (search for DOS interrupt in Google), but is only of real value if you plan to write larger and more powerful assembly language programs.

Example program 3, P3.ASM

This program extends P2.ASM by including a 'loop' that will output the letter 'A' 10 times.

```
        MOV DL, 'A'    ;letter to be printed
        MOV AH, 2      ;DOS output routine number 2
        MOV CH, 10     ;start counter at 10
TOP:    INT 021        ;Call DOS routine number 2.
                       ;it outputs whatever is in DL
        DEC CH         ;count down by 1
        CMP CH, 0      ;see if counter has reached zero
        JNZ TOP        ;if counter has not reached zero,
                       ;jump to top of loop
        INT 020        ;if counter has reached zero, terminate
                       ;program
```

BTEC National Study Guide: IT Practitioners. See page 293 for order details of individual texts

45

Points to note about P3.ASM

The first two lines are the same as for program P2.ASM.

The third line starts a register off at 10, ready to count down to 0.

The fourth line starts with TOP: This is called a **symbolic address** and the name TOP is called a **label**. When the program is assembled this address is converted into a real numerical address; in this case the address is 0106, but we would not have known that when the program was written, hence the use of a symbolic address. This is one of the services offered by an assembler and explains the appearance of the .SYM files in your directory; it is a file of the symbolic and numerical addresses to be used when reversing the assembly process – **un-assembly**.

The fifth line simply counts down by 1.

The sixth line checks to see if the counter has reached zero. When the DEC instruction is executed, the 8086 sets a **flag** in the **flag register** to record the result. A flag is simply a binary digit that is either 1 or 0 depending on the result.

Line seven is short for Jump if Not Zero to address TOP (remember the assembler converts the address TOP to the real numeric address at assembly time, in this case address 0106).

Lines five, six and seven form an 'if' statement.

Taking P3.COM apart with DEBUG

Supplied with DOS is a very odd but useful program called DEBUG. You can use DEBUG to look into your executable code. Assuming you have P3.COM in your directory, you just type DEBUG P3.COM and you will get a '-' character! You can then supply the command u for **u**nassemble. The result (all in hex) should look like this:

```
C:\>DEBUG P3.COM
-u
0E92:0100 B241      MOV   DL,41
0E92:0102 B402      MOV   AH,02
0E92:0104 B50A      MOV   CH,0A
0E92:0106 CD21      INT   21
0E92:0108 FECD      DEC   CH
0E92:010A 80FD00    CMP   CH,00
0E92:010D 75F7      JNZ   0106
0E92:010F CD20      INT   20
0E92:0111 06        PUSH  ES
0E92:0112 1000      ADC   [BX+SI],AL
0E92:0114 75E2      JNZ   00F8
0E92:0116 56        PUSH  SI
0E92:0117 BF0400    MOV   DI,0004
0E92:011A B5FF      MOV   CH,FF
0E92:011C B000      MOV   AL,00
0E92:011E 43        INC   BX
0E92:011F 3DF2AE    CMP   AX,AEF2
-q
C:\>
```

Points to note about the unassembly of P3.ASM

Ignore the first column that starts with 0E92, this is called a **segment address** and need not concern us here.

BTEC National Study Guide: IT Practitioners. See page 293 for order details of individual texts

46

The next column tells us that the assembler has placed the program starting at address 0100 in RAM.

The third column is the **machine code**, the actual code that the processor uses to execute the program.

The last two columns contain almost the same code as you started with except that the symbolic address TOP has been converted to address 0106. DEBUG has unassembled the code, almost back to its original.

The value loaded into DL in the first line is still an 'A' because 41 hex = ASCII 'A'; DEBUG always outputs in hex.

All the bytes after the program, i.e. at address 0111 onwards are 'snow', i.e. meaningless data left over from whatever was in addresses 0111 to 011F when the machine used to prepare this book last used those addresses.

You quit from DEBUG with the command q.

Reverse engineering

The process of taking parts of an executable program and unassembling them is called **reverse engineering**. It is used to take code from other people or companies for use in new programs. Most of the time this is illegal as it contravenes the licence agreement. For example, Microsoft licence agreements refer specifically to 'Reverse Engineering, Decompilation, and Disassembly'. In the past, people have taken some useful parts of commercial programs, unassembled them, put this with their own code and re-assembled it for sale. There are ways to discover this has taken place and the programmers prosecuted.

Operating systems

This book is being prepared on a machine running Microsoft Windows 98. This operating system has as its core the older operating system called DOS, the Disc Operating System, with additions and modifications to suit Windows 98. Machines running Windows 2000 still offer a 'command prompt' but the underlying operating system is different. In this case calls to DOS services are emulated so should still work, but some things **may** not work correctly. For the exercises in this section it is preferable to use Windows 98 or older. Unfortunately, the more modern operating systems are not so easy to program using assembly language.

Example program 4, P4.ASM

This program extends P3.ASM by incrementing the letter to print ABCDEFGHIJ.

```
        MOV DL, 'A'    ;letter to be printed
        MOV AH, 2      ;DOS output routine number 2
        MOV CH, 10     ;start counter at 10
TOP:    INT 021        ;call DOS routine number 2.
```

BTEC National Study Guide: IT Practitioners. See page 293 for order details of individual texts

47

```
                              ;it outputs whatever is in DL
        INC DL               ;represent next letter in alphabet
        DEC CH               ;count down by 1
        CMP CH, 0            ;see if counter has reached zero
        JNZ TOP              ;if counter has not reached zero,
                             ;jump to top of loop
        INT 020              ;if counter has reached zero,
                             ;terminate program
```

Points to note about P4.ASM

The only difference from P3.ASM is the addition of INC DL. INC means increment, or 'add 1 to'. Since DL started by containing 65, or hex 41, it will become 66 then 67 etc., i.e. ASCII for ABC etc.

When DOS outputs the contents of DL, this is the first time that 65 means 'A'; before that it was simply a number. This is often hard to come to terms with; all the data in RAM are simply numbers, it is not until they are used that they have 'meaning'. An 'A' is for humans to read; to a computer it is no more than a pattern of dots on a screen produced by the DOS Interrupt 021.

Exercise 2.2

Modify program P4.ASM to print letters MNOPQRSTUVWXYZ, i.e. 14 letters starting at M. The answer is in Appendix A.

Exercise 2.3

Modify program P4.ASM to print numbers 0123456789. The answer is in Appendix A.

Example program P5.ASM

This program will output the string 'Mary had a little lamb', followed by a Carriage Return and Line Feed characters.

```
top:      jmp start
buffer:   db 'Mary had a little lamb',10,13,0
start:    mov si,buffer
L1:       mov dl,[si]    ;get first character
          cmp dl,0       ;see if end of string
          jz finprint    ;finish if end of string
          mov ah,2       ;initialize subroutine
                         ;int21 DOS call next
          int 021        ;write char using DOS
                         ;interrupt 021
          inc si         ;point to next char
          jmp L1         ;back for more chars
finprint: int 020        ;back to DOS
```

Points to note about P5.ASM

Data and instructions all occupy the same address space, so the string 'Mary had a little lamb' is stored with the code used to

BTEC National Study Guide: IT Practitioners. See page 293 for order details of individual texts

48

process it. The code db in front of the line stands for **Define Byte** and tells the assembler to find some space in RAM and to keep the symbolic address as 'buffer'. There are four other symbolic addresses. Defining byte storage like this is done with an **assembler directive**, i.e. it **directs** the assembler how to behave, it does not generate machine code. Another assembler directive is DW, short for Define Word, in this case a 16-bit value. The Carriage Return is coded as 13 and the Line Feed is coded as 10. The 0 byte at the end is used to detect the end of the string. This kind if string, known as an ASCIIZ string, is common in programming languages such as C. It avoids the need to know the length of the string in order to control the loop that outputs it.

Terminology

As stated elsewhere in this book, some of the terms used in computing are confusing or downright silly. It is common to use the term 'word' to refer to a whole piece of storage. In the case of the 8086 microprocessor, this is a 16-bit value; in other processors it is 8 bits, 32 bits, 64 bits etc. The term 'word' has no bearing on the normal usage of the term – i.e. it is nothing to do with English **words**.

On the fourth line, use is made of the SI general purpose register. The op. code MOV DL, [SI] says 'put into DL the byte stored at the address that is in SI'. So if SI contains the address 0103, the instruction will have the same effect as MOV DL, [0103]. The reason this is used is so that SI can be incremented in order to **point** at the next address in memory. In this case, SI is being used as a **pointer**, an idea that is much used in high-level programs such as C or C++.

Addressing modes

In assembly language programming, much is made of **addressing modes**. This is to draw attention to such things as MOV DL, [SI] being different from MOV DL, 3 or MOV DL, [0103]. Each of these op. codes has a different effect, but a full discussion of addressing modes is best left until you wish to write larger and more complex assembler programs.

A different kind of loop from that used in program P3.ASM is in use here. In P3.ASM, the decision to terminate the loop was at the **bottom** of the loop, i.e. decrement the counter and see if it has finished; if not, jump back to the top of the loop. In P5.ASM, the **top** of the loop is marked with the symbolic address L1:. It contains the code that checks for the byte 0 at the end of the string; if it is found, the loop is terminated.

The line 'top: jmp start' is there because the processor cannot distinguish between data and machine instructions; they are all just numbers. If 'jmp start' was not there, the processor would attempt to execute the byte codes for 'Mary had a little lamb'. The hex dump of P5.COM is below to show this.

BTEC National Study Guide: IT Practitioners. See page 293 for order details of individual texts

49

Hex dumps and binary files

A **hex dump** is when a file is presented as hex bytes. This is usually because the file is not made up of simple ASCII characters. Files that need to be shown this way are often called **binary files**. For example, if a program file contained the byte 08, 'printing' the file to the screen would result in a backspace (ASCII 8 is backspace) and not the character 8, a hex dump would show 08.

Hex dump of P5.COM

```
E9 19 00 4D 61 72 79 20 68 61 64 20 61 20 6C 69      ;e..Mary had a li
74 74 6C 65 20 6C 61 6D 62 0A 0D 00 BE 03 01 8A      ;ttle lamb.../.._
14 80 FA 00 74 07 B4 02 CD 21 46 EB F2 CD 20         ;._u.t.'.I!FeoI
```

As you can see, the machine code (written in hex bytes) does not seem to mean very much!

As assembly is a simple process of converting mnemonics directly to machine code; it can be reversed, the machine code can be 'turned back' to assembly code. Table 2.13 shows the result of this process, and provides a comment on what most of the bytes mean.

Unassembly of P5.ASM

Table 2.13   *Unassembly of P5.ASM*

Address	Contents	Mnemonic	Comments
0100	E91900	JMP 011C	;jump to the first instruction after the data
0103	4D	M	;data
0104	61	a	;data
0105	72	r	;data
0106	79	y	;data
0107	20	(space character)	;data
0108	68	h	;data
0109	61	a	;data
010A	64	d	;data
010B	20	(space character)	;data
010C	61	a	;data
010D	20	(space character)	;data
010E	6C	l	;data
010F	49	i	;data
0110	74	t	;data
0111	74	t	;data
0112	6C	l	;data
0113	65	e	;data
0114	20	(space character)	;data
0115	6C	l	;data
0116	61	a	;data
0117	6D	m	data
0118	62	b	;data
0119	0A	(line feed)	;data

(Contd)

BTEC National Study Guide: IT Practitioners. See page 293 for order details of individual texts

50

Table 2.13 *(Contd)*

Address	Contents	Mnemonic	Comments
011A	13	(carriage return)	;data
011B	00	(0 used as end of string marker)	;data
011C	BE0301	MOV SI,103	;point to start of data at address 103
011F	8A14	MOV DL,[SI]	;get the data pointed to in DL ;processor register
0121	80FA00	CMP DL,00	;test to see if data is last in the string
0124	7407	JZ 012D	;if so, jump to last instruction in program
0126	B402	MOV AH,02	;put 2 into AH register, required for DOS ;function 2 call next
0128	CD21	INT 21	;call DOS int 21 function 2 to write ;character to screen
012A	46	INC SI	;point to next character in data string ;at next address
012B	EBF2	JMP 011F	;go back to address 11F to start again
012D	CD20	INT 20	;terminate program and return to DOS ;CLI (the DOS prompt)

Points to note about the unassembled program

There seem to be gaps in the addresses. This is not so, it is just that some instructions take up more than one address location. For instance, starting at address 011C there is the machine code instruction BE 03 01, which, when unassembled, gives the mnemonic MOV SI, 103. This instruction takes up the addresses 011C, 011D and 011E so the next instruction starts at address 011F. Some instructions only occupy 1 byte; for instance, at address 012A the instruction to add 1 to the SI register has the machine code 46 only.

Experiment with program P5.ASM

If you remove the top line (top: jmp start) and re-assemble the program, the first byte of the 'code' will be the ASCII code for 'M'. When you execute the program, most likely the machine will crash as the 4 bytes 'Mary' will be interpreted as op. codes DEC BP, DB 61, JB 017D.

Example program 6, P6.ASM

This program demonstrates that assembly language programmers must do everything for themselves! If a register holds a value such as 173, to print this to the screen will take a small program and not a single instruction as would be the case in a high-level language. The reason is that no op. code exists to convert the value 173 to the **three** ASCII characters required to print this to the screen.

Suppose at some point you wish to output the contents of the AX register as a multi-digit number. The code to do this is contained as a subroutine called OUTINT in the file LIB.ASM supplied in Appendix 1 and at www.anderh.com/repp. For the purposes of the National Certificate/Diploma in Computing, the detail of this

BTEC National Study Guide: IT Practitioners. See page 293 for order details of individual texts

51

subroutine takes assembly language too far; students would not be expected to write such code but would be expected to use it as a subroutine.

```
MOV AX, 173      ;the number to be printed by sub routine
CALL OUTINT      ;print the multi digit number
INT 020          ;terminate program
```

That's it!

To assemble the program with the file called LIB.ASM, just type at the DOS prompt

C:\>P6.ASM LIB.ASM P6.COM

This will assemble P6.ASM **with** LIB.ASM, and output the executable in P6.COM.

The only new op. code is CALL. This op. code causes the current address to be stored (on a **stack**) and a jump to be made to the address of the subroutine (remember the assembler will convert the symbolic address OUTINT to a real numerical address). When the RET instruction is reached, a jump is made back to the return address (held on the stack).

Stacks

A stack is simply a section of RAM that is handled in a particular way. A stack pointer (usually held in register SP) holds the address at the top of the stack. This is usually described as **pointing** to the top of the stack. If a value is to be stored on the stack, the op. code PUSH is used; this puts the value into the **address pointed to by the stack pointer** then **decrements** the stack pointer ready for the next use. In this way, the next value goes into the next location. To reverse the process, the instruction POP is used.

Example program P7.ASM

Now we know how to use a pre-written subroutine, we can practise with outputting a string:

```
        MOV SI, buffer
        CALL printstring
        INT 020
buffer: db 'I love Computing', 13,10,0
```

The string is terminated with a 0 byte as before, and SI is used to point to the string.

Assemble the program with:

C:\>A86 P7.ASM LIB.ASM P7.COM

BTEC National Study Guide: IT Practitioners. See page 293 for order details of individual texts

52

Example program P8.ASM

This uses a DOS interrupt to get the current time and then the OUTINT subroutine to display it. It also demonstrates a common problem in assembly language, that of avoiding accidentally corrupting a register value. The OUTINT subroutine will not output a leading 0, so if the value to be output should be 02 instead of just 2, the program must check this first. To find the system time, a list of DOS interrupts is consulted to find out the 'rules' of the interrupt. This is what was found:

DOS interrupt 21 Function 2C, read system time.
Calling registers

  AH = 2C

Return registers

  CH = hours (0-23) in decimal
  CL = minutes (0-59) in decimal
  DH = seconds (0-59) in decimal
  DL = hundredths of a second (0-99) in decimal

This means that 02C is put into AH before a call to the interrupt, then the values in registers CH, CL, DH and DL are used as hours, minutes and seconds.

```
      MOV AH, 02C  ;DOS interrupt 21 Function 2C,
                   ;read system time.
      INT 021      ;call DOS
                   ;now CH=hours, CL=Minutes
                   ;DH=seconds,DL=hundredths/sec

;..... now store to prevent overwriting by subroutine

      MOV hours, CH
      MOV mins, CL
      MOV secs, DH

      ;..... display the hours.................

      MOV AH,0     ;AX is AH and AL so clear top
      MOV AL, hours ;of AX (AH) ready for OUTINT
      CMP AX, 10   ;see if leading zero is needed
      JAE L20      ;jump if 10 or more without
                   ;outputting 0 first
      CALL leadingzero
L20: CALL OUTINT   ;output the time in hours

      ;..... now output a h:m:s separator...........

      MOV DL, ':'  ;hour:min:sec separator
      MOV AH, 2    ;DOS interrupt 21 function 2
      INT 021      ;call DOS to output ':'

      ;..... display the minutes.................
```

BTEC National Study Guide: IT Practitioners. See page 293 for order details of individual texts

53

```
        MOV AH,0      ;AX is AH and AL so clear top
        MOV AL, mins  ;of AX (AH) ready for OUTINT
        CMP AX, 10    ;see if leading zero is needed
        JAE L21       ;jump if 10 or more without
                      ;outputting 0 first
        CALL leadingzero
L21: CALL OUTINT      ;output the time in minutes

        ;..... now output a h:m:s separator............

        MOV DL, ':'   ;hour:min:sec separator
        MOV AH, 2     ;DOS interrupt 21 function 2
        INT 021       ;call DOS to output ':'

        ;..... display the seconds.................

        MOV AH,0      ;AX is AH and AL so clear top
        MOV AL, secs  ;of AX (AH) ready for OUTINT
        CMP AX, 10    ;see if leading zero is needed
        JAE L22       ;jump if 10 or more without
                      ;outputting 0 first
        CALL leadingzero
L22: CALL OUTINT      ;output the time in seconds

        INT 020       ;terminate program

hours DB 0            ;define some space
mins DB 0             ;for variables
secs DB 0             ;to store values
```

Exercise 2.4

Modify program P8.ASM to output the system date. The following information is required:

DOS interrupt 21 Function 2A, read system date
Calling registers

 AH = 2A in hex

Return registers

 AL = day of the week (0=Sunday, 1=Monday etc.)
 CX = year
 DH = month
 DL = day.

Hint, for storing the year you will need a DW directive to define a 16-bit word in place of the DB directive to define an 8-bit byte. The answer is in Appendix A.

Exercise 2.5

Modify program P8.ASM to output the DOS version number for your machine, preceded by the string 'DOS version number= '. The following information is required:

BTEC National Study Guide: IT Practitioners. See page 293 for order details of individual texts

54

DOS interrupt 21 Function 30, return DOS version number
Calling registers

AH = 30 in hex

Return registers

AL = Major version number (2,3 etc.)
AH = Minor version number (2.1 returns 2 in AL and 10 in AH).

The answer is in Appendix A.

Exercise 2.6

Modify programs P8.ASM and your answer to Exercise 2.4 to output both the system time and date on the same line with strings saying 'Time is now' and 'Date= '.

The answer is in Appendix A.

2.7 Operating systems

An operating system has a number of functions:

- to provide an interface with the user
- to provide a range of services that are used by application software, such as disk management, printer control, time/date functions etc.
- to provide a development environment, i.e. compilers and run-time systems etc.

It is usual in operating systems (OS) to consider a layered architecture in a similar manner to layering in networks. The layers in a typical OS are:

- layer 4, applications
- layer 3, kernel
- layer 2, drivers
- layer 1, hardware.

Layer 1 is how the operating system communicates with the hardware, rather than the hardware itself. In PCs, this is generally the BIOS – the Basic Input Output System.

Layer 2, drivers, refers to pieces of software that 'talk' to specific device types such as disk drives. For example, in a PC, an ATAPI CD-ROM needs a device driver loaded because the operating system at layers 3 and 4 does not 'know about' CDs and how the data are organized in detail. The device driver provides this service.

Layer 3, the kernel, organizes the way that processes are controlled – i.e. if an application requests service from a printer, other application requests must not interfere.

Layer 4, applications, are the programs the user wishes to run in the machine. The OS must load them into memory and start them running.

BTEC National Study Guide: IT Practitioners. See page 293 for order details of individual texts

55

Various operating systems have a layered architecture different in detail from that described here. No matter; the idea is that application software is supported or supplied with services by the OS. This means that an application programmer need not know how to control a printer or a disk drive; all that is needed is to ask the OS for these services. In the case of Microsoft Windows, this is done by the Windows API or **Application Programme Interface**. Application software calls for service from the Win API; the actual code for this is stored in .DLL files or **Dynamic Link Libraries**.

User interface

In the past, what the user saw was a screen prompt (or even a printer prompt!) like C:\>. This 'prompted' the user to type a command such as DIR to gain a service. (DIR requests a listing of the files on the current disk drive.) This style of user interface is called a CLI, or Command Line Interpreter, because the text typed at the prompt (the command line) is interpreted by the CLI and either a request is made to the kernel for service or an error message is issued. In Microsoft's DOS, the CLI is called COMMAND.COM. In the unix world there are many different command line interpreters; they are called 'shells' but do essentially the same thing -- they provide a command line–user interface.

More modern PC operating Systems use a **Graphical User Interface**, or GUI. This is what you see when you use Windows, but it is **only** an interface; what underlies Windows 95 or 98 is mostly DOS. Windows NT or 2000 are very different although they look similar. Here the underlying kernel is not DOS but the GUI 'talks' to the kernel in a related fashion. If you run **Linux** on a PC, you use either a shell (the CLI) or a GUI that has a similar 'look and feel' to Microsoft Windows. There are several on the market.

Kinds of OS

Quite independently of the user interface, the OS must provide for ideas such as multi-tasking, and for multiple users.

Multi-tasking is not quite what it seems. To the user the machine is running multiple tasks all at once so, for instance, a download from the Internet is running at the same time as the user types into a wordprocessor. Of course the PC only has a single CPU, which can only do one thing at a time. The solution is to switch between tasks so quickly that the user is not aware of the switching. This is achieved using a number of system software techniques.

Multi-user operating systems must provide additional services to allow the identification of users; i.e. they must 'log in'. The OS must also provide security so that malicious or careless users cannot affect the work of others.

If more than one task or more than one user needs service from the OS, it must provide memory management. This means that the physical RAM must be organized so that users and applications are not able to infringe other areas. When using Windows, you may

BTEC National Study Guide: IT Practitioners. See page 293 for order details of individual texts

56

have seen the error message 'This program has performed an illegal operation'. A common cause of this is an application that attempts to access an address in memory that belongs to a different application or process. Windows cannot resolve the problem, so it shuts down the errant process.

2.8 ASCII and Unicode character sets

Before the days of computing, communication systems required each character to be sent as a code. Simple systems used 1s and 0s for transmission just like today, so binary numbers were used to encode characters. You could not send an 'A' character directly, but you could send binary 1000001 in its place. This eventually led to a 'standard' set of characters that were used to control printing devices before the widespread use of VDUs. ASCII stands for American Standard Code for Information Interchange, but there are other character encoding systems around like EBCDIC and LICS that work in a similar way. However, ASCII is the most widespread.

In ASCII, the codes from 0 to 31 are called 'Control Characters'. These were originally used to control the movement of the old mechanical printers, so we have terms like 'Carriage Return' (now known as Enter or just Return) that actually caused the carriage that held the paper to return to the left-hand side. Understanding this historical basis of the control characters helps you to understand the names they are given, which now seem a little odd. If a Control Character (written as CTRL A etc.) is sent to a printer or screen, it usually results in an action rather than a printable character. Because some of the codes only have real meaning for mechanical printers, the original names do not always make sense in modern usage.

Before the widespread use of Microsoft Windows, most machines responded directly to these control characters. As an experiment, try opening a DOS window and typing a command. Instead of pressing the Enter key, press CTRL M instead; you should find it does the same thing as pressing Enter. The Enter key is just a CTRL M key in DOS. (If you try this using Microsoft Word, CTRL M has a different effect.) If you are using Unix or Linux, try using CTRL H in place of the backspace key; it should work unless it has been re-mapped on your machine.

Table 2.14 lists the ASCII control characters.

Characters in ASCII are easy to remember; they run from A = 65 to Z = 90. This may look like an odd choice of numbers until you convert the 65 into binary and get 1000001, i.e. 64 + 1. This means that any letter is easy to calculate; it is 64 plus its position in the alphabet. M is the thirteenth letter in the alphabet, so in ASCII, M = 64 + 13 = 77. To make it lower case, just add 32. This is a good choice, as 32 encodes as a single binary digit. Lower case m is then 64 + 32 + 13 = 109. Of course it would be better to use hex, so A = 41, M = 4D, a = 61, m = 6D etc. Numerals are just as easy; '0' encodes as 48, '1' encodes as 48 + 1 = 49, etc.

The full set of 7-bit printable ASCII characters is shown in Table 2.15.

You will notice that the codes only extend to 127. This is because the original ASCII only used 7-binary digits and was referred to as a 7 bit code. Whilst there is some standardization of the codes 128 to 255; some machines will give different characters for codes 128

BTEC National Study Guide: IT Practitioners. See page 293 for order details of individual texts

57

Table 2.14 *The ASCII control characters*

Dec	Hex	Keyboard	Binary		Description
0	0	CTRL @	00000	NUL	Null Character
1	1	CTRL A	00001	SOH	Start of Heading
2	2	CTRL B	00010	STX	Start of Text
3	3	CTRL C	00011	ETX	End of Text
4	4	CTRL D	00100	EOT	End of Transmission
5	5	CTRL E	00101	ENQ	Enquiry
6	6	CTRL F	00110	ACK	Acknowledge
7	7	CTRL G	00111	BEL	Bell or beep
8	8	CTRL H	01000	BS	Back Space
9	9	CTRL I	01001	HT	Horizontal Tab
10	A	CTRL J	01010	LF	Line Feed
11	B	CTRL K	01011	VT	Vertical Tab
12	C	CTRL L	01100	FF	Form Feed
13	D	CTRL M	01101	CR	Carriage Return
14	E	CTRL N	01110	SO	Shift Out
15	F	CTRL O	01111	SI	Shift In
16	10	CTRL P	10000	DLE	Date Link Escape
17	11	CTRL Q	10001	DC1	Device Control 1
18	12	CTRL R	10010	DC2	Device Control 2
19	13	CTRL S	10011	DC3	Device Control 3
20	14	CTRL T	10100	DC4	Device Control 4
21	15	CTRL U	10101	NAK	Negative Acknowledge
22	16	CTRL V	10110	SYN	Synchronous Idle
23	17	CTRL W	10111	ETB	End of Transmission Block
24	18	CTRL X	11000	CAN	Cancel
25	19	CTRL Y	11001	EM	End Medium
26	1A	CTRL Z	11010	SUB	Substitute or EOF End Of File
27	1B		11011	ESC	Escape
28	1C		11100	FS	File Separator
29	1D		11101	GS	Group Separator
30	1E		11110	RS	Record Separator
31	1F		11111	US	Unit Separator

to 255; for instance, older machines will give an é for code 130 whilst more modern machines will give an é for code 233.

It is not important to remember ASCII codes but it is often useful, especially when writing text- or string-handling parts of programs. If you remember that 'A' = 64 + alphabet position (40 in hex) and that 'a' = 'A' + 32 ('A' + 20 in hex), you can work out all of the alphabet. The '0' character is 48, and the digits are 48 + their value. If you also remember that a Carriage Return is 13 (0D hex) and that Line Feed is 10 (0A hex), you will be able to remember about half the codes and interpret some hex-dumped files.

Question 2.3

Write down the ASCII values in decimal and hex for the string 'I Love Computing'. Try to work it out without looking at the code table. Don't forget the spaces are ASCII characters as well.

	I		L	o	v	e		C	o	m	p	u	t	i	n	g
Dec																
Hex																

BTEC National Study Guide: IT Practitioners. See page 293 for order details of individual texts

58

Table 2.15 *Seven-bit printable ASCII characters*

Char	Dec	Hex	Binary	Char	Dec	Hex	Binary	Char	Dec	Hex	Binary
Space	32	20	100000								
!	33	21	100001	A	65	41	1000001	a	97	61	1100001
"	34	22	100010	B	66	42	1000010	b	98	62	1100010
#	35	23	100011	C	67	43	1000011	c	99	63	1100011
$	36	24	100100	D	68	44	1000100	d	100	64	1100100
%	37	25	100101	E	69	45	1000101	e	101	65	1100101
&	38	26	100110	F	70	46	1000110	f	102	66	1100110
'	39	27	100111	G	71	47	1000111	g	103	67	1100111
(	40	28	101000	H	72	48	1001000	h	104	68	1101000
)	41	29	101001	I	73	49	1001001	i	105	69	1101001
*	42	2A	101010	J	74	4A	1001010	j	106	6A	1101010
+	43	2B	101011	K	75	4B	1001011	k	107	6B	1101011
,	44	2C	101100	L	76	4C	1001100	l	108	6C	1101100
−	45	2D	101101	M	77	4D	1001101	m	109	6D	1101101
.	46	2E	101110	N	78	4E	1001110	n	110	6E	1101110
/	47	2F	101111	O	79	4F	1001111	o	111	6F	1101111
0	48	30	110000	P	80	50	1010000	p	112	70	1110000
1	49	31	110001	Q	81	51	1010001	q	113	71	1110001
2	50	32	110010	R	82	52	1010010	r	114	72	1110010
3	51	33	110011	S	83	53	1010011	s	115	73	1110011
4	52	34	110100	T	84	54	1010100	t	116	74	1110100
5	53	35	110101	U	85	55	1010101	u	117	75	1110101
6	54	36	110110	V	86	56	1010110	v	118	76	1110110
7	55	37	110111	W	87	57	1010111	w	119	77	1110111
8	56	38	111000	X	88	58	1011000	x	120	78	1111000
9	57	39	111001	Y	89	59	1011001	y	121	79	1111001
:	58	3A	111010	Z	90	5A	1011010	z	122	7A	1111010
;	59	3B	111011	[	91	5B	1011011	{	123	7B	1111011
<	60	3C	111100	\	92	5C	1011100	|	124	7C	1111100
=	61	3D	111101	]	93	5D	1011101	}	125	7D	1111101
>	62	3E	111110	^	94	5E	1011110	~	126	7E	1111110
?	63	3F	111111	_	95	5F	1011111	del	127	7F	1111111
@	64	40	1000000	`	96	60	1100000				

Answer

	I		L	o	v	e		C	o	m	p	u	t	i	n	g
Dec	73	32	76	111	118	101	32	67	111	109	112	117	116	105	110	103
Hex	49	20	4C	6F	76	65	20	43	6F	6D	70	75	74	69	6E	67

Unicode

ASCII characters, although universally accepted, present one serious problem; there are not sufficient characters to cover all the symbols and characters from different languages. The solution adopted until the introduction of **Unicode** was to set up each computer with its own character set according to the country or language. This makes it harder to communicate files from computers set up for different countries; try finding the pound sign on an American keyboard! 'Normal' Unicode uses 16-bit characters, so there are $2^{16} = 65536$ possible characters, more than enough to cover all the world's main languages. The ASCII character set has been incorporated so character 65 is still an 'A', but the 65 is a 16-bit value. There is also a byte-oriented Unicode that allows for more than a million

BTEC National Study Guide: IT Practitioners. See page 293 for order details of individual texts

59

characters. The Unicode standard is developing all the time; the latest situation is presented on their web page at http://www.unicode.org/. This describes the current version, and the work in progress to add more.

Conversion of ASCII to Unicode is very easy as the codes are simply changed from 8 bit into 16 bit. Conversion from Unicode to ASCII may result in the loss of data as ASCII cannot support more than 256 different characters. Some operating systems will work with both character sets; the more modern ones will use Unicode as the native code.

2.9 Number bases

The Romans used a number system based on symbols, so I was 1 and V was 5. The number IV means 5 – 1, or 4, and VI means 5 + 1, or 6. This is a very difficult system to use if you want to do mathematics. In contrast, we use the Arabic system, which is based on **numbers by position**.

Consider the number 264. We all know this is two hundred and sixty-four because we have been brought up to be very familiar with numbers in this format. If you break it down, it means two hundreds, six tens and four units or 200 + 60 + 4. The digit 6 only means 60 because of its **position** in the number 264.

If you remember back to primary school days, you will recognize the sum

```
  h    t    u
  2    6    4
 +1    2    2
 _____
  3    8    6
```

The headings mean **h** for hundreds, **t** for tens and **u** for units.

A more mathematical approach would be to recognize that 100 is 10^2, 10 is 10^1, and units are 10^0 (any number to power 0 is 1). The sum then looks like this:

```
 10²   10¹   10⁰
  2     6     4
 +1     2     2
 _____
  3     8     6
```

This is the basis for numbers by position to a base, in this case, base 10. Each column is simply then number base raised to an integer power.

If you add 392 to 264 and set it out as below, the second column results in a **carry** operation.

```
 10²      10¹   10⁰
 2        6     4
 3        9     2
 carry 1
 _____
 6        5     6
```

BTEC National Study Guide: IT Practitioners. See page 293 for order details of individual texts

60

This is how we are taught to 'carry 1' into the next column. What we are doing is simply using numbers by position; the sum of the second column, 6 + 9, is 15, the digit 1 in 15 refers to **10** rather than **1** so it belongs in the next column to the left.

> The only reason we use numbers to the base 10 is that humans are born with 10 fingers. If we were all born with, say, 12 fingers, we would use numbers to base 12 and think numbers to base 10 to be very odd indeed! The way we manipulate numbers, do addition, multiplication, division etc. is exactly the same in any number base.

Other number bases

The 6 in 264 means 60, or 6 tens, because we use numbers to the base 10. We could just as easily use numbers to any other base. If we used numbers to base 8 (called octal numbers), then the number 64 would mean 6 eights plus 4, not 6 tens plus 4.

If we were to use numbers to the base 8, the column headings would be $8^2\,8^1\,8^0$; if numbers to the base 5, the headings would be $5^2\,5^1\,5^0$.

The powers simply increase by 1 for each column to the left or decrease by 1 to the right.

The number of symbols required

To use any given number base, you need that number of symbols to write it down. As we use numbers to base 10, we use symbols 0–9. Binary numbers use base 2, so we need only two symbols, 0 and 1.

The common bases in computing are 2, 10 and 16. Binary is used because the electronic circuits operate in two states that can be modelled using 1 or 0; 1 for 'on' and 0 for 'off'.

Hex or hexadecimal numbers are often used in computing. This is because conversion to or from binary is very simple, and those people who need to work with 'bits and bytes' find hex convenient. Since hex numbers are to the base 16, we need 16 symbols, 0–9 and A–F. This makes numbers look a little odd, but 5D simply means 5 times 16^1 plus D, (or 13) times 1, so 5D hex is $(5 \times 16) + 13 = 93$ in base 10 numbers.

Table 2.16 shows the same value in each row, but in various number bases.

Binary numbers

Knowing that binary uses the same **rule** as base 10 numbers, i.e. numbers by position, it is easy to understand a binary number.

The value shown in Table 2.17 in binary is 10110001010, or $2^{10} + 2^8 + 2^7 + 2^3 + 2^1 = 1024 + 256 + 8 + 1 = 1289$ base 10. Ignore the leading zeros.

BTEC National Study Guide: IT Practitioners. See page 293 for order details of individual texts

61

Table 2.16   *Various number bases showing the same value in each row*

Base 2 binary	Base 8 octal	Base 10 decimal	Base 16 hex
0	0	0	0
1	1	1	1
10	2	2	2
11	3	3	3
100	4	4	4
101	5	5	5
110	6	6	6
111	7	7	7
1000	10	8	8
1001	11	9	9
1010	12	10	A
1011	13	11	B
1100	14	12	C
1101	15	13	D
1110	16	14	E
1111	17	15	F
10000	20	16	10
10001	21	17	11
10010	22	18	12
10011	23	19	13

Table 2.17   *Decimal and binary numbers*

	2^{11}	2^{10}	2^9	2^8	2^7	2^6	2^5	2^4	2^3	2^2	2^1	2^0
Decimal value	2048	1024	512	256	128	64	32	16	8	4	2	1
Binary	0	1	0	1	1	0	0	0	1	0	1	0

Question 2.4

(a) Convert 110110011 to decimal.

Answer

2^{11}	2^{10}	2^9	2^8	2^7	2^6	2^5	2^4	2^3	2^2	2^1	2^0
0	0	0	1	1	0	1	1	0	0	1	1

$2^8 + 2^7 + 2^5 + 2^4 + 2^1 + 2^0 = 256 + 128 + 32 + 16 + 2 + 1 = 435$

(b) Convert 110001101 to decimal.

Answer

2^{11}	2^{10}	2^9	2^8	2^7	2^6	2^5	2^4	2^3	2^2	2^1	2^0
0	0	0	1	1	0	0	0	1	1	0	1

$2^8 + 2^7 + 2^3 + 2^2 + 2^0 = 256 + 128 + 8 + 4 + 1 = 397$

There are many way to convert backwards. One is to use knowledge of the values in each column, like this:

BTEC National Study Guide: IT Practitioners. See page 293 for order details of individual texts

62

2^{11}	2^{10}	2^9	2^8	2^7	2^6	2^5	2^4	2^3	2^2	2^1	2^0
2048	1024	512	256	128	64	32	16	8	4	2	1

When converting 106 to binary, it is clear that all the columns 128 and higher have the value zero as 106 is lower than 128. A '1' is entered into the 2^6 column, and 64 subtracted from 106 to give 106 − 64 = 42. Because 42 is higher than the next number down, a '1' goes into the 2^5 column and 32 is subtracted from 42 to give 10; as 10 is 8 + 2, a '1' will go in each of the 8 and 1 columns as shown in Table 2.18. Therefore, 106 base 10 is 1101010.

Table 2.18 *Converting 106 to binary*

2^{11}	2^{10}	2^9	2^8	2^7	2^6	2^5	2^4	2^3	2^2	2^1	2^0
2048	1024	512	256	128	64	32	16	8	4	2	1
0	0	0	0	0	1	1	0	1	0	1	0

Checking backwards, 1101010 is 64 + 32 + 8 + 2 = 106.

Another way to convert a decimal number to binary is successive division by 2. In Table 2.19, the number 106 is divided by 2 using **integer arithmetic** – i.e. the fractional part of the answer is ignored. Also using integer arithmetic, the remainder after division is shown. This is known as MOD, so 106 MOD 2 = 0, i.e. there is no remainder after division by 2. Each quotient is then divided by 2 in the same way until a quotient of 0 is obtained. The binary value of the original number is now shown in the remainder column, **read from the bottom**. In this example, the value 106 is shown to be 1101010 as above.

Table 2.19 *Using integer arithmetic to convert a decimal number to binary*

	Quotient	Remainder
106 DIV 2 =	53	0
53 DIV 2 =	26	1
26 DIV 2 =	13	0
13 DIV 2 =	6	1
6 DIV 2 =	3	0
3 DIV 2 =	1	1
1 DIV 2 =	0	1

Hex and octal numbers

If we have an octal number, it is easy to convert it to base 10. Taking 523 as an octal number, this is:

5×8^2, or $5 \times 64 = 320$

plus

2×8^1, or $2 \times 8 = 16$

plus

BTEC National Study Guide: IT Practitioners. See page 293 for order details of individual texts

63

3×8^0, or $3 \times 1 = 3$ (any number to power 0 is 1)

equals

$320 + 16 + 3 = 339$ (base 10).

As a further example, what is the octal number 1000 in decimal? The answer is easy to see if it is laid out as before:

8^3	8^2	8^1	8^0
1	0	0	0

so 1000 octal $= 1 \times 8^3 = 512$ base 10.

Converting numbers

You can convert numbers using Microsoft Excel spreadsheets. The functions OCT2BIN OCT2HEX, OCT2DEC, HEX2BIN, HEX2OCT, HEX2DEC, BIN2HEX, BIN2OCT, BIN2DEC, DEC2BIN, DEC2OCT, DEC2HEX can be used. If they do not work first time, see the help file about installing the Analysis Tool Pack 'add-in'.

The same rules apply if using hex or any other base. For example, the hex number 26A is:

2×16^2, or $2 \times 64 = 128$

plus

6×16^1, or $6 \times 16 = 96$

plus

A (or 10) $\times 16^0$, or $16 \times 1 = 16$

equals

$128 + 96 + 16 = 618$ base 10.

Converting Octal and hex to and from binary

As stated above, one reason that Hex or Octal numbers are used is that conversion to or from binary is simple.

Examples

1. To convert the hex number 4A7 to binary:
    Take each digit and write it down in 4-bit binary.

    4 = 0100
    A = 1010
    7 = 0111

    so 4A7 = 0100 1010 0111, usually written with no spaces as 010010100111.

2. To convert the hex number F0FF to binary:

    F = 1111

BTEC National Study Guide: IT Practitioners. See page 293 for order details of individual texts

64

0 = 0000
F = 1111
F = 1111

so F0FF = 1111 0000 1111 1111.

3. To convert the other way, simply break the binary number into 4-bit sections **from the right** and write down the hex digit equivalent for each of the 4-bit groups. For examples to convert 10011000100111010100 to hex:

1001 1000 1001 1101 0100
9   8   9   D   4

so 10011000100111010100 = 989D4 in hex.

4. To convert 11110111001000000011011 to hex:

1 1110 1110 0100 0001 1011
1 E   E   4   1   B

so 11110111001000000011011 = 1EE41B in hex.

5. The only difference with octal numbers is that you use 3-bit groups instead of 4-bit groups. For example, to convert the octal number 216 to binary:

2 = 010
1 = 001
6 = 110

So 216 octal = 010001110 in binary.

6. To convert 110010011100001 to octal:

110 010 011 100 001
6   2   3   4   1

So 110010011100001 = 62341 octal.

7. One way to convert a hex number to an octal number is to convert to binary as an intermediary. For example, to convert 23FA to octal (notice that 23FA cannot be octal as octal only uses the digits 0–7):

23FA = 0010 0011 1111 1010, which when split into groups of three gives

0 010 001 111 111 010 = 21772 octal (ignore leading zeros).

If you have access to a PC running Windows and you do not have a scientific calculator that can handle numbers to different bases, you can check your answers with the Windows calculator. Go to start, programs, accessories, calculator. When started, click on the view menu and choose Scientific.

Question 2.5

Fill in table without using a calculator or any other aid.

BTEC National Study Guide: IT Practitioners. See page 293 for order details of individual texts

65

Binary	Octal	Decimal	Hex
	233	155	9B
111110011		499	
		40	
			2E
101001010			
			BE
110111010			
	527		
	714		
		138	
		16	
		57	
			13E
		400	
			1FB
100011110			

Answer

Binary	Octal	Decimal	Hex
10011011	233	155	9B
111110011	763	499	1F3
101000	50	40	28
101110	56	46	2E
101001010	512	330	14A
10111110	276	190	BE
110111010	672	442	1BA
101010111	527	343	157
111001100	714	460	1CC
10001010	212	138	8A
10000	20	16	10
111001	71	57	39
100111110	476	318	13E
110010000	620	400	190
111111011	773	507	1FB
100011110	436	286	11E

BTEC National Study Guide: IT Practitioners. See page 293 for order details of individual texts

66

Fixed point fractional numbers

In numbers to the base 10 using numbers by position, fractional numbers are represented in the same way, so

10^2	10^1	10^0	10^{-1}	10^{-2}	10^{-3}	10^{-4}
2	6	4	2	7	8	4

gives 264.2784 because

10^{-1} is $1/10^1$ or 0.1
10^{-2} is $1/10^2$ or 1/100 or 0.01
10^{-3} is $1/10^3$ or 1/1000 or 0.001 etc.

so $0.2784 = 2 \times 10^{-1}$ plus 7×10^{-2} plus 8×10^{-3} plus 4×10^{-4}.

In numbers by position, each power increases to the right and decreases to the left.

Question 2.6

Write down 452.0625 as a fixed point binary number.

Answer

452 = 256 + 128 + 64 + 4 = 111000100
$0.0625 = 2^{-4}$ or 0.0001

	2^8	2^7	2^6	2^5	2^4	2^3	2^2	2^1	2^0	2^{-1}	2^{-2}	2^{-3}	2^{-4}
Dec.	256	128	64	32	16	8	4	2	1	0.5	0.25	0.125	0.0625
	1	1	1	0	0	0	1	0	0	0	0	0	1

so 452.0625 = 111000100.0001.

Here the point is a bicemal point instead of a decimal point.

Just as one-third = 0.3333 recurring in decimal, i.e. 0.333 is not exactly one-third, it is possible to get inexact binary fractions. The decimal 1/100 or 0.01 gives an inexact binary fraction, which is unfortunate because £0.01, or one penny, cannot be represented exactly as a simple binary fraction. This can lead to errors, as will be shown in section 2.10. Decimal 0.01 is

0.00000010100011110101110000101000111101011100001010001111 to 56 binary places, **approximately**!

2.10 Floating point numbers

A floating point number (called a 'real' in Pascal) stores the number in several parts. For example, to change 382.070556640625 to a floating point number:

Step 1, convert to **fixed** point binary

382.070556640625 = 101111110.000100100001000000000000000

Step 2, move the binary point to the left until there is a leading '1'. This is called **normalizing**, and the number it produces is called the **mantissa**. Record the power of 2 required to achieve this; in this case it is 8. This value is called the **exponent**.

BTEC National Study Guide: IT Practitioners. See page 293 for order details of individual texts

67

$$1.01111111000010010000100000000000000 \times 2^8$$

Step 3, to avoid the possibility of negative powers, add a fixed value to the exponent. This is called an **excess** value. A standard value to add is 127, and such a system would be called 'Excess 127'. Use the excess 127 rule on the exponent and convert to binary

$8 + 127 = 135$

$135 = 10000111.$

Step 4, store values, stripping the leading 1 of the mantissa. Since the mantissa will always have a leading '1' there is no point storing it.

Step 5, assign a 0 to a positive number or a 1 to negative number; this is called the **sign bit**.

Sign	Exponent	Fraction or mantissa
0	10000111	01111110000100100001000
bit 31	bits 30–23	bits 22–0

So as a floating point number,

$382.070556640625 = 0100\ 0011\ 1011\ 1111\ 0000\ 1001\ 0000\ 1000$

which viewed as hex would be:

0100	0011	1011	1111	0000	1001	0000	1000
4	3	B	F	0	9	0	0

or 43 BF 09 00.

IEEE floating point format

It is often said that the nice thing about standards in computing is that there are so many to choose from! Floating point numbers can and are represented in a wide variety of formats, which usually means the only program that can read them is the one that created them in the first place. Clearly it is desirable to have a common standard so all programs can read/write floating point numbers. The Institute of Electrical and Electronic Engineers (IEEE, home page http://standards.ieee.org/) has issued a floating point number standard, which is usually referred to as simply IEEE 754 (see http://grouper.ieee.org/groups/754/).

The IEEE standard defines several formats for floating point numbers, but for simplicity the most common is shown here. It is supported by many software providers.

Numbers are stored in the format $N = 1.F * 2^{(E-127)}$, where

N = floating point number
F = fractional part in binary
E = exponent in excess 127 format, also known as bias 127 representation.

One bit represents the sign of the number and is known as the sign bit. 0 = positive. The next 8 bits contain the exponent field, and the

BTEC National Study Guide: IT Practitioners. See page 293 for order details of individual texts

68

last 23 bits contain the mantissa as a normalized number, leading zero not stored:

Sign	Exponent	Fraction
0	00000000	00000000000000000000000
bit 31	bits 30–23	bits 22–0

Floating point experiments

The following experiments with a spreadsheet, Visual Basic and Pascal demonstrate that floating point numbers are not always exact and that small errors can exist in their representation. These errors are small, but can be significant if appropriate steps are not taken to avoid them.

Use of a spreadsheet

This example is produced from Microsoft Excel 97.

In this experiment, the spreadsheet adds a value (called an increment) to a number and then adds itself again and again to the result. If the increment is itself not an exact floating point number, any errors get amplified to the point that they become visible. Once you have set up the spreadsheet, look at the first column in Table 2.20. You will see that the values increase at first as they should; each line is just 0.001 larger than the last, and any errors are not visible. If you look several hundred rows down, you will see that errors have appeared. Column 2 uses another simple floating point operation to make the errors appear larger. In this case an error is obvious in the very first row, as the answer should be 1, not 0.999999999999890.

Stage 1, set up the spreadsheet

1. Starting at cell A1, insert the values and formulas shown in Table 2.21. The cell that contains the string 'Starting value' is cell A1.
2. Format all rows from 4 onwards to 'Number' and 15 decimal places.
3. Copy down for more than 1000 rows.

Your results should be similar to those in Table 2.20.

(The $ characters in the formulas of Table 2.21 are to avoid indexing the cell reference during copying down; they have no effect on the calculation. The result will be that any reference with $ will not change; $B$2 remains a reference to B2, and will not become B3, B4 etc. as the formula is copied down. They are known as **absolute cell references**.)

> **Hiding rows**
>
> You may want to hide a large number of rows. To do this, select these rows by clicking on the first row number (shown on a grey background) and then moving to the last row and clicking again **whilst holding down the shift key**. Then use the menu sequence (in Excel) of Format-> Row->Hide.

BTEC National Study Guide: IT Practitioners. See page 293 for order details of individual texts

69

Stage 2, experiment with different values

If you choose a starting value of 1, try different values for the increment. Increments that are exact binary fractions yield no error. For example, $2^{-3} = 0.125$, which in binary is 0.001. When normalized and converted to floating point, there is no error. Values that are not exact binary fractions, such as 1/100 or 1/1000, will cause a (small) error as shown in the Tables 2.20 and 2.21. Try these increments and decide if the resulting stored floating point numbers are exact:

0.0625
0.063
0.06
0.015625
0.05078125
0.0001.

Reduction of errors

Look at the last column in Table 2.20. It produces the values 1.001, 1.002, 1.003 etc. with no apparent errors. This is because there is no successive addition of inaccurate floating point numbers, so any error never gets any larger. Errors in floating point numbers are usually only significant when they are added, multiplied etc. many times. In the design of spreadsheets or when writing programs, effort should be made to avoid errors being amplified by unnecessary iteration. The same mathematical result can usually be achieved with smaller errors by avoiding successive operations.

Table 2.20   *Values*

Starting value	Amount to increment at each step		
1	0.001		
Results of successive additions	Results minus starting value multiplied by 1/increment	Number of additions	Alternative calculation avoiding floating point errors
1.001000000000000	0.999999999999890	1	1.001000000000000
1.002000000000000	1.999999999999780	2	1.002000000000000
1.003000000000000	2.999999999999670	3	1.003000000000000
1.004000000000000	3.999999999999560	4	1.004000000000000
1.005000000000000	4.999999999999450	5	1.005000000000000
1.006000000000000	5.999999999999340	6	1.006000000000000
1.007000000000000	6.999999999999230	7	1.007000000000000
1.008000000000000	7.999999999999120	8	1.008000000000000
1.009000000000000	8.999999999999010	9	1.009000000000000
1.010000000000000	9.999999999998900	10	1.010000000000000
1.011000000000000	10.999999999998800	11	1.011000000000000
1.012000000000000	11.999999999998700	12	1.012000000000000
1.013000000000000	12.999999999998600	13	1.013000000000000
	1000 rows hidden to save space!		
2.013999999999890	1013.999999999890000	1014	2.014000000000000
2.014999999999890	1014.999999999890000	1015	2.015000000000000
2.015999999999890	1015.999999999890000	1016	2.016000000000000
2.016999999999890	1016.999999999890000	1017	2.017000000000000
2.017999999999890	1017.999999999890000	1018	2.018000000000000
2.018999999999890	1018.999999999890000	1019	2.019000000000000
2.019999999999890	1019.999999999890000	1020	2.020000000000000

BTEC National Study Guide: IT Practitioners. See page 293 for order details of individual texts

70

Table 2.21 *Formulas*

Starting value	Amount to increment at each step		
1	**0.001**		
Results of successive additions	Results minus starting value multiplied by 1/increment	Number of additions	Alternative calculation avoiding floating point errors
=A2+$B$2	=(A4−$A$2)*(1/$B$2)	1	=1+$A$2*(C4*$B$2)
=A4+$B$2	=(A5−$A$2)*(1/$B$2)	=C4+1	=1+$A$2*(C5*$B$2)
=A5+$B$2	=(A6−$A$2)*(1/$B$2)	=C5+1	=1+$A$2*(C6*$B$2)
=A6+$B$2	=(A7−$A$2)*(1/$B$2)	=C6+1	=1+$A$2*(C7*$B$2)
=A7+$B$2	=(A8−$A$2)*(1/$B$2)	=C7+1	=1+$A$2*(C8*$B$2)
=A8+$B$2	=(A9−$A$2)*(1/$B$2)	=C8+1	=1+$A$2*(C9*$B$2)
=A9+$B$2	=(A10−$A$2)*(1/$B$2)	=C9+1	=1+$A$2*(C10*$B$2)
=A10+$B$2	=(A11−$A$2)*(1/$B$2)	=C10+1	=1+$A$2*(C11*$B$2)
=A11+$B$2	=(A12−$A$2)*(1/$B$2)	=C11+1	=1+$A$2*(C12*$B$2)
=A12+$B$2	=(A13−$A$2)*(1/$B$2)	=C12+1	=1+$A$2*(C13*$B$2)
=A13+$B$2	=(A14−$A$2)*(1/$B$2)	=C13+1	=1+$A$2*(C14*$B$2)
=A14+$B$2	=(A15−$A$2)*(1/$B$2)	=C14+1	=1+$A$2*(C15*$B$2)
=A15+$B$2	=(A16−$A$2)*(1/$B$2)	=C15+1	=1+$A$2*(C16*$B$2)
1000 rows hidden to save space!			
=A1016+$B$2	=(A1017−$A$2)*(1/$B$2)	=C1016+1	=1+$A$2*(C1017*$B$2)
=A1017+$B$2	=(A1018−$A$2)*(1/$B$2)	=C1017+1	=1+$A$2*(C1018*$B$2)
=A1018+$B$2	=(A1019−$A$2)*(1/$B$2)	=C1018+1	=1+$A$2*(C1019*$B$2)
=A1019+$B$2	=(A1020−$A$2)*(1/$B$2)	=C1019+1	=1+$A$2*(C1020*$B$2)
=A1020+$B$2	=(A1021−$A$2)*(1/$B$2)	=C1020+1	=1+$A$2*(C1021*$B$2)
=A1021+$B$2	=(A1022−$A$2)*(1/$B$2)	=C1021+1	=1+$A$2*(C1022*$B$2)
=A1022+$B$2	=(A1023−$A$2)*(1/$B$2)	=C1022+1	=1+$A$2*(C1023*$B$2)

Visual Basic

Start a new project and add the following controls:

- a text box called TxtIncrement with the initial value of the text property as 0.001
- a text box called TxtStartingvalue with the initial value of the text property as 1
- a list box called LstOutput
- a command button called cmdGo with a caption of Go
- a command button called cmdClear with a caption of Clear.

Add the code shown below:

```
Private Sub cmdClear_Click()
LstOutput.Clear
End Sub

Private Sub cmdGo_Click()
Dim i As Integer
Dim x As Double
Dim y As Double

x = Val(TxtIncrement.Text)
y = Val(txtStartingvalue.Text) + x
For i = 1 To 1050
  LstOutput.AddItem Str$(y)
  y = y + x
Next i

End Sub
```

BTEC National Study Guide: IT Practitioners. See page 293 for order details of individual texts

71

When you run the resulting program, you should get something like Figure 2.26. Scroll though the list box to see the output. Errors due to successive additions of inexact floating point numbers are easily seen. Use the same increments as above to see if you get the same results:

0.0625
0.063
0.06
0.015625
0.05078125
0.0001.

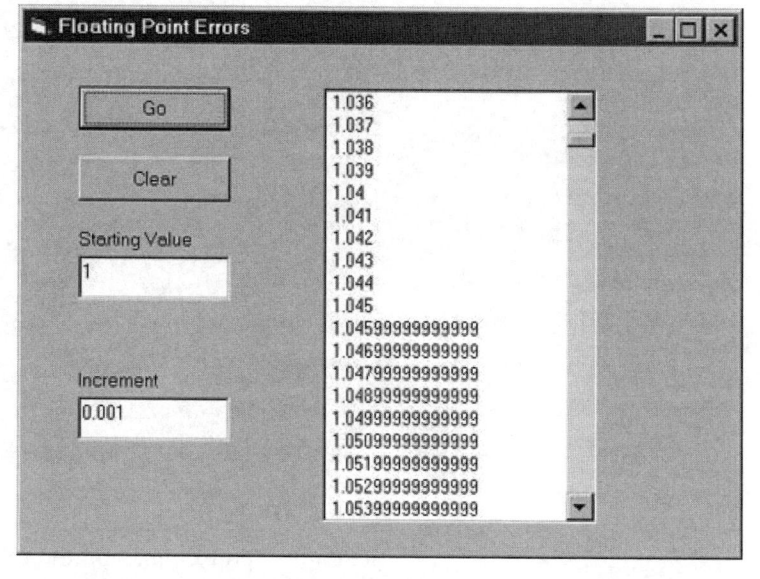

Figure 2.26 *Visual Basic experiment with floating point errors*

Pascal (Free Pascal or Borland Turbo Pascal version 6 or 7)

Start Turbo Pascal with a blank program editing screen, and enter the code below. Compile and run the code in a DOS screen. Errors in the output are easily seen; the program pauses every 100 rows until you press the Enter key (Carriage Return).

```
program fperror;

var i:integer;
  x,y,stvalue:real;

begin
  write('Starting value ');readln(stvalue);
  write('Increment ');readln(x);
  y:=stvalue+x;

  for i:=1 to 1050 do
    begin
      writeln(y:0:15);
      if (i mod 100)=0 then readln; {provides a
      pause every 100 lines}
      y:=y+x;
    end;
end.
```

BTEC National Study Guide: IT Practitioners. See page 293 for order details of individual texts

72

Experiment with the same increments as before:

0.0625
0.063
0.06
0.015625
0.05078125
0.0001

You should get similar results.

2.11 User requirements

When considering the specification of PCs and associated equipment, there is more to consider than the machine itself. How do you know if you need the wonderful model on sale for £2000, or the lesser model selling for £500? A major reason for the ever-increasing power of computers being purchased is 'upgradeitus'. Some people will buy the latest computer/software simply because it is available. Operating systems like Windows are very hungry for disk space and RAM, and work very slowly unless run in a powerful machine. People often lose sight of the fact that Windows and many Windows applications offer features most do not even realize are present, let alone use or need. In a competitive commercial environment, a sound knowledge of why computers and software are specified is very important. There is no real point in upgrading a system just because it becomes available. As an example, if an application in one office is running perfectly well using an old 80286 PC running MSDOS and a dot-matrix printer, why change it? What **need** is there to change? Simply upgrading the computer is very easy, as is upgrading the software, but successfully running and paying for the change in work practice and staff training is often difficult and very expensive.

Cost of ownership

In order to own and run computers in a business for a period of time, the following items of value must be considered:

* hardware
* software licences
* staff training
* installation and maintenance
* business-specific data and documents
* staff experience and knowledge

Which of these are more significant? After working for some time, many data are generated in the normal course of the business and much knowledge and experience of the computer systems is built up in the staff. After a very short time, these data and the staff knowledge are much more valuable than the costs of the computers. Although the ongoing cost of IT support and maintenance is high, the value of the staff knowledge is probably greater. The cost of the hardware is often the lowest of these, and its value falls to zero in a very short time.

Therefore, **it is not sensible to upgrade unless there is a clear business need**.

BTEC National Study Guide: IT Practitioners. See page 293 for order details of individual texts

73

Over the last few years, companies like Microsoft, Lotus, Corel etc. have put more and more features into their software. This has resulted in the perceived 'need' to upgrade the machines and staff training, often without any real thought. It is interesting to note that the 'cost of ownership' issue has become very prominent in recent times, and that these software companies have started to change their policies, making their software easier to use rather than having more features that require ever more powerful machines.

Figure 2.27 shows typical proportions of the cost of ownership found in many companies. The cost of the machines themselves is just one-fifth of the total. Simply upgrading machines and then upgrading the software often causes grief for no real benefit to the organization, because the extra training required and the cost of data conversion outweigh any benefits of newer machines. It makes sense to 'over specify' for a new installation so the machines will perform well for a reasonable period, but it does not always make sense to upgrade when new hardware or software become available.

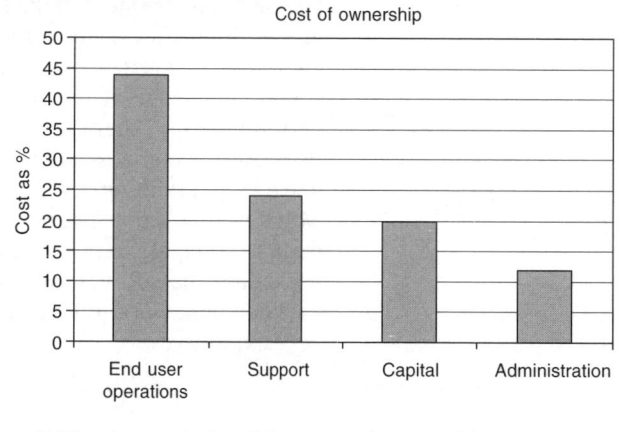

Figure 2.27 *An analysis of the cost of ownership*

General guidelines

Microprocessor

Do not be over-awed by CPU clock speeds. In practice, when running business software you are very unlikely to see the difference between a 1.2- and a 1.7-GHz machine; 1.7 is only 1.7/1.2 = 1.42 (or 42 per cent) faster, and the overall speed of a machine is a result of much more than the CPU speed. A 1.1-GHz machine has only a 10 per cent faster clock speed then a 1-GHz machine – an even smaller difference. Machines fitted with faster CPUs are generally fitted with faster subsystems at the same time, so naïve users may be fooled into thinking it is all due to the heavily advertised processor 'inside'.

RAM

If running Microsoft Windows as a desktop operating system, performance improves up to about 128 Mb of RAM. Above this it is not likely to show a **marked** improvement unless the applications

BTEC National Study Guide: IT Practitioners. See page 293 for order details of individual texts

74

to be run all need simultaneous open windows or are themselves very demanding on memory. Running a PC as a server is very different, but is not in the scope of this part of the book. You will probably not **see** much difference between the latest RAM types unless you enjoy running benchmark software or timing long tasks with a stopwatch.

Video

The amount of RAM fitted to the video card depends on what you need the machine for. Running standard office applications does not usually require animated 3D, so you can calculate the RAM required from the resolution you intend to set. Many people do not like the highest resolution set for office applications as they cannot see the screen fonts, so if the target is the typical 800×600 you will see no benefit from an 8-Mbyte video card over a 4-Mb version. If you plan to use 3D applications and high-speed animated games, the more video RAM the better, but you will only see the benefit if the software designers make use of the hardware. More memory will have no effect on older software.

Monitor

Buy a good one! Overall, when using a PC it is better to have a good stable image with crisp resolution and well-saturated colours than something that is a few per cent faster. Spend the money you saved by not specifying the 'latest, fastest processor' on the monitor. Users will thank you for it. If you run a price comparison on machines with the latest CPU, you will see the price rises dramatically towards the faster end of the market. If one machine is 50 per cent more expensive but only 20 per cent faster, spend the difference on the monitor.

Disk Drive

A while ago it was thought that you could not buy a disk that was too large! This was mainly due to the ever-increasing size of the software and data files. Now that MP3, graphics and video are becoming more important, it looks as though the demand for disk space will now be dictated more by your data than the software. At one extreme, if you are only using the machine for typing plain text and you type at a good 'office' speed of 45 words a minute all day and all night, 7 days a week without a break for 40 years, apart from being tired and hungry, you will still only generate less than 5 Gb of data! At the other extreme, you are likely to fill a 60 Gb drive in a few months if you store MP3, graphics and video files. One hour of full broadcast quality video can be stored on a 10-Gb drive. The best option is to go for size, and only buy the more expensive fast drives if the applications really need it.

Floppy Disk Drive

Almost every PC has one, it is hardly ever used now but as soon as you specify a machine without a floppy drive, someone will arrive with an important file on a floppy disk.

BTEC National Study Guide: IT Practitioners. See page 293 for order details of individual texts

75

CD-ROM

Almost all PCs are fitted with a CD-ROM or DVD drive. CD-R is now cheap and is an excellent system for backups of key data. Unless the budget is very tight, specify a CD-RW compatible drive wherever possible and use it for CD-R writing. DVD drives are gaining acceptance and offer much larger capacity, but most software is still distributed on CD. Speed is only an issue if you intend to use the drive as a continuous source of data; software installation speed is not seriously limited by CD-ROM drive speed. Do not get carried away with a '×40' drive; for most uses a '×20' is fine. Buy quality rather than speed.

Sound

Specify the cheapest possible sound if the system is for office use. Most users turn it off after a while, especially if the office is open plan. If you need good quality sound to support games or to edit music etc., it is better to output sound to a sound system than to spend on expensive PC speakers. In this case, buy a high quality sound card and leave the speakers in the shop.

Modem

Modems will soon be a thing of the past, at least if the promised ADSL connections become available for home use. Most offices use a direct LAN connection. Until this happens, 56 K modems are adequate. Buy quality, and avoid the 'plain wrapper' kind.

Modems

A modem is a 'MOdulator–DEModulator'. In English, to **modulate** means to **change** (like modify). The old telephone system (known to some as POTS, Plain Old Telephone System!) could carry only analogue sound signals. It was not possible to put a digital signal through such a system. Modern digital telephone systems are very different, but modems were designed for the POTS. A modem modulates a sound with digital information and demodulates this sound for received signals. The speed of a modem is given in bits/second; most are now 56 Kbits/sec. As each byte is encoded in either 9 or 10 bits, this means a 56 K modem will transmit about 5.6 Kb of data per second in an ideal world. Real world rates are nearly always slower. Having CPUs that are claimed to 'speed up the Internet' will make no difference at all!

Printer

For home or SOHO (Small Office Home Office) use, inkjets are fine; they are expensive to run if your output is high and are not as reliable as laser printers. For office use, the only real choice is a laser printer; they are fast, quiet, and reasonably cheap to run. Even for small offices, a printer with a large paper capacity will be appreciated by the users.

BTEC National Study Guide: IT Practitioners. See page 293 for order details of individual texts

76

How to specify and buy a computer

First, clearly specify why you need a computer, what do you want to do with it, and who needs to be able to share your data. Next, decide on your budget.

The next step is to decide what software you will need to satisfy your business requirements, and only then should you specify what hardware is required to run that software. It is a great mistake to think 'I will need a 1.7 GHz Pentium IV' just because they are available and heavily advertised.

Due to the ever-increasing efficiency of hardware production and changes in Far Eastern economies, the actual costs of hardware are getting lower and lower. This means that the 'lowest' specification of some computer components now on sale is more than adequate for most people. For example, many machines now come with a disk drive with a 10 Gb capacity as standard. If you only need a wordprocessor this will meet your needs for a very long time. Some people seem to think that if they specify a 40 Gb drive the machine will be 'better' in some respect, but this is not true. Many machines are fast enough for normal business activities, and more speed is simply not required. A lot of people find that to run Windows 98 and Word 97 on a Pentium 266 with 32 Mb RAM fitted is quite adequate; why specify any more? In any case, what do you mean by 'more speed' in respect of a wordprocessor; always assuming that a Pentium IV is somehow 'faster', will it enable you to type faster?

Consider these typical applications:

- wordprocessing
- spreadsheets
- databases
- graphic arts
- technical design.

Now consider these things that would appear on a list of components when specifying a computer:

- disk speed
- disk capacity
- video resolution
- video RAM size
- monitor size
- monitor resolution
- monitor slot pitch
- monitor refresh rate
- main RAM size
- processor type
- processor clock speed
- internal bus speed
- internal bus type
- motherboard features, buses, expansion slots etc.

Now write down what is required (allowing for future expansion), rather than what you might 'like' to have. You will find that if you focus more on quality than on performance, the benefits will be higher. Clearly you need a machine that has sufficient performance, but you should next consider:

BTEC National Study Guide: IT Practitioners. See page 293 for order details of individual texts

77

- cost/budget
- performance
- expandability
- ergonomics, i.e. how well the components 'fit' with the people who will use them
- needs of specific or specialist software, e.g. Autocad.

Some people are specifying notebook computers in place of desktop machines, but you should consider these points:

- they cost at least 50 per cent more for the same 'power', and often twice as much.
- sometimes, they will not run specialist software
- they are not as reliable as desktop machines, and are easy to damage
- they are not as expandable or configurable as desktops
- they are very portable
- they have an LCD screen (many people prefer this)
- newer versions of software make ever greater demands on the hardware, so notebooks go out of date quicker.

Now consider the questions shown in the sample assignment below and discuss your thoughts with your lecturer and fellow students. Keep your mind focused on what is **needed**, not on what is **desirable**, or what you may see advertised as 'The Computer Deal of the Century!'.

Sample assignment tasks

You are asked to specify computers for the six users below. For each of the users listed, choose a suitable machine and justify your choice. You should give a detailed explanation of your choices in terms of:

- cost
- capabilities
- performance
- upgrade path.

Very useful sources of information are the many computer magazines available at most newsagents. You should buy two or three of these and look at their buying advice; this is often very sound. Avoid the titles that are aimed at games players. The other useful source of information is the Internet; sites such as www.zdnet.com give excellent information.

The simplest way is to list the items fitted or specified in your chosen machine, and then explain the significance of each item and how it relates to the user's requirements. Write down the machine specification as a list of components in the same way as you would present it to a supplier.

User 1

This company supplies artwork, graphics etc. to the advertising industry, especially the glossy magazine trade. Their main expertise is in photo retouching, using very high resolution images. They only need machines for five graphic artists; the management function in the company is already computerized.

BTEC National Study Guide: IT Practitioners. See page 293 for order details of individual texts

78

User 2

A small college runs 200 stand-alone PCs. A network company has offered a sponsorship deal and supplied a full network with cabling and servers to support the college, with the proviso that the college upgrades the user's machines. The current 200 machines are to be scrapped. The plan is to run the latest versions of Windows, MS Office and similar software on each user machine, but with the software stored on the servers; they have an **extremely tight budget** where every penny counts. You must achieve the **cheapest possible machine** that will run the software.

User 3

The PA to the Finance Director of a large shipping company requires a machine to do wordprocessing and e-mail. All the other computerized functions in the company are already running elsewhere.

User 4

A very experienced design engineer working on petrochemical plant designs has been on an Autocad course. The projects she works on involve 3D drawings of very complex pipework etc. During the course of the next year she will employ two assistants to computerize the existing paper drawings and to use Autocad themselves, so she needs three new networked PCs to run Autocad. The application requires that large amounts of data are stored and that the hidden line removal and other performance critical functions in Autocad are used to full effect.

User 5

A local private genealogy society has computer links to help in their research; they use an old PC with a 56-Kb/s modem. To reduce costs and speed up enquiries, they have decided to start a large database of family genealogy details. The eventual size of the database may be 200 Gb with the requirement of at least one level of back-up. Funds are very tight, but users will require a good service. To limit the expenditure, only one member will use the machine at a time, linked via a fixed modem on a pre-arranged time slot.

User 6

A financial accountant uses spreadsheets to model the financial behaviour of companies. The spreadsheets are very large and she is hoping to make them even larger, but is impatient with the recalculation time obtained with her current computer.

2.12 How to build a PC

There are so many options to consider when building a PC that it is difficult to provide specific instructions in a book of this nature. However, presented below are some of the main points.

A PC is generally fitted into a **system box** that contains several main components:

1. A **power supply**. This takes the AC mains voltage and converts it to 12 V DC for electric motors in the disk drives and 5 V DC for the logic circuits.

BTEC National Study Guide: IT Practitioners. See page 293 for order details of individual texts

79

2. A **motherboard**. This is the main circuit board of a computer. When IBM first introduced a PC in the late 1980s, their design took no account of video graphics. For this reason a lot of PC motherboards do not contain any circuitry for video graphics, so a video card is added as an extra.
3. Peripheral items such as **hard disk drives**, **floppy disk drives** and similar accessories. Even the most basic PC now has one hard drive, one floppy drive and at least a **CD-ROM drive**.

Motherboards

On motherboards there is usually a set of parallel slots that are amongst the largest visible features. These slots house the bus that connects devices to the motherboard, and it is into these slots that accessories like a video cards, modems, television cards etc. are plugged. Over the history of the development of the PC motherboard there have been a number of types of these bus expansion slots. The first type, which is no longer made, had 8 data bits; later ones had 16 data bits, and this type became so common that it was called the industry standard architecture (or ISA) bus.

Several attempts were made by IBM and others to improve upon the speed of the ISA bus, and this has resulted in what is now called the PCI bus; it does the same job as the ISA bus but faster.

An expansion bus allows data to pass from the motherboard to the accessory cards and back again. As will as data, the bus also contains address information so that the data can be stored in particular places and has control wires to provide such things as the timing of events etc.

Electrostatic discharge

Installing the motherboard is very straightforward, but precise instructions must come from the manufacturer. It is very easy to damage the chips on the motherboard; this is done by accidentally applying very large voltages from your fingers when you touch the board. If you are wearing clothes made of nylon or similar synthetic materials and if the atmosphere is very dry it is extremely easy for you to build up a very large static voltage on your body. This can be of many thousands of volts. The problem with many silicon chips is that 30 or 40 volts will damage them. If you touch the board and have a static charge, it will discharge into the board and damage the electronics. One solution is to attach a copper wire from your wrist to a good earth; this will cause any static build-up from your body to be discharged, so you'll have zero volts on your body and cannot discharge into the electronics. If you are unable to take this precaution, simply touching a good earth like the screws in a light switch, or a heating radiator or some pipes, will at least reduce the static charge on your body and minimize the possibility of damage to electronics. If static electricity discharges from your body into the electronics, it is known as an **electrostatic discharge** (ESD).

BTEC National Study Guide: IT Practitioners. See page 293 for order details of individual texts

80

To assemble the PC, the motherboard is fixed on some plastic pegs. The hard disk drive, CD-ROM drive and floppy disk drive are fixed into custom-made brackets and generally connected via a ribbon cable. This contains a large number of wires that are effectively an extension to the bus. Other wires coloured red, black, yellow etc. are to supply the 12 V or 5 V to motors in the disk drives or to the logic circuits.

Once these main components are in place, the accessory or expansion boards can be plugged in, again according to the manufacturer's instructions. You may have some components that plug into an ISA slot; these are the old-fashioned so-called **legacy devices**. The ISA bus is slower than the PCI bus, but if the device happens to be a modem the data rate is so slow that you will see no advantage from using a PCI version.

One application that requires very high-speed data transfer is video, and on many motherboards there is a special video slot called an **AGP slot**. This slot is dedicated to video data transfer from the processor to the video card and back again.

On the back of the PC there will be **legacy ports**. These are for connecting external devices to the PC; typically there is a **serial port** or possibly two serial ports, and a **printer port** (also known as a **parallel port**). Most modern PCs have more modern communication ports; the most common is called the **Universal Serial Bus** (USB), but you may find **FireWire** or **SCSI** ports. They are different in the way they work in detail, but in general are for communicating with external devices. SCSI stands for Small Computer Systems Interface, it is a standard that was designed not for the PC world but for larger computers. It has been adapted for PCs and is commonly used for such devices as disk drives and scanners. USB ports are used for connecting almost any peripheral devices such as scanners and even mice. FireWire is generally used to connect digital cameras. The older serial ports are used for connecting modems and mice, and the parallel port is used for connecting the printer. One reason for introducing USB was to reduce the number of different connections, but until USB is completely universal the old so-called legacy ports will be around.

Once the main PC box is assembled with the motherboard, drives, a power supply etc., the external devices are plugged in (the keyboard, monitor and printer). Once this is done the main electronic nature of the PC build is finished, but it is a long way from being a useful computer. At least three more things need to be done:

1. The BIOS of the computer needs to be configured. The **BIOS** is the **Basic Input Output System**. When you first turn on the PC, you will be instructed to press a particular key combination, e.g. ALT S or just the del key. This will present you with the BIOS control screen. The items on this screen must be configured according to the manufacturer's instructions for the components in your PC.
2. As part of the basic configuration of the PC, a hard disk must be **partitioned**. Partitioning involves taking a **physical disk** and creating one or more **logical disks**. In this way, the operating system is able to treat one physical disk as several logical disks. Disk partitioning is done with a program called **fdisk**. There are different versions of this supplied with different versions of Microsoft operating systems; you should use the

BTEC National Study Guide: IT Practitioners. See page 293 for order details of individual texts

81

one that comes with the operating system that you intend to install. Unfortunately, the business of partitioning a disk is fraught with problems. A good source of information on using fdisk can be found from the Microsoft web site at http://support.microsoft.com/default.aspx?scid=kb;EN-US;q255867. Once the disk partitioning is complete, it must be **formatted** using the format program supplied with the operating system. Formatting means that details specific to the operating system are written to the disk. These things are **track and sector numbering**, the **file allocation table** and the **root directory** etc. The details of disk formatting are beyond the scope of this book; see http://support.microsoft.com/default.aspx?scid=kb;EN-US;q255867.

3. Once formatted, the operating system can be installed on the main disk. The operating system installation software is usually stored on CD-ROM. The operating system is sometimes supplied with a **bootable floppy disk**. This floppy disk is used to boot the machine, and contains **driver** software that will allow the CD-ROM to be visible to the installation program. There are many different operating systems available; the most common are the Microsoft Windows series (3.1, 95, 98, ME, 2000 and XP) the Microsoft NT series (NT Workstation and NT Server), and then there is **linux** from a whole range of suppliers. Linux is free and is based on the older **unix** operating system.

Switching the computer on

Simply turning on a computer and making the electronics come to life is not sufficient to get the computer working. Since everything in the computer is controlled by software, including the loading of software itself, simply turning on the computer with no software will cause a problem. The problem is that there is no software to control the loading process! In very old-fashioned computers there was a special program called a **loader**, which was set in the machine via switches. In other words, an operator set ones and zeros with the switches to load a very simple program into memory. The simple program, called a loader, simply loaded the rest of software into memory. In PCs this loader program is already placed in the BIOS chip. This loader will load whatever software it finds on the first sectors of the bootable or main disk. The software in these first few sectors is usually the operating system. Once this starts to load, it takes over and loads the rest of the operating system.

Booting

Why is starting a computer called **booting**?
There is an ancient philosophical problem that goes something like this:

'If I stand in front of you and I pull up very hard on your bootstraps, I notice that I can lift you off the floor. Now if you bend down and pull just as hard on your own bootstraps, you do not rise above the floor. Why is this?'

BTEC National Study Guide: IT Practitioners. See page 293 for order details of individual texts

82

To the modern mind trained in engineering mechanics the problem is quite straightforward, but it puzzled the ancient philosophers. It is a problem that is related to computers because in one sense they have to 'pull themselves up with their own bootstraps', i.e. they need a program to load a program. The original loaders were called **bootstrap loaders** from this problem. There is more to starting the PC than simply turning it on!

The BTEC Unit 2 specifies that students undertake maintenance of software and hardware using appropriate disk tools, and locate and repair faults using appropriate faultfinding techniques. As there is a huge range of possible configurations of hardware and software, it is not possible to provide specific help on these topics.

2.13 Software licensing

It is very important to understand the legal position you are in when you install or use software on a computer. Software is generally supplied with a **licence**; it may come as a surprise that you generally cannot 'buy' software, it will only come with a licence to **use** the software. The software itself is called **intellectual property** and, except in a few rare circumstances, this intellectual property remains with the company that wrote or supplied the software.

There are various kinds of software licences. The first kind is called **freeware**. Here, a programmer has written a program and places it in the **public domain** for use according to the licence agreement that comes with it. There is no payment to be made, but the author usually asks that the software is not changed and that credit is given if the software is used in conjunction with a business. Some software is supplied under a licence written by the Free Software Foundation. This is known as the GNU General Public Licence. It generally means you can use the software free of charge unless you are using it for business (see http://www.gnu.org/copyleft/gpl.html).

The second kind is called **shareware**. This usually means you are free to load software on a machine and test it. If you like it, you pay some money to the software writer; if not, you delete it from the machine. Some shareware comes without any restriction and simply relies on your honesty to pay. Other kinds of shareware come with some kind of restriction, for instance, the inability to print or a restriction on the number of items you can use. Once you have paid the software writer the (usually small) sum of money to register the shareware, this restriction is lifted. Selling shareware is a very efficient way of supplying software. There are a large number of shareware download sites available on the net, including:

- http://www.shareware.com/
- http://www.jumbo.com/
- http://www.tucows.com/
- http://download.cnet.com/
- http://www.zdnet.com/

Alternatively, search for 'shareware download' on www.google.com.

Finally, there is the normal commercial software purchased online or from a software supplier, for instance Microsoft Office. This comes with a long and detailed licence agreement that sets out

BTEC National Study Guide: IT Practitioners. See page 293 for order details of individual texts

83

precisely how you can use the software and how you can't. Remember, all you have purchased is a licence to use the software, so in order to remain within the law you must use that software according to the licence agreement. Generally you are not free to let other people have a copy; this is in contrast to shareware, where most shareware authors encourage you to supply copies to your friends and colleagues.

Appendix A: answers

Exercise 2.1

(a)

A	B	C	D	E	F	G	R
0	0	0	0	0	0	1	1
0	0	0	1	0	0	0	0
0	0	1	0	0	1	0	1
0	0	1	1	0	1	0	1
0	1	0	0	0	1	1	1
0	1	0	1	0	1	0	1
0	1	1	0	0	1	0	1
0	1	1	1	0	1	0	1
1	0	0	0	0	0	1	1
1	0	0	1	0	0	0	0
1	0	1	0	0	1	0	1
1	0	1	1	0	1	0	1
1	1	0	0	1	1	1	1
1	1	0	1	1	1	0	1
1	1	1	0	1	1	0	1
1	1	1	1	1	1	0	1

Logic function = $(A \bullet B) + (B + C) + \overline{(C + D)}$

(b)

A	B	C	NOT A	D	E	R
0	0	0	1	0	1	1
0	0	1	1	0	0	0
0	1	0	1	1	0	1
0	1	1	1	1	0	1
1	0	0	0	0	1	1
1	0	1	0	0	0	0
1	1	0	0	0	0	0
1	1	1	0	0	0	0

Logic function = $(\overline{A} \bullet B) + \overline{(B + C)}$

BTEC National Study Guide: IT Practitioners. See page 293 for order details of individual texts

84

(c)

A	B	C	D	E	R
0	0	0	1	0	0
0	0	1	1	1	1
0	1	0	0	1	0
0	1	1	0	0	0
1	0	0	0	0	0
1	0	1	0	1	0
1	1	0	0	1	0
1	1	1	0	0	0

Logic function $= \overline{(A \bullet B)} \bullet (B \oplus C)$

Exercise 2.2

Change the first line to MOV DL, "M" or MOV DL, 'M' or MOV DL, 77 or MOV DL, 04D ;(hex) or MOV DL, 01001101b ;(binary) as all these produce the same machine code output.
Change the third line to MOV CH, 14

Exercise 2.3

Change the first line to MOV DL, '0' (or 48 or 030 or 00110000b). Note, putting MOV DL, 0 is not correct; the result will be the first 10 control codes in the ASCII character set.

Exercise 2.4

```
        MOV AH, 02A     ;DOS interrupt 21 Function 2A,
                        ;read system date
        INT 021         ;call DOS
                        ;AL= day of the week (0=Sunday,
                        ;1=Monday etc.)
                        ;CX=year
                        ;DH=month
                        ;DL=day

; now store to prevent overwriting when subroutine
is used

        MOV year, CX
        MOV month, DH
        MOV day, DL

;..... display the day.................

        MOV AH,0        ;AX is AH and AL so clear top
```

BTEC National Study Guide: IT Practitioners. See page 293 for order details of individual texts

85

```
        MOV AL, day     ;of AX (AH) ready for OUTINT
        CMP AX, 10      ;see if leading zero is needed
        JAE L20         ;jump if 10 or more without
                        ;outputting 0 first
        CALL leadingzero
L20:    CALL OUTINT     ;output the day

;..... now output a day/month/year separator
............

        MOV DL, "/"     ;hour:min:sec separator
        MOV AH, 2       ;DOS interrupt 21 function 2
        INT 021         ;call DOS to output "/"

;..... display the month...................

        MOV AH,0        ;AX is AH and AL so clear top
        MOV AL, month   ;of AX (AH) ready for OUTINT
        CMP AX, 10      ;see if leading zero is needed
        JAE L21         ;jump if 10 or more without
                        ;outputting 0 first
        CALL leadingzero
L21:    CALL OUTINT     ;output the month

;..... now output a day/month/year separator ........

        MOV DL, "/"     ;hour:min:sec separator
        MOV AH, 2       ;DOS interrupt 21 function 2
        INT 021         ;call DOS to output "/"

;..... display the year...................

        MOV AX, year
        CALL OUTINT     ;output the year

        INT 020         ;terminate program

year  DW 0              ;define some space
month DB 0              ;for variables
day   DB 0              ;to store values
```

Exercise 2.5

```
        MOV AH,030      ;DOS interrupt 21 Function 30,
                        ;return DOS version number
        INT 021         ;call DOS

; now store values away to avoid overwriting by
subroutine

        MOV major, AL
        MOV minor, AH

; now output the string. Point SI to string for
subroutine

        MOV SI, string ;copies ADDRESS of string to SI
```

BTEC National Study Guide: IT Practitioners. See page 293 for order details of individual texts

86

```
        CALL
        printstring      ;printstring subroutine in
                          LIB.ASM

; now output major version ......................

        MOV AH,0          ;clear top of AX
        MOV AL, major     ;AX now contains
                          ;major version ready
                          ;for subroutine
        CALL outint       ;output to screen

; now output a separator .......................

        MOV AH,2          ;DOS interrupt 21 function 2
        MOV DL,"."        ;separator character
        INT 021           ;call DOS

; now output minor version......................

        MOV AH,0          ;clear top of AX
        MOV AL, minor     ;AX now contains
                          ;minor version ready
                          ;for subroutine
        CMP AX, 10        ;see if leading zero is
                          ;needed
        JAE L20           ;jump if 10 or more without
                          ;outputting 0 first
        CALL leadingzero
L20:    CALL outint       ;output to screen

;........terminate program......................

        INT 020

major   db 0              ;variable to store major
                          ;version
minor   db 0              ;variable to store minor
                          ;version
string: db "DOS version number= ",0
```

Exercise 2.6

```
;Assembly language program exercise 2.8. File ex5.asm
;Assemble with LIB.ASM for subroutines
;Modify programs P8.ASM and answer to exercise 2.6
;to output both the system time
;and date on the same line with strings saying 'Time
;is now'
;and 'Date= '.

; output string 1 "Time is now " .................

        MOV SI, string1
        CALL printstring

; now output the time
```

BTEC National Study Guide: IT Practitioners. See page 293 for order details of individual texts

87

```
        MOV AH, 02C      ;DOS interrupt 21 Function 2C,
                         ;read system time.
        INT 021          ;call DOS
                         ;now CH=hours, CL=Minutes
                         ;DH=seconds, DL=hundredths/sec

;now store to prevent overwriting when subroutine
;is used

        MOV hours, CH
        MOV mins, CL
        MOV secs, DH

; display the hours.................

        MOV AH,0         ;AX is AH and AL so clear top
        MOV AL, hours    ;of AX (AH) ready for OUTINT
        CMP AX, 10       ;see if leading zero is needed
        JAE L20          ;jump if 10 or more without
                         ;outputting 0 first
        CALL leadingzero
L20:    CALL OUTINT      ;output the time in hours

; now output a h:m:s separator...........

        MOV DL, ":"      ;hour:min:sec separator
        MOV AH, 2        ;DOS interrupt 21 function 2
        INT 021          ;call DOS to output ":"

; display the minutes.................

        MOV AH,0         ;AX is AH and AL so clear top
        MOV AL, mins     ;of AX (AH) ready for OUTINT
        CMP AX, 10       ;see if leading zero is needed
        JAE L21          ;jump if 10 or more without
                         ;outputting 0 first
        CALL leadingzero
L21:    CALL OUTINT      ;output the time in minutes

; now output a h:m:s separator...........

        MOV DL, ":"      ;hour:min:sec separator
        MOV AH, 2        ;DOS interrupt 21 function 2
        INT 021          ;call DOS to output ":"

; display the seconds.................

        MOV AH,0         ;AX is AH and AL so clear top
        MOV AL, secs     ;of AX (AH) ready for OUTINT
        CMP AX, 10       ;see if leading zero is needed
        JAE L22          ;jump if 10 or more without
                         ;outputting 0 first
L22:    CALL leadingzero
        CALL OUTINT      ;output the time in seconds

; now output string 2 "Date= ".....................

        MOV SI, string2
        CALL printstring
```

BTEC National Study Guide: IT Practitioners. See page 293 for order details of individual texts

88

```
; now output the date...............................

        MOV AH, 02A      ;DOS interrupt 21 Function 2A,
                         ;read system date
        INT 021          ;call DOS
                         ;AL= day of the week
                         ; (0=Sunday, 1=Monday etc.)
                         ;CX=year
                         ;DH=month
                         ;DL=day

; now store to prevent overwriting when subroutine
; is used

        MOV year, CX
        MOV month, DH
        MOV day, DL

; display the day..................

        MOV AH,0         ;AX is AH and AL so clear top
        MOV AL, day      ;of AX (AH) ready for OUTINT
        CMP AX, 10       ;see if leading zero is needed
        JAE L23          ;jump if 10 or more without
                         ;outputting 0 first
        CALL leadingzero
L23:    CALL OUTINT      ;output the day

; now output a day/month/year separator...........

        MOV DL, "/"      ;hour:min:sec separator
        MOV AH, 2        ;DOS interrupt 21 function 2
        INT 021          ;call DOS to output "/"

; display the month..................

        MOV AH,0         ;AX is AH and AL so clear top
        MOV AL, month    ;of AX (AH) ready for OUTINT
        CMP AX, 10       ;see if leading zero is needed
        JAE L24          ;jump if 10 or more without
                         ;outputting 0 first
        CALL leadingzero
L24:    CALL OUTINT      ;output the month

; now output a day/month/year separator...........

        MOV DL, "/"      ;hour:min:sec separator
        MOV AH, 2        ;DOS interrupt 21 function 2
        INT 021          ;call DOS to output "/"

; display the year..................

        MOV AX, year
        CALL OUTINT      ;output the year

        INT 020          ;terminate program

; variable declarations....................

year                    DW 0
month                   DB 0
```

BTEC National Study Guide: IT Practitioners. See page 293 for order details of individual texts

89

```
day                   DB 0
hours                 DB 0
mins                  DB 0
secs                  DB 0

; string declarations........................
string1:   db 'Time is now ',0  ;note trailing
                                 ;space

string2:   db ' Date= ',0       ;note leading space
```

This code can be downloaded from http://www.bh.com/companions/0750656840.

Appendix B: Assembly language subroutine library

```
;Library of subroutines in file LIB.ASM

;PRINTSTRING prints a string pointed to with SI
;register
;OUTINT writes a 16 bit number in AX to the screen
;as integer
;PRINTNUM writes a string as PRINTSTRING but with
;no spaces
;SHOWBITS writes a 16 bit number in AX to the screen
;as binary
;leadingzero writes a single 0 to the screen
;crlf writes an ASCII 13 Carriage Return
;then ASCII 10 Line Feed


rem       dw 0          ;16 bit variable for remainder
quo       dw 0          ;16 bit variable for quotient
space     equ " "       ;defines "space" as ASCII 32
numbuff: db 5 dup
          (space)       ;5 duplicates of "space"
          db 0          ;to give zero byte string
                        ;terminator
row       db 0          ;for MOVECURSOR
col       db 0          ;for MOVECURSOR

;.......... Subroutines ...................

printstring:           ;assume pointer to
                       ;string is in SI register
          mov ah,02
L1:       mov dl,[si]  ;get first character
          cmp dl,0     ;see if end of string
          jz finprint  ;finish if end of string
          int 021      ;write char
          inc si       ;point to next char
          jmp L1       ;back for more chars
finprint: ret          ;end of subroutine

;...... end of printstr .....................

; subroutine to show a 16 bit number in AX as binary

showbits:
          mov si,ax    ;copy of equipment config
                       ;number
          mov bl.16    ;counter for 16 bits
```

BTEC National Study Guide: IT Practitioners. See page 293 for order details of individual texts

90

```
L1:        mov cx,si    ;cx is working register
           and cx,08000 ;mask off all but top bit
           cmp cx,0     ;if zero
           jz nought    ;then write a '0'

one:       mov dl,'1'
           mov ah,02     ;DOS write to screen function
           int 021
           jmp next

nought:    mov dl,'0'
           mov ah,02     ;DOS write to screen function
           int 021

next:      shl si,1     ;move all bits left one space
           dec bl       ;
           jnz L1       ;see if all 16 bits done
           ret          ;end of showbits subroutine

;..............end if showbits...................

;OUTINT subroutine
;this prints out a number in decimal held in AX
;register by storing it
;as ascii into a buffer and then pointing to this
;buffer with bx.
;Needs numbuff and space equ at top of file. A86
;seems to fall over if these are included within the
;code.

outint:
           mov cx,5     ;for each place in the buffer
           mov si,
           numbuff      ;
           mov dl,space ;
L21:       mov[si],dl   ;fill it with spaces
           inc si
           loop L21     ;the LOOP instruction
                        ;uses CX and does the
                        ;increment for you first
           mov si,
           numbuff +4   ;ready to start filling the
                        ;array

L22:
           mov dx,0     ;clear DX since DIV works on
                        ;DX:AX
           mov cx,10    ;divisor of 10
           div cx       ;divide by 10 and store
                        ;remainder
           mov quo,ax   ;store quotient for next time
           or dl,48     ;change remainder to ascii
           mov [si],dl  ;and store in buffer
           dec si       ;point to next location in
                        ;buffer
           mov ax,quo   ;ready for next div
           cmp ax,0     ;see if any numbers left
           jne L22      ;if there are, process them
```

BTEC National Study Guide: IT Practitioners. See page 293 for order details of individual texts

91

```
                                      ;if not, write result to
                                      ;screen
                    mov si,
                    numbuff           ;point to the buffer
                    call
                    printnum          ;output the result
                    ret               ;return to whence you came
printnum:                             ;assume pointer to string
                                      ;is in SI register
                    mov ah,02
L51:                mov dl,[si]       ;get first character
                    cmp dl,0          ;see if end of string
                    jz
                    finprintnum       ;finish if end of string
                    cmp dl,32         ;see if space char
                    jz L52            ;do not print spaces
                    int 021           ;write char
L52:                inc si            ;point to next char
                    jmp L51           ;back for more chars

finprintnum:                  ret

;..............end if outint...................

;..............crlf subroutine...................

crlf:               pusha             ;save gen purpose registers
                    mov ah,2          ;DOS write char function
                    mov dl,13         ;Carriage Return (CR)
                    int 021           ;print it
                    mov dl,10         ;Line Feed (LF)
                    int 021           ;print it
                    popa              ;restore registers
                    ret               ;return from subroutine

leadingzero:
                    PUSH AX           ;keep AX to prevent
                                      ;overwriting
                    MOV AH, 2         ;DOS int 20 function 2
                    MOV DL, "0"       ;zero character to be output
                    INT 021           ;call DOS
                    POP AX            ;restore value to AX
                    RET               ;return to address after
                                      ;calling address
```

BTEC National Study Guide: IT Practitioners. See page 293 for order details of individual texts

92

Unit 4: Introduction to software development

Assessment Guidance

To achieve a PASS	To achieve a MERIT	To achieve a DISTINCTION
Write a brief report for a given specification stating the requirements and data needs based on what the system is to do.	Determine appropriate data types for a program and show how they are declared.	Enhance programs with validation and appropriate graphical elements; include end-user enhancements..
Design a solution for a given set of requirements using appropriate text and graphical documentation tools.	Identify and use appropriate selection and iteration methods for programming problems.	Demonstrate that the program has expansibility.
Write simple working programs that include suitable input/output statements, variable assignments and operators.	Produce technical documentation for a program.	
Produce well designed programs that are clearly laid out and appropriately commented.	Use an appropriate tool to analyse a piece of code to ascertain its semantic correctness.	
Produce user documentation for a completed program including the user interface design.		
Produce suitable test data for a working program.		

BTEC National Study Guide: IT Practitioners. See page 293 for order details of individual texts

94

Chapter 23

Program design

The single most important requirement of a computer program is that it runs without error at all times, since a program that either produces erroneous results or hangs up under certain circumstances is almost useless. Because of this stringent requirement, computer program design and production is a very skilled activity demanding meticulous attention to detail. It is not sufficient to address only the relatively easy problem of designing and implementing a program which produces the correct output when provided with ideal data. Rather, the program must be able to cope with non-ideal data such as that provided by a user who may be unfamiliar with its operation or data input requirements. Such a user might supply inappropriate input by, for example, entering alphabetic instead of numeric characters, and even experienced operators of the program might accidentally enter invalid data on occasions.

In fact there are many ways that a program could be presented with exceptional - that is, invalid or unreasonable - data and it is the responsibility of the program designer to allow for such. Consequently, the program design stage of program production, in which possible problems - and their solutions - are identified, is of vital importance. As a result, there are now a number of established program design methodologies to aid the program designer to produce well-crafted, error-free programs. The design method described here is a form of *structured programming* using *top-down, stepwise refinement*.

Two forms of notation that we will use to express solutions to design problems are *pseudocode* and *structure charts*; these are called *program design languages* (PDLs). Structure charts provide a graphical representation of a program, allowing its logical structure to be easily appreciated, whereas pseudocode, having a form similar to program instructions, aids program writing and testing.

Problem solving

Whether a problem is computer-related or otherwise, the strategy for solving it has essentially the same three main stages:(1) *understand the problem*, (2) *devise a solution*, and (3) *test the solution*. In addition, for program design tasks there is a further stage which is to (4) *document the solution*.

1. Understand the problem

This first stage requires a *thorough* understanding of the problem being addressed so that you can identify what assumptions can be made and what can't in order to test your solution in the correct context. Some problems are apparently straightforward but, when analysed with a view to producing a program design, become much more complex. As an example, consider the following outline program specification:

> *Write a program to read in a date and convert it to the number of days from the start of the calendar year.*

It sounds simple enough until you start to consider what the problem implies. For example, what format is to be used for the date? - 15th January, 1995 or 15 Jan 95, or 15/1/95, or 15-01-95 or 150195, or 950115, and so on. Is a particular format to be adopted and incorrectly formatted dates to be rejected, or is the program to attempt to interpret different formats? Are

BTEC National Study Guide: IT Practitioners. See page 293 for order details of individual texts

95

leap years to be considered when calculating the day number? Do you assume that the date is for the current year or can the date be for a different year? You may be able to think of more problems that could arise.

2. Design a solution

The method adopted here to design the solution involves tackling the problem in a number of steps. An outline program is designed first, showing the main modules of the program, and the order in which they are to be executed. Each main module is then reduced to a number of smaller, simpler, and more manageable components, and this process of refinement continues until the program designer judges that there is sufficient detail in the design for a programmer to be able to convert the design directly into a programming language. The process of reducing components into sequences of smaller components in stages is often termed *stepwise refinement*. Top-down, stepwise refinement encourages program design to be tackled methodically in a number of stages of increasing detail. Although structure charts and pseudocode are both suitable program design languages, we recommend that you adopt our approach of first using structure charts to produce your program designs in outline form and then translating them into detailed pseudocode prior to testing and subsequent conversion to program code.

An example of a simple structure chart and the equivalent pseudocode for the addition of two real numbers are shown in Figure 23.1. (Note that a *real* number is a number with a fractional part such as 23·456, whereas an *integer* is a whole number such as 32). Answer, a and b are called variables which serve a similar function to the symbols used in algebra - they are general, symbolic representations of data that is to be processed. Thus, the pseudocode statement 1

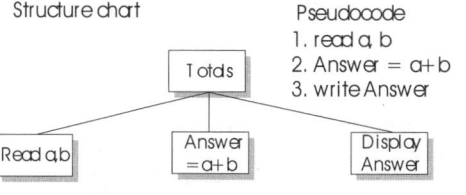

Figure 23.1. *Simple program design for addition of two real numbers*

in Figure 23.1 means 'read two values from the input device (such as a keyboard) and call them a and b respectively'. Statement 2 adds the two values and calls the result Answer. Statement 3 displays Answer on the output device (such as a display screen). By using variables rather than actual numbers, this sequence of statements defines how a computer is to deal with the addition of *any* two numbers. In addition to the problem solution itself, another part of the design is a *data table* which defines the purpose and type of the variables used in the solution. The data table (Table 23.1) would identify whether these variables were integers or real numbers and their purpose.

name	description	type
Answer	Holds the sum of the two numbers	real variable
a	First number entered	real variable
b	Second number entered	real variable

Table 23.1

3. Test the solution

This involves using test data to manually step through the solution statements so that the computed output can be compared with the expected output. For instance, the date example mentioned earlier should give an answer of 70 for 10th March 2000, assuming that the days are calculated from 1st January, 2000. This value would be compared with that provided by the design - if the answer was different then the apparent design fault would need to be investigated and corrected before continuing with further testing. The design of test data is considered in Chapter 24.

BTEC National Study Guide: IT Practitioners. See page 293 for order details of individual texts

96

4. Document the solution

The documentation contains the following: (i) the problem statement; (ii) the top-level program design; (iii) the final detailed program design; (iv) the data table. These are produced during the course of the first three stages of program design. The examples in later sections show the form of this documentation.

Structured programming

Most current program design methodologies are based on *structured programming* concepts. Structured programming is generally associated with certain basic principles:

1. **Restricted use of control structures**. These are limited to three types: *sequence* consisting of instructions which are performed one after the other in the order that they appear in the program; *selection* of one set of instructions from several possible sets of instructions so that the program is able to deal with a number of different circumstances; *repetition*, or *iteration,* of a set of instructions using some kind of program loop. Restricting design to using only these three constructs does not necessarily produce error-free code, but it does help to produce a program which is clear and relatively easy to test.

2. **Modularity**. This is the subdivision of a program into easily identifiable and manageable segments, or *modules*. Each module should require no more than about one page of code. A module may be realised in the final program as one or more small subprograms. Using modules helps to clarify the logical structure of a program for human readers and, by incorporating subprograms, aids its construction.

3. **Top-down, stepwise refinement**. This program design method was described in the earlier section *Problem Solving.*

4. **Clear program format**. This is concerned with the layout of the program instructions. Each page of coding should contain clearly identifiable control structures and blocks of code. One main method of achieving this clarity of structure is by the consistent use of indentation showing the limits of loops, selections and blocks of instructions. Formatting standards apply both to pseudocode and actual program code.

5. **Comments**. The thorough use of comments within the pseudocode design and the actual program in order to explain the purpose of each variable and each few lines of logically related code.

6. **Simplicity**.Where there is a choice between a simple solution to a problem and a slightly more efficient solution which perhaps uses less code, then the simple solution is to be preferred. Straightforward, simple code is easier to test, modify and understand than obscure, 'clever' code.

Basic control structures

As explained earlier, structured programs are constructed using the three control structures sequence, selection and iteration. In order to illustrate how each of these is expressed and used in program design, consider the following programming problem:

Read a set of ten positive and negative numbers entered from a keyboard and find the separate totals of the positive numbers and the negative numbers. Print the two totals.

It is assumed that only valid real numbers such as $1 \cdot 2$, $-7 \cdot 3$, 25, -6 will be entered. The program can be considered to be a *sequence* of three simple modules:

1. **Initialise variables**. Two variables will be required: one for the total of the positive numbers and the other for the total of the negative numbers.

BTEC National Study Guide: IT Practitioners. See page 293 for order details of individual texts

97

2. **Process the numbers**. This involves a loop to read numbers typed in from the keyboard until ten values have been entered. A count will be incremented every time a number is read in.

3. **Display the results**. This will involve writing out the two totals.

This top-level design is illustrated by the structure chart shown in Figure 23.2. The equivalent pseudocode for the top-level design is in Listing 23.1.

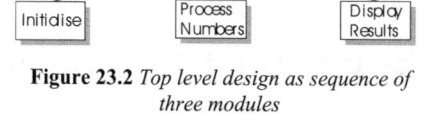

Figure 23.2 *Top level design as sequence of three modules*

Listing 23.1.

```
{Totals}
1     Initialise
2     Process numbers
3     Display results
```

The first refinement of the design results in the structure chart shown in Figure 23.3.

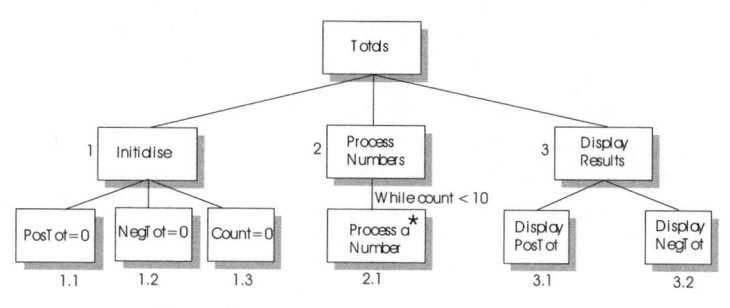

Figure 23.3. *First refinement showing an iteration*

The loop that reads the ten numbers, in other words the *iteration*, is indicated in the structure chart by an asterisk in the top right-hand corner of the component that is to be repeated. The condition governing the loop is written above this component; in this case the loop continues while the count variable has a value less than ten. The equivalent pseudocode is shown in Listing 23.2.

Listing 23.2.

```
{Totals}
1.1   PosTot=0
1.2   NegTot=0
1.3   Count=0
2     while Count < 10
2.1      Process Number
2     endwhile
3.1   write PosTot
3.2   write NegTot
```

Each of the Listing 23.1 statements, numbered *1*, *2* and *3*, have all been refined in Listing 23.2; statement *1* (initialise) has been replaced by three detailed instruction, *1.1*, *1.2* and *1.3*.

BTEC National Study Guide: IT Practitioners. See page 293 for order details of individual texts

98

Similarly, statements *2* and *3* in Listing 23.1 have also been refined in Listing 23.2. (These statement level numbers reflect the depth of the structure diagram; a single statement level such as *1* indicates a top-level module, a statement number such as *1.2* indicate the second step of a refinement of level *1*. Number *2.3.1* indicates the first step of a refinement of statement *2.3*, and so on. A refinement of a statement is denoted by adding another level to the statement number.) Notice that the end of the loop is indicated by endwhile and the instruction inside the loop, Process Number, is indented. A loop thus translates into three pseudocode statements: one statement for the type of loop and the condition that governs it, another for the item that is to be repeated, and the third for the end of the loop. The final refinement is to expand Process Number, since this is the only statement that has not yet been fully defined: we need to show *how* a number is to be processed. The structure chart for the full design is shown in Figure 23.4.

The structure chart shows that the repeated component Process Number involves three steps: increment the count, read a number, and test the number to determine its sign. Positive numbers are to be accumulated in Pos-Tot and negative numbers are to be accumulated in NegTot. The test involves a *selection*, each independent choice being indicated by a small circle in the top right-hand corner of the box. The condition governing each choice is written

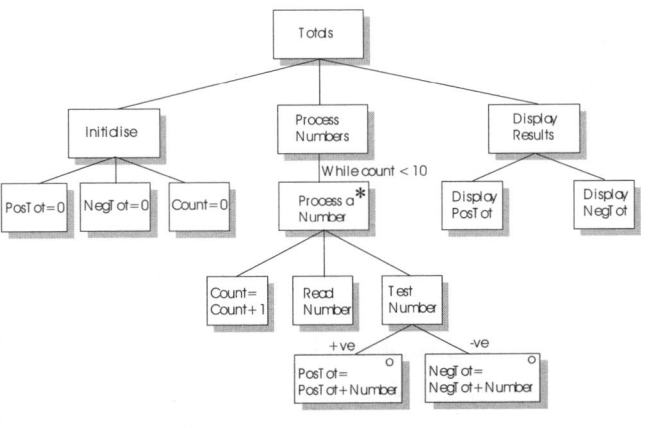

Figure 23.4. *Final refinement showing a selection*

above the appropriate box as shown. This version of the design needs no further refinement since it is now in a suitable form for conversion to pseudocode and subsequently to a programming language such as COBOL or C. The pseudocode in Listing 23.3 uses a select statement for the selection. If the condition following the first select is true, the statement or statements following are obeyed, otherwise the next select is considered. The endselect statement must be used to terminate the select statement. Note that the number of alternative sets of statements is not limited to two - as many as necessary can be chained together in this way. If some action is necessary when none of the select statements is true then the select when otherwise statement can be included before endselect.

Listing 23.3. Totalling positive and negative numbers

```
        {Totals}
1.1        PosTot = 0
1.2        NegTot = 0
1.3        Count = 0
2          while Count < 10
2.1          Count = Count + 1
2.2          Read Number
2.3          select
2.3.1a          when Number > 0
2.3.1b              PosTot = PosTot + Number
```

BTEC National Study Guide: IT Practitioners. See page 293 for order details of individual texts

99

```
2.3.2a        when Number < 0
2.3.2b            NegTot = NegTot + Number
2.3         endselect
2        endwhile
3.1        write PosTot
3.2        write NegTot
```

The numbering follows the refinement levels of the structure charts. Thus if the first module is refined as a sequence of two statements, these statements are labelled *1.1* and *1.2*. In the case of an iteration, the start and end statements are given the same number. Thus in Listing 23.3, the `while` and `endwhile` both are labelled *2* showing that the iteration is the second top-level module in the program. The start and end statements of a selection are similarly labelled, but each option, which might involve a number of steps, has a small letter added to indicate that it is a step within the option. (For example, *2.3.1a* and *2.3.1b*).

In addition, in the examples that follow, where a structure chart step has been expanded in the pseudocode, each part of the expansion is also designated with a lower case letter. This frequently occurs when the structure chart shows that a value is to be entered by a user through a keyboard; the pseudocode might be expanded thus: *5.1* `read Number` becomes

```
5.1a    write 'Enter a number'
5.1b    read Number
```

This helps to prevent the structure chart from becoming too detailed and thus unclear. To complete the design, the three variables must be defined in a data table (see Table 23.2).

name	description	type
Count	Counts how many numbers have been entered	integer variable
PosTot	The sum of the positive value numbers	real variable
NegTot	The sum of the negative value numbers	real variable

Table. 23.2. *Definition of variables*

Summary

Figure 23.5 summarises the structure chart and pseudocode notation used for the three basic control structures, sequence, selection and iteration.

Iteration is shown in a commonly used alternative form in which the condition is expressed as `repeat..until <condition>`. In this form the condition is tested at the end of the loop rather than at the beginning; this means that the statements within the loop will be repeated at least once.

The `repeat..until` loop is illustrated in the worked examples.

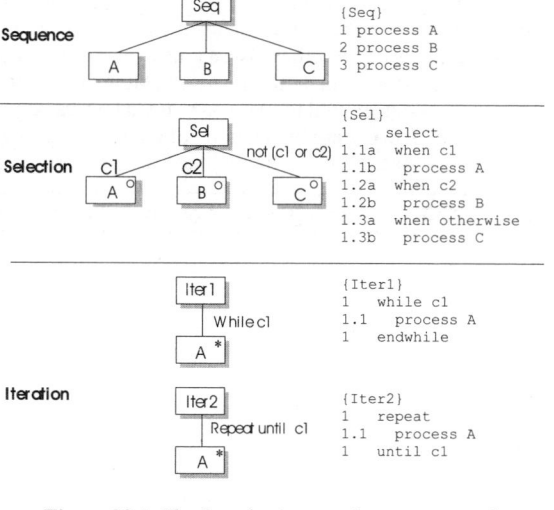

Figure 23.5. *The three basic control structures used in structured programming*

BTEC National Study Guide: IT Practitioners. See page 293 for order details of individual texts

100

Worked examples

The worked examples presented in the next sections use a combination of structure charts and pseudocode to arrive at the final program design. Structure charts are used for the design refinements in order to express the overall logic in a clear, easily understandable form. The design is then presented in pseudocode, a form more suitable for testing and subsequent conversion to a programming language. At this stage some fine detail may also be added to the design. The program design technique presented here, rather than being targeted at a particular programming language such as COBOL, is in a form suitable for conversion to any one of a number of quite different high-level languages. Each of the following worked examples is in the format:

- (i) the problem statement;
- (ii) any assumptions that have been made;
- (iii) structure charts showing the top-level design and any further refinement stages;
- (iv) pseudocode for the final design;
- (v) the data table for the complete design;
- (vi) comments.

Reading and displaying information

Problem statement

Design a program which will accept from the keyboard a value representing a number of inches and display the equivalent number of centimetres.

Assumptions

1. The input is a valid real number.   2. There is no preferred format for the output.

Top-level design

The top-level design, shown on the right, now requires only minor refinements concerned with the precise form that the output is to take. This can be accomplished conveniently in pseudocode without the need to draw another structure chart.

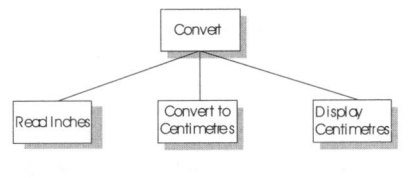

Pseudocode

```
{Convert inches to centimetres}
1a   write 'Enter the length in inches: ', <newline>
1b   read Inches
2    Centimetres = Inches*2.54
3a   write <newline>
3b   write 'A length of ', Inches, ' inches is equivalent to ',
                   centimetres, ' centimetres', <newline>
```

Data table

name	description	type
Inches	Value entered at the keyboard and converted to centimetres	real variable
Centimetres	The value to be output	real variable

BTEC National Study Guide: IT Practitioners. See page 293 for order details of individual texts

101

Comments

`<newline>` indicates that the cursor is to move to the beginning of the next line.

Loops - Running totals

One very frequent programming task is to keep a running total when a number of values are read within an iteration (that is, *loop*). This next example illustrates the technique usually adopted to accumulate a total in a variable.

Problem statement

Design a program to read ten numbers from a keyboard and display their sum.

Assumptions

1. Exactly ten valid real numbers will be entered using a keyboard.

2. The sum of the numbers is to be accumulated as the numbers are entered, and thus there is no requirement to store them.

Top-level design

The top-level design is a simple sequence of three modules. The second module, `Process Numbers`, involves a loop which is to repeat a known number of times (namely 10). It can therefore be implemented using a count variable as shown in refinement #1.

Refinement #1

The variable `Total` is to be used to accumulate the sum of the ten numbers and therefore must start with an initial value of zero. `Count` is to start at 1 because it must be increased by one each time a new number is read. Each time through the loop a new number is read into the variable `Number` and then added to `Total` which accumulates the numbers. When `Count` reaches 10, the loop terminates.

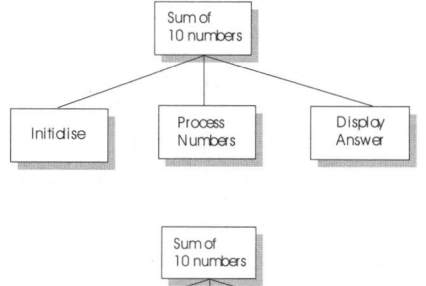

Refinement #2

The statements required for processing a number and incrementing the loop control variable have been added; this represents the final structure chart form of the design.

Pseudocode

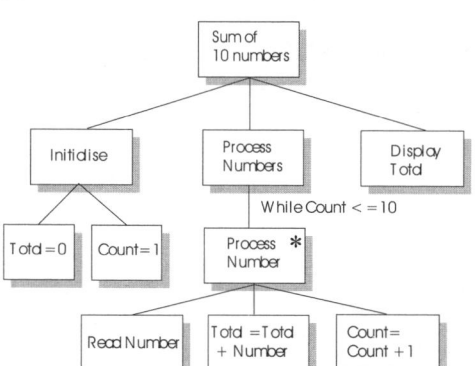

```
{Sum of 10 numbers}
1.1     Total = 0
1.2     Count = 1
2       while Count <= 10
2.1a      write <newline>, 'Enter
          number #', Count
```

BTEC National Study Guide: IT Practitioners. See page 293 for order details of individual texts

102

```
2.1b     read Number
2.2       Total = Total + Number
2.3       Count = Count + 1
2       endwhile
3       write <newline> , 'The sum of the 10 numbers is: ', Total
```

This pseudocode form of the final refinement is to make the program a little more user friendly by adding some text to prompt the user to enter a number - this is much better than presenting the user with a blank screen and expecting him/her to know exactly what to do. The final instruction adds some text to announce the answer.

Data table

name	description	type
Total	Accumulates the ten numbers	real variable
Number	Stores the latest number input	real variable
Count	The control variable for the loop	integer variable

Comments

1. Variables that are used as running totals and counts must always be initialised before a loop commences.

2. Control variables for loops are always of type `integer`.

3. A count variable is used to control the duration of a loop when the number of repetitions is known before the loop commences.

Loops - Rogue values

There are many occasions when the exact number of repetitions of a loop is not known in advance. Frequently loops are terminated when a special value is entered by the user. Such special values are often called 'rogue values'.

Problem statement

Design a program to read a set of numbers representing the cost of some purchased items. The end of the list is to be indicated by entering 0 for the cost. Display how many items were purchased and the total cost of the items.

Assumptions

1. The values entered will be valid real numbers entered

2. No negative numbers will be

Top-level design

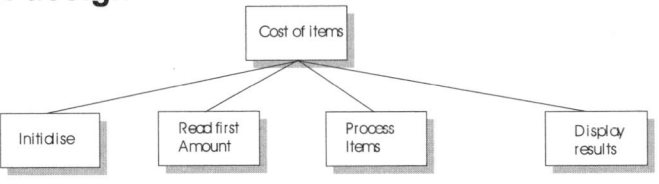

The strategy used in this instance is to read a value before the loop represented by the module, `Process Items`, is started. The condition governing the continuation of the loop will be

BTEC National Study Guide: IT Practitioners. See page 293 for order details of individual texts

103

`While Amount > 0` and this means that `Amount` must have been assigned a value before the loop starts.

Refinement #1

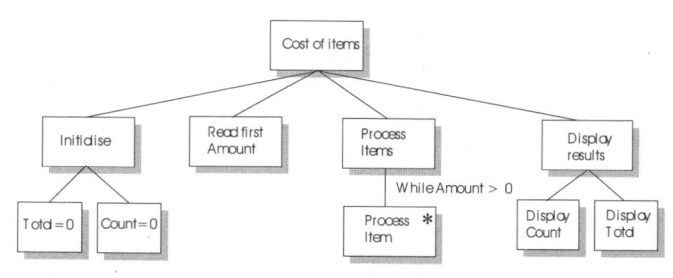

This refinement now shows that if the user initially enters zero for the amount, the loop is not executed at all because the condition, `Amount > 0`, is false. This is a very important characteristic of the `while` loop and a reason for not using the `repeat..until` loop construct in this instance.

Refinement #2

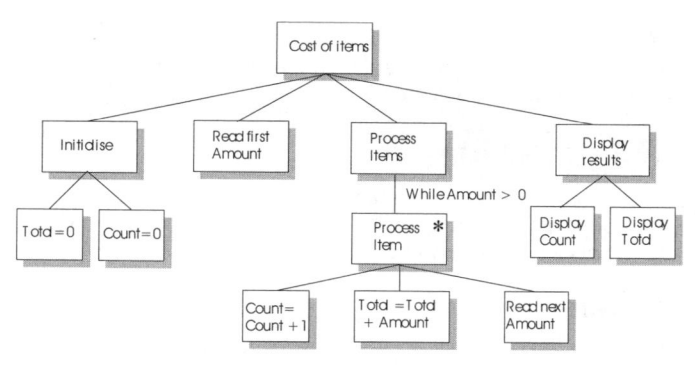

Processing an item requires a sequence comprising incrementing a count for the number of items, adding the current item's cost to the running total and finally obtaining another item cost. Again, if this latter amount is zero, the condition for continuing the loop becomes false and the loop is terminated. The results are then displayed.

Notice that the last statement executed in the loop is a `read` statement which obtains the data to be processed next. Since no further detail is required for the structure chart, this is the final refinement before writing the pseudocode.

Pseudocode

```
{Enter and total costs}
1.1     Total = 0
1.2     Count = 0
2.1a    write 'Enter the cost of the first item, or 0 to end'
2.1b    read Amount
3       while Amount > 0
3.1        Count = Count + 1
3.2        Total = Total + Amount
```

BTEC National Study Guide: IT Practitioners. See page 293 for order details of individual texts

104

```
3.3a    write <newline>, 'Enter cost of next item, or zero to end'
3.3b    read Amount
3       endwhile
4.1a    write  <newline>,
4.1b    write  <newline>, Count, 'items were purchased'
4.2a    write <newline>
4.2b    write 'The total cost was: £', Total
```

The detail added to the pseudocode is again to improve communication with the user by displaying prompts such as that in statement *2.1a* and by using blank lines (that is, `write <newline>`) to improve the clarity of the output.

Data table

name	description	type
Total	Accumulates the cost of the items	real variable
Amount	Stores the current item's cost	real variable
Count	Counts the number of items	integer variable

Comments

Try to avoid using a `while` condition such as `Amount <> 0` (not equal to zero) instead of `Amount > 0` because real numbers may not be represented exactly within a computer; the representation of zero might not be **exactly** zero and the condition `Amount <> 0` may still be true even when zero is entered for `Amount`.

Making decisions - the select statement

This example introduces the idea of taking one of several courses of action depending on the value of a variable read in from the keyboard. A loop is again terminated by testing for a rogue value, this time a negative value.

Problem statement

Design a program to accept a number of values representing student examination marks. Each mark is to be displayed as a grade as shown alongside. A negative value is to be used to indicate the end of the set of marks.

Mark	Grade
80 or over	Distinction
60 or over	Merit
40 or over	Pass
less than 40	Fail

Assumptions

The marks are entered as valid integers.

Top-level design

The third module in this sequence is an iteration which repeatedly reads and grades a mark until a negative mark is entered.

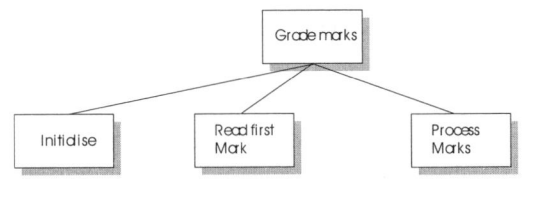

BTEC National Study Guide: IT Practitioners. See page 293 for order details of individual texts

105

Refinement #1

The threshold values for the grades are assigned to integer constants. Any negative value entered will be regarded as the signal to terminate the program.

Refinement #2

The four actions comprising the selection statement, Grade, which determine the message to be displayed should not be considered as a sequence of tests; the selection notation simply shows which action is to be taken depending on the one condition which is true, and as such the four actions could have been drawn in any order.

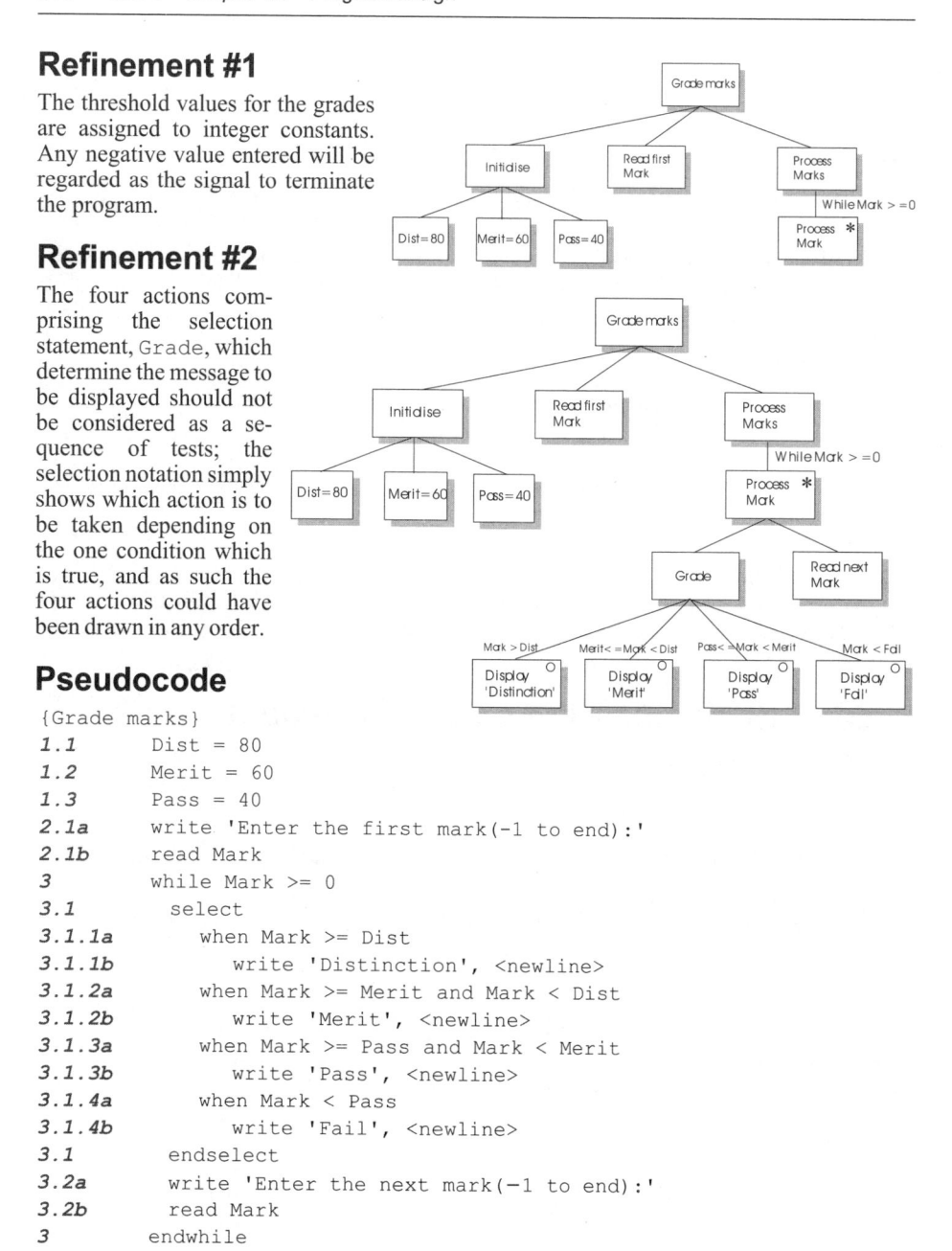

Pseudocode

```
{Grade marks}
1.1        Dist = 80
1.2        Merit = 60
1.3        Pass = 40
2.1a       write 'Enter the first mark(-1 to end):'
2.1b       read Mark
3          while Mark >= 0
3.1          select
3.1.1a         when Mark >= Dist
3.1.1b            write 'Distinction', <newline>
3.1.2a         when Mark >= Merit and Mark < Dist
3.1.2b            write 'Merit', <newline>
3.1.3a         when Mark >= Pass and Mark < Merit
3.1.3b            write 'Pass', <newline>
3.1.4a         when Mark < Pass
3.1.4b            write 'Fail', <newline>
3.1          endselect
3.2a         write 'Enter the next mark(−1 to end):'
3.2b         read Mark
3          endwhile
```

The three thresholds for the grades are stored in the integer constants Dist, Merit and Pass. The advantage of doing this rather than using the actual values 80, 60 and 40 respectively is that if any of these values need to be modified, they need only be changed in the initialisation module and nowhere else.

BTEC National Study Guide: IT Practitioners. See page 293 for order details of individual texts

106

Data table

name	description	type
Dist	The distinction mark	integer constant = 80
Merit	The merit mark	integer constant = 60
Pass	The pass mark	integer constant = 40
Mark	The student's exam mark	integer variable

Comments

The precise form of a selection statement in a programming language can vary considerably; it is the responsibility of the programmer to choose the most appropriate form available in the target language that exactly represents the required logic.

Decisions - A menu program

Where a program offers a user a number of different options, a menu-based program structure is often employed. The options are displayed and the user is invited to choose one of them by, for example entering its first letter. The program then performs the requested operation and re-displays the menu after it is completed. One of the options always allows the user to exit the program. This example illustrates the structure of a program which presents the user with four options concerned with currency conversion.

Problem statement

Design a menu-based program to allow a user to choose between converting pounds sterling to German marks, American dollars or French francs. The program will ask the user to enter the number of pounds and it will display the equivalent amount in the chosen currency before returning to the menu. The menu is to appear at the top of a blank screen and appear as follows:

```
Currency conversion program

(M)arks
(D)ollars
(F)rancs
e(X)it

Which currency do you want to convert to Pounds?
```

Assumptions

1. Invalid choices (that is entering a letter other than M, D, F or X) will produce an error message and an invitation to try again.

2. Upper and lower case letters will be allowed.

3. The amount in pounds entered by the user will be a valid real number.

4. A single statement, ClearScreen, is available to blank the display screen.

Top-level design

The top-level design in this instance is very simple: the initialisation module sets the values for the three currency conversion factors and the remaining module, Main, repeatedly displays the user options and executes the one chosen.

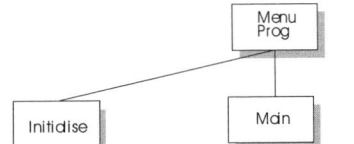

BTEC National Study Guide: IT Practitioners. See page 293 for order details of individual texts

107

Refinement #1

Three constants used for the currency conversion calculations are defined at this point (don't rely on these figures for holiday plans!).

Further, the iteration is defined as a `repeat..until` loop with condition `c1`. Logical conditions governing loops and selections can be coded in this way so that defining their precise form can be deferred until the design has been completed. We will see later in refinement #3 that `c1` is the condition that indicates the user has chosen the exit option.

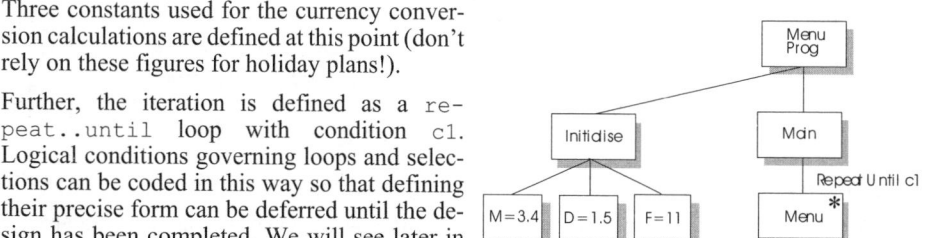

Remember that the `repeat` loop causes the statements within the loop to be repeated at least once, and that the test for continuing to repeat the statements is made at the end of the loop.

Refinement #2

This refinement now shows that the loop controls a sequence of two modules. The first, `Display menu`, repeatedly clears the display screen, shows the menu of options and then reads the user's choice. The second module is a selection statement which processes the option chosen. The final refinement defines the operation of each of the options and under what circumstances each is chosen.

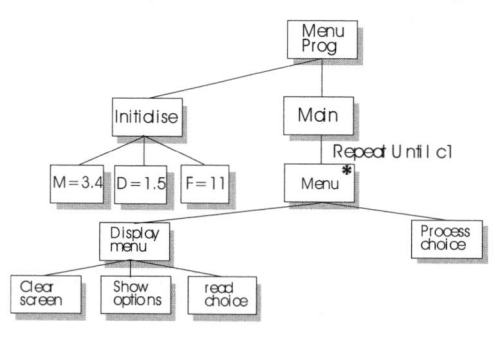

Refinement #3

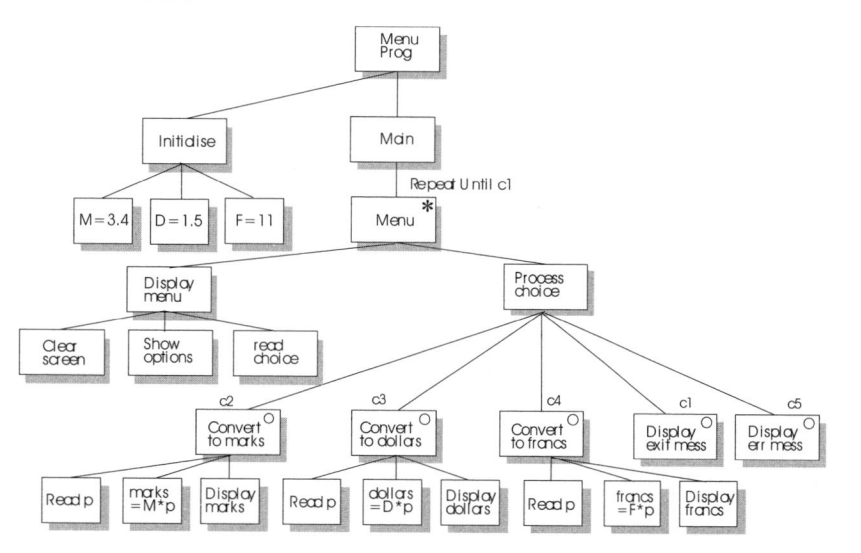

The first three options are concerned with the actual currency conversions. The fourth option displays a message to confirm that the user has chosen to exit the program. The final `select`

BTEC National Study Guide: IT Practitioners. See page 293 for order details of individual texts

108

statement is only invoked if the user has entered an invalid choice, that is, the letter entered is not 'M', 'D', 'F' or 'X'. The condition codes c1-c5 are defined in the next table.

c1	choice = ('X' or 'x')
c2	choice = ('M' or 'm')
c3	choice = ('D' or 'd')
c4	choice = ('F' or 'f')
c5	choice <> ('X' or 'x')or ('M' or 'm')or ('D' or 'd')or ('F' or 'f')

Pseudocode

```
{Menu currency conversion}
1.1      M = 3.4
1.2      D = 1.5
1.3      F = 11
2        repeat
2.1.1      ClearScreen
2.1.2a     write 'Currency conversion program', <newline>
2.1.2b     write <newline>
2.1.2c     write '(M)arks'
2.1.2d     write '(D)ollars'
2.1.2e     write '(F)rancs'
2.1.2f     write <newline>
2.1.2g     write 'Which currency do you want to convert to pounds?'
2.1.3      read Choice
2.2        select
2.2.1a       when Choice = ('M' or 'm')
2.2.1b         write <newline>, 'Enter amount'
2.2.1c         read p
2.2.1d         Currency = M*p
2.2.1e         write ' = ', Currency, ' Marks'
2.2.1f         write <newline> 'Press <Enter> to return to menu'
2.2.1g         read key
2.2.2a       when Choice = ('D' or 'd')
2.2.2b         write <newline>, 'Enter amount'
2.2.2c         read p
2.2.2d         Currency = D*p
2.2.2e         write ' = ', Currency, ' Dollars'
2.2.2f         write <newline> 'Press <Enter> to return to menu'
2.2.2g         read key
2.2.2a       when Choice = ('F' or 'f')
2.2.3b         write <newline>, 'Enter amount'
2.2.3c         read p
2.2.3d         Currency = F*p
2.2.3e         write ' = ', Currency, ' Francs'
2.2.3f         write <newline> 'Press <Enter> to return to menu'
2.2.3g         read key
2.2.4a       when Choice = ('X' or 'x')
2.2.4b         write 'Exiting program..'
2.2.5a       when otherwise
2.2.5b         write 'Invalid option. Please try again'
2.2.5c         write <newline> 'Press <Enter> to return to menu'
2.2.5d         read key
2.2        endselect
2.3      until Choice = ('X' or 'x')
```

BTEC National Study Guide: IT Practitioners. See page 293 for order details of individual texts

109

Data table

name	description	type
M	Conversion factor for pounds to marks	real constant = 3.4
D	Conversion factor for pounds to dollars	real constant = 1.5
F	Conversion factor for pounds to francs	real constant = 11
P	The number of pounds to convert	real variable
Choice	The user's menu choice	character variable
Currency	The equivalent value in the currency chosen	real variable
key	Dummy variable to accept the <Return> key	character variable

Comments

1. This is a good model for constructing menu-driven programs.

2. The manner of implementing the `select` statement can vary considerably with the target programming language. Pascal provides `if` and `case` statements which each have their particular advantages and disadvantages. The programmer is responsible for choosing the most appropriate selection construct from those available.

BTEC National Study Guide: IT Practitioners. See page 293 for order details of individual texts

110

Chapter 24

Program testing, debugging and documenting

Once a program has been written, it must go through two stages in order to remove errors which almost inevitably will be present. No matter how much care has been taken in the design and coding of a program, it is still very likely to contain *syntax* errors, that is incorrectly formed statements, and probably errors in *logic* as well. *Debugging* is the term given to the process of detecting and correcting these errors or *bugs*.

The first stage in the removal of errors is the correction of syntax errors. Fortunately for the programmer, modern interpreters and compilers will provide a large amount of assistance in the detection of syntax errors in the source code. Badly formed statements will be reported by a compiler after it has attempted to compile the source code; an interpreter will report illegal statements as it attempts to execute them.

Logic errors, however, are largely undetectable by the translating program. These are errors which cause the program to behave in a manner contrary to expectations. The individual statements in the program are correctly formed, but when executed it does not operate correctly; it may give incorrect answers, or terminate prematurely, or not terminate at all. Hopefully, even the most puzzling logic errors, having been detected, eventually can be removed. But how can the programmer be confident that the program will continue to behave properly when it is in use? The answer is that the programmer never can be absolutely certain that the program will not fail. However, by the careful choice of test data in the second stage of the debugging process, the programmer can test the program under the conditions that are most likely to occur in practice.

Test data is designed to determine the robustness of the program: how well it can cope with unexpected or spurious inputs, as well as those for which it has been designed specifically to process. The purpose of *documentation* is to provide the user with all the information necessary to fully understand the purpose of the program and how that purpose has been achieved. The precise form that the documentation takes will be determined by a number of factors:

- ❏ The type of program.
- ❏ Who is likely to use the program.
- ❏ Whether it will be necessary to modify the program coding after it has been finally tested and accepted.

General guidelines for the contents of program documentation are at the end of this chapter.

Detecting logic errors

If after examining program code for a reasonable amount of time the cause of an error remains a mystery, there are a number of courses of action which probably will be much more productive than continuing to pore over the listing:

1. Ask a fellow programmer to listen while you explain the operation of the program and

BTEC National Study Guide: IT Practitioners. See page 293 for order details of individual texts

111

the way it is behaving. Quite often you will see the cause of the error as you are making the explanation. Alternatively, your helper might recognise the type of error and its probable cause from his/her own experience, or might ask a question which makes you reconsider some aspect of the program which you have assumed to be correct or had no direct bearing on the problem. It is surprising how often this simple approach works.

2. Examine the values of key variables while the program is running by inserting temporary lines of code throughout the program to display the values of key variables. Comparison of the values actually displayed with expected values will normally identify the likely source of the error.

3. Use debugging utilities provided in the language itself or separately in the system software. Most high-level language development systems provide debugging aids. These allow the programmer to do such things as step through the program line by line and display the value of variables, or to insert break-points to interrupt the execution of the program so that the state of variables can be examined. It is the responsibility of the programmer to investigate the debugging aids available and make good use of them.

Test data

When the programmer feels that the more obvious program errors have been detected and removed, the next stage is to test the program using carefully selected data. The nature of the test data should be such that:

❏ every statement in the program is executed at least once;
❏ the effectiveness of every section of coding devoted to detecting invalid input is verified;
❏ every route through the program is tried at least once;
❏ the accuracy of the processing is verified;
❏ the program operates according to its original design specification.

In order to achieve these aims, the programmer must be inventive in the design of the test data. Each test case must check something not tested by previous runs; there is no point in proving that a program which can add successfully a certain set of numbers can also add another similar set of numbers. The goal is to strain the program to its limit, and this is particularly important when the program is to be used frequently by a number of different people. There are three general categories of test data:

1. *Normal data.* This is the general data which the program was designed to handle.

2. *Extreme values.* These test the behaviour of the program when valid data at the upper and lower limits of acceptability are used. The process of using extreme values is called 'boundary testing' and is often a fruitful place to look for errors. For numeric data this could be the use of very large or very small values. Text could be the shortest or longest sequence of characters permitted. A program for file processing could be tested with a file containing no records, or just a single record. The cases where zero or null values are used are very important test cases, frequently highlighting programming oversights.

3. *Exceptional data.* Programs are usually designed to accept a certain range or class of inputs. If invalid data is used, that is data which the program is not designed to handle, the program should be capable of rejecting it rather than attempting to process it. This is particularly important when the program is to be used by people other than the programmer, since they may be unaware of what constitutes invalid data. A programmer should from the outset assume that incorrect data will be used with the program; this may save a great deal of time looking for program errors which may actually be data errors.

BTEC National Study Guide: IT Practitioners. See page 293 for order details of individual texts

112

Test logs

Once test cases have been devised, the program must be executed using the test data. The effect of using the test data is recorded in a *test log*. Since the point of program testing is to find errors, the log will indicate a <u>successful</u> test <u>if an error is found</u>, and an unsuccessful test otherwise.

The test log will form part of the documentation of the program so that if the program is subsequently modified, the same test data can be re-applied to ensure that no program errors have been accidentally introduced by the modifications. For each set of test data, the expected output must be determined before running the program so that it can be compared with the actual output produced by the program. The test log could be set out in tabular form as follows.

TEST LOG		Date:		
Program name:		Version:		
Author:		Tested by:		

Test case	Expected output	Observed output	Result	Comments
1				
2				
3				
4				
etc				

Validation

At some point the programmer must decide that the program has had sufficient testing. He or she will be confident that the program will operate according to specification and without 'crashing' or 'hanging up' under extreme or unexpected circumstances; the reputation of a professional programmer relies on this. Prior to release, the final testing is then performed by the user for whom the program was developed. The programmer may have overlooked areas of difficulty because it is often hard to consider a problem objectively or entirely from the viewpoint of the user. If this is the case, that the operation of the program is not entirely satisfactory, the program will be modified and re-tested until all user requirements are met.

Program documentation requirements

The documentation produced for a program will depend on a number of factors. For instance, a program which validates a temporary file prior to creating it permanently will probably require a minimum of user interaction and only a small number of user instructions. However, at some later date, it might be necessary for the author of the program, or a different programmer, to modify it. This possibility means that the structure of the program will have to be explained in great detail, and test procedures to ensure its correct operation will need to be provided.

A general purpose program such as a spreadsheet, designed for people who just want to use the computer as a tool, will require extremely detailed instructions regarding its function and use. Such programs are generally accompanied by detailed user manuals and tutorials. On the other hand, users would not be expected (and definitely not encouraged) to modify the program coding; thus no details would be provided regarding the way the program has been written. This latter type of documentation would only be required for the people responsible for producing the program. In addition to the documentation requirements of users and programmers, there is a third category of person to be considered. These are people such as managers who are neither likely to use programs extensively nor want to attempt to modify them. They merely need to have an overview of the program - its function, capabilities, hardware requirements etc. Thus there are many factors governing the coverage of documentation, and for this reason in the next section it is only possible to provide a checklist of items which might reasonably be included.

Documentation checklist

The documentation for a simple program generally falls into four sections:

❏ Identification.   ❏ General specification.

❏ User information.   ❏ Program specification.

Most users will need access to the first three sections; in general the fourth section will only be needed if the program is to be modified. The amount of detail in each section will depend entirely on the particular application and, to some extent, the implementation language. COBOL, for example, is largely self-documenting: it contains an Identification Division containing all the information listed in the first section below; the Data Division of a COBOL program contains precise details regarding all of the files used by the program and which devices are required; the Procedure Division is written in 'English-like' sentences which are generally easy to understand, even by a non-programmer. Consequently, a program written in COBOL will generally require less documentation than one written in Pascal or C, languages which are not self-documenting. The following checklist is a guide to what might reasonably be included in the documentation for a program.

1. Identification.

❏ Title of program and short statement of its function.

❏ Author.

❏ Date written.

❏ Language used and version if relevant.

❏ Hardware requirements.

2. General specification.

❏ Description of the main action(s) of the program under normal circumstances.

❏ File specifications.

❏ Restrictions and/or limitations of the program.

❏ Equations used or references to texts explaining any complex procedures /techniques involved.

3. Program specification.

❏ Structure charts/flowcharts/decision tables.

❏ Annotated listing.

❏ Testing procedure including test classes and data with expected output and a test log.

4. User Guide.

❏ Installation instructions.

❏ Detailed explanation of the operation of the program.

❏ Tutorial.

❏ Screen shots.

❏ Troubleshooting guide.

BTEC National Study Guide: IT Practitioners. See page 293 for order details of individual texts

114

Chapter 25
Pascal programming

This chapter addresses the task of developing a piece of software using the programming language Pascal. Here we look at Pascal in enough depth for you to be able to develop your own simple programs, provided of course that you have access to a Pascal compiler. The programs presented in this unit were written and tested using Borland's Turbo Pascal. However, apart from a small number of possible exceptions, the programs should work with any standard version of Pascal. Any special features of Turbo Pascal used in example programs are noted and explained; if you are not using Turbo Pascal, your version will most likely have very similar features that you can substitute, but you will need to refer to the appropriate language reference manual for the precise instruction format required. Turbo Pascal was chosen because it provides an ideal, easy to use environment for developing programs since it combines in one package all the tools required for the task. For example, it has: (i) an *editor* for creating and editing source programs; (ii) a *compiler* to check the syntax of a program, to report and identify errors and to produce object code; (iii) a *linker* to produce executable code; (iv) a *debugger* to help with locating runtime errors; (v) a *file manager* to allow you to quickly save, retrieve and print source programs.

The structure of a Pascal program

A Pascal program consists of four main parts: (i) the *name* of the program; (ii) a *declarations* section in which the programmer defines global *identifiers*. These are the variables and constants used in the program; (iii) *function* and *procedure definitions*; (iv) The main *procedural* part of the program which defines the sequence of instructions to be performed by the program. This section uses the identifiers, functions and procedures defined in the previous two sections of the program. It starts with the word begin and ends with end. Listing 25.1. shows the general structure of a Pascal program.

Listing 25.1. General structure of a Pascal program

```
program Name(input, output);

   {Declarations of global variables and  and constants}

   {Procedures and functions definitions}

begin
   {The main body of the program containing a sequence of
   instructions to be performed}
end.
```

As a simple example to illustrate these ideas, Listing 25.2 shows a program which calculates the total cost of a purchased item by calculating VAT and adding it to the price of the item. The algorithm on which the program is based is as follows:

1. *Ask the user to enter the price of the item*

2. *Store the price*

BTEC National Study Guide: IT Practitioners. See page 293 for order details of individual texts

115

3.   *Calculate the VAT at 17.5% (i.e. multiply the price by 0.175)*

4.   *Calculate the total price by adding the VAT to the price*

5.   *Display the total cost on the screen.*

Note that the line numbers preceding each line in the program are included in the example programs presented in this chapter simply for ease of reference to specific lines when describing them. ***Line numbers are not part of the Pascal language and should not be included if you intend to compile and run the example programs.***

The operation of program `Example1`

Line *1* declares that this program is called `Example1` and (`input`, `output`) indicates that the program uses the keyboard for the input of data and the screen for the display of data.

Lines *2* **and** *3* declare that VAT is a *constant* value.

Listing 25.2.	A simple program to calculate the total cost of a purchase
1	`program Example1(input, output);`
2	`const`
3	`  VAT = 0.175;`
4	`var`
5	`  Price :real;`
6	`  Tax :real;`
7	`  TotalCost :real;`
8	`begin`
9	`  write('Enter price of the item');`
10	`  readln(Price);`
11	`  Tax:= Price*VAT;`
12	`  TotalCost:= Price + Tax;`
13	`  writeln('The total cost is:' , TotalCost:8:2);`
14	`  end.`

Lines *4 - 7* declare three *variables* `Price`, `Tax` and `TotalCost` (hence the word `var` on line *4*) each as being of type `real`. Variables are used to store data, which in this case are in the form of real numbers, that is, numbers which are not whole numbers. Every variable used in a Pascal program must be declared in this way. Up to this point the programmer has defined a number of *identifiers* that will be used in the procedural part of the program which follows.

Line *8* indicates the beginning of the procedural part of the program, that is, the section of the program which states what operations are to be performed. This is the part of the program in which the tasks identified by the algorithm are coded.

Line *9* causes the message Enter price of the item to be displayed on the screen.

Line *10* causes the computer to pause and accept numeric data typed in to be stored in the variable `Price` before continuing.

Line *11* stores the result of `Price` multiplied by `VAT` in the variable `Tax`.

Line *12* stores the result of adding `Price` and `Tax` in `TotalCost`.

Line *13* then displays the text, 'The total cost is: ' followed by the value stored in `TotalCost`. The total cost is shown in a field of eight characters with two figures after the decimal point.

BTEC National Study Guide: IT Practitioners. See page 293 for order details of individual texts

116

Finally in **Line *14***, the word end followed by a full stop indicates the end of the program.

Some general remarks

Before going on to explore Pascal in more depth, it is worth mentioning a few general points at this stage:

1.　Pascal does not distinguish between the use of capitals and lower-case letters. Thus it regards BEGIN, begin and Begin as being exactly the same.

2.　Pascal uses the semicolon to indicate the end of an instruction, which is why you will see a semicolon at the end of most of the lines in a program. (You will quickly learn where a semicolon is not necessary). If you forget to terminate a complete instruction with a semicolon, the compiler will 'think' that the instruction is continued on the next line and, more often than not, it will say that there is an error in the next line.

3.　It is a good idea to include comment lines (that is, text enclosed between '{' and '}') to describe the purpose of lines or sections of your program. Particularly for large, complex programs, this is very helpful if it is necessary to change the program at some later date.

4.　Using spaces, blank lines and indentation can greatly improve the appearance and the clarity of a program, thus making the program easier to read and understand if it has to be modified later for any reason.

5.　Programming involves meticulous attention to detail; omitting punctuation marks, including them in the wrong place or making spelling mistakes will usually lead to the compiler reporting syntax errors, but sometimes such slips might cause serious errors which are more difficult to detect, so be very careful to form instructions precisely.

Identifiers and data types

The term *identifier* is a general term used for *variables*, *constants* and other programmer-defined names such as *procedures* and *functions*. Variables and constants are always associated with a data *type*. Pascal requires that variables are given a type such as integer or real so that the necessary amount of memory can be reserved for their use.

Variables

A variable, which represents an item of data such as a single number, has a name and a current value. Variables are given names such as Amount, Total or Numb3 and are assigned values by program instructions. These values are stored in the memory of the computer and they are accessed whenever a variable is referenced in a program instruction. So, for example, in the instruction

```
Total := Price + Tax;
```

the value associated with the variable Price is added to the value of the variable Tax and the sum is then assigned to the variable Total. If in a previous instruction total had already been assigned a value, that value would be replaced by the new one.

Constants

Constants too are assigned values but only once after the word const preceding the main program. The constant VAT in Listing 25.2 is an example. Constants retain their values throughout the execution of a program; Pascal does not allow you to use a constant in an instruction which

BTEC National Study Guide: IT Practitioners. See page 293 for order details of individual texts

117

tries to change the value of the constant. Thus, if in Listing 25.2, you included an instruction such as

```
VAT := 0.2;
```

in the main program, the Pascal compiler would report an error. Notice that a constant is assigned a value using only the '=' sign without the ':'.

Special identifiers and reserved words

Certain words in Pascal are classed as *special*, or *standard*, *identifiers* because they perform the same function as programmer-defined identifiers but they are recognised by the compiler as being pre-defined and they are therefore to be used only in a certain context. Examples of special identifiers are the words `write`, `writeln`, `read`, `readln`, `input` and `output`. If you use any of these words for identifiers, for example by declaring

```
var
    Read :integer;
```

then Pascal will not necessarily regard this as a mistake, but you will have overridden the standard definition of `read` as an input instruction, and you will have to use it as an integer variable; you will not be able then to use read as an input instruction since, in effect, you will have redefined its function. The moral is to avoid using these special identifier names for your own, programmer-defined identifiers. Reserved words such as `begin`, `end`, `real` and `program` are words which are actually part of the Pascal language and are unavailable for use as identifiers. Pascal's reserved words and special identifiers are shown below.

Reserved words

and	array	begin	case	const
div	do	downto	else	end
file	for	function	goto	if
in	label	mod	nil	not
of	or	packed	procedure	program
record	repeat	set	then	to
type	until	var	while	with

Special identifiers

abs	arctan	boolean	char	chr
cos	dispose	eof	eoln	exp
false	get	input	integer	ln
maxint	new	odd	ord	output
pack	page	pred	put	read
readln	real	reset	rewrite	round
sin	sqr	sqrt	succ	text
true	trunc	unpack	write	writeln

Rules for naming identifiers

Pascal imposes a number of restrictions concerning the formation of names for identifiers:

1. The name must consist only of alphabetic and numeric characters.

2. The name must start with an alphabetic character.

3. The name must not be a special identifier or a reserved word.

Examples of valid identifiers

firstNum	NUMBER1	abc31	Counter	x

BTEC National Study Guide: IT Practitioners. See page 293 for order details of individual texts

118

Examples of invalid identifiers

`12abc`	(starts with a numeric character)
`first-number`	(contains a non-alphabetic/numeric character)
`var 1`	(contains a space)
`End`	(a reserved word)
`READ`	(a special identifier)

Data types

As well as having names and values, variables are also given a *type*. Three commonly used types are `integer`, `real` and `char` (character). Data types are declared before the main program. For variables, the type must be shown after the name of the variable, as illustrated on lines *5-7* of Listing 25.2. More examples of type declarations are shown below.

```
var
    Amount              :real;
    CodeLetter          :char;
    NumberOfItems       :integer;
```

The type `real` means that these variables can be used for numbers such as 123.456, 0.22 or –9.93, that is, *signed* numbers that are not whole numbers. The computer holds `real` numbers in floating-point form so that very large, and very small numbers can be stored.

Signed whole numbers, that is, `integer` values are stored as two's complement binary values in the computer. Some examples of integers are 23, 0, –1, 32767 and –559.

Type `char` means that the named variable (`CodeLetter` in the example above) stores a single character such as 'a', 'D', '6' or '?'.

Turbo Pascal provides a further data type to handle *strings*. A string is simply a number of characters which are collected together and used as a unit. For example, a person's name is a string of alphabetic characters, and a stock number such as 100-234/ABC in a mail order catalogue is a string containing a mixture of alphabetic, numeric and special characters. String variable declarations are illustrated in the examples below.

```
    Surname             :string[20];
    StockNumber         :string[12];
    Address1            :string[30];
```

The number inside the brackets specifies the maximum number of single characters to be handled by the named variable.

A further standard data type is the type `boolean`. This type of variable has only one of two possible values, namely `true` or `false`. A boolean variable declaration is made as follows:

```
    Morevalues          :boolean;
```

Pascal provides the two reserved words `true` and `false` which can be used to assign a value to a boolean variable, as in:

```
    Morevalues:= true;
```

The use of boolean variables will be explored in a later section.

Performing calculations

Probably every program that you will ever write will contain at least one calculation, and this is

BTEC National Study Guide: IT Practitioners. See page 293 for order details of individual texts

119

true of the majority of programs. It is not surprising therefore that Pascal and other high-level languages make calculations easy to perform. Arithmetic instructions simply involve defining what arithmetic operations are to be performed on numeric identifiers and constants. The four common arithmetic operations: add; subtract; multiply; divide, use the symbols +, –, * and /, respectively. The examples of arithmetic operations provided in Table 25.1 assume that the following data declarations have been made.

```
const
   PI       =3.14;
var
   Length, Width, Perimeter                :integer;
   Area, Radius, Gallons, Miles, Mpg       :real;
   a, b, c, x, y                           :real;
```

Expression	Pascal statement
$Area = length \times width$	`Area:= Length*Width;`
$Area = \pi r^2$	`Area:= PI*Radius*Radius;`
$Perimeter = 2 \times (length + width)$	`Perimeter:= 2*(Length + Width);`
$Mpg = gallons \div miles$	`Mpg:= Gallons/Miles;`
$x = 0$	`x:= 0;`

Table 25.1. Examples of arithmetic operations with real variables

All of the statements in Table 25.1 involve calculating a value using `real` or `integer` variables or a combination of `reals` and `integers`. Pascals rules concerning how such calculations may be expressed are called *assignment compatibility* rules. They state that a calculation which involves: (i) a mixture of integers and reals must be assigned to a real variable; (ii) only integers may be assigned to either an integer variable or a real variable. Another point to note is that Pascal provides two divide operators. The '/' divide operator may be used with any values, `real` or `integer`, but if both values are `integers`, the result is a `real` value and must be assigned to a `real` variable. The second divide operator, `div`, is only allowed to be used with integers. If the result of a division does not produce a whole number, the fractional part is ignored. In other words, the result is rounded down to the nearest integer. The remainder when one integer is divided by another is produced by the `mod` operator. Some examples should help to clarify these points and these are shown in Table 25.2.

Operands	Example	Answer	Answer type
real/real	7.3/0.2	36.5	real
	0.5/0.25	2.0	real
real/integer	13.9/5	2.78	real
integer/real	1116/7.2	155.0	real
integer/integer	33/11	3.0	real
	33/10	3.3	real
	3/5	0.6	real
integer div integer	33 div 11	3	integer
	33 div 10	3	integer
	3 div 5	0	integer
integer div real	Not allowed		
real div integer	Not allowed		
real div real	Not allowed		

BTEC National Study Guide: IT Practitioners. See page 293 for order details of individual texts

120

integer mod integer	33 mod 10	3	integer
	10 mod 33	10	
integer mod real	Not allowed		
real mod integer	Not allowed		
real mod real	Not allowed		

Table 25.2. *Examples of divide operations*

Listing 25.3 is an example of the use of integer division. The program converts a number of seconds into hours, minutes and seconds.

Listing 25.3.	The `div` and `mod` integer division operators

```
1    program ModAndDiv(input, output);
2      {Program to convert a time given in seconds
3      to hours, minutes and seconds}
4
5    const
6      SECONDSPERMINUTE    =60;
7      MINUTESPERHOUR      =60;
8
9    var
10     Hours          :integer;
11     Minutes        :integer;
12     Seconds        :integer;
13     Duration       :integer;
14     Temp           :integer;
15
16   begin
17     writeln;
18     write('Enter the time in seconds: ');
19     readln(Duration);
20     Seconds := Duration mod SECONDSPERMINUTE;
21     Temp := Duration div SECONDSPERMINUTE;
22     Minutes := Temp mod MINUTESPERHOUR;
23     Hours := Temp div MINUTESPERHOUR;
24
25     writeln;
26     writeln(Duration, ' seconds is: ');
27
28
29     write(Hours, ' hours ');
30     write(Minutes, ' minutes ');
31     writeln(Seconds, ' seconds.');
32   end.
```

On line *19* the user is requested to enter the time to be converted from seconds to hours, minutes and seconds. The number of seconds is stored in the variable Duration. The first stage in the calculation is to calculate the remainder when Duration is divided by the number of seconds per minute stored in the constant SECONDSPERMINUTE which has the value 60. Suppose, for example, the user entered the number 6573 when asked for the time in seconds. Line *20* would produce the value 6573 mod 60, that is, 33. This is assigned to the variable,

BTEC National Study Guide: IT Practitioners. See page 293 for order details of individual texts

121

Seconds. Next, the temporary variable Temp is given the value 6573 div 60, that is, 109. The remainder when this last number is divided by the number of minutes per hour, that is 60, gives the value for Minutes: 109 mod 60 = 49. The number of hours is calculated using 109 div 60 = 1. Thus, when the program is run, it produces the following output:

```
Enter the time in seconds: 6573

6573 seconds is: 1 hours 49 minutes 33 seconds.
```

Operator precedence

The term *operator precedence* applies to the order in which the operators in an arithmetic expression are used. For example, to evaluate the expression

$$x = y + 3z$$

z is multiplied by 3 before the result is added to *y*; the multiply operator thus has precedence over the addition operator. If *y* had a value of 2 and *z* had a value of 4, *x* would be calculated as

$$x = 2 + 3 \times 4 = 2 + 12 = 14$$

The higher the precedence of an operator, the sooner it is used in the evaluation of an expression. The use of parentheses within an expression can alter the way a calculation is performed. So, in the above expression, to force the addition to be performed before the multiplication, we would write x = (y + 3) $\times$ z. This would result in y being added to 3 before multiplying by z. Thus,

$$x = (2 + 3) \times 4 = 5 \times 4 = 20$$

In Pascal, the operators * and / have equal precedence; this means that in an expression involving two or more of them, they are simply used in the order that they appear in the expression. These two operators have higher precedence than + and –. Again, + and – have the same precedence. As a further example, consider the program in Listing 25.4.

Listing 25.4.	Illustration of operator precedence

```
1       program Example2(input, output);
2       var
3         x1 :real;
4         y1 :real;
5         n :integer;
6       begin
7         n:= 11;
8         y1:= 5;
9         x1:= 1.0/2.0*(y1 + n div y1);
10        writeln(x1:8:2);
11      end.
```

The order of evaluation of line *9* is as follows:

1.	1.0/2.0	i.e.	0.5
2.	n div y1	i.e.	11 div 5 = 2
3.	y1 + n div y1	i.e.	5 + 2 = 7
4.	1.0/2.0*(y1 + n div y1)	i.e.	0.5*7 = 3.5

BTEC National Study Guide: IT Practitioners. See page 293 for order details of individual texts

122

Reading and displaying information

Practically every program requires that data are provided by some input device such as a keyboard and that results are produced on an output device such as a monitor. Pascal provides a number of instructions to simplify these operations. The example program in Listing 25.4 used three input-output instructions, namely `readln`, `writeln` and `write`. In this section we examine these instructions in a little more detail.

The `readln` instruction uses data provided by a standard input device such as a keyboard to assign values to variables . The word `input` inside the brackets after the program name at the beginning of a Turbo Pascal program tells the Pascal compiler that a keyboard is to be used to enter character-based data (see Listing 25.4 for an example). You use the readln instruction to read real numbers, integers, single characters or strings into appropriately declared variables. For example, the statement

```
readln(Price);
```

would cause the program to wait for the user to enter a number to be stored in the real variable price. The user presses the ENTER key to signify the end of data entry. It is good practice to include a write instruction to precede readln to inform the user what information is required. So, for example, the statements

```
write('Please enter the price of the item: ');
readln(Price);
```

would cause the computer to display

```
Please enter the price of the item:
```

on the display screen and then, with the text cursor remaining on the same line, wait for the user to type in a value and press the Enter key. The `writeln` instruction is almost identical to `write`, except that the text cursor is automatically moved to the beginning of the line immediately following the line on which the message is displayed. Which one of the instructions `write` and `writeln` you use depends on how you want your output to appear. Listing 25.5 illustrates the use of `write`, `writeln` and `readln`.

Listing 25.5.	Using `write`, `writeln` and `readln` instructions

```
1     program convert1(input, output);
2       {Program to convert inches to centimetres }
3     const
4       CENTIMETRESPERINCH =2.54;
5     var
6       Centimetres  :real;
7       Inches       :real;
8     begin
9       write('Enter the length in inches: ');
10      readln(Inches);
11      Centimetres := Inches*CENTIMETRESPERINCH;
12      writeln;
13      write('A length of ', Inches:5:2,' inches');
14      write(' is equivalent to ');
15       writeln(Centimetres:5:2, ' centimetres');
16    end.
```

The program would produce the following output when run:

BTEC National Study Guide: IT Practitioners. See page 293 for order details of individual texts

123

```
Enter the length in inches: 12

A length of 12.00 inches is equivalent to 30.48 centimetres
```

Notice the different form of the `writeln` instruction on line *12*: it simply produces a single blank line when the round brackets are not used. This is useful for making your output clear and easy to read. The output shows that the user entered the number *12* followed by Enter when prompted to type in the length in inches.

In line *13*, `write('A length of ', Inches:5:2,' inches');`, the purpose of the numbers after the variable `Inches` is to control the number of characters printed, that is, the *field width* and the number of decimal places of the displayed variable. In this instance the field width, including the decimal point, is to be restricted to five, with two figures after the decimal point. When the variable is of type `integer`, only one figure representing the total number of digits to be displayed is provided. If the field width is larger than the item to be displayed, the output is padded with blanks. Using a field width of zero, as in `Inches:0`, or less than the number of digits in the number, causes the minimum number of digits to be displayed. Table 25.3 contains a number of examples using various output formats.

value	type	format	output	remarks
15.234	real	:10:1	`******15.2`	Six leading spaces are added
6.6666	real	:10:1	`*******6.7`	The figure after the decimal point is rounded up
6.6666	real	:0:2	`6.67`	The minimum number of digits is displayed
−8.3124	real	:0:3	`−8.312`	As above
234.56	real	:1	`2.3E+02`	Number is displayed in floating-point form
234.56	real	none	`2.3456000000E+02`	The maximum number of decimal places is displayed
123	integer	:5	`**123`	Two leading spaces included in the field
123	integer	:2	`123`	Minimum number of figures displayed and no leading spaces
'hello'	string	:10	`*****hello`	Strings are treated like integers
'hello'	string	:0	`hello`	As above

Table 25.3. *Examples of various output formats and their effects*

Note that the instructions that we have covered in this section, namely `readln`, `write` and `writeln`, are actually implemented as *standard procedures* which are explored later.

Loops

A very frequent programming requirement is to perform a set of instructions several times. Rather than writing the set of instructions several times (which is impractical for all but a small number of repetitions), they are controlled by a special instruction which causes them to be repeated as many times as desired. Such program constructs are called *loops*, and each repetition of a set of statements is often called an *iteration*. For example, suppose a program is required to read 10 numbers, add each one to a running total and then display the final total. The program in Listing 25.6 accomplishes this task using a loop.

BTEC National Study Guide: IT Practitioners. See page 293 for order details of individual texts

124

Listing 25.6.   Using a loop to add numbers

```
1    program RunningTotal2(input, output);
2     {Program to add ten numbers }
3    var
4      Number       :real;
5      Total        :real;
6      Count        :integer;
7    begin
8      Total:= 0;
9      writeln('Enter ten numbers: ');
10     for Count:= 1 to 10 do
11     begin
12        readln(Number);
13        Total:= Total + Number;
14     end;
15     writeln('The total is: ', Total:10:2);
16   end.
```

Listing 25.6 uses a `for` loop to repeat the two instructions which repeatedly read a number and add it to a running total. The `for` loop requires that a control variable, called `Count` in this example, is defined as type `integer`. The control variable is automatically given the first value specified (1 in this example) and, each time the statements within the loop are repeated, it is increased by 1 until it finally reaches the second value specified (10 in this example). Thus the same program, but with the value 10 replaced by the required number, could be used to add any number of numbers. Statements to be repeated are enclosed between `begin` and `end`. Listing 25.7 is a further example of the use of the `for` loop.

Listing 25.7.   Using a `for` loop to display a conversion table

```
1    program ConvTab(input, output);
2     {Program to display a conversion table for inches to
3        centimetres using a for loop}
4    const
5      CONVERSIONFACTOR =2.54;
6      MAXINCHES =12;
7    var
8      Inches :integer;
9      Centimetres :real;
10
11   begin
12     writeln;
13     writeln('Inches':20, 'Centimetres':20);
14     writeln('——':20, '———':20);
15
16     for Inches:= 1 to MAXINCHES do
17        begin
18           Centimetres:= Inches*CONVERSIONFACTOR;
19           writeln(Inches:17, Centimetres:20:2);
20        end;
21   end.
```

BTEC National Study Guide: IT Practitioners. See page 293 for order details of individual texts

125

The output produced looks like this:

```
Inches        Centimetres
------        -----------
  1              2.54
  2              5.08
 etc             etc
 12             30.48
```

Notice that the end value in the `for` statement on line *16* is a `constant` called `MAXINCHES`; this could also have been defined as a variable used in a `readln` instruction.

A slight variation in the format of a `for` statement allows the count variable to go down from a high value to a low value. For example, you could write

```
for i:= 12 downto 1 do ....
```

which would cause the variable `i` to start at 12 and go down to 1 in steps of 1.

The `for` statement is a very useful means of implementing a loop, but certain programming problems require a different approach to repeating a set of instructions. For example, consider the following outline program description:

> *Read a set of real numbers representing the cost of a number of items. Accumulate the total cost of the items until a value of zero is entered, then display the number of items purchased and their total cost.*

Here it is not known how many times the loop is to be repeated: the user decides when to terminate the loop by entering a *rogue value*, (zero in this case). The rogue value is used in another type of loop instruction, the `while` instruction. Listing 25.8 shows how a `while` loop can be used in conjunction with a rogue value. The rogue value is defined as a constant on line *5*. Because the user may want to terminate the program immediately, without entering any values, the program asks for a purchase amount before entering the loop starting on line *18*. The `while` instruction requires that a true/false expression is included after the word 'while'. Thus the expression, `Amount > ROGUEVALUE`, will be true if `Amount` entered is greater than zero, and it will be false if `Amount` is not greater than zero, that is if it is equal to, or less than zero. When the expression is true, the statements between the immediately following `begin` and `end`, that is lines *20* to *23*, will be executed; as soon as the expression becomes false, the loop terminates and the program goes on to line *26*.

Notice that the last instruction in the lines to be repeated is the `readln` instruction to read another value: this means that because the next instruction to be executed is the `while` instruction, the value typed in by the user is immediately compared with the rogue value. This ensures that the rogue value is not processed as an actual data item.

Listing 25.8.   Using a `while` loop and a rogue value

```
1     program RogueVal(input, output);
2        {program to illustrate the use of a rogue value
3           to terminate a loop}
4     const
5        ROGUEVALUE =0;
6     var
7        Count :integer;
8        Amount :real;
9        Total :real;
10
11    begin
12       Total:= 0;
13       Count:= 0;
```

BTEC National Study Guide: IT Practitioners. See page 293 for order details of individual texts

126

```
14
15        write('Enter the cost of the first item, or 0 to end :');
16        readln(Amount);
17
18        while Amount > ROGUEVALUE do
19          begin
20            Count:= Count + 1;
21            Total:= Total + Amount;
22            write('Enter the cost of the next item, or 0 to end :');
23            readln(Amount);
24          end;
25
26          writeln;
27          writeln(Count, ' items were purchased.');
28          writeln;
29          writeln('The total cost was: £', Total:0:2);
30      end.
```

Here is a typical output from the program:

```
Enter the cost of the first item, or 0 to end :23.45
Enter the cost of the next item, or 0 to end :6.12
Enter the cost of the next item, or 0 to end :5.99
Enter the cost of the next item, or 0 to end :0

3 items were purchased.
The total cost was: £35.56
```

Notice that the assignment instruction on line *20*, Count:= Count + 1, is used as a means of counting the number of times the loop is executed. The instruction simply adds 1 to the variable, Count, each time the instructions within the loop are repeated. The true/false expression on line *18* in the while statement uses the *relational operator*, >, meaning 'greater than', to compare Amount with ROGUEVALUE. There are in fact six different relational operators that can be used in such logical expressions, and these are shown in Table 25.4.

relational operator	meaning
>	Greater than
>=	Greater than or equal to
<	Less than
<=	Less than or equal to
=	Equal to
<>	Not equal to

Table 25.4. *Relational operators used in logical expressions*

The operators in Table 25.4 are used according to the relationship to be established between two values. Whatever logical expression is used, the result of the comparison will either be true or false - if true, the while loop will repeat; if false the loop will terminate. More examples of the use of these operators are provided in the next section, which deals with the use of logical expressions in making program decisions.

Decisions

Suppose a program is required to display multiple-choice questions with one correct answer out of three possible choices. For example, one of the questions could be:

BTEC National Study Guide: IT Practitioners. See page 293 for order details of individual texts

127

```
        A BYTE is the name given to

           (a) Four bits
           (b) Eight bits
           (c) Sixteen bits

        Your answer is:
```

The program is also required to display the message

```
        Correct - well done!
```

if the answer is correct, and display a message such as

```
        Sorry, the correct answer is (b)
```

if the answer provided is incorrect.

The program must therefore be able to take two alternative courses of action depending on the answer supplied. An `if` statement is one possible way of achieving this requirement. The appropriate form of the `if` statement is illustrated in Listing 25.9 which shows the Pascal code required to display the question above and provide the response appropriate to the letter `'a'`, `'b'` or `'c'`, typed in.

Listing 25.9.   Using an `if` statement

```
 1      program Decisions1(input,output);
 2        {Program to illustrate the use of the if statement}
 3      var
 4        Answer      :char;
 5      begin
 6        writeln('Enter the letter corresponding to the ');
 7        writeln('correct answer for the following question:');
 8        writeln;
 9
10        writeln('A BYTE is the name given to');
11        writeln(' (a) Four bits');
12        writeln(' (b) Eight bits');
13        writeln(' (c) Sixteen bits');
14        writeln;
15        write('Your answer is: ');
16        readln(Answer);
17
18        if Answer = 'b' then
19           writeln('Correct - well done!')
20        else
21           writeln('Sorry, the correct answer is (b)');
22      end.
```

The `if` statement extending over lines *18* to *21* shows how the program can take one of two possible courses of action depending on the value of a variable. We saw in the last section concerning the use of the `while` statement that logical expressions are either true or false. This is also the case with the logical expression `Answer = 'b'` in the `if` statement on line *18*. If the letter stored in the character variable `Answer` is the letter 'b', then the logical expression `Answer = 'b'` will be true, otherwise it will be false. If it is true, the statement following the word `then` is executed (that is, line *19*), otherwise the statement after `else` is executed (that

BTEC National Study Guide: IT Practitioners. See page 293 for order details of individual texts

128

is, line *21*). The general form of the if statement is

```
if {logical expression} then
    {statement 1}
else
    {statement 2}
```

Note that {statement 1} is the instruction that is performed if {logical expression} is true; {statement 2} is performed if {logical expression} is false. Note also that either {statement 1} or {statement 2}, or both of them, can be a block of instructions enclosed between begin and end as follows.

```
if Answer = 'b' then
  writeln('Correct - well done!')
else
  begin
     writeln('Sorry, the correct answer is (b)');
     writeln('There are eight bits in a byte');
  end;
```

Sometimes it is necessary to choose between more than just two courses of action in a program. For example, Listing 25.10 shows a program which converts a percentage mark to a pass, merit, distinction or fail grade. The program repeatedly accepts marks and converts them to grades until the mark entered is the rogue value –1 (or any negative integer value) signifying the end of the mark inputs. The rules that are used to determine the grade are as follows:

For a distinction the mark must be over 80.

For a merit the mark must be greater than or equal to 60 and less than 80.

For a pass the mark must be greater than or equal to 40 and less than 60.

Below 40 is a fail.

Listing 25.10. The if..else if construction

```
1     program Decision2(input, output);
2       const
3         DIST    =80;
4         MERIT   =60;
5         PASS    =40;
6
7       var
8         Mark      :integer;
9
10      begin
11        writeln;
12         write('Please enter the first mark(-1 to end): ');
13        readln(Mark);
14
15        while Mark >=0 do
16          begin
17            if Mark >= DIST then
18               writeln('Distinction')
19            else if (Mark >= MERIT) and (Mark < DIST) then
20                     writeln('Merit')
```

BTEC National Study Guide: IT Practitioners. See page 293 for order details of individual texts

129

```
21                        else if (Mark >= PASS) and (Mark < MERIT) then
22                                writeln('Pass')
23                                else writeln('Fail');
24           write('Please enter the next mark(-1 to end): ');
25           readln(Mark);
26       end;
27     end.
```

The if statement between lines *17* and *23* reflects this logic exactly. It is possible to chain if statements in this way to cope with quite complex lines of reasoning. Added flexibility is provided by the use of the logical and operator used for the the logical expressions on lines *19* and *21*. The and operator requires that both of the minor logical expressions it connects are true for the complete logical expression to be true. If either or both are false, then the whole expression is false. Logical operators are discussed in more detail in the next section. Here is a typical output from the program:

```
Please enter the first mark(-1 to end):46
Pass
Please enter the next mark(-1 to end):68
Merit
Please enter the next mark(-1 to end):32
Fail
Please enter the next mark(-1 to end):83
Distinction
Please enter the next mark(-1 to end):-1
```

Logical operators

Logical operators allow you to combine logical expressions. There are three logical operators in Pascal : and, or and not. An example of the use of the and operator was provided in Listing 25.10. The and and the or operators are always placed between two logical expressions, and they each combine these logical expressions to produce a value of true or false. Table 25.5 shows the rules that are applied by Pascal to determine whether a compound logical expression is true or false. This type of table is usually called a *truth table*.

(Expr 1)	(Expr 2)	(Expr 1) or (Expr 2)	(Expr 1) and (Expr 2)
true	true	true	true
true	false	true	false
false	true	true	false
false	false	false	false

Table 25. 5. *Truth table for the* **and** *and* **or** *logical operators*

Referring back to Listing 25.10 in the previous section, on line *19*, where the compound logical expression (Mark >= MERIT) and (Mark < DIST) is used to determine whether the mark is equivalent to a merit grade. In the expression, (Mark >= MERIT) is an example of (Expr 1) and (Mark < DIST) is an example of (Expr 2) shown in Table 25.5. The next table (Table 25.6) shows how the and operator combines these two logical expressions for a number of cases.

BTEC National Study Guide: IT Practitioners. See page 293 for order details of individual texts

130

Mark	(Mark >= MERIT)	(Mark < DIST)	(Mark >= MERIT and (Mark < DIST)
45	false	true	false
86	true	false	false
67	true	true	true

Table 25. 6. *Truth table for the* and *logical operator.*

Thus, both logical expressions must be true for the complete expression to be true; with the or operator, however, only one of the expressions needs to be true for the complete expression to be true. For example, consider the program in Listing 25.11 which reads some text and counts how many vowels it contains. The program uses a for loop to test each letter in turn in the text against each possible vowel. If the current letter is a vowel, that is 'a', 'e', 'i', 'o' or 'u', a count is incremented.

Listing 25.11. Illustrating the use of the or logical operator

```
1      program Vowels(input, output);
2      var
3       VowelCount     :integer;
4       Letters        :string[80];
5       LengthOfText   :integer;
6       c              :integer;
7      begin
8       VowelCount:= 0;
9       writeln('Type text followed by ENTER: ');
10      readln(Letters);
11      LengthOfText:= length(Letters);
12
13      for c:= 1 to LengthOfText do
14        if (Letters[c] = 'a') or
15             (Letters[c] = 'e') or
16             (Letters[c] = 'i') or
17             (Letters[c] = 'o') or
18             (Letters[c] = 'u')
19         then
20            VowelCount:= VowelCount + 1;
21
22         writeln;
23         writeln('The text contained ', VowelCount, '
       vowels');
24      end.
```

The text is held in a string variable called Letters. Each letter in Letters is accessed by specifying its position within the text. For example, if the text entered was the string 'hello there', then Letters[1] is the letter 'h', Letters[2] is the letter 'e', Letters[3] is the letter 'l', and so on. The for loop control variable, c, starts at 1 and goes up in steps of 1 to the length of the string (11 for the string 'hello there'). The length of the string is determined by the pre-defined Pascal function length(), on line *11*, which requires a string as its single argument. (See the later section on Pascal functions for more detail about functions). Here is the output from the program when the string, 'the cat sat on the mat' is typed in:

```
Type text followed by ENTER: the cat sat on the mat
```

BTEC National Study Guide: IT Practitioners. See page 293 for order details of individual texts

131

```
The text contained 6 vowels
```

Note that the program will only work with lower-case text. The reason is that lower-case letters 'a', 'b', 'c', etc are represented in a computer using a different set of codes from the equivalent upper-case letters 'A', 'B', 'C', etc.

The third logical operator is the `not` operator which simply reverses the logical value of a logical expression. Thus, the logical expression `not (x > 3)` is true only when x is less than or equal to 3. Similarly, the logical expression `not (Balance <= 0)` is true only when `Balance` has a value that is greater than zero. The truth table shown in Table 25.7 defines the operation of the `not` logical operator.

Expr	not Expr
true	false
false	true

Table 25.7. *Truth table for* **not** *logical operator*

More control statements

Listing 25.12 draws together two further Pascal control statements, namely the `repeat..until` and the `case` statements using a progam which allows you to convert Pounds Sterling into one of three foreign currencies: American Dollars, German Marks or French Francs. The `repeat..until` statement provides a third method of constructing a loop. It is similar to the `while` statement in that it uses a logical condition to determine when to exit the loop, but the difference is that the condition appears at the end rather than at the beginning of the loop. This means that the loop will be executed at least once, which is appropriate for this example in which the loop repeatedly executes instructions which display a menu and ask the user to choose one of the menu options. In this example, the `repeat` statement repeats the statements between lines *13* to *63* until the condition following the word `until` is true, that is, when the user enters the letter 'X' or 'x' to indicate the desire to exit the program.

Listing 25.12.   Using the `case` and `repeat` statements in a menu program.

```
1     program menu1(input, output);
2     uses CRT;
3     const
4       DOLLARS    =1.5;
5       MARKS      =3.4;
6       FRANCS     =11;
7     var
8       Choice     :char;
9       Currency   :real;
10      Pounds     :real;
11    begin
12     repeat
13       clrscr'
14        writeln('Currency conversion program');
15       writeln;
16       writeln('(M)arks');
17       writeln('(D)ollars');
18       writeln('(F)rancs');
19       writeln('e(X)it');
20       writeln;
21       write('Which currency do you want to convert to Pounds? ');
22       readln(Choice);
23       writeln;
24
25       case Choice of
26          'D', 'd':
27                begin
```

BTEC National Study Guide: IT Practitioners. See page 293 for order details of individual texts

132

```
28              writeln('Enter the amount to convert to Dollars');
29              readln (Pounds);
30              Currency:=Pounds*DOLLARS;
31              writeln('You would get ',Currency:0:0,
32                   ' Dollars for',Pounds:0:0, ' Pounds');
33              writeln('Press ENTER to return to the menu');
34              readln;
35            end;
36         'M', 'm':
37            begin
38              writeln('Enter the amount to convert to Marks');
39              readln(Pounds);
40              Currency:=Pounds*Marks;
41              writeln('You would get ',Currency:0:0,
42                   ' Marks for ',Pounds:0:0, ' Pounds');
43              writeln('Press ENTER to return to the menu');
44              readln;
45            end;
46         'F', 'f':
47            begin
48              writeln('Enter the amount to convert to Francs');
49              readln(Pounds);
50              Currency:= Pounds*FRANCS;
51              writeln('You would get ',Currency:0:0,
52                   ' Francs for ',Pounds:0:0, ' Pounds');
53              writeln('Press ENTER to return to the menu');
54              readln;
55            end;
56         'X', 'x':
57            writeln('Exiting program..');
58         else
59            begin
60              writeln('Invalid option. Please try again');
61              writeln('Press ENTER to return to the menu');
62              readln;
63            end;
64      end;
65    until (Choice = 'X') or (Choice = 'x');
66  end.
```

The case statement is an alternative method to the if statement for choosing between alternative courses of action wihin a program. It has the following general format:

```
case {variable name} of
    value list 1: statement 1;
    value list 2: statement 2;
    etc...
    ......
else statement N
end;
```

The variable name after the word case can be of type integer, character or boolean, but string and real variables *are not allowed*. Pascal matches the value of the variable against the values specified on the subsequent lines; when a match is found, the corresponding statement is executed after which the case statement is immediately exited without considering any remaining values. If there are no values that match the variable, the case statement does nothing unless the else option is used, in which circumstances, the supplied statement (shown as statement N above) is executed. Note that some versions of Pascal may not support the use of the else option: you may need to consult the language manual for

BTEC National Study Guide: IT Practitioners. See page 293 for order details of individual texts

133

your version of Pascal. In Listing 25.12, the `case` statement is used to select the block of statements corresponding to the menu option chosen by the user. The user can choose one of four options using the letters 'D', 'M', 'F' or 'X'; to allow for the possibility of either upper or lower case letters being entered, both are included in the `case` statement value lines. Here are some program fragments which should help to clarify the use of the `case` statement:

Example 1

```
var
  Month, Days    :integer;
.......
.......
case Month of
  1, 3, 5, 7, 8, 10, 12   :Days:= 31;
  4, 6, 9, 11             :Days:= 30;
  2                       :Days:= 28;
end;
```

`Month` contains a number corresponding to the month of the year, where January = 1, February = 2 ..... December = 12. The `case` statement is used to store, in the variable, `Days`, the number of days in the month whose number is stored in `Month`. Thus if `Month` contained the number 8 corresponding to August, `Days` would be assigned the value 31.

Example 2

```
var
  Smoker :boolean;
  ......
   ......
case Smoker of
  true :writeln('Smoking seriously damages your health!');
  false :writeln('Good for you!');
end;
```

If the boolean variable, `Smoker`, has been assigned a value of `true` prior to the `case` statement, the health warning will be displayed, otherwise the complimentary message 'Good for you!' will be displayed. This is equivalent to using the `if` statement

```
if Smoker then
  writeln('Smoking seriously damages your health!')
else
  writeln('Good for you!');
```

Note that it is because `Smoker` is a boolean variable having a value of `true` or `false`, that it can be used as a logical expression in an `if` statement as illustrated above.

Example 3

```
var
  Letter :char
  VowelCount :integer;
  ConsonantCount :integer;
  .....
  .....
case Letter of
  'a', 'e', 'i', 'o', 'u' : VowelCount:= VowelCount + 1;
```

BTEC National Study Guide: IT Practitioners. See page 293 for order details of individual texts

134

```
            'A', 'E', 'I', 'O', 'U' : VowelCount:= VowelCount + 1;
            ',', '.', ';', ':', '(', ')', ' ':{No action required}
          else ConsonantCount:= ConsonantCount + 1;
          end;
```

Here the program adds one to a vowel count if `Letter` contains either an upper or lower case letter; otherwise it adds one to a consonant count. Punctuation marks, brackets and spaces are ignored. Note that using `if` statements to perform this task would be much more difficult.

Arrays

An *array* is a data structure which allows you to store a number of items of data without having to allocate separate variable names to them. Arrays, like all other identifiers, must be declared before they are used. For example, the following declaration is for an array of five integers:

```
var
   Array1    :array[1..5] of integer;
```

This single declaration is in effect defining five variables called `Array[1]`, `Array[2]`, `Array[3]`, `Array[4]` and `Array[5]`, each of which can store a single integer value. The integer value inside the square brackets is called the array's index, and it is allowed only to take the range of values specified in the declaration (1 to 5 inclusive in this example). Each of these identifiers can be used just like any ordinary integer variable. For instance, to set each of them to zero could be accomplished as follows:

```
Array[1]:= 0;
Array[2]:= 0;
Array[3]:= 0;
Array[4]:= 0;
Array[5]:= 0;
```

However, we could accomplish the same operation by using an integer variable as an *index* and by putting a single assignment statement in a `for` loop:

```
for i:= 1 to 5 do Array[i]:= 0;
```

Now the count variable i takes on the integer values 1 to 5 and again each element in the array is set to zero. The obvious advantage of using a variable for an index is that arrays can then be used very effectively within loops, and they allow the manipulation of as many or as few numbers as appropriate to the task in hand; notice that the same `for` loop could initialise 5000 array elements as easily as 5 elements:

```
for i:= 1 to 5000 do Array[i]:= 0;
```

This would be an exceedingly difficult task to accomplish without the use of an array. Listing 25.13 illustrates the use of an array of real numbers. The program reads five numbers into an array and then finds the position within the array of the smallest number. It then swaps this number with the first number in the list before displaying the re-ordered array.

Listing 25.13.   Using an array.

```
1    program TopList(input, output);
2    uses CRT;
3    const
4      MAXNUMS      =5;
5    var
6      Array1       :array[1..MAXNUMS] of real;
```

BTEC National Study Guide: IT Practitioners. See page 293 for order details of individual texts

135

```
7       Temp           :real;
8       i              :integer;
9     begin
10      clrscr;
11      writeln('Enter ', MAXNUMS, ');
12      writeln;
13      for i:= 1 to MAXNUMS do
14         begin
15            write('Enter number ', i, ' and press ENTER :');
16            readln(Array1[i]);
17         end;
18      for i:= 2 to MAXNUMS do
19         if Array1[i] < Array1[1] then
20            begin
21                Temp:= Array1[1];
22                Array1[1]:= Array1[i];
23                Array1[i]:= Temp;
24            end;
25      writeln;
26      writeln('The new list is as follows:');
27      for i:= 1 to MAXNUMS do write(Array1[i]:10:2);
28    end.
```

Line *2* contains a non-standard statement which allows you to clear the screen by using the pre-defined *procedure* clrscr shown on line *10*. You may have to omit these two lines if you are not using Turbo Pascal. Note that *procedures* and the uses statement are discussed later.

The program first defines a constant MAXNUMS to be the maximum size of the real array, Array1. Lines *11* to *17* are to read in the ten numbers with appropriate user prompts. Thus the first number is read into Array1[1], the second into Array1[2], and so on up to the last number which is read into Array1[10]. The second for loop starting on line *18* compares each number in the array in turn with the first number; if one is found that is greater than the first, they are swapped over. By the time the last number in the array has been compared with the first one, the largest number is in the first position in the array.

A typical output from the program might be as follows:

```
Enter 5 numbers

Enter number 1 :5.7
Enter number 2 :3.9
Enter number 3 :9.1
Enter number 4 :1.7
Enter number 5 :98.4

The new list is as follows: 1.7   3.9   9.1   5.7   98.4
```

As a final example in this section on arrays, Listing 25.14 shows a program which uses a random number generator to select five lottery numbers in the range 1 to 49.

Listing 25.14.   Using random numbers and an array to generate lottery numbers

```
1       program Lottery(input, output);
```

BTEC National Study Guide: IT Practitioners. See page 293 for order details of individual texts

136

```
2    uses CRT;
3
4    const
5      NUMOFNUMS      =5;
6      MAXNUM         =49;
7    var
8      LuckyNums      :array[1..MAXNUM] of integer;
9      Num            :integer;
10     i              :integer;
11     Count          :integer;
12
13   begin
14     clrscr;
15     writeln('Lottery random number generator');
16      writeln;
17
18     randomize;
19
20     for i:= 1 to MAXNUM do LuckyNums[i]:= 0;
21
22     for Count:= 1 to NUMOFNUMS do
23       begin
24         Num:= random(MAXNUM + 1);
25         while LuckyNums[Num] <>  0 do
26              Num := random(MAXNUM + 1);
27
28         LuckyNums[Num]:= Num;
29         write(Num:5);
30       end;
31
32     writeln;
33     writeln;
34     write('Press ENTER to exit program');
35     readln;
36   end.
```

The random numbers are generated using the pre-defined function random(N) which produces a random number in the range specified by its single integer argument, N, within the brackets. For example, random(11) would produce a random number between 1 and 10 inclusively. Thus the statement

```
Num:= random(MAXNUM + 1);
```

assigns a random number between 1 and 49 to the variable Num. The randomize instruction on line *18* simply initialises the random number generator so that it does not produce the same sequence of random numbers every time the program is run. Line *20* initialises each element to zero in the array LuckyNums[] which is to be used to store the five random numbers. The reason for the while loop on lines *25* and *26* is to ensure that the same random number is not used more than once. The loop keeps generating random numbers until it finds one that has not been generated previously. For instance, if the first random number generated on line *24* was the number 36, then this would be stored in Num. The while loop will only generate another random number if Luckynums[36] contains zero, showing that 36 has not previously been

BTEC National Study Guide: IT Practitioners. See page 293 for order details of individual texts

137

generated. As soon as the `while` loop finds an empty slot, the number is stored in the array and immediately displayed on the screen. The process repeats until five different numbers have been generated.

Pre-defined procedures and functions

High-level languages almost invariably provide libraries of useful pre-written programs that are available to the programmer. These programs, which are often termed *pre-defined procedures* and *functions*, have previously been written, compiled and thoroughly tested so that they can be used by programmers with confidence that they are error-free.

In Turbo Pascal such libraries of programs are declared with the nonstandard instruction, `uses`, followed by the name the library file, or *unit*, as it is called. We have already used a unit called `Crt` containing the procedure `clrscr` which was used to clear the display screen Some library programs require you to provide information in the form of *parameters* at the time they are called. An example of such a program is the `delay(T)` procedure which requires you to supply a delay, `T`, in milliseconds inside the brackets. Functions always return an item of information when they are used. For example, in Listing 25.14 we saw that the function `random(N)` returned to the calling program a random number in the range 1 to $N-1$, where N is an integer value. Whatever the version, however, Pascal always provides a number of *standard procedures* and *functions* which are available without the need to declare them in programs. They comprise procedures and functions which are considered to be the most frequently used. It was noted earlier that `readln`, `write` and `writeln` are in fact such standard procedures, rather than instructions such as `for` and `if` which are integral parts of the Pascal language. Turbo Pascal keeps the standard procedures and functions, plus quite a few more, in a library unit called `System` which is automatically available when a program is compiled. Pascal's standard functions are described at the end of this chapter, and in addition we have provided further descriptions of a selection of procedures and functions that are available in some of Turbo Pascal's other units.

Simple user-defined procedures

Procedures are often called *subprograms* or *subroutines* because they form only part of a complete program. We saw in the previous section that Pascal provides a number of pre-written functions and procedures that you can use in your own programs, but it is also possible for you to write your own. These are called *user-defined* procedures and functions.

A Pascal procedure is very similar to a Pascal program, the main difference being that a procedure cannot stand by itself - it must form part of another program. Like identifiers such as constants and variables, procedures must also be declared at the beginning of the program before they are used. The structure of a program containing two procedures, called `Procname1` and `Procname2`, would have the outline structure shown in Listing 25.15.

Listing 25.15.   The structure of a program containing two procedures.

```
1    program Progname(input, output);
2    const
3      {Progname constants are declared here}
4    var
5      {Progname variables are declared here}
6
7    procedure Procname1;
8    const
9      {Procname1 constants are declared here}
```

BTEC National Study Guide: IT Practitioners. See page 293 for order details of individual texts

138

```
10    var
11      {Procname1 variables are declared here}
12    begin
13      {Procname1 code goes here}
14    end;
15
16    procedure Procname2;
17    const
18      {Procname2 constants are declared here}
19    var
20      {Procname2 variables are declared here}
21    begin
22      {Procname2 code goes here}
23    end;
24    begin
25      ........
26      ........
27      Procname1;
28      ........
29      ........
30      Procname2;
31      ........
32    end.
```

The two procedure definitions, shown in the shaded sections of the program, appear after the constants and variables declarations of the main program. The definitions of the procedures look exactly like a main program, each having their own `constant`s and `variable`s declarations (if required) and their own main code between `begin` and `end`.

The program in Listing 25.16 illustrates the use of simple procedures to cycle through three rudimentary pictures of faces in order to give the appearance of a face winking alternate eyes. The program uses three procedures, `Face1`, `Face2` and `Face3`, each of which uses keyboard characters to display a face. The procedures are executed in the main program by simply naming them. Thus line *36* `Face1` causes the instructions in procedure `Face1` to be executed. The program then continues with line *37* `delay(500)`, a pre-defined procedure which causes a delay of 500 milliseconds.

Listing 25.16.   Using procedures to make a face wink.

```
1     program Winker(input, output);
2     uses CRT;
3     var
4       i      :integer;
5
6     procedure Face1;
7     begin
8       clrscr;
9       writeln('   _ _   ');
10      writeln(' < 0 0 > ');
11      writeln(' | ^ | ');
12      writeln('   \_/   ');
13    end;
```

BTEC National Study Guide: IT Practitioners. See page 293 for order details of individual texts

139

```
14
15    procedure Face2;
16    begin
17     clrscr;
18     writeln('   _ _    ');
19     writeln(' < 0 o > ');
20     writeln(' | ^ |  ');
21     writeln('   \_/    ');
22    end;
23
24    procedure Face3;
25     begin
26     clrscr;
27     writeln('   _ _    ');
28     writeln(' < o 0 > ');
29     writeln(' | ^ |  ');
30     writeln('   \_/    ');
31     end;
32
33    begin
34    for i:= 1 to 10 do
35     begin
36        Face1;
37        delay(500);
38        Face2;
39        delay(500);
40        Face1;
41        delay(500);
42        Face3;
43        delay(500);
44     end;
45    end.
```

Each of the procedures uses the pre-defined clrscr procedure to clear the screen so that the face stays in the same place and appears to wink. Notice that the logic of the main program is easy to follow by the use of procedures - this is one of their major advantages. Another feature of this program is that although the procedure Face1 is used twice, the code required for it appears only once in its definition. This economical use of program code is another major advantage of using procedures in programs.

Global vs local variables

Earlier we said that a procedure is allowed to have its own var declarations. When this is the case, the variables declared in the procedure are termed *local* variables. This means that these variables only have values while the procedure is being executed; once the procedure has been completed and control has returned to the main program, local variables cannot be accessed. On the other hand, *global* variables which are defined in the main program are always available, even to procedures, while the program is running. Note, however, that if a variable declared in a procedure has the same name as a variable declared in the main program, the local variable only, can be used in the procedure. These ideas are best illustrated with the aid of an example such as that shown in Listing 25.17.

BTEC National Study Guide: IT Practitioners. See page 293 for order details of individual texts

140

Listing 25.17. A program to illustrate the difference between global and local variables

```
1    program Scope(input, output);
2    uses CRT;
3    var
4      Greeting1      :string[20];
5
6    procedure Proc1;
7    var
8      Greeting1      :string[20];
9    begin
10     Greeting1:= 'How do';
11     writeln('Proc1':15, 'Greeting1':15, 'local ':15,
       Greeting1:15);
12    end;
13
14   procedure Proc2;
15   var
16     Greeting2      :string[20];
17      begin
18     Greeting2:= 'Hi ';
19     writeln('Proc2':15, 'Greeting2':15, 'local ':15,
       Greeting2:15);
20     writeln('Proc2':15, 'Greeting1':15, 'global':15,
       Greeting1:15);
21    end;
22
23   begin
24     clrscr;
25     writeln('Source':15, 'Variable':15, 'Scope':15, 'Value':15);
26      writeln;
27      Greeting1:= 'Hello ';
28     writeln('Main ':15, 'Greeting1':15, 'global':15,
       Greeting1:15);
29     Proc1;
30     Proc2;
31      end.
```

The program declares three string variables: Greeting1 which is a global variable defined on line *4*, Greeting1 a variable local to procedure Proc1 and declared on line *8*, and finally Greeting2, a local variable declared in Proc2 on line *16*. The main program assigns a value ('Hello') to Greeting1 on line *27* and displays it. Then, when Proc1 is executed, the local variable Greeting1 is assigned a different value ('How do') on line *10* and then displays that string. Finally, when Proc2 is executed, it displays the contents of the local variable Greeting2 followed by the global variable Greeting1. Note that an attempt to include a line such as

```
writeln(Greeting2);
```

after line *30* in the main program would result in an error since, once Proc2 has terminated, the local variable Greeting2 does not exist. Here is what the program produces as its output:

```
Source          Variable        Scope          Value
```

BTEC National Study Guide: IT Practitioners. See page 293 for order details of individual texts

141

```
Main              Greeting1        global        Hello
Proc1             Greeting1        local         How do
Proc2             Greeting2        local         Hi
Proc2             Greeting1        global        Hello
```

Each line of the output indicates the source of the line, that is whether it is generated from the main program or from a procedure, the name of the variable whose value is being displayed, whether the variable is local or global, and the contents of the variable.

Using parameters in procedures

The 'wink' program shown in Listing 25.16 uses the simplest form of procedure which performs a task without any need to communicate with the main program. However, there will be many instances when you will want to use information available in the main program. As we saw in the previous section, global variables provide one means of accomplishing this, but for sound reasons current programming practice discourages the use of global variables for this purpose. Usually a much better method is to use procedures which have either *value parameters* or *variable parameters*.

Value parameters

Listing 25.18 is a modification of the program shown in Listing 25.16. Notice that another procedure, `Wink()`, has been included. This new procedure uses a *value parameter*, called `Eye`, which is defined within brackets after the procedure name on line *34*. A value parameter allows you to pass a value to a procedure from the main program or from another procedure. Thus, on line *47*, the value of the `for` loop variable `k` is passed to the procedure `Wink`. `k` takes the values 1, 2 and 3 which are used to decide which of the three procedures, `Face1`, `Face2` or `Face3` to execute. In effect, this causes each of the latter three procedures to be executed in turn. The outer `for` loop makes this cycle of three procedures repeat ten times. When one loop is controlled by an outer loop in this fashion, they are called *nested loops*.

Listing 25.18.   A program to illustrate the use of value parameters

---

```
1      program Winker2(input, output);
2      uses CRT;
3      var
4        i      :integer;
5        k      :integer;
6
7      procedure Face1;
8      begin
9        clrscr;
10       writeln('    _ _    ');
11       writeln('  < 0 0 >  ');
12       writeln('  | ^ |   ');
13       writeln('   \_/    ');
14     end;
15
16     procedure Face2;
17     begin
18       clrscr;
19       writeln('    _ _    ');
20       writeln('  < 0 o >  ');
```

BTEC National Study Guide: IT Practitioners. See page 293 for order details of individual texts

142

```
21      writeln(' | ^ |  ');
22      writeln('  \_/   ');
23    end;
24
25    procedure Face3;
26      begin
27      clrscr;
28      writeln('  _ _    ');
29      writeln(' < o 0 > ');
30      writeln(' | ^ |  ');
31      writeln('  \_/   ');
32      end;
33
34    procedure Wink(Eye:integer);
35    begin
36      case Eye of
37        1 :Face1;
38        2 :Face2;
39        3 :Face3;
40      end;
41    end;
42
43    begin
44    for i:= 1 to 10 do
45      for k:= 1 to 3 do
46        begin
47          Wink(k);
48          delay(500);
49        end;
50    end.
```

The number of parameters that you can use in a procedure is not limited to one - you can use as many as you like as long as you declare them in the procedure definition and include them within the brackets when you call the procedure from the main program. For example, suppose that we wanted to include the pre-defined delay procedure on line *48* within the procedure Wink() as shown in the program fragment below.

```
procedure Wink(Eye:integer, Time:integer);
begin
  case Eye of
    begin
      1 :begin
          Face1;
          delay(Time);
        end;
      2 :begin
          Face2;
          delay(Time);
        end;
      3 :begin
```

BTEC National Study Guide: IT Practitioners. See page 293 for order details of individual texts

143

```
                    Face3;
                    delay(Time);
                end;
        end;
```

Now `Wink()` has two value parameters and these would both be included in any call to the procedure, as shown in the example below.

```
        for i:= 1 to 10 do
            for k:= 1 to 3 do Wink(k, 500);
```

An important point about value parameters is that they provide a *one-way transfer of information* from the main program to a procedure. Variables used as value parameters when a procedure is called are unaffected by any processing that has occurred within the procedure; this is not the case, however, with *variable parameters*.

Variable parameters

Listing 25.19 is an example of a program which incorporates a procedure that uses a variable parameter.

Listing 25.19. A program to illustrate the use of variable parameters.

```
1    program VarParam(input, output);
2    var
3      Smaller      :real;
4      Larger       :real;
5
6    procedure Sort(var a, b:real);
7    var
8      Temp         :real;
9    begin
10     if a > b then
11       begin
12          Temp:= a;
13          a:= b;
14          b:= Temp;
15       end;
16    end;
17
18   begin
19     write('Enter two numbers: ');
20     readln(Smaller, Larger);
21     Sort(Smaller, Larger);
22     write('The sorted numbers are: ');
23     writeln(Smaller:10:2, Larger:10:2);
24   end.
```

The program simply sorts two numbers into ascending order of magnitude using a procedure. The procedure has two variable parameters, a and b, which it compares: if a is greater than b, the values in a and b are swapped over. The main program asks the user to enter two numbers, it calls the procedure using the two numbers stored in `Smallest` and `Largest`, and then displays them when the procedure has finished. Here is a typical run of the program:

```
Enter two numbers: 34.6 17.32
```

BTEC National Study Guide: IT Practitioners. See page 293 for order details of individual texts

144

```
The sorted numbers are: 17.32 34.6
```

Notice that the values contained in Smallest and Largest, which were exchanged in the procedure using the variables a and b, have been swapped over. Thus, *variable parameters allow a two-way exchange of data* between a program and a procedure.

User-defined functions

As well as being able to write your own procedures you can also devise your own functions. Functions also accept value or variable parameters, but in addition they require that you declare what type of value they return. So, for a function, you would need to write its first line using the following format:

```
function FunctionName(parameters):return type;
```

In addition, you must assign the return value to FunctionName somewhere within the function. For example, for a function called TriangleType which accepts three positive real numbers, in ascending order of magnitude, representing the three sides of a triangle and which returns an integer value of 0, 2 or 3 indicating how many of its sides are equal, the function definition in Listing 25.20 might be appropriate.

Listing 25.20. A function to determine the type of triangle represented by three numbers

```
20    function TriangleType(a, b, c:real):integer;
21      var
22        Count      :integer;
23      begin
24        Count:= 0;
25        if a = b then Count:= Count + 1;
26          if b = c then Count:= Count + 1;
27          if c = a then Count:= Count + 1;
28        case Count of
29          0 :TriangleType:= 0;
30          1 :TriangleType:= 2;
31          2 :{not possible}
32          3 :TriangleType:= 3;
33        end;
34      end;
```

The three sides are passed as value parameters to the variables a, b and c. The if statements on lines *25* to *27* increment Count if any two sides are the same. The values that Count can assume are 0 for no sides equal, 1 if two sides are equal and 3 if all three sides are equal; a value of 2 is not possible when the three sides are arranged in ascending order of magnitude. The number of equal sides is stored in TriangleType by the case statement and it is this value which is returned by the function to the calling program. Note that because a function always returns a value it can be used like a variable in an arithmetic expression or in a logical expression or in a write statement. For example, it would be perfectly valid to write

```
if TriangleType(x, y, z) = 3 then writeln('Equilateral triangle');
```

Writing programs using procedures and functions

Listing 25.21 illustrates the use of user-defined procedures and functions in a program which allows two people to use the computer to play noughts and crosses. The program illustrates the

BTEC National Study Guide: IT Practitioners. See page 293 for order details of individual texts

145

use of procedures and functions appropriate to a variety of situations. The main program alternately gets X and O moves, checking each time for a winning or drawn position. The program terminates when someone has won or after nine moves have been made.

Listing 25.21.   Noughts and crosses game

```
1    program Oxo(input, output);
2
3    {----------------------------------------------------------------}
4    {A program which makes use of functions and procedures to allow }
5    {two players to play noughts and crosses. The computer checks   }
6    {for a win  or draw automatically, and ensures that illegal     }
7    {moves are not made. The board is a grid numbered 1 to 9. Each  }
8    {Player in turn selects a number and the grid is redrawn with   }
9    {the X or O in that position. X always starts first.            }
10   {----------------------------------------------------------------}
11
12   uses CRT;{The screen handling unit to allow screen to be cleared}
13
14   var
15     Grid       :array[1..9] of char;
16     Move       :integer;
17     Count      :integer;
18      Winner    :boolean;
19      XMove     :boolean;
20
21   procedure InitGrid;
22   {----------------------------------------------------------------}
23   {Sets up the board with the positions numbered from 1 to 9      }
24   {----------------------------------------------------------------}
25
26   begin
27      Grid[1]:='1';
28      Grid[2]:='2';
29      Grid[3]:='3';
30      Grid[4]:='4';
31      Grid[5]:='5';
32      Grid[6]:='6';
33      Grid[7]:='7';
34      Grid[8]:='8';
35      Grid[9]:='9';
36   end;
37
38   procedure DrawGrid;
39   {----------------------------------------------------------------}
40   {This draws the current board after every move                  }
41   {----------------------------------------------------------------}
42
43   begin
44     clrscr;
45     writeln(' ',Grid[1], ' | ', Grid[2], ' | ', Grid[3]);
46     writeln('--|--|--');
47     writeln(' ',Grid[4], ' | ', Grid[5], ' | ', Grid[6]);
48     writeln('--|--|--');
49     writeln(' ',Grid[7], ' | ', Grid[8], ' | ', Grid[9]);
50     writeln;
51   end;
52
53   function CheckMove(Move:integer):boolean;
54   {----------------------------------------------------------------}
```

BTEC National Study Guide: IT Practitioners. See page 293 for order details of individual texts

146

```
55  {This validates every move to make sure that a number      }
56  {from 1 to 9 is chosen and that the selected position is     }
57  {not already occupied by an X or O.                          }
58  {Parameters: Move - integer value parameter                  }
59  {Return value:boolean - true if valid, false if invalid move }
60  {-----------------------------------------------------------}
61
62  begin
63    CheckMove:= true;
64    if (Move < 1) or (Move > 9) then
65      begin
66         writeln('Invalid position - number between 1 and 9');
67         CheckMove:= false;
68      end
69    else if (Grid[Move] = 'X') or (Grid[Move] = 'O') then
70      begin
71         writeln('This position has already been used');
72         CheckMove:= false;
73      end;
74  end;
75
76  function GetXmove:integer;
77  {-----------------------------------------------------------}
78  {Accepts the X move from the player. If the move is invalid, the}
79  {player is required to enter the move again.                 }
80  {Parameters: None                                            }
81  {Return value: Integer in the range 1 to 9                   }
82  {-----------------------------------------------------------}
83  var
84    Xpos          :integer;
85    ValidXMove     :boolean;
86  begin
87    repeat
88      writeln;
89      writeln('Enter position( 1 to 9 ) for X move');
90      readln(Xpos);
91      ValidXMove:= CheckMove(Xpos);
92    until ValidXMove;
93    GetXmove := Xpos;
94  end;
95
96  function GetOmove:integer;
97  {-----------------------------------------------------------}
98  {This accepts the O move from the player. If the move is     }
99  {invalid the player is required to enter the move again.     }
100 {Parameters: None                                            }
101 {Return value: Integer in the range 1 to 9                   }
102 {-----------------------------------------------------------}
103 var
104    Opos          :integer;
105    ValidOMove     :boolean;
106 begin
107    repeat
108      writeln;
109      writeln('Enter position( 1 to 9 ) for O move');
110      readln(Opos);
111      ValidOMove:= CheckMove(Opos);
112    until ValidOMove;
113    GetOmove:= Opos;
114 end;
```

BTEC National Study Guide: IT Practitioners. See page 293 for order details of individual texts

147

```
115
116 function CheckForWinner :boolean;
117 {----------------------------------------------------------------}
118 {Checks for a line of Xs or Os in one of the 7 possible ways    }
119 {Determines whether row, column or diagonal contains the same   }
120 {character (ie an X or an O)                                    }
121 {Parameters: None                                              }
122 {Return value: Boolean - true if there is a winner, else false }
123 {----------------------------------------------------------------}
124
125 begin
126    if  (Grid[1]=Grid[2]) and (Grid[2]=Grid[3]) or
127        (Grid[4]=Grid[5]) and (Grid[5]=Grid[6]) or
128        (Grid[7]=Grid[8]) and (Grid[8]=Grid[9]) or
129        (Grid[1]=Grid[4]) and (Grid[4]=Grid[7]) or
130        (Grid[2]=Grid[5]) and (Grid[5]=Grid[8]) or
131        (Grid[3]=Grid[6]) and (Grid[6]=Grid[9]) or
132        (Grid[1]=Grid[5]) and (Grid[5]=Grid[9]) or
133        (Grid[3]=Grid[5]) and (Grid[5]=Grid[7])
134    then
135        CheckForWinner:= true
136    else CheckForWinner:= false;
137 end;
138
139 begin   {Main program }
140    InitGrid;           {Call procedure to initialise the board }
141    Count:= 0;          {Counts the number of valid moves made  }
142    Winner:= false;     {Boolean variable which becomes true    }
143                        {when there is a winner                 }
144    XMove:= true;       {Keeps track of whose move it is:       }
145                                    {true for X move            }
146                                    {false for Y move           }
147    DrawGrid;           {Display the initial board position     }
148
149    {Loop to repeat the playing sequence                        }
150    while (Count < 9) and not Winner do
151      begin
152        case XMove of
153        true:               {Do this if it is X's move      }
154            begin
155              Move:= GetXmove;{Get the X move position        }
156              Grid[Move]:='X';{Store it in the data structure}
157              XMove:= false;  {Make it O's move next          }
158            end;
159        false:              {Do this if it is O's move      }
160            begin
161              Move:= GetOmove; {Get the O move position       }
162              Grid[Move]:= 'O';{Store it in the data structure}
163              XMove:= true;   {Make it X's move next          }
164            end;
165      end;
166
167    Count:= Count + 1;          {Increment count after every move}
168
169    DrawGrid;                   {Show the current board position }
170
171    {Check to see if the game is a win or draw                  }
172    Winner:= CheckForWinner;
173    if Winner
174      then writeln('End of Game:', Grid[Move], ' has won')
```

BTEC National Study Guide: IT Practitioners. See page 293 for order details of individual texts

148

```
175        else if Count=9
176          then writeln('A draw');
177        end;
178
179      readln;
180 end.
```

The two procedures, InitGrid and DrawGrid, and the four functions, CheckMove, GetXMove, GetYMove and CheckForWinner, are described in the following sections.

InitGrid

This procedure initialises the character array, Grid[], which is a global array used throughout the program by every procedure and function. The procedure is used once only and does not require any parameters.

DrawGrid

This procedure draws the current board position. Initially the board is displayed like this:

```
1 | 2 | 3
--|---|--
4 | 5 | 6
--|---|--
7 | 8 | 9
```

The numbers are replaced by Xs and Os as the game progresses.

CheckMove

This function has a single integer value parameter called Move which represents the current player's choice of board position. The function first checks that the integer is in the range 1 to 9 before checking the contents of Grid[Move] to ensure that the position is not already occupied with an X or an O. If the move is valid, the function returns a boolean value of true, otherwise it returns false. CheckMove is used by the following two functions.

GetXMove

This function asks the X player to type in a number from 1 to 9 representing a board position. If the move is valid, the function terminates and the position entered by the player is returned as an integer value; if the move is invalid (see function CheckMove) the player is requested to try again.

GetOMove

This function asks the O player to type in a number from 1 to 9. Otherwise it is structurally identical to GetXMove.

CheckForWinner

This function checks individually the three rows, three columns and two diagonals, to see that they contain the same character. If one of these lines does contain the same character, then one of the players has won. For example, if the diagonal represented by Grid[1], Grid[5] and Grid[9] all contain an X, then the X player has won.

Advantages of using procedures and functions

All good programmers make full use of procedures and functions, and in fact their use is essential to the development of all but the most trivial programs. There are a number of good reasons for making this statement, including the following: (i) they allow a large, complex program to

BTEC National Study Guide: IT Practitioners. See page 293 for order details of individual texts

149

be built up from a number of smaller or more manageable units. This facilitates a team approach to program development by allowing each unit to be written and tested independently of the rest of the program; (ii) they can reduce the amount of code required for a program. Once a subprogram has been developed, it can be used as many times as required within a program using the same code; (iii) they can reduce the amount of time required to write a program if libraries of re-usable functions and procedures are available. This is much the same as building electronic circuits using standard electronic components.

Screen handling

Turbo Pascal's CRT unit contains a number of useful screen handling functions and procedures. We have already used two of the procedures in the unit: clrscr to clear the screen and delay() to make the computer pause while executing a program. More functions and procedures in the CRT unit are described below.

Window procedure

Defines a text window on the screen. The syntax of the procedure is

Window(X1,Y1,X2,Y2) where the four parameters are explained by the following diagram.

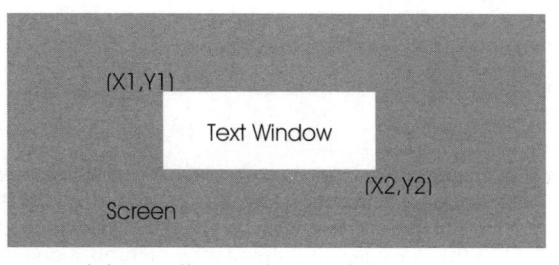

To set a text window containing ten lines at the top of the screen use

```
window(1,1,80,10)
```

To return the current window to the full screen size use

```
window(1,1,80,25)
```

ClrEol procedure

Clears all characters from the cursor position to the end of the line without moving the cursor. It uses the current text window.

DelLine procedure

Deletes the line containing the cursor in the current text window.

GotoXY procedure

Moves the cursor to X, Y, where X is the column and Y is the row relative to the top left corner of the current window which has the coordinates (1, 1). Thus to move the cursor to row 5, column 10, you would use GotoXY(10,5).

InsLine procedure

Inserts a line in the current text window, above the line that the cursor is on.

BTEC National Study Guide: IT Practitioners. See page 293 for order details of individual texts

150

`TextColor` **procedure**

This sets the colour for subsequently displayed text. There are sixteen colours and you can specify each one by name or by using the equivalent number as shown in the Table 25.8. Thus, to set the text colour to red, you could use either `TextColor(Red)` or `TextColor(4)`.

By using the pre-defined constant, `blink`, you can make the text flash, for example, `TextColor(Blue + Blink)`.

colour	value	colour	value	colour	value	colour	value
Black	0	Red	4	DarkGray	8	LightRed	12
Blue	1	Magenta	5	LightBlue	9	LightMagenta	13
Green	2	Brown	6	LightGreen	10	Yellow	14
Cyan	3	LightGray	7	LightCyan	11	White	15

Table 25.8.

`TextBackGround` **procedure**

This allows you to set one of sixteen different colours for the text background. The colours are shown in the table. Thus to set the background colour to light grey you could use either `TextBackGround(LightGray)` or `TextBackGround(7)`. Note that if you clear the screen using `clrscr` after setting the background colour, the whole of the current text window will change to that colour.

Example program 1

The example shown in Listing 25.22 illustrates the use of text windows and text colours by drawing random windows of different colours.

Listing 25.22.   Using text windows

```
1    program Screen1(input,output);
2
3      {----------------------------------------------------------}
4      {Illustrates some screen handling facilities by            }
5      {drawing randomly sized and coloured windows               }
6      {----------------------------------------------------------}
7
8       uses CRT;
9      var
10       x       :integer;
11       y       :integer;
12       i       :integer;
13
14     begin
15       textbackground(Black);    {Clear screen}
16       clrscr;
17
18       for i:= 1 to 100 do
19         begin
20         {Draw random windows}
21           x := Random(60);       {Random x position}
22           y := Random(15);       {Random y position}
```

BTEC National Study Guide: IT Practitioners. See page 293 for order details of individual texts

151

```
23              window(x, y, x + Random(10), y + Random(8));
24              textbackground( Random(16) + 1);
25              clrscr;    {Set window to random colour}
26                                    {in the range 1 to 16}
27              delay(200); {Pause for 200 millisecs}
28          end;
29
30      end.
```

KeyPressed and Readkey

Two other useful functions to be found in Turbo Pascal's CRT unit are KeyPressed and ReadKey. KeyPressed returns a boolean value of true if there is a character in the keyboard buffer and false if the buffer is empty. The keyboard buffer is simply an area of memory which is used to store, temporarily, characters entered through the keyboard. KeyPressed can therefore be used to detect any use of the keyboard. A common application of KeyPressed is as a means of terminating a loop, as illustrated by the following program fragment.

```
repeat
      {instructions to be repeated}
until keypressed;
```

Each time through the repeat loop KeyPressed tests the keyboard buffer: if a key has been pressed, the keyboard buffer will have at least one entry, KeyPressed returns true and the loop terminates, otherwise KeyPressed returns false and the loop repeats once more.

Readkey allows you to capture a keystroke by reading the first character in the keyboard buffer. If the keyboard buffer is empty, it waits until a character is available and then returns its value. The advantage of using ReadKey rather than read or readln is that it is not necessary to press Enter.

Example program 2

The program shown in Listing 25.23 echoes only numeric characters to the screen, ignoring characters that are not in the range 0 to 9. The repeat loop terminates as soon as the space bar is pressed.

Listing 25.23.   Using readkey.

```
1    program EchoNumbers(input,output);
2    {-----------------------------------------------------------}
3    {Program to display numeric digits entered at keyboard      }
4    {and to ignore any other characters typed. The program      }
5    {terminates when the space bar is pressed.                  }
6    {-----------------------------------------------------------}
7
8    uses CRT;
9
10    var
11     key      :char;
12
13    begin
14       repeat
15         key:= readkey;
```

BTEC National Study Guide: IT Practitioners. See page 293 for order details of individual texts

152

```
16        if (key >= '0') and (key <='9') then write(key);
17     until key = ' ';
18     end.
```

Sound and NoSound

Finally, these two procedures allow you to use your computer's built-in speaker. Sound(Pitch) causes the speaker to emit a tone whose pitch is determined by the integer parameter, Pitch. Thus, Sound(500) produces a tone with pitch 500Hz. NoSound terminates the tone produced by Sound. Thus to produce a tone of 300Hz for half a second within a program you could use:

```
sound(300);
delay(500);
nosound;
```

Example program 3

As a final example Listing 25.24 uses all of the screen handling functions and procedures discussed in a program which measures how quickly you are able to press a key after being given a signal.

Listing 25.24. Screen handling example.

```
1    program reflexes(input, output);
2
3    {---------------------------------------------------------------}
4    {A program to illustrate some screen handling facilities.       }
5    {The user is invited to test his/her reflexes by pressing a key }
6    {as quickly as possible. The average of three attempts is       }
7    {calculated and displayed in millisecond units.                 }
8    {---------------------------------------------------------------}
9
10   uses crt;
11    const
12    ROW          =2; {The row base position for screen text        }
13    COLUMN       =5; {The column base position for screen text     }
14
15    var
16     i              :integer; {A for loop control variable         }
17     Total          :integer; {The total time for the three attempts }
18   {............................oOo.............................}
19
20    procedure FlushKeyboardBuffer;
21
22   {---------------------------------------------------------------}
23   {This makes sure that there are no characters in the standard   }
24   {input buffer. The function readkey removes a single character  }
25   {from the keyboard buffer. Keypressed is true while there is at }
26   {least one character in the buffer                              }
27   {---------------------------------------------------------------}
28
29    var
30     key :char;
31
32    begin
33      while keypressed do
34        key:= readkey;
35   end;
36   {............................oOo.............................}
```

BTEC National Study Guide: IT Practitioners. See page 293 for order details of individual texts

153

```
37
38   procedure PressAnyKey;
39
40   {-----------------------------------------------------------------}
41   {A procedure that waits until a key is pressed before             }
42   {continuing with the next instruction                            }
43   {-----------------------------------------------------------------}
44
45   begin
46     FlushKeyboardBuffer;       {Ensure that the keyboard buffer is   }
47                                 {empty                               }
48     repeat until keypressed;  {Do nothing until a key is pressed   }
49   end;
50   {...........................oOo............................}
51
52   procedure instructions;
53
54   {-----------------------------------------------------------------}
55   {Displays the instructions for using the program                 }
56   {-----------------------------------------------------------------}
57
58   begin
59     window(10,10,70,20);       {Define the text window              }
60     textcolor(yellow);         {Text colour set to yellow           }
61     textbackground(blue);      {Background text clour is blue       }
62     clrscr;
63     gotoxy(COLUMN, ROW);
64     writeln('Put your finger on any key and as soon as');
65     gotoxy(COLUMN, ROW+1);
66     writeln('this window changes colour, press it');
67     gotoxy(COLUMN, ROW+3);
68     writeln('You will get three tries and the program');
69     gotoxy(COLUMN, ROW+4);
70     writeln('will calculate your average response time');
71     gotoxy(COLUMN +5, ROW+6);
72     write('Press any key to begin');
73     PressAnyKey;
74   end;
75   {...........................oOo............................}
76
77   function Time(attempt:integer):integer;
78
79   {-----------------------------------------------------------------}
80   {Uses the delay() procedure to determine the response time in    }
81   {milliseconds required for hitting the space bar.                }
82   {-----------------------------------------------------------------}
83
84   var
85      Millisecs :integer;
86
87   begin
88     clrscr;
89     textcolor(yellow);
90     gotoxy(COLUMN, ROW);
91     case attempt of
92        1:write('First attempt starting..');
93        2:write('Second attempt starting..');
94        3:write('Third attempt starting..');
95     end;
96     randomize;                 {Initialise the random number generator }
```

BTEC National Study Guide: IT Practitioners. See page 293 for order details of individual texts

154

```
97
98    Millisecs:= 0;
99    delay(1000);                    {Pause for one second before timing  }
100     textcolor(red + blink);
101     write(' NOW!');
102     delay(random(5000));   {Random delay of up to 5 seconds       }
103     FlushKeyboardBuffer;   {Make sure that there are no           }
104                            {characters in the keyboard buffer  }
105     textbackground(Red);
106     clrscr;                 {The signal to press the space bar   }
107
108     repeat
109       delay(1);
110       Millisecs:= Millisecs + 1;{Count how many msecs expire   }
111     until keypressed;               {Look for user hitting any key }
112     Time:= Millisecs;               {Return time taken to respond  }
113   end;
114 {.............................oOo...........................}
115
116 procedure Results(Average:real);
117
118 {─────────────────────────────}
119 {Displays the average time taken over the three attempts       }
120 {─────────────────────────────}
121
122 begin
123   textbackground(LightGray);
124   textcolor(Black);
125   clrscr;
126   gotoxy(COLUMN, ROW);
127   write('Your average response time was ', Average:5:0,
128        ' milliseconds');
129   gotoxy(COLUMN, ROW + 5);
130   write('Press any key to continue');
131   PressAnyKey;
132 end;
133
134 begin
135   Total:= 0; {Set the total time to 0 }
136   for i:= 1 to 3 do          {Repeat the trial three times        }
137   begin
138     Instructions; {Display the user instructions }
139     Total:= Total + Time(i);{Accumulate time for each trial     }
140   end;
141   Results(Total/3);               {Display result of the three trials}
142 end.
```

The main program starts on line *134*. The procedure Instructions explains that the user is to press a key as quickly as he/she can when a rectangular window changes colour. The function Time() times how long it took to do so in milliseconds. This time is added to a running total which accumulates the times for three attempts. Results() displays the average time the user took to respond. The program makes good use of user-defined functions and procedures, and the comments in the program Listing 25.24 explain their operation, but it is worth adding some further explanation regarding the procedure PressAnyKey and associated functions and procedures. As mentioned earlier, the buffer memory associated with the keyboard

temporarily stores the values of key depressions made while the program is running, and these values can be accessed using the ReadKey function which extracts the first available

BTEC National Study Guide: IT Practitioners. See page 293 for order details of individual texts

155

character in the buffer. By repeatedly using this function to read single characters until there are no more left in the buffer, `FlushKeyboardBuffer` empties the buffer in preparation for using the `KeyPressed` function. This is to ensure that `KeyPressed` will detect only the next key depression and not any that have been made previously.

Reference section

This section describes a number of Pascal's standard functions and some of the additional functions provided by Turbo Pascal.

Standard Pascal functions

abs

Returns the absolute, that is unsigned, value of a real or integer value.

Examples

If x is a real variable then

1. `x:= abs(-3.7)`   gives   x = 3.7
2. `x:= abs(24.3)`   gives   x = 24.3

If i is an integer variable then

3. `i:= abs(-6)`   gives   i = 6
4. `i:= abs(3.232)`

    is not allowed since the type of the returned value (real) is not the same as the type of the argument (integer).

exp

Returns the exponential of the argument, that is e^a, where a is the value of the parameter supplied in brackets and e is a mathematical constant approximately equal to 2.72.

Example

If x is a real variable then

   `x:= exp(2)`   gives   x = 7.39 (that is, $x=e^2$)

ln

Returns the natural logarithm of the argument, that is, the inverse of the `exp` function.

Example

If x is a real variable then

   `x:= ln(7.39)`   gives   x = 2

sqr

Returns the square of the argument, that is x^2 , where x is the argument.

Examples

If x is a real variable then

1. `x:= sqr(-3.1)`   gives   x = 9.61

BTEC National Study Guide: IT Practitioners. See page 293 for order details of individual texts

156

2.   `x:=sqr(3.1)`   gives   x = 9.61

If `i` is an integer variable then

3.   `i:=sqr(-6)`   gives   i = 36

4.   `i:=sqr(3.232)`

is not allowed since the type of the returned value (real) is not the same as the type of the argument (integer).

Sqrt

Returns the square root of the operand, that is Öx, where x is a positive valued argument.

Examples

If `x` is a real variable then

1.   `x:=sqrt(16.3)`   gives   x = 4.04

2.   `x:=sqrt(-16.3)`   is not allowed since x is negative

If `i` is an integer variable then

3.   `i:=sqrt(16)`   gives   i = 4

4.   `i:=sqrt(-16)`   is not allowed since i is negative

sin

Returns the sine of the argument which must be in radians.

Example

Since 1 radian $= \dfrac{180}{\pi}$ degrees, to convert an angle from degrees to radians we must divide the angle by $\dfrac{180}{\pi}$ where p » 3.1416

Thus, if x is a real variable and we want the sine of 30^0, then

`x:=sin(30/(180/3.1416))`   gives $x = \text{sine}(30^0) = 0.5$

cos

Returns the cosine of the argument which must be in radians. See sin above for converting degrees to radians.

Example

If x is a real variable and we want the cosine of 30^0, then

`x:=cos(30/(180/3.1416))`   gives $x = \text{cosine}(30^0) » 0.87$

Note that the `sin` and the `cos` functions can be used together for finding the tangent of an angle, since tan q = sin q/cos q

arctan

Returns the arc tangent of the argument in radians. This is the inverse of finding the tangent of an angle.

BTEC National Study Guide: IT Practitioners. See page 293 for order details of individual texts

157

Example

If x is a real variable and we want to find the arc tangent of 1 then

$$x := \text{arctan}(1) * (180/3.1416) \quad \text{gives} \quad x = \text{arctangent}(1) = 45^0$$

round

Returns the nearest integer type value to the real type value provided.

Examples

If i is an integer variable then

1. i := round(34.3)   gives   i = 34
2. i := round(34.8)   gives   i = 35

trunc

Converts a real type value to an integer type value by removing the fractional part of the real value.

Examples

If i is an integer variable then

1. i := trunc(34.3)   gives   i = 34
2. i := trunc(34.8)   gives   i = 34
3. i := trunc(.975)   gives   i = 0

ord

This gives the ASCII numeric value for characters.

Examples

If c is an integer variable then

1. c := ord('a')   gives   c = 97
2. c := ord('A')   gives   c = 65
3. c := ord('?')   gives   c = 63

chr

Returns the character equivalent of a numeric code in the range 0 to 255

Examples

If c is an character variable then

1. c := chr(97)   gives   c = 'a'
2. c := chr(65)   gives   c = 'A'
3. c := chr(63)   gives   c = '?'

The following program prints the full character set:

```
program CharSet(input, output);
var
c :char;
i :integer;
begin
```

BTEC National Study Guide: IT Practitioners. See page 293 for order details of individual texts

158

```
        for i:= 0 to 255 do
        writeln(i:10, chr(i):10);
end.
```

odd

Returns TRUE if the argument is an odd number and FALSE if it is an even number. The argument must be an integer. The sign of the argument is ignored.

Examples

If t is a boolean variable then

1.   t:=odd(23)   gives   t = TRUE
2.   t:=odd(22)   gives   t = FALSE
3.   t:=odd(-23)   gives   t = TRUE
4.   t:=odd(0)   gives   t = FALSE
3.   t:=odd(7.5)   is not allowed since the argument must be an integer.

Some Turbo Pascal functions

These functions are always available in Turbo Pascal and do not require a unit declaration.

Length

Returns the length of a string.

Example

If s1:= '1234567' and len is an integer variable then

        len:=length(s1)   gives   len = 7;

Concat

Joins together a number of strings. The strings are provided as arguments to the function.

Examples

If string variables s1, s2 and s3 have the values

```
s1= 'One, two, three o clock '
s2= 'four o clock '
s3= 'rock'
```

and s4 is another string variable then

        s4:=concat(s1, s2, s3) gives s4= 'One, two, three o clock four o clock rock'

Copy

This allows a set of characters, or a *substring*, to be copied from a string. It has the form:

        copy(Str, StartChar, NumOfChars)

where Str is the string from which the substring is to be copied,

StartChar is the position within Str from which to start copying and NumOfChars is how many characters are to be copied.

BTEC National Study Guide: IT Practitioners. See page 293 for order details of individual texts

159

Examples

If s1 = 'Copy me please'

1. s2:= copy(s1, 6, 2)   gives   s2 = 'me'

2. s3:= copy(s1, 1, length(s1)) gives   s3= 'Copy me please'

Pos

Returns the starting position of a substring within a string. Returns zero if the substring is not found.

Examples

1. p:= pos('Koteikan, Windsor Tce', ',') gives p=9

2. p:= pos('abcde', 'z')   gives p=0

Upcase

Converts a letter to capitals, that is, upper case. Non letters are not affected.

Examples

1. Capital:= upcase('x');   gives   Capital='X'

2. Capital:= upcase('X');   gives   Capital='X'

3. Capital:= upcase('3');   gives   Capital='3'

4. readln(Answer);

5. if upcase(Answer) = 'Y' then writeln('The Y key was pressed');

(This is a good way to ensure that pressing both 'y' and 'Y' can be detected).

Random

Generates a random number in the range 0 to n-1 where n is the integer value supplied to the function.

Example

```
writeln(random(10) + 1)
```

generates a random number between 1 and 10 inclusively.

Randomize

This is a procedure used in conjunction with random function described above. It initialises the random number generator using the system clock so that each time a program is run it does not generate exactly the same set of random numbers.

BTEC National Study Guide: IT Practitioners. See page 293 for order details of individual texts

160

Programming Exercises

For each of the following problems, design, implement and thoroughly test the program.

Decisions

1. Read a number and display a message which states whether the number is positive, negative or zero.

2. Read a number and print it only if it is between 10 and 20.

3. Read a number followed by a single letter code. The number represents the price of an item and the code indicates whether tax is to be added to the price. If the code is "V" then the tax is 20% of the item's cost. If the code is "X" then the item is not taxed. Print out the total cost of the item.

4. Read three positive, non-zero integers which may represent the sides of a triangle. The numbers are in ascending order of size. Determine whether or not the numbers do represent the sides of a triangle.

5. Read in a single character and print a message indicating whether or not it is a vowel.

Loops

6. Write separate programs to produce conversion tables for:
    (i) Inches to centimetres (1 to 20 inches, 1 inch = 2.54 centimetres);
    (ii) Pounds to kilograms (1 to 10 pounds, 2.2 pounds per kilogram);
    (iii) Square yards to square metres (10, 20 ,30,..., 100 sq yds 1yd = .91 m)

7. The cost and discount code of a number of items are to be entered by a user. The program must print out each item's cost, discount and cost less discount. The discount codes are as shown alongside. The program will terminate when the user enters 0 for the cost of the item. The program must then print the total cost of all the items entered.

Code	Discount
A	5%
B	10%

8. Write a program to repeatedly display a menu containing a number of options for converting between different units, plus one option to exit the program. The user must enter a number or letter corresponding to a menu item. Valid entries are to accept a numeric value from the user and apply and display the appropriate conversion, invalid entries are reported and the user is reminded about what choices are valid, and the exit option terminates the program. An example follows.

> Menu
>
> 1 Inches to centimetres
>
> 2 Centimetres to inches
>
> 3 Pounds to Kilograms
>
> etc
>
> 4 Exit
>
> Please enter option number :

9. A program reads an integer representing the number of gas bills to be processed, followed by that number of customer details. Each set of customer details consists of a customer number, a single character code representing the type of customer and the number of units used. Customers are of type 'D' (domestic) or 'B' (business). Domestic customers are charged 8p per unit and business customers are charged 10p per unit. For each customer print the customer number, the number of units used and the cost of the gas used. Print the total number of units used for this batch of customers and the total amount charged.

BTEC National Study Guide: IT Practitioners. See page 293 for order details of individual texts

161

10. Repeat the previous question assuming that all the domestic users are first and that separate totals are required for domestic and business users.

Strings

11. Read two strings and compare them. Print a message to indicate whether or not they are identical.

12. Repeat the previous problem but ignore case. For example, your program should regard the strings

    "Hello There", "HELLO THERE", and "hello there" as being identical.

13. Read a string representing a sentence and print the number of words in the sentence. Assume that words are separated by no more than one space and that there are no punctuation marks in the text.

14. Write separate programs to enter and store a string of up to 80 characters and then:
    (i)   Count the number of leading spaces;
    (ii) Count the number of trailing spaces;
    (iii) Count the number of embedded spaces;
    (iv) Count the number of leading, trailing and embedded spaces;
    (v)   Remove leading and trailing spaces from a string, and reduce multiple embedded spaces to single spaces.

15. Read a string containing a sentence and print the words in reverse order. For example, the sentence "the cat sat on the mat" would become, "mat the on sat cat the".

16. Read a string and determine whether it is purely alphabetic, purely numeric or a mixture of alphabetic and numeric characters.

Arrays

17. Read 15 values into a numeric array and then:
    (i)   print the contents the array;
    (ii) find the average of the numbers stored in the array;
    (iii) copy the array into a duplicate array, but in reverse order. Print the contents of both arrays.

18. Read a set of numbers and swap the first number with the largest in the set. Then, starting from the second value, find the largest number in the remaining list and swap it with the second value.

    Repeat this process until the list has been sorted into ascending order of magnitude.

Validation

19. Post codes have the following possible formats:
    (i)   aa99 9aa
    (ii) aa9 9aa
    (iii) a9a 9aa

    where *a* represents an alphabetic character and *9* represents a numeric character. Write a program to validate a post code, assuming that only uppercase letters are used and there is a single space separating the two parts of the post code.

20. As for the previous problem but allow upper and lower case letters, leading spaces, trailing spaces and more than one space between the two parts of the code.

BTEC National Study Guide: IT Practitioners. See page 293 for order details of individual texts

162

Encoding

21. Many names that sound the same are often spelled differently and this can cause problems in information systems. For example, Waites, Waits and Whaites all sound the same though they are all spelled differently and contain different numbers of letters. A coding system called Soundex can be used to solve this problem by converting a name into a code based on the following algorithm.

(i) The first letter of the name is used as the first letter of the code.

(ii) All subsequent vowels, and the letters H, W and Y are ignored.

(iii) Double letters are replaced by single instances of the letter.

(iv) Then this code, apart from the first character, is converted into a number by substituting the letters in the following table by numeric digits.

Letter	Substitute
BFPV	1
CGJKQSXZ	2
DT	3
MN	4
L	5
R	6

(v) The code is restricted to four characters including the leading letter.

(vi) If the code is less than four characters it is padded with zeros.

22. Write a program to convert a name into its equivalent Soundex code. Some examples are given below.

Morton becomes M635

Morten becomes M635

Waites becomes W320

Whaites becomes W320

Waits becomes W320

23. The table illustrates the Morse code.

A	. –	N	– .
B	– . . .	O	– –
C	– . – .	P	. – – .
D	– . .	Q	– . –
E	.	R	. – .
F	. . – .	S	. . .
G	– .	T	–
H	. ....	U	. . –
I	. .	V	. . . –
J	. – –	W	. –
K	– . –	X	– . . –
L	. – . .	Y	– . – –
M	–	Z	– . .

(i) Write a program to read in a word (or a sentence) and output it in Morse code.

(ii) Add sound so that when a letter is pressed on the keyboard the appropriate Morse code is heard.

BTEC National Study Guide: IT Practitioners. See page 293 for order details of individual texts

163

24. A form of encoding used on the Internet is called "rot13" encoding. It involves taking each letter of the alphabet and replacing it by the letter 13 positions further on in the alphabet as shown in the following table.

Letter	Replace with	Letter	Replace with	Letter	Replace with
A	N	J	W	S	F
B	O	K	X	T	G
C	P	L	Y	U	H
D	Q	M	Z	V	I
E	R	N	A	W	J
F	S	O	B	X	K
G	T	P	C	Y	L
H	U	Q	D	Z	M
I	V	R	E		

(i)   Write a program to read a block of text and encode it using rot13. Spaces and punctuation marks do not need to be encoded.

(ii) Write a program to decode text which has been encoded using rot13.

(iii) Invent and implement your own encoding and decoding scheme using a different form of substitution.

BTEC National Study Guide: IT Practitioners. See page 293 for order details of individual texts

164

Chapter 26

Introduction to Visual Basic

Overview

Even for experienced programmers, creating a program that runs under the latest Microsoft Windows *Operating System* can be a daunting task, particularly when using traditional programming languages such as Pascal, C or C++. Consequently, many program developers are using Visual Basic (VB) for application prototype development, or even for producing the final application program. The reason for the widespread adoption of VB is that it hides the complexities of Windows programming by the use of special graphical tools. These tools provide a convenient graphical user interface allowing complex windows components to be incorporated in a program with great ease.

Typically, a Visual Basic program is a collection of control objects that respond to user actions such as mouse operations and keyboard use. These actions generate events that are linked to program code. For example, a commonly used control is a *command button* that simulates a physical switch such as that used for door bells. 'Pushing' the button by clicking the mouse over it is a mouse-click event that can cause a specific section of code to be executed. Each type of control has one or more related events, each of which can be programmed. For this reason Visual Basic is classed as an *event-driven programming language*. The collection of control objects forms the user interface, the basis of most Visual Basic programs. Program design starts with creating the user interface which defines the functionality of the program. Then code is written to perform the required functions. Because control objects can be added to the user interface independently of other control objects, programs can be developed and tested in a modular fashion. A new control can be created, configured, modified, programmed and tested independently of existing controls. Moreover, the effects of any changes to the program can be examined immediately simply by clicking a button on the Visual Basic toolbar. This is one of the great strengths of Visual Basic, that programs can be created and modified very quickly and easily.

However, although VB can help novice programmers to produce professional-looking Windows programs relatively easily, it introduces a number of concepts additional to other more traditional languages. The VB programmer needs to know about objects, methods, properties and events in addition to such traditional programming concepts as variables, constants, control structures, files and subprograms. This brief introduction to programming in Visual Basic is in three parts:

1. **VB Programming Environment.** Later in this chapter we describe the VB environment and provide instructions for creating and running simple programs.

2. **Programming Basics**. Traditional programming concepts are examined using VB as the programming language. Once VB has been set up for the tutorial, the first example programs that illustrate programming concepts can be run without the complications of having to create procedures or screen objects.

3. **Introduction to Event-driven Programming**. A number of simple programs illustrate elementary event-driven programming principles. Objects such as Forms, Command buttons, List boxes and Text boxes are introduced.

BTEC National Study Guide: IT Practitioners. See page 293 for order details of individual texts

165

Pre-requisites

To use this Visual Basic tutorial you need access to Microsoft Visual Basic version 4 or above running under Windows 95 or above, and you must be familiar with the Microsoft Windows 95/98/ME/2000 operating system. You should know how to run applications, maximise, minimise, resize and scroll windows, use a mouse to select and drag items and be able to save and load documents using standard File menu commands.

You also need to set up a simple project in Visual Basic, as explained after the next section, to be able to run the example programs in the next chapter, "Programming Basics".

The Visual Basic Programming Environment

The screenshot of the Visual Basic 6 programming environment shows the main features (described below) used in this introduction to VB. Note that in other versions of Visual Basic the toolbox, project window, properties window and form may initially appear in separate, movable windows.

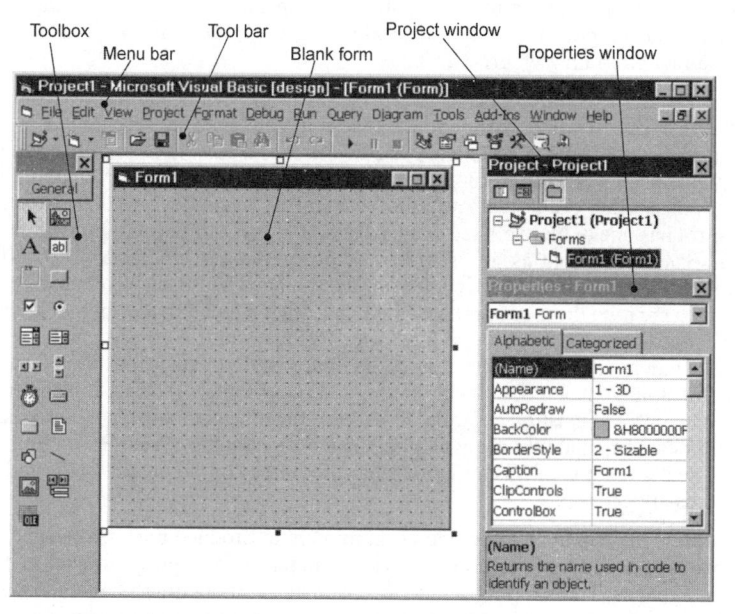

Menu and Toolbar

The Menu bar provides access to all of VB's utilities. We will mostly make use of the File, Edit, Debug and Run menus. The Toolbar provides quick access to some VB features. We will use some of these features in example programs.

Form

A Form is the container for user interface controls. These controls can be visually positioned and moved by using the mouse. Example programs that use forms are provided in *Event-driven Programming*.

BTEC National Study Guide: IT Practitioners. See page 293 for order details of individual texts

166

Toolbox

The Toolbox allows you to select, position and configure various controls on a Form. It displays all the standard Visual Basic controls plus any custom controls and insertable objects you have added to your project with the Custom Controls dialog box. You can display ToolTips for the Toolbox buttons by selecting the Show ToolTips option in the Environment tab of the Options dialog box. To open the Toolbox, choose Toolbox from the View menu.

The tools used in this introduction to Visual Basic are briefly described below. You can learn about other tools from VB Help.

Pointer. This is the only item in the Toolbox that doesn't draw a control. Use it to resize or move a control after it has been drawn on a form.

PictureBox. Use to display graphical images (either decorative or active), as a container that receives output from graphics methods, or as a container for other controls.

Label. Use for text that you don't want the user to change, such as a caption under a graphic.

TextBox. Use to hold text that the user can either enter or change.

Frame. Use to create a graphical or functional grouping for controls. To group controls, draw the Frame first, and then draw controls inside the frame.

CommandButton. Use to create a button the user can choose to carry out a command.

CheckBox. Use to create a box that the user can easily choose to indicate if something is true or false, or to display multiple choices when the user can choose more than one.

OptionButton. Use in a group of option buttons to display multiple choices from which the user can choose only one.

ComboBox. Use to draw a combination list box and text box. The user can either choose an item from the list or enter a value in the text box.

ListBox. Use to display a list of items from which the user can choose one. The list can be scrolled if it has more items than can be displayed at one time.

Timer. Use to generate timer events at set intervals. This control is invisible at run time.

DriveListBox. Use to display valid disk drives.

DirListBox (directory list box). Use to display directories and paths.

FileListBox. Use to display a list of files.

Shape. Use to draw a variety of shapes on your form at design time. You can choose a rectangle, rounded rectangle, square, rounded square, oval, or circle.

Line. Use to draw a variety of line styles on your form at design time.

Image. Use to display a graphical image from a bitmap, icon, or metafile on your form. Images displayed in an Image control can only be decorative and use fewer resources than a PictureBox.

OLE Container. Use to link and embed objects from other applications in your Visual Basic application.

BTEC National Study Guide: IT Practitioners. See page 293 for order details of individual texts

167

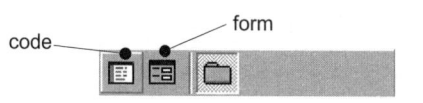 CommonDialog. Use to create dialog boxes for operations such as opening, saving, and printing files, or selecting colours and fonts. CommonDialog is a custom control.

Project window

The Project window shows the project forms and modules and allows you to view code or forms.

To view the code associated with a form, click the code icon. To view the form itself, click the form icon.

Creating a project allows you to keep all of the files associated with the project together.

Properties window

Objects such as forms and controls used in a project have properties associated with them. For instance, the width, height and colour of a form are properties. The Properties window allows you to set and modify all of the properties associated with an object.

Setting up Visual Basic to run example programs in "Programming Basics"

You will need to create a simple project called "VBConcepts.vbp" to allow you to create and run the example programs given later in the chapter. To create the VBConcepts project, follow the instructions below:

First launch VB and start a new project.

1. Open the project window by pressing Ctrl+R.

2. If there is a Form in the project window delete it by clicking the mouse right-hand button and selecting "Remove".

3. Create a new Module (Menu: Insert|Module, VB4 or Menu: Project|Add Module, VB6). The code window for the module should appear.

4. Create a procedure called "Main" (Menu: Insert|Procedure.. VB4 or Tools|Add procedure.. VB6)

The code window should look much like this on the right.

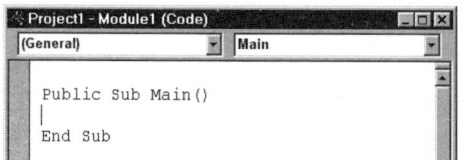

5. Finally, open the Debug window by pressing Ctrl+G.

Now save the project as "VBConcepts".

Create and run example programs in "Programming Basics"

In the next chapter, we will create example programs by first opening project *VBConcepts.vbp* and then entering code between the lines `Public Sub Main()` and `End Sub` in the code window. To run the program you click the ***Run*** button on the toolbar. Any output from the program will be shown in the Debug window. (**Note**: if the Debug window is not visible prior to running a program, press Ctrl+G.)

BTEC National Study Guide: IT Practitioners. See page 293 for order details of individual texts

168

Chapter 27

VB programming basics

This chapter introduces basic programming concepts common to languages such as Pascal and C/C++ as well as Visual Basic, the language used here. We cover the following subjects:

- Variables and Constants
- Performing calculations
- Arrays
- Data Types
- Loops
- Strings
- Simple input and output
- Decisions
- Visual Basic functions

A first VB program

As a simple example to illustrate creating and running a program, Listing 27.1 shows a program which calculates the total cost of a purchased item by calculating VAT and adding it to the price of the item.

The algorithm on which the program is based is as follows:

1. *Ask the user to enter the price of the item*

2. *Store the price*

3. *Calculate the VAT at 17.5% (i.e. multiply the price by 0.175)*

4. *Calculate the total price by adding the VAT to the price*

5. *Display the total cost on the screen.*

Listing 27.1.   A simple program to calculate the total cost of a purchase

```
Public Sub Main()
' ====== Program to calculate the total cost of an item ======
10 Const VAT = 0.175
20 Dim Price As Single
30 Dim Tax As Single
40 Dim TotalCost As Single
50 Price = InputBox("Enter price of the item")
60 Tax = Price * VAT
70 TotalCost = Price + Tax
80 Debug.Print "The total cost is: "; TotalCost
End Sub
```

Note: line numbers are optional in VB, and we have used them to allow us to describe the operation of the example programs in detail.

The operation of the program

The first two lines (without line numbers) identify the program. "Sub" stands for *Sub*program or *Sub*routine and "Main" is the name of the program (this will be the name of all our example programs in this tutorial). The single quotation mark identifies the rest of the line as a comment. Comments are ignored by VB and are used to annotate programs.

BTEC National Study Guide: IT Practitioners. See page 293 for order details of individual texts

169

Lines *10* declares that VAT is a *constant* value.

Lines *20 - 40* declare three *variables* Price, Tax and TotalCost each as being of type single. (This means *single* precision real number - ie a number having figures after the decimal point). Variables are used to store data, which in this case are in the form of real numbers, that is, numbers which are not whole numbers. Every variable used in a VB program must be declared in this way.

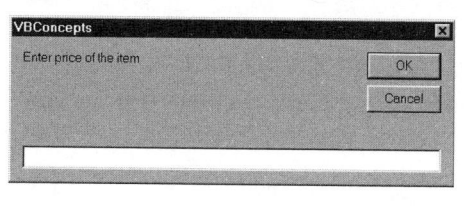

Up to this point the programmer has defined a number of *identifiers* that will be used in the procedural part of the program which follows.

Line *50* causes the message 'Enter price of the item' to be displayed on the screen in an input box. That appears like this:

The user types in the value for the price of the item and then clicks OK or presses the Enter key on the keyboard. The value entered by the user is stored in the variable Price.

Line *60* stores the result of Price multiplied by VAT in the variable Tax.

Line *70* stores the result of adding Price and Tax in TotalCost.

Line *80* then displays the text, 'The total cost is: ' followed by the value stored in TotalCost in the Debug window. The Debug.Print statement indicates that the variables and/or text following is to be printed in the Debug window. As its name suggests, the Debug window is generally used for debugging, that is finding and correcting programs, but it is used in this context to simplify learning VB concepts. Print is known as a *Method* of the Debug window *Object*. We will be discussing *Objects* and *Methods* later in the tutorial.

Finally, End sub indicates the end of the program. When the program is run, if the user entered the value 20 in the input box, the output from the program would look like this:

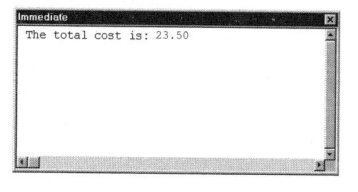

Some general remarks

Before going on to explore VB in more depth, it is worth mentioning a few general points at this stage:

1. VB does not distinguish between the use of capitals and lower-case letters. Thus it regards Price, PRICE and price as being exactly the same.

2. It is a good idea to include comment lines - text beginning with a single quote (') - to describe the purpose of lines or sections of your program. Particularly for large, complex programs, this is very helpful if it is necessary to change the program at some later date.

3. Using spaces, blank lines and indentation can greatly improve the appearance and the clarity of a program, thus making the program easier to read and understand if it has to be modified later for any reason.

4. Programming involves meticulous attention to detail; omitting punctuation marks, including them in the wrong place or making spelling mistakes will usually cause VB to report a syntax error on a program line, but sometimes such slips might cause errors which are more difficult to detect, so be very careful to form instructions precisely.

5. Line numbers are used in VB as labels for the GOTO instruction. Our example programs contain line numbers only so that we can identify lines that we want to explain; you do not need to include these line numbers in your own programs.

BTEC National Study Guide: IT Practitioners. See page 293 for order details of individual texts

170

6. The Debug window (also called the Immediate window) is mainly used as a debugging aid. In this tutorial we are using it to simplify showing the output from example programs. When VB programs are compiled into stand-alone applications, the debug window would not appear. Topics later in the tutorial will deal with more usual methods of displaying program output.

Identifiers and data types

The term *identifier* is a general term used for *variables*, *constants* and other programmer-defined names such as *procedures* and *functions*. Variables and constants are normally associated with a data *type*. *VB does not require that variables are given a type* such as `Integer` or `Single` but it is good practice do so by using `Dim` and `Const` declarations.

Variables

A variable, which represents an item of data such as a single number, has a name and a current value. Variables are given names such as `Amount`, `Total` or `Numb3` and are assigned values by program instructions. These values are stored in the memory of the computer and they are accessed whenever a variable is referenced in a program instruction. So, for example, in the instruction

```
Total = Price + Tax
```

the value associated with the variable `Price` is added to the value of the variable `Tax` and the sum is then assigned to the variable `Total`. If in a previous instruction `Total` had already been assigned a value, that value would be replaced by the new one.

Constants

Constants too are assigned values but only once after the word `Const`. The constant `VAT` in Listing 1 is an example. Constants retain their values throughout the execution of a program; VB does not allow you to use a constant in an instruction which tries to change the value of the constant. Thus, if in Listing 1, you included an instruction such as

```
VAT = 0.2;
```

in the main program, VB would report an error.

Reserved words

Words that form part of the VB language are not allowed to be used as identifier names. For instance, if you included in your program the line

```
Print = 3
```

VB would report an error because `Print` is a reserved word that is part of the VB language. VB also provides a large number of predefined constants that programmers can use but not change. Many, but not all, of these constants start with the letters vb, for example,

```
vbMultiSelectNone
```

Some of VB's reserved words are shown in the next table. You will soon learn to avoid using reserved words as identifiers by careful choice of identifier names, but be aware that illegal use of reserved words will cause an error.

BTEC National Study Guide: IT Practitioners. See page 293 for order details of individual texts

171

Reserved words		
And	Wend	Not
Case	Next	Xor
End	Set	Until
Dim	To	Do
Or	Step	
If	Then	
For	Goto	
While	On	

VB imposes a number of restrictions concerning the formation of names for identifiers:

1. The name must consist only of alphabetic and numeric characters.

2. The name must start with an alphabetic character.

3. The name must not be a reserved word or predefined VB constant.

Examples of valid identifiers

```
firstNum    NUMBER1    abc31    Counter    x
```

Examples of invalid identifiers

```
12abc              (starts with a numeric character)
first-number       (contains a non-alphabetic/numeric character)
var 1              (contains a space)
End                (a reserved word)
```

As well as having names and values, variables are also given a *type*. Three commonly used types are Integer, Single and String. Variable data types are declared before the variables are used in the program. For the purposes of this tutorial, we will use the Dim statement to declare variables, but note that this is not the only way it can be done.

The *type* must be shown after the name of the variable in the Dim statement. Some examples of type declarations are shown below.

```
Dim Amount As Single
Dim Address as String
Dim NumberOfItems As Integer, Count As Integer
```

The third example illustrates that more than one variable can be declared in a single Dim statement.

The type single means that these variables can be used for numbers such as $123 \cdot 456, 0 \cdot 22$ or $-9 \cdot 93$, that is, *signed* numbers that are not whole numbers. The computer holds Single numbers in 32-bit floating-point form so that very large, and very small numbers can be stored.

Signed whole numbers, that is, Integer values are stored as two's complement binary values in the computer. Some examples of integers are 23, 0, −1, 32767 and −559.

Type String means that the named variable (Address in the example above) can store a number of alphanumeric characters such as "24 Railway Terrace, Shilbottle, Countyshire".

A further standard data type is the type Boolean. This type of variable has only one of two

BTEC National Study Guide: IT Practitioners. See page 293 for order details of individual texts

172

possible values, namely `True` or `False`. A boolean variable declaration is made as follows:

```
Dim MoreValues As Boolean
```

VB provides the two reserved words `True` and `False` which can be used to assign a value to a boolean variable, as in:

```
Morevalues = True
```

The use of boolean variables will be explored in a later section. The following table shows all the data types supported by VB, including their storage sizes and ranges.

Data type	Storage size	Range
Byte	1 byte	0 to 255
Boolean	2 bytes	True or False.
Integer	2 bytes	−32,768 to 32,767
Long (long integer)	4 bytes	−2,147,483,648 to 2,147,483,647
Single (single-precision floating-point)	4 bytes	−3.402823E38 to -1.401298E−45 for negative values; 1.401298E-45 to 3.402823E38 for positive values
Double (double-precision floating-point)	8 bytes	−1.79769313486232E308 to −4.94065645841247E-324 for Negative values; 4.94065645841247E-324 to 1.79769313486232E308 for positive values.
Currency (scaled integer)		−922,337,203,685,477.5808 to 922,337,203,685,477.5807
Date	8 bytes	January 1, 100 to December 31, 9999
Object	4 bytes	Any Object reference
String (variable-length)	10 bytes + string length	0 to approximately 2 billion
String (fixed-length)	Length of string	1 to approximately 65,400
Variant (with numbers)	16 bytes	Any numeric value up to the range of a Double
Variant (with characters)	22 bytes + string length	Same range as for variable-length String
User-defined	Number required by elements	The range of each element is the same as the range of its data type

Performing calculations

Probably every program that you will ever write will contain at least one calculation, and this is true of the majority of programs. It is not surprising therefore that VB and other high-level languages make calculations easy to perform. Arithmetic instructions simply involve defining what arithmetic operations are to be performed on numeric identifiers and constants. The four common arithmetic operations: add; subtract; multiply; divide, use the symbols +, −, * and /, respectively.

The examples of arithmetic operations provided in Table 27.1 on the next page assume that the following data declarations have been made.

BTEC National Study Guide: IT Practitioners. See page 293 for order details of individual texts

173

```
Const PI = 3.14
Dim Length As Integer, Width As Integer, Perimeter As Integer
Dim Area as Single, Radius as Single, Gallons as Single, Miles As
Single, Mpg As Single
Dim x As Single
```

Expression	VB statement
Area = length × width	`Area = Length*Width`
Area = $\pi \times$ radius^2	`Area = PI*Radius*Radius`
Perimeter = 2 × (length + width)	`Perimeter = 2*(Length + Width)`
Mpg = gallons ÷ miles	`Mpg = Gallons/Miles`
x = 0	`x = 0`

Table 27.1. *Examples of arithmetic operations with real variables*

Another point to note is that VB provides two divide operators. The '/' divide operator may be used with any values, real or integer, and it produces a real result, that is a non-integer value. The second divide operator, '\', produces an integer result. If the result of a division does not produce a whole number, the fractional part is ignored. In other words, the result is rounded down to the nearest integer. The remainder when one integer is divided by another is produced by the Mod operator. Some examples of different combinations of real and integer divisions are shown in Table 27.2. VB automatically rounds any non-integer values used with \ and Mod.

Operands	Example	Answer	Answer type
real / real	7.3 / 0.2	36.5	real
	0.5 / 0.25	2.0	real
real / integer	13.9 / 5	2.78	real
integer / real	1116 / 7.2	155.0	real
integer / integer	33 / 11	3.0	real
	33 / 10	3.0	real
	3 / 5	0.6	real
integer \ integer	33 \ 11	3	integer
	33 \ 10	3	integer
	3 \ 5	0	integer
integer \ real	33\3.3	11	integer
	33\3.8	8	integer
real \ integer	15.9\4	4	integer
real \ real	14.9/3.3	5	integer
integer mod integer	33 mod 10	3	integer
	10 mod 33	10	integer
integer mod real	10 mod 3.3	1	integer
real mod integer	14.4 mod 4	2	integer
real mod real	13.9 mod 3.3	4	integer

Table 27.2. *Examples of divide operations*

BTEC National Study Guide: IT Practitioners. See page 293 for order details of individual texts

174

Listing 27.2 is an example of the use of integer division. The program converts a number of seconds into hours, minutes and seconds.

Listing 27.2. The \ and Mod integer division operators

```
Public Sub Main()
' ====== Program to illustrate integer division ======

' Declare identifiers
10 Const SECONDSPERMINUTE = 60
20 Const MINUTESPERHOUR = 60
30 Dim Hours As Integer
40 Dim Minutes  As Integer
50 Dim Seconds As Integer
60 Dim Duration As Integer
70 Dim Temp  As Integer

' Get the duration in seconds
80 Duration = InputBox("Enter the length of time in seconds")

'Calculate equivalent hours minutes and seconds
90 Seconds = Duration Mod SECONDSPERMINUTE
100 Temp = Duration \ SECONDSPERMINUTE
110 Minutes = Temp Mod MINUTESPERHOUR
120 Hours = Temp \ MINUTESPERHOUR

'Display the results
130 Debug.Print Duration; " seconds is: "
140 Debug.Print Hours; " hours "
150 Debug.Print Minutes; " minutes "
160 Debug.Print Seconds; " seconds."

End Sub
```

On line *80* the user is requested to enter the time to be converted from seconds to hours, minutes and seconds:

The number of seconds is stored in the variable Duration. The first stage in the calculation is to calculate the remainder when Duration is divided by the number of seconds per minute stored in the constant SECONDSPERMINUTE which has the value 60. Suppose, for example, the user entered the number 6573 when

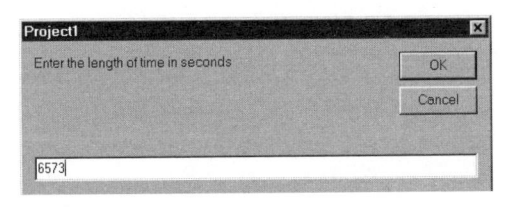

asked for the time in seconds. Line *90* would produce the value 6573 mod 60, that is, 33. This is assigned to the variable, Seconds. Next, the temporary variable Temp is given the value 6573 \ 60, that is, 109. The remainder when this last number is divided by the number of minutes per hour, that is 60, gives the value for Minutes: 109 mod 60 = 49. The number of hours is calculated using 109 \ 60 = 1. Thus, when the program is run, it produces the following output:

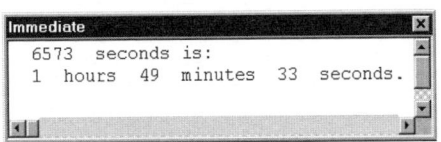

BTEC National Study Guide: IT Practitioners. See page 293 for order details of individual texts

175

Operator precedence

The term *operator precedence* applies to the order in which the operators in an arithmetic expression are used. For example, to evaluate the expression

$$x = y + 3z$$

z is multiplied by 3 before the result is added to *y*; the multiply operator thus has precedence over the addition operator. If *y* had a value of 2 and *z* had a value of 4, *x* would be calculated as

$$x = 2 + 3 ' 4 = 2 + 12 = 14$$

The higher the precedence of an operator, the sooner it is used in the evaluation of an expression. The use of parentheses within an expression can alter the way a calculation is performed. So, in the above expression, to force the addition to be performed before the multiplication, we would write x = (y + 3) ' z. This would result in y being added to 3 before multiplying by z. Thus,

$$x = (2 + 3) ' 4 = 5 ' 4 = 20$$

In VB, the operators *, /, div and mod have equal precedence; this means that in an expression involving two or more of them, they are simply used in the order that they appear in the expression. These four operators all have higher precedence than + and –. Again, + and – have the same precedence. As a further example, consider the program in Listing 27.3.

Listing 27.3.   Illustration of operator precedence

```
Public Sub Main()
' ====== Program to illustrate operator precedence ======

10 Dim x1 As Single
20 Dim y1 As Integer
30 Dim n As Integer

40 n = 11
50 y1 = 5
60 x1 = 1 / 2 * (y1 + n \ y1)

70 Debug.Print x1

End Sub
```

The order of evaluation of line *60* is as follows:

1.	½	i.e.	0.5
2.	n \ y1	i.e.	11 \ 5 = 2
3.	y1 + n \ y1	i.e.	5 + 2 = 7
4.	½* (y1 + n \ y1)	i.e.	0.5*7 = 3.5

The For..Next statement

A very frequent programming requirement is to perform a set of instructions several times. Rather than writing the set of instructions several times (which is impractical for all but a small number of repetitions), they are controlled by a special instruction which causes them to be repeated as many times as desired. Such program constructs are called *loops*, and each repetition of a set of statements is often called an *iteration*. For example, suppose a program is required to read 10 numbers, add each one to a running total and then display the final total. The program

BTEC National Study Guide: IT Practitioners. See page 293 for order details of individual texts

176

in Listing 27.4 accomplishes this task using a loop.

Listing 27.4.   Using a loop to add numbers

```
Public Sub Main()
' ====== Program to add ten numbers   ======

' Declare variables
10 Dim Number  As Single
20 Dim Total As Single
30 Dim Count As Integer

' Initialise running total variable
40 Total = 0

' Get numbers and add to running total
50 For Count = 1 To 10
60    Number = InputBox("Please enter a number")
70    Total = Total + Number
80 Next Count

' Display final total
90 Debug.Print "The total is: "; Total

End Sub
```

Listing 27.4 uses a For loop to repeat the two instructions which repeatedly read a number and add it to a running total. The For loop requires that a control variable, called Count in this example, is defined as type integer. The control variable is automatically given the first value specified (1 in this example) and, each time the statements within the loop are repeated, it is increased by 1 until it finally reaches the second value specified (10 in this example). Thus the same program, but with the value 10 replaced by the required number, could be used to add any number of numbers. Statements to be repeated are enclosed between For and Next Count.

Listing 27.5 is a further example of the use of the For loop.

Listing 27.5.   Using a For loop to display a conversion table

```
Public Sub Main()
' ====== Program to display a conversion table for
'        inches to  centimetres using a For loop   ======

' Declare constants and variables
10 Const CONVERSIONFACTOR = 2.54, MAXINCHES = 12
20 Dim Inches As Integer
30 Dim Centimetres As Single


50 Debug.Print "Inches", "Centimetres"
60 Debug.Print "——", "———-"


70  For Inches = 1 To MAXINCHES
80    Centimetres = Inches * CONVERSIONFACTOR
90    Debug.Print Inches, Centimetres
100 Next Inches

End Sub
```

BTEC National Study Guide: IT Practitioners. See page 293 for order details of individual texts

177

The output looks like this alongside. Notice that the end value in the `For` statement on line *100* is a constant called `MAXINCHES`; this could also have been defined as a variable, its value to be supplied by the user using an `InputBox` instruction.

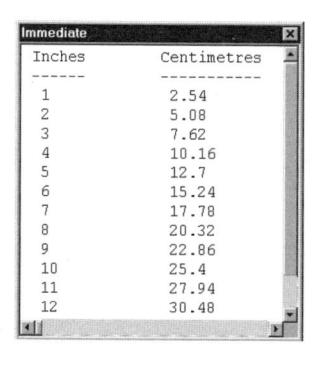

A variation in the format of a `For` statement allows the count variable to go down from a high value to a low value. For example, you could write

```
For i= 12 To 1 Step -1
```

which would cause the variable `i` to start at 12 and go down to 1 in steps of 1.

The While..Wend statement

The `For` statement is a very useful means of implementing a loop, but certain programming problems require a different approach to repeating a set of instructions. For example, consider the following outline program description:

> *Read a set of real numbers representing the cost of a number of items. Accumulate the total cost of the items until a value of zero is entered, then display the number of items purchased and their total cost.*

Here it is not known how many times the loop is to be repeated: the user decides when to terminate the loop by entering a *rogue value*, (zero in this case). The rogue value is used in another type of loop instruction, the `While` instruction.

Listing 27.6 shows how a `While` loop can be used in conjunction with a rogue value.

Listing 27.6.   Using a While loop and a rogue value

```
Public Sub Main()
' ====== Program to illustrate the use of a rogue value
'        to terminate a loop                      ======

' Declare constants and variables
10 Const ROGUEVALUE = 0
20 Dim Count As Integer
30 Dim Amount As Single
40 Dim Total As Single

' Initialise variables
50 Total = 0
60 Count = 0
' Get the cost of the first item
70 Amount = InputBox("Enter the cost of the first item, or 0 to end:")
' Loop to get the remaining items
80   While Amount > ROGUEVALUE
90     Count = Count + 1
100    Total = Total + Amount
110    Amount = InputBox("Enter the cost of the next item, or 0 to
end:")
120 Wend
' Display the restults
130 Debug.Print Count; "items were purchased"
140 Debug.Print "The total cost was: £"; Total
End Sub
```

BTEC National Study Guide: IT Practitioners. See page 293 for order details of individual texts

178

The rogue value is defined as a constant on line *10*. Because the user may want to terminate the program immediately, without entering any values, the program asks for a purchase amount before entering the loop starting on line *80*. The While instruction requires that a true/false expression is included after the word 'while'. Thus the expression, Amount > ROGUEVALUE, will be true if Amount entered is greater than zero, and it will be false if Amount is not greater than zero, that is if it is equal to, or less than zero. When the expression is true, the statements between While and Wend, that is lines *90* to *110*, will be executed; as soon as the expression becomes false, the loop terminates and the program goes on to line *130*. Notice that the last instruction in the lines to be repeated is the instruction to read another value: this means that because the next instruction to be executed is the While instruction, the value typed in by the user is immediately compared with the rogue value. This ensures that the rogue value is not processed as an actual data item. Here is a typical run of the program:

```
Enter the cost of the first item, or 0 to end :23.45
Enter the cost of the next item, or 0 to end :6.12
Enter the cost of the next item, or 0 to end :5.99
Enter the cost of the next item, or 0 to end :0
```

Notice that the assignment instruction on line *90*, Count = Count + 1, is used as a means of counting the number of times the loop is executed. The instruction simply adds 1 to the variable, Count, each time the instructions within the loop are repeated. The true/false expression on line *80* in the While statement uses the *relational operator*, >, mean-

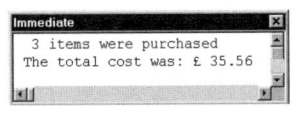

ing 'greater than', to compare Amount with ROGUEVALUE. There are six different relational operators that can be used in such logical expressions, and these are shown in Table 27.4.

relational operator	meaning
>	Greater than
>=	Greater than or equal to
<	Less than
<=	Less than or equal to
=	Equal to
<>	Not equal to

Table 27.4. *Relational operators used in logical expressions*

The operators in Table 27.4 are used according to the relationship to be established between two values. Whatever logical expression is used, the result of the comparison will either be true or false - if true, the While loop will repeat; if false the loop will terminate. More examples of the use of these operators are provided in the next part of this Topic, which deals with the use of logical expressions in making program decisions.

The If statement

Suppose a program is required to display multiple-choice questions with one correct answer out of three possible choices. For example, one of the questions could be:

```
A BYTE is the name given to

(a)  Four bits
(b)  Eight bits
(c)  Sixteen bits
```

BTEC National Study Guide: IT Practitioners. See page 293 for order details of individual texts

179

```
        Your answer is:
```

The program is also required to display the message

```
        Correct - well done!
```

if the answer is correct, and display a message such as

```
        Sorry, the correct answer is (b)
```

if the answer provided is incorrect. The program must therefore be able to take two alternative courses of action depending on the answer supplied. An If statement is one possible way of achieving this requirement. The appropriate form of the If statement is illustrated in Listing 27.7 which shows the VB code required to display the question above and provide the response appropriate to the letter 'a', 'b' or 'c', typed into the Input box that appears.

Listing 27.7.   Using an If statement

```
Public Sub Main()
' ====== Program to illustrate the use of the If statement =======


' Declare constants and variables
10 Dim Answer As String

' Ask the question
20 Debug.Print "Please enter a, b, c or d"
30 Debug.Print "in the Answer Box provided:"
40 Debug.Print
50 Debug.Print "A BYTE is the name given to"
60 Debug.Print "(a) Four bits"
70 Debug.Print "(b) Eight bits"
80 Debug.Print "(c) Sixteen bits"
90 Debug.Print

' Get the answer and display it
100 Answer = InputBox("Your answer is?", "Answer Box")
110 Debug.Print "You answered ("; Answer; ")"

' Check the answer and report
120 If Answer = "b" Then
130    Debug.Print "Correct - well done!"
140 Else
150    Debug.Print "Sorry, the correct answer is (b)"
160 End If

End Sub
```

The If statement extending over lines *120* to *160* shows how the program can take one of two possible courses of action depending on the value of a variable. We saw in the last Topic concerning the use of the While statement that logical expressions are either true or false. This is also the case with the logical expression Answer = "b" in the If statement on line *120*. If the letter stored in the character variable Answer is the letter 'b', then the logical expression Answer = "b" will be true, otherwise it will be false. If it is true, the statement following the word Then is executed (that is, line *130*), otherwise the statement after Else is executed (that is, line *150*). Notice the different form of the input box on line *100*:

BTEC National Study Guide: IT Practitioners. See page 293 for order details of individual texts

180

```
100 Answer = InputBox("Your answer is?", "Answer Box")
```

The text after the prompt text ("Your answer is?") is the title of the input box shown alongside. The general form of the If statement is

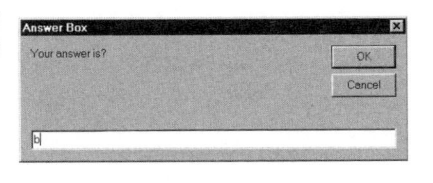

```
If {logical expression} Then
   {statement 1}
Else
   {statement 2}
End If
```

Note that {statement 1} is the instruction that is performed if {logical expression} is true; {statement 2} is performed if {logical expression} is false. Note also that either {statement 1} or {statement 2}, or both of them, can contain more than a single instruction, as illustrated below:

```
If Answer = "b" Then
   Debug.Print "Correct - well done!"
Else
   Debug.Print "Sorry, the correct answer is (b)"
   Debug.Print "There are eight bits in a byte"
End If
```

Sometimes it is necessary to choose between more than just two courses of action in a program. For example, Listing 27.8 shows a program which converts a percentage mark to a pass, merit, distinction or fail grade. The program repeatedly accepts marks and converts them to grades until the mark entered is the rogue value –1 (or any negative integer value) signifying the end of the mark inputs. The rules that are used to determine the grade are as follows:

For a distinction the mark must be equal to or over 80.

For a merit the mark must be greater than or equal to 60 and less than 80.

For a pass the mark must be greater than or equal to 40 and less than 60.

Below 40 is a fail.

Listing 27.8.   The If..Else If construction

```
Public Sub Main()
' ====== Program to illustrate the use of the If statement =======


' Declare constants and variables
10 Const DIST = 80, MERIT = 60, PASS = 40
20 Dim Mark As Integer, Grade As String

'Get the first mark
30 Mark = InputBox("Please enter the first mark(-1 to end): ",
"Marks")

' Check the grade
40 While Mark >= 0
50    If Mark >= DIST Then
60       Grade = "Distinction"
70    Else
80       If (Mark >= MERIT) And (Mark < DIST) Then
90        Grade = "Merit"
100      Else
110       If (Mark >= PASS) And (Mark < MERIT) Then
```

BTEC National Study Guide: IT Practitioners. See page 293 for order details of individual texts

181

```
120        Grade = "Pass"
130      Else
140        Grade = "Fail"
150      End If
160   End If
170  End If


'Report mark and grade
180 Debug.Print "Mark: "; Mark, "Grade: "; Grade

' Get the next mark
190 Mark = InputBox("Please enter the next mark(-1 to end): ",
"Marks")
200 Wend

End Sub
```

The `If` statement between lines *50* and *170* reflects this logic exactly. It is possible to chain `If` statements in this way to cope with quite complex lines of reasoning. Added flexibility is provided by the use of the logical `And` operator used for the logical expressions on lines *80* and *110*. The `And` operator requires that both of the minor logical expressions it connects are true for the complete logical expression to be true. If either or both are false, then the whole expression is false. Logical operators are discussed in more detail in the next section. The output from the program for a set of four marks is shown on the right.

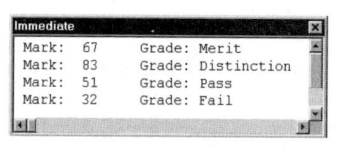

Logical operators

Logical operators allow you to combine logical expressions. There are three logical operators in VB: `And`, `Or` and `Not`. An example of the use of the `And` operator was provided in Listing 27.8. The `And` and the `Or` operators are always placed between two logical expressions, and they each combine these logical expressions to produce a value of true or false. Table 27.5 shows the rules that are applied by VB to determine whether a compound logical expression is true or false. This type of table is usually called a *truth table*.

(Expr 1)	(Expr 2)	(Expr 1) Or (Expr 2)	(Expr 1) And (Expr 2)
true	true	true	true
true	false	true	false
false	true	true	false
false	false	false	false

Table 27.5. *Truth table for the* **And** *and* **Or** *logical operators*

Look at Listing 27.8, on line *80*, where the compound logical expression (`Mark >= MERIT`) `And` (`Mark < DIST`) is used to determine whether the mark is equivalent to a merit grade. In the expression, (`Mark >= MERIT`) is an example of (`Expr 1`) and (`Mark < DIST`) is an example of (`Expr 2`) shown in Table 27.5.

The next table (Table 27.6) shows how the `And` operator combines these two logical expressions for a number of cases.

BTEC National Study Guide: IT Practitioners. See page 293 for order details of individual texts

182

Mark	(Mark >= Merit)	(Mark < Dist)	(Mark >= Merit And (Mark < Dist)
45	false	true	false
86	true	false	false
67	true	true	true

Table 27.6. *Truth table for the* **And** *logical operator*

Thus, both logical expressions must be true for the complete expression to be true; with the Or operator, however, only one of the expressions needs to be true for the complete expression to be true. For example, consider the program in Listing 27.9 which reads some text and counts how many vowels it contains. The program uses a For loop to test each letter in turn in the text against each possible vowel. If the current letter is a vowel, that is 'a', 'e', 'i', 'o' or 'u', a count is incremented.

Listing 27.9.   Illustrating the use of the Or logical operator

```
Public Sub Main()
' ====== Program to illustrate the use of the Or operator =======

' Declare constants and variables
10 Dim VowelCount As Integer
20 Dim Letters As String
30 Dim LengthOfText As Integer
40 Dim c As Integer

' Initialise vowel count variable
50 VowelCount = 0

' Get the text to process
60 Letters = InputBox("Type text followed by ENTER: ", "Vowel count")
70 LengthOfText = Len(Letters)

' Count the number of vowels
80  For c = 1 To LengthOfText
90    If (Mid(Letters, c, 1) = "a") Or
         (Mid(Letters, c, 1) = "e") Or
         (Mid(Letters, c, 1) = "i") Or
         (Mid(Letters, c, 1) = "o") Or
         (Mid(Letters, c, 1) = "u") Then
100     VowelCount = VowelCount + 1
110   End If
120 Next c

'Display the results
130 Debug.Print "You entered "; Letters
140 Debug.Print "The text contains "; VowelCount; " vowels"
End Sub
```

The text is held in a string variable called Letters. Each letter in Letters is accessed by specifying its position within the text. For example, if the text entered was the string 'hello there', then Mid(Letters,1,1) is the letter 'h', Mid(Letters,2,1) is the letter 'e', Mid(Letters,3,1) is the letter 'l', and so on.

The function Mid allows us to access one or more characters from a string. The first item in the brackets is the string to search, the second is the position in the string to start, and the third is the number of characters to access. So Mid(Letters,5,2) would return two characters

BTEC National Study Guide: IT Practitioners. See page 293 for order details of individual texts

183

starting at position 5 and `Mid(Letters,c,1)` returns the single character at position `c`. The `For` loop control variable, c, starts at 1 and goes up in steps of 1 to the length of the string (11 for the string 'hello there'). The length of the string is determined by the VB function `len()`, on line *70*, which requires a string as its single argument. The output from the program when the string, 'the cat sat on the mat' is typed in, is shown on the right.

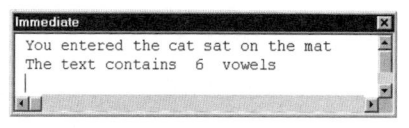

Note that the program will only work with lower-case text. The reason is that lower-case letters 'a', 'b', 'c', etc are represented in a computer using a different set of codes from the equivalent upper-case letters 'A', 'B', 'C', etc.

The third logical operator is the `Not` operator which simply reverses the logical value of a logical expression. Thus, the logical expression `Not (x >3)` is true only when x is less than or equal to 3. Similarly, the logical expression `Not (Balance <= 0)` is true only when `Balance` has a value that is greater than zero. The truth table shown in Table 27.7 defines the operation of the `Not` logical operator.

Expr	not Expr
true	false
false	true

Table 27.7. *Truth table for not logical operator*

The Select..Case statement

The `Select` statement is an alternative method to the `If` statement for choosing between alternative courses of action within a program. It has the following general format:

```
Select Case {expression}
Case value list 1
   statement 1
             Case value list 2
                statement 2
   etc...
   ......
Case Else
   statement N
Select End
```

The expression after `Select Case` can be a single variable or an expression involving several variables. VB matches the value of this single variable or expression against the values specified in the `Case` value lists; when a match is found, the corresponding statements are executed after which the `Select` statement is immediately exited without considering any remaining values. If there are no values that match the variable, the `Select` statement does nothing unless the `Else` option is used, in which circumstances the supplied statement or statements (shown as `statement N` above) are executed.

In Listing 27.10, the `Select` statement is used to find the number of days in a month given the month number (1 to 12):

Listing 27.10.   Illustrating the use of the Select statement
---

```
Public Sub Main()
' ====== Program to illustrate the use of the Or operator =======


' Declare constants and variables
10 Const Title = "Days in month"
20 Const Buttons = vbOKOnly
```

BTEC National Study Guide: IT Practitioners. See page 293 for order details of individual texts

184

```
30 Dim Month As Integer
40 Dim Response As Integer

' Get month number
50 Month = InputBox("Enter a month number(1 to 12)", Title)

' Determine days in month
60   Select Case Month
     Case 1, 3, 5, 7, 8, 10, 12
70    Msg = "There are 31 days in month " & Month
     Case 4, 6, 9, 11
       Msg = "There are 30 days in month " & Month
     Case 2
       Msg = "There are 28 days in month " & Month
80   Case Else
90    Msg = "Invalid month number: " & Month
     End Select

' Report days in month using a message box
100 Response = MsgBox(Msg, Buttons, Title)
End Sub
```

Month contains a number corresponding to the month of the year, where January = 1, February = 2 ..... December = 12. The Select..Case statement is used to store, in the variable, Days, the number of days in the month whose number is stored in Month. Thus if Month contained the number 8 corresponding to August, Days would be assigned the value 31. The example uses a Message Box function on line *100* to display the number of days in the specified month. The message box displays a window with a title, a message and a single OK button as illustrated alongside.

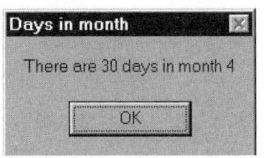

A Message box can display a variety of different buttons that can be specified by using appropriate VB constants as shown below:

Constant	Value	Description
vbOKOnly	0	Display OK button only
vbOKCancel	1	Display OK and Cancel buttons
vbAbortRetryIgnore	2	Display Abort, Retry, and Ignore buttons
vbYesNoCancel	3	Display Yes, No, and Cancel buttons
vbYesNo	4	Display Yes and No buttons
vbRetryCancel	5	Display Retry and Cancel buttons

The function returns the value corresponding to the button that the user selects:

Constant	Value	Button chosen
vbOK	1	OK
vbCancel	2	Cancel
vbAbort	3	Abort
vbRetry	4	Retry
vbIgnore	5	Ignore
vbYes	6	Yes
vbNo	7	No

BTEC National Study Guide: IT Practitioners. See page 293 for order details of individual texts

185

This allows us to take different forms of action depending on the button clicked. (See Listing 27.11). However, in our example this value is not used - we simply display a message and stop.

The message to display is stored in the variable `Msg` and is set according to the Case clause that corresponds to the `Month` entered by the user. Notice that to join together strings (*concatenate*) we use the & operator, as in line *70*:

```
70   Msg = "There are 31 days in month " & Month
```

In the next example we use another form of the Message box function in combination with the `Select` statement.

Listing 27.11.   Illustrating the use of the Select statement

```
Public Sub Main()
' ====== Program to illustrate the use of Select..Case =======

' Declare constants and variables
10 Const Title = "Smoking"
20 Const MsgYes = "Smoking is bad for you!"
30 Const MsgNo = "Good for you!!"
40 Dim Response As Integer

' Display message box
50 Response = MsgBox("Do you smoke?", vbYesNo, Title)

' Determine whether smoker or non-smoker and report
60   Select Case Response
     Case vbNo
70     Response = MsgBox(MsgNo, vbOKOnly, Title)
     Case vbYes
80     Response = MsgBox(MsgYes, vbOKOnly, Title)
     End Select

End Sub
```

If the user clicks the **Yes** button in the Message box that is displayed by line *70* variable, `Response` is assigned the value `vbYes`(6) ; if the user clicks the No button, Response is assigned the value `vbNo` (7). The `Select` statement then determines which button was clicked and displays the appropriate message.

Arrays

An *array* is a data structure which allows you to store a number of items of data without having to allocate separate variable names to them. Arrays must be declared before they are used. For example, the following declaration is for an array of five integers:

```
        Dim Array(5) As Integer
```

This single declaration is in effect defining five variables called `Array(1)`, `Array(2)`, `Array(3)`, `Array(4)` and `Array(5)`, each of which can store a single integer value. The integer value inside the brackets is called the array's index, and it is allowed only to take the range of values specified in the declaration (1 to 5 inclusive in this example). Each of these identifiers can be used just like any ordinary integer variable. For instance, to set each of them to zero could be accomplished as follows:

```
        Array(1) = 0
        Array(2) = 0
        Array(3) = 0
```

BTEC National Study Guide: IT Practitioners. See page 293 for order details of individual texts

186

```
          Array(4) = 0
          Array(5) = 0
```

However, we could accomplish the same operation by using an integer variable as an *index* and by putting a single assignment statement in a `For` loop:

```
     For i = 1 to 5
       Array(i)= 0
     Next i
```

Now the count variable i takes on the integer values 1 to 5 and again each element in the array is set to zero. The obvious advantage of using a variable for an index is that arrays can then be used very effectively within loops, and they allow the manipulation of as many or as few numbers as appropriate to the task in hand; notice that the same `For` loop could initialise 5000 array elements as easily as 5 elements:

```
     For i = 1 to 5000
       Array(i) = 0
     Next i
```

This would be an exceedingly difficult task to accomplish without the use of an array.

Listing 27.12 illustrates the use of an array of real numbers. The program reads five numbers into an array and then finds the position within the array of the smallest number. It then swaps this number with the first number in the list before displaying the re-ordered array.

Listing 27.12.   Using an array

```
Public Sub Main()
' ====== Program to illustrate the use an array =======

' Declare constants and variables
10 Const MAXNUMS = 5
15 Dim Array1(MAXNUMS) As Integer
   Dim Temp As Integer
   Dim i As Integer

' Get the numbers
20 For i = 1 To MAXNUMS
30   Array1(i) = InputBox("Enter number " & i & " of " & MAXNUMS)
35 Next i

' Find the smallest and store in first array element
40 For i = 2 To MAXNUMS
50   If Array1(i) < Array1(1) Then
60     Temp = Array1(1)
70     Array1(1) = Array1(i)
80     Array1(i) = Temp
     End If
   Next i

' Print the new list
   Debug.Print "The new list is as follows: "
90 For i = 1 To MAXNUMS
   Debug.Print Array1(i);
   Next i
 End Sub
```

BTEC National Study Guide: IT Practitioners. See page 293 for order details of individual texts

187

The program first defines a constant MAXNUMS to be the maximum size of the integer array, Array1. Lines *20* to *35* are to read in the five numbers with appropriate user prompts. Thus the first number is read into Array1(1), the second into Array1(2), and so on up to the last number which is read into Array1(5). The second For loop starting on line *40* compares each number in the array in turn with the first number; if one is found that is less than the first, they are swapped over. By the time the last number in the array has been compared with the first one, the smallest number is in the first position in the array. A typical run of the program might be:

```
Enter number 1 of 5 :5
Enter number 2 of 5 :3
Enter number 3 of 5 :9
Enter number 4 of 5 :1
Enter number 5 of 5 :8
```

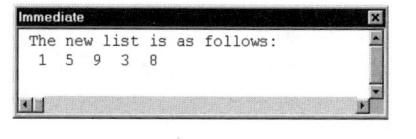

The output appears as shown alongside.

As a final example in this section on arrays, Listing 27.13 shows a program which uses a random number generator to select five lottery numbers in the range 1 to 49.

Listing 27.13.   Random numbers and array to generate lottery numbers

```
Public Sub Main()
' ====== Program to use random numbers
'        to generate 5 lottery numbers               =======

' Declare constants and variables
10  Const NUMOFNUMS = 5
20  Const MAXNUM = 49
30  Dim LuckyNums(MAXNUM) As Boolean
40  Dim Num As Integer
50  Dim i As Integer
60  Dim Count As Integer

'Display heading
    Debug.Print "Lottery random number generator"
    Debug.Print

' Initialise array
70  For i = 1 To MAXNUM
80     LuckyNums(i) = False
90  Next i

' Initialise count for numbers generated
100 Count = 0

' Initialise random number generator
110 Randomize

' Generate the lottery numbers
120 While Count < NUMOFNUMS
130   Num = Int(MAXNUM * Rnd()) + 1
140   If LuckyNums(Num) = False Then
150     Debug.Print Num;
160     LuckyNums(Num) = True
170     Count = Count + 1
180   End If
```

BTEC National Study Guide: IT Practitioners. See page 293 for order details of individual texts

188

```
190   Wend

200   End Sub
```

The random numbers are generated using the function `Rnd()` which produces a random number less than 1 but greater than or equal to 0. To produce a random number in the range 0 to `MAXNUM`, we use the statement

```
130   Num = Int(MAXNUM * Rnd()) + 1
```

This instruction multiplies the random number by `MAXNUM` (i.e. 49) to produce a number in the range 0 to less than 49. The `Int` function then rounds this number down to the nearest integer, thus giving a number in the range 0 to 48. Then 1 is added to produce a number in the range 1 to 49. The `randomize` instruction on line *110* simply initialises the random number generator so that it does not produce the same sequence of random numbers every time the program is run. Lines *70-90* initialises each element to `False` in the array `LuckyNums()` which is to be used to record the five numbers that are generated.

The reason for the `If` statement on lines *140* to *180* is to ensure that the same random number is not used more than once. When a number is generated, the appropriate element in the `LuckyNums` array is checked to see if it has a value of `False` which indicates that the number has not been generated before. Then, to record that the number has been generated, that element is set to `True` in the `LuckyNums` array. For example, if the first random number generated on line *130* was the number 36, then this would be stored in `Num`. The `If` statement checks that 36 has not been used already by checking if `LuckyNums(36)` still has its initial value of `False`. If this is the case, 36 is displayed (line *150*), `LuckyNums(36)` is set to `True` and `Count` is increased by 1. Thus if 36 is generated again, the `If` statement will prevent it from being used. The `While` loop repeats until five different numbers have been generated. Here is an example from the output of Example 13:

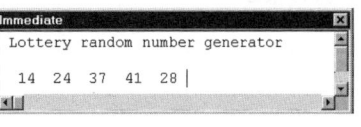

Strings

A string is a set of characters such as "24, Railway Terrace, Willington" or "Hello" or "123abc". Strings can be stored by string variables and they can be manipulated in various ways using special Visual Basic functions. In this section we will briefly review a number of common functions used for handling strings and then apply them in an example program.

Declaring strings and assigning strings to variables

Use the `Dim` statement to declare a variable as a string variable. For example, to declare the variable "Myname" as a string use the statement

```
Dim Myname As String
```

Declare `Myname` before it is used in the program.

There is no practical limit on the size of a string (up to about 2 billion characters).

To store characters in a string you simply use an assignment statement such as

```
Myname = "Ivar Peregrine Trews"
```

The right-hand side of this statement, that is the text in quotation marks, is called a string *literal*. To clear a string variable, store the empty string , "" (double quotes with nothing between), in it:

```
Myname = ""
```

BTEC National Study Guide: IT Practitioners. See page 293 for order details of individual texts

189

To join strings together (concatenate) use the & operator. The following example illustrates how to concatenate strings:

```
Dim Firstname As String,  Surname As String, Fullname As String
Firstname = "John"
Surname = "Smith"
Fullname = Surname &  ", " & Firstname
```

The variable `Fullname` would then contain the string "Smith, John"

String length - Len()

This function returns the length of a string, that is, the number of characters in the string.

Example

```
Mystring = "Hello there"
L = Len(Mystring)
```

(`L` would be assigned the value 11)

Substrings - Left(), Right() and Mid()

These three functions are used to extract parts of strings (*substrings*) from strings.

`Left(string, length)` returns a specified number of characters (`length`) from the left side of a string (`string`).

Examples

```
MyString = "Hello There"        ' Define string.
Str1 = Left(MyString, 1)        ' Returns "H".
Str2 = Left(MyString, 7)        ' Returns "Hello T".
Str3 = Left(MyString, 20)       ' Returns "Hello There".
```

`Right(string, length)` returns a specified number of characters (`length`) from the right side of a string (`string`).

Examples

```
MyString = "Hello There"        ' Define string.
Str1 = Right(MyString, 1)       ' Returns "e".
Str2 = Right(MyString, 5)       ' Returns "There".
Str3 = Right(MyString, 20)      ' Returns "Hello There".
```

`Mid(string, start, [length])` returns a specified number of characters (`length`) starting from position start in a string (`string`). `length` is optional and if omitted all characters from start to the end of the string are returned.

Examples

```
MyString = "Hello There"        ' Create text string.
Str1 = Mid(MyString, 1, 3)      ' Returns "Hel".
Str2 = Mid(MyString, 7, 5)      ' Returns "There".
Str3 = Mid(MyString, 7)         ' Returns "There".
Str4 = Mid(MyString, 5, 1)      ' Returns "o".
```

BTEC National Study Guide: IT Practitioners. See page 293 for order details of individual texts

190

Searching strings - Instr()

InStr([start,]string1, string2[, compare]) returns the position of the first occurrence of string2 within string1 starting from position start in string1. The optional parameter compare can be used to specify whether the search is to be case sensitive (compare = 0) or not (compare = 1). If compare is omitted the comparison is case sensitive (binary comparison). The start value is also optional - if omitted the search starts from the first character in string1. If the search string, string2, is not found in string1, the function returns a value of 0, otherwise it returns the position of the first character of string2 within string1.

Examples

```
MyString = "Information and Communications Technology"
Pos1 = Instr( MyString, "c", 0)      ' Returns 24 - case sensitive
Pos2 = Instr( MyString, "com", 1)    ' Returns 17 - case insensitive


Pos3 = Instr( MyString, "com")       ' Returns 0 - case sensitive
Pos4 = Instr( 25, MyString, "c")     ' Returns 34 - start position 25
```

Example program to illustrate string handling

This example program splits a sentence into separate words by looking for a space at the end of a word. It is assumed that there are no extra spaces between words or any spaces at the beginning or end of the sentence, and that the sentence contains no punctuation marks.

Listing 27.14.   String handling

```
Public Sub Main()
' ====== Program to use illustrate the use of some string
'        handling functions                              =======
' Declare constants and variables
 Dim Sentence As String, Word As String
 Dim CurPos As Integer, SpacePos As Integer, L As Integer

' Get the sentence
10 Sentence = InputBox("Please type in a sentence")

' Add space at end to simplify coding
20 Sentence = Sentence & " "

' Set the starting point for searching sentence
30 CurPos = 1

' Get the length of the sentence
40 L = Len(Sentence)

' Look for spaces and extract words
50   While CurPos < L
60     SpacePos = InStr(CurPos, Sentence, " ")
70     Word = Mid(Sentence, CurPos, SpacePos - CurPos)
80     Debug.Print Word
90     CurPos = SpacePos + 1  ' update search start position
100 Wend
End Sub
```

BTEC National Study Guide: IT Practitioners. See page 293 for order details of individual texts

191

The user is requested to type in the sentence on line *10*. Line *20* adds a single space to the end of the sentence to simplify the programming required to extract single words. (this allows us to assume that all words in the sentence are followed by a space).

The starting position for the search is set at the beginning of the sentence on line *30*. `CurPos` will store the start position of each new word located.

On line *40* the length of the sentence is stored in the variable `L`.

The main part of the program is the `While` loop from lines *50* to *100*. The position of the next space in the sentence is located using the `Instr()` function. It is not necessary to use the `compare` option because a space does not have upper and lower case.

Line *70* extracts a word using the `Mid()` function. `SpacePos` contains the position of the space at the end of the word and `CurPos` is the position of the first letter in the word; thus the length of the word is given by `SpacePos - CurPos`.

Finally, the extracted word is printed, `CurPos` is set to the beginning of the next word and the loop repeats.

The loop ends when `CurPos` exceeds `L`, the length of the sentence.

Some Visual Basic Functions

We have already used a few functions in the example programs. The previous lottery number program used `rnd()` to generate random numbers and `int()` to convert a real number to an integer. We have also used the `MsgBox()` function to display a window and return a value to indicate which button the user clicked. Functions are pre-written subprograms that perform frequently required tasks. There are a great number of Visual Basic functions available to the programmer, and you can use the VB Help facility to research them and to see examples of how they can be used. Here we list and briefly describe a selection of them.

Function	Purpose
Abs	Returns the absolute value of a number
Asc	Returns the character code corresponding to the first letter in a string
Atn	Returns the arctangent of a number
Chr	Returns the character associated with the specified character code.
Cos	Returns the cosine of a number
CurDir	Returns the current path
Date	Returns the current system date.
Dir	Returns the name of a file or directory that matches a specified pattern or file attribute, or the volume label of a drive.
DoEvents	Yields execution so that the operating system can process other events
EOF	Returns a value that indicates whether the end of a file has been reached
Error	Returns the error message that corresponds to a given error number.

BTEC National Study Guide: IT Practitioners. See page 293 for order details of individual texts

192

Exp	Returns e (the base of natural logarithms) raised to a power
Input	Returns characters from an open sequential or binary file
InStr	Returns the position of the first occurrence of one string within another
Int	Returns the integer portion of a number
IsNumeric	Returns a Boolean value indicating whether an expression can be evaluated as a number
Left	Returns a specified number of characters from the left side of a string
Len	Returns the number of characters in a string or the number of bytes required to store a variable
Log	Returns the natural logarithm of a number
Ltrim, Rtrim, Trim	Returns a copy of a string without leading spaces (LTrim), trailing spaces (RTrim), or both leading and trailing spaces (Trim)
Mid	Returns a specified number of characters from a string
MsgBox	Displays a message in a dialog box, waits for the user to choose a button, and returns a value indicating which button the user has chosen
Now	Returns the current date and time according to the setting of your computer's system date and time
Right	Returns a specified number of characters from the right side of a string
Rnd	Returns a random number
Sgn	Returns an integer indicating the sign of a number
Shell	Runs an executable program
Sin	Returns the sine of an angle
Space	Returns a string consisting of the specified number of spaces
Sqr	Returns the square root of a number
Str	Returns a string representation of a number
StrComp	Returns a value indicating the result of a string comparison
String	Returns a repeating character string of the length specified
Tan	Returns the tangent of an angle.
Timer	Returns the number of seconds elapsed since midnight.
Val	Returns the numbers contained in a string

BTEC National Study Guide: IT Practitioners. See page 293 for order details of individual texts

193

4.1.

A program is required to read in three numeric values representing the three sides of a triangle. The numbers are to be entered from a keyboard one after the other, separated by one or more spaces and followed by pressing the Enter key. The program outputs a number of messages regarding the type of triangle that the three numbers represent:

- ❏ Invalid data: these values cannot be used to form a triangle;
- ❏ Invalid data: non-numeric input;
- ❏ Scalene;
- ❏ Isosceles;
- ❏ Equilateral;
- ❏ Obtuse;
- ❏ Right-angled.

The program may print out more than one message. For instance, if the three values were 3, 3, 5, the program should say that the triangle is 'Obtuse' and 'Isosceles'.

Task 1

Using a standard design methodology design the program. Your design should adhere to top-down, structured design principles and should include a data dictionary specifying the name, type, size and use of all identifiers used in the design.

Task 2

1. Use appropriate testing methods to devise test cases which would test the program thoroughly.
2. For each test case specify the expected output from the program.
3. You should assume that the program has code to validate the input so that it can detect invalid inputs. Your test data should cover every possible output from the program for invalid and valid data.

Task 3

Write the program using the design in Task 1.

After identifying and removing syntax and runtime errors, test the program using the test cases devised in Task 2. Keep a log of test results and of how errors were corrected and the program re-tested.

You will need to research the characteristics of each type of triangle in order to devise test data that represents each possible type of triangle.

BTEC National Study Guide: IT Practitioners. See page 293 for order details of individual texts

194

UNIT 10: APPLICATIONS SOFTWARE DEVELOPMENT

Most PCs include a wide range of applications available for effective data processing, such as databases, spreadsheets, word processors and presentation applications. To demonstrate your skills in applications software development, you are going to enhance an application using programming facilities to provide customised functions and adapt the user interface to provide a professional, easy-to-use application.

This unit concentrates on developing applications by writing macros within spreadsheet software, but similar development could be applied to word processing applications, database applications or presentations. Database programs like Microsoft Access offer more sophisticated facilities than can be found in any spreadsheet programs. So, if you would like to demonstrate your programming skills for a 'heavier' database application, refer to Unit 13 for details of how this could be

Learning objectives

- To use appropriate methods to plan and design a system
- To customise the way an application processes data
- To customise an application's user interface
- To use programming facilities to enhance an application

367

BTEC National Study Guide: IT Practitioners. See page 293 for order details of individual texts

195

10.1 Planning and design

The familiar general-purpose applications such as word processing, spreadsheets and databases are often bundled together in a complete suite of applications such as Microsoft Office. These 'office' applications are designed to be 'jacks of all trades' with a wide range of in-built facilities. However, there are times when you may want to add to some of the facilities provided by these programs so that novice users can use them more easily:

- in word processing, automating a procedure such as a mail merge
- in a spreadsheet, automating some complex formulae and building a user interface
- in a database, providing forms and a menu system as a user interface.

Database applications tend to require lots of customisation and so the applications software provides a query language called SQL (details of this can be found in Unit 13).

Each of the standard applications offers a common, built-in programming facility using macros, and this unit concentrates on how to use these in the following ways to demonstrate your programming skills:

- controlling what the user can and cannot do, to prevent a user from doing things with which they are unfamiliar
- making sure that users carry out actions in a certain order, e.g. completing data entry before printing the spreadsheet

Each individual macro provides a single facility, such as a button to click which results in saving and printing a spreadsheet or document. Several macros can be combined to create a complete application.

The first step in creating any application-based program, as with creating any program, is to understand the user requirements. The stages in the development of a system (investigation, analysis and design) are described in detail in Unit 6 so they are not repeated again here.

✓ **Check your understanding 10.1**

1 Refer to Unit 6 to refresh your memory of the stages of development for a system.
2 In a group of five or six, hold a brainstorming session to discuss options for enhancing applications software to meet user needs. The user may be an experienced user who is looking to save time or a novice user; the latter may provide more options to customise an application.
3 Draw up a short list of users and the user requirements for systems that you may decide to provide as a demonstration of your ability to develop applications software.

368

BTEC National Study Guide: IT Practitioners. See page 293 for order details of individual texts

196

Once the user requirement has been investigated and understood, the next step is to design the way the application program will work. There are number of aspects of the system that you will need to design:

- the system plan, showing the objects in the system (such as forms), the links between them and how the user will progress through them while using the application
- the methods of input and output, including the user interface, and items such as customised reports
- the processing which will be carried out, including any calculations required.

Creating a plan of the system

This stage involves creating an overall plan of how the system will work, including:

- the **objects** that are to be provided
- how the different objects in the system are linked together, e.g. on one form
- the logical progression through the system
- for larger, more complex system involving a number of different forms, how the user is to navigate around the system
- any procedures and functions.

? What does it mean?

The **objects** in a system are the tables, forms and customised outputs.

Case study: Cellphone World

Cellphone World sell a range of mobile phones to the public. They need a system to estimate customer phone bills, based on their expected duration of peak and off-peak calls per month. They decide to use a spreadsheet application, but need this to be customised so that it guides the shop assistant through the process of estimating a customer's monthly bill. The system should allow the shop assistant to choose different networks and to see the monthly bill for that network.

The solution to this user's needs involves the use of menus and buttons, and will need to incorporate validation to prevent the shop assistant entering invalid data.

This solution requires five separate steps (Figure 10.1):

- Display an opening screen.
- Show a form where the user can select which service company is to be used and enter the number of minutes of calls made.
- Display total estimated bill.
- Print a record of the calculation.
- Exit or do another calculation.

1 Check that you understand the plan for the Cellphone World system.
2 Working with others, sketch plans for systems that you might develop and discuss them.

BTEC National Study Guide: IT Practitioners. See page 293 for order details of individual texts

197

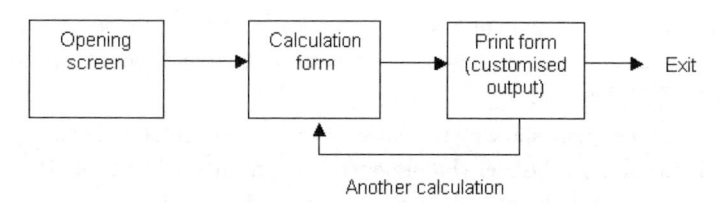

Figure 10.1 The steps involved in solving Cellphone World's problem

The plan is shown as a simple diagram as in Figure 10.1, with boxes representing the different objects and arrows showing how they are linked. This type of diagram is sometimes called a **state diagram** because it shows the different states that the application can be in. The procedures and functions required depend on the **controls** that are added to the forms to make the application work.

? What does it mean?

A **control** may be a button or a field on a form or a field on a report.

Designing system controls

For any system being designed, the investigation stage should provide a clear idea of what the

- **Buttons** are used to indicate that some action should be carried out, such as a calculation to be done or results to be printed.
- **Text boxes** are used to allow the user to make text (or numeric) entries. They may also be used to display a text or numeric result.
- **Radio buttons** are used to allow the user to make a choice between a number of different options.
- **List boxes** (or combo boxes) allow the user to see a list of values, and the user can select an item from the list.
- **Text labels** are included to provide the user with information about what each particular control is to be used for.

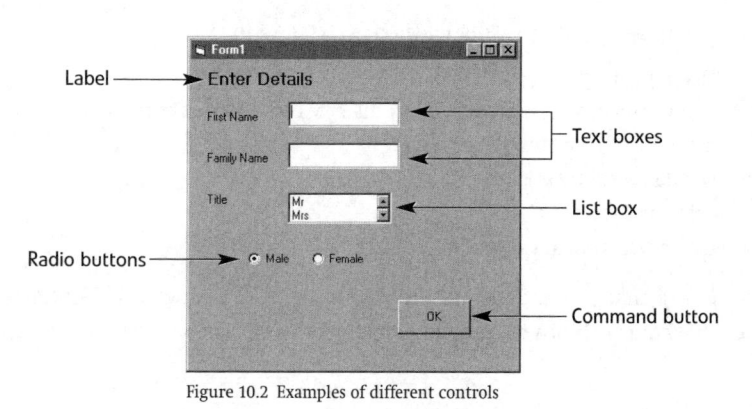

Figure 10.2 Examples of different controls

370

BTEC National Study Guide: IT Practitioners. See page 293 for order details of individual texts

198

In designing the layout of these controls, you could use graphic software, but it is simpler to sketch it by hand on a piece of paper, and to refer to this when placing the controls on-screen.

The way that the input data should be processed also needs designing. There are number of different techniques available for designing data processing, some of which were covered in Units 4 and 6:

- dataflow diagrams
- structure diagrams
- flow charts
- pseudo code.

Grouping controls logically

When designing the user interface, it is important to remember that the layout needs to be clear and logical for the user.

- Make sure that the layout is neat and consistent.
- Identify controls that are related to each other (e.g. title, first name and surname) and group these together, perhaps surrounding them by a box to focus the user's attention.
- Include labels to identify what the various controls are for. For many controls, you might have one label per control; where controls are related, a single label may serve the whole group, e.g. title/first name/surname may be given the label 'Customer name'.

Headers and footers

dates. Page numbers should be included for reports of more than one page, and headings may need to be repeated.

- When filtering and/or sorting data, it should be clear which field has been used for sorting purposes, e.g. in the column headings of a table or as part of the title of a screen.

Commercial standards

When creating a system for a particular organisation, appropriate commercial standards will need to be met, such as:

- company colour schemes
- use of particular logos and the positioning of these.

Further research 10.1

1 Identify five different organisations, who have a recognised company brand/image, such as a car manufacturer (e.g. Ford), a charity (e.g. The Prince's Trust), a sportswear company (e.g. Nike), a corporation (e.g. the BBC) and a service company (e.g. your local accountant or solicitor).
2 Working with others, collect material that shows the corporate image of each of these organisations. You could visit websites or collect hard copy examples such as brochures, business cards and business letters.
3 Identify how these organisations use graphics to convey a company image.

371

BTEC National Study Guide: IT Practitioners. See page 293 for order details of individual texts

199

Case study: Cellphone World

More detail can now be added to the plan shown in Figure 10.1. For each of the forms, a separate Excel worksheet is needed.

■ To display the opening screen, a worksheet can be displayed with a title and a button attached to a macro which takes the user to the next sheet (Figure 10.3).

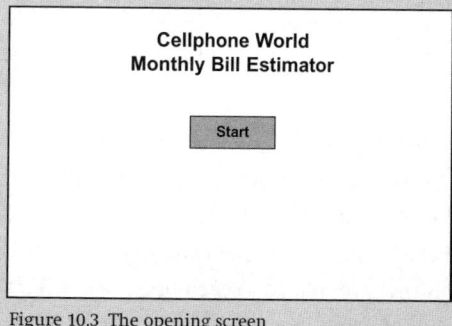

Figure 10.3 The opening screen

■ For the next step, to select which service company is to be used, another worksheet is needed with buttons to allow the user to select the service company (Figure 10.4). These buttons need to be attached to macros that set the charges for the particular network chosen.

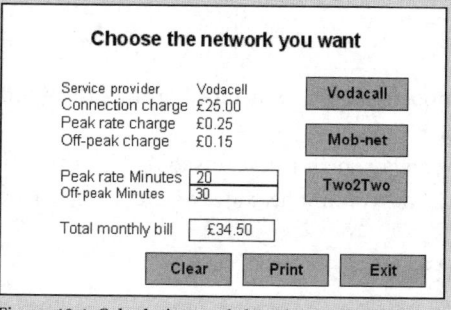

Figure 10.4 Calculation worksheet layout

■ The same worksheet is used to enter the number of minutes at peak and cheap rates. It needs to display an input box to allow the user to enter the number of minutes of use at peak and then at cheap rates. Validation is needed to make sure the user enters only a numeric value (i.e. not text).

■ Buttons will be needed on the calculation worksheet to allow the user to select the service provider and then display the total estimated bill.

■ Printing a record of the calculation will involve transferring the data from the main worksheet on to a separate worksheet laid out for printing and **Exit options** must offer the user the choice of redoing the calculation, perhaps for a different service, or with different numbers of minutes usage, or to exit to the initial screen, ready to do a calculation for a different customer.

1 Check that you know how to place labels and text boxes on a worksheet.
2 Sketch a layout for the printing sheet.

BTEC National Study Guide: IT Practitioners. See page 293 for order details of individual texts

200

Note that the Cellphone World case study presents the user with a series of screens in a predefined sequence; it produces results from calculations on values input by the sales assistant. To achieve this, the programming will involve setting up a number of worksheets (forms), adding controls (titles, boxes), incorporating validation of data that is input, writing macros to perform calculations and printing out the results. This is just one example of enhancing applications software to meet a user's needs. The next case study gives another example, involving interrogation of a table of data via the filter function.

Case study: Car-Call

Car-Call are an agency who match up people who want to buy sports cars with dealers. They use a Microsoft Excel spreadsheet (Figure 10.5) to store details of the cars that are for sale. They need to provide an easy way for their telesales people to find the car that matches the customer's requirements.

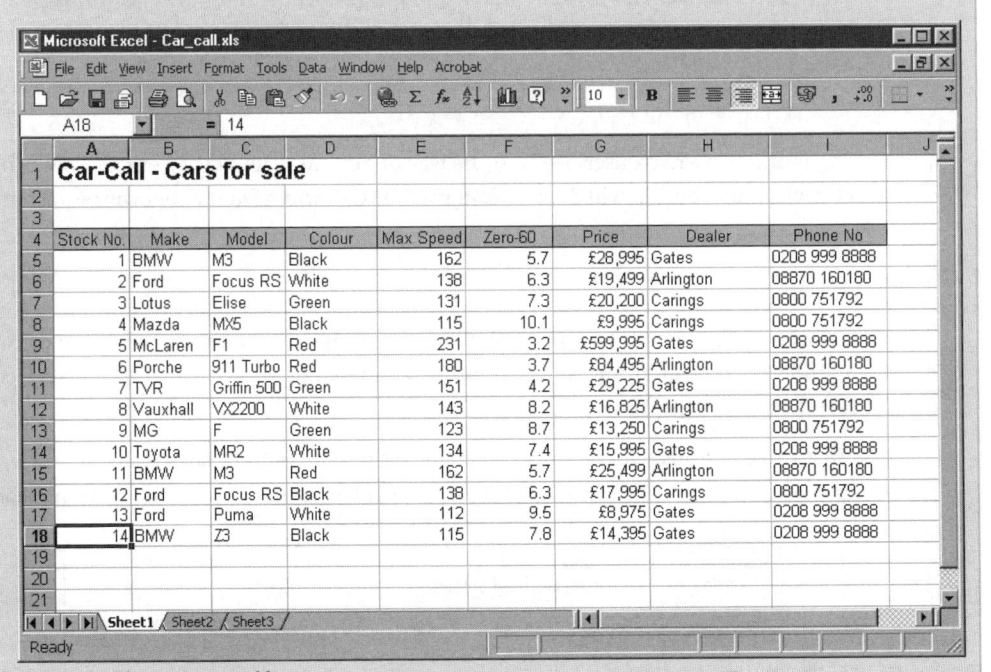

Figure 10.5 The sports cars table

The telesales people would like buttons on the form to carry out certain functions:

- A button is needed to filter the display of cars so only those of a certain make are shown (e.g. Ford). This should be combined with a text box where they can type in the make they want, and another button to remove the filter, displaying all the records again.
- A button is needed to sort the list of cars displayed by price, showing the lowest priced car first.
- A button is needed to print out the current list of cars on a customised form.

Figure 10.6 shows a suggested design for the layout of these buttons and the text box needed to enter the make of car.

373

BTEC National Study Guide: IT Practitioners. See page 293 for order details of individual texts

201

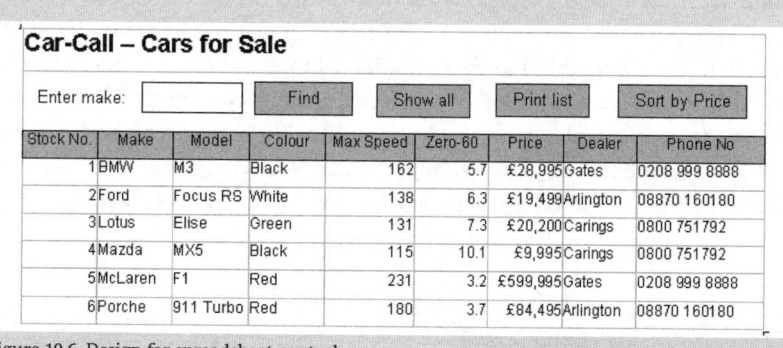

Figure 10.6 Design for spreadsheet controls

1 With others, discuss your short list of possible users, and consider what functions could be automated in a similar way.

2 Review your sketch plans for systems that you might develop and choose one to concentrate on. For this system, sketch a more detailed plan of the objects involved and how they might be linked. Identify buttons that you would need, and how the user would navigate through the system.

Having found out what a user needs in the way of buttons, you, as the designer, need to decide exactly what each button will do. For example, Car-Call will need the following four buttons:

■ a 'Sort by price' button to sort the data in ascending order (lowest first) on the price field

■ a 'Print list' button to copy the current list to a separate sheet, formatted with appropriate labels, as shown in Figure 10.7.

The first three buttons require functions (apply filter, remove filter, sort) which are all available using the auto-filter facility within Excel, but which will need to be automated using macros.

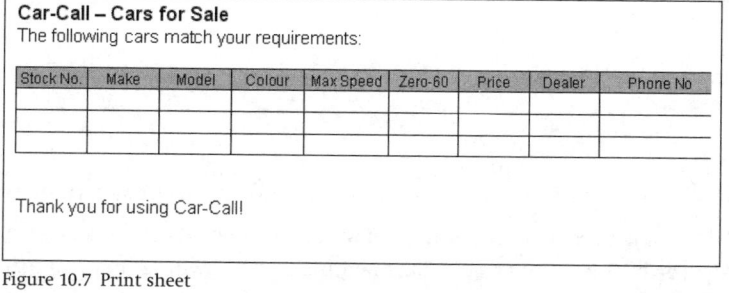

Figure 10.7 Print sheet

374

BTEC National Study Guide: IT Practitioners. See page 293 for order details of individual texts

202

Start up

Consideration also needs to be given to how the application will appear to the user when it is first started and how access will be given to the various options and facilities within the application. To a certain extent, this will depend of the type of application. Some applications may follow a logical flow through a series of forms; others may present the user with a series of options at the outset, presented using a **switchboard** type form.

? What does it mean?

A **switchboard** is an opening screen from which all other screens/forms are accessed.

Special spreadsheet macros can be created which automatically run when the spreadsheet file is opened, so these can be used to set up toolbars or menus. This approach is explained in detail on page 395. When an Excel spreadsheet is opened, the first worksheet is always displayed, so if an opening menu is to be displayed as in the Cellphone World case study, then this menu needs to be placed on the first worksheet.

Assessment activity 10.1

Create a plan and design for the application you will develop. Include a state diagram and sketches for the forms the application will use, and include details of how the application will start up.

10.2 Customising data processing

Having designed the application, the next step is to create it, using the design as a guide. This section looks at creating some simple applications that concentrate on automating the processing of data. Before beginning to write some spreadsheet applications, we must first look at some basic concepts of spreadsheets.

Spreadsheets

A spreadsheet presents the user with a worksheet made up of rows and columns (Figure 10.8). **Columns** are named letters of the alphabet and **rows** are numbered. The box where a row and column meet is called a **cell** and the **cell reference** or address is made up of its column letter and row number.

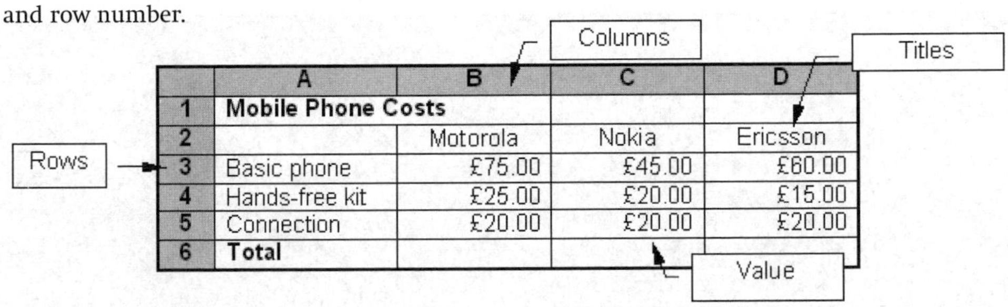

	A	B	C	D
1	Mobile Phone Costs			
2		Motorola	Nokia	Ericsson
3	Basic phone	£75.00	£45.00	£60.00
4	Hands-free kit	£25.00	£20.00	£15.00
5	Connection	£20.00	£20.00	£20.00
6	Total			

Figure 10.8 Spreadsheet basics: mobile phone costs

375

BTEC National Study Guide: IT Practitioners. See page 293 for order details of individual texts

203

Each cell in a worksheet can be empty, or can contain one of three things:

1 **Text**: Sometimes called row or column titles or labels, these are used to help the spreadsheet user to understand what the numeric data in the spreadsheet shows and how to use the spreadsheet. In Figure 10.8, cell A1 contains a main title, cells A3, A4, A5, A6 contain row titles, and cells B2, C2 and D2 contain column titles.

2 **Numbers**: Sometimes called **values**, these can be formatted in a number of ways. For example, a number can be displayed in **currency format** (as shown columns B–D in Figure 10.8). Another example would be a **percentage format**. The value 0.12 formatted as percentage would be displayed as 12%.

3 **Formulas**: Formulas are the real power of a spreadsheet. They allow calculations not only of a fixed value but by reference to a cell address. For example =B2+B3 will add together the values found in cell addresses B2 and B3.

✓ Check your understanding 10.3

1 Columns are labelled A to Z. What happens after 26 columns, i.e. when there are no more letters of the alphabet left? What is the maximum number of rows and columns on the spreadsheet you are using?

2 Find out what other formats are available for numbers on your spreadsheet. Hint: You will probably find these listed in the help facility.

3 Cellphone World need simple spreadsheet as shown in Figure 10.8 to calculate the total

    b To calculate the total cost of a Motorola phone, enter a formula into cell B6 to add together the contents of the cells, B3, B4 and B5. What formula did you put into cell B6?

B3+B4+B5 gives the correct result to question 3b (above), but an alternative spreadsheet facility, called a **function** could be used. The SUM function adds up all the values between two cells, so =SUM(B3:B5) has the same effect as =B3+B4+B5.

To total the costs of the other phones, another important spreadsheet facility is needed: copying formulas. Rather than entering another formula in C6 and yet another in D6, the existing formula could be copied and pasted.

✓ Check your understanding 10.4

The formula entered in cell B6 should be =SUM(B3:B5).

1 Copy this to cells C6 and D6.

2 Inspect the formula in C6 and check how it has changed. Copying across a column (from column B to column C) changes the columns in the cell addresses so, in cell C6, the formula should now read =SUM(C3:C5). When copied into D6 the formula should read =SUM(D3:D5).

3 Check that your spreadsheet totals match those in Figure 10.8.

376

BTEC National Study Guide: IT Practitioners. See page 293 for order details of individual texts

204

The way the cell addresses change when the formula is copied is called relative referencing (or **relative addressing**), because the address changes relative to where it is copied. Note that if you copy a formula down the rows rather than across the columns then the row number will change rather than the column letter. There are circumstances when you will not want this to happen. For example, when calculating the VAT that is to be added to the total cost of the phone, this depends on a fixed rate (currently 17.5%).

	A	B	C	D	E
1	**Mobile Phone Costs**				
2		Motorola	Nokia	Ericsson	VAT rate
3	Basic phone	£75.00	£45.00	£60.00	17.5%
4	Hands-free kit	£25.00	£20.00	£15.00	
5	Connection	£20.00	£20.00	£20.00	
6	**Total**	**£120.00**	**£85.00**	**£95.00**	
7	VAT				
8	**Grand Total**				

Figure 10.9 VAT rate

The formula needed in B7 to calculate the VAT is =B6*E3 (the total cost for the Motorola phone multiplied by the VAT rate). However, if you copy this formula to C6, it would change (due to relative addressing) to =C6*F3. The C6 is fine, that is the total cost of the of the Nokia phone, but F3 does not contain the VAT rate. In this situation, where the VAT is stored in a fixed cell, you need to turn off the relative referencing effect on the E3 cell address. The $ sign can be used to turn off relative addressing, so that **absolute referencing** can be used instead.

✓
1   Enter the text shown in rows 7 and 8 and column E on Figure 10.9.
2   In B7 enter the formula =B6*$E$3.
3   Copy B7 across to C7 and D7.
4   Check the contents of C7 (should be =C6*$E$3) and D7 (D6*$E$3).

In some circumstances, when you copy a formula, you may want the column address to change (relative referencing), but the row address to be fixed (absolute referencing) or vice versa. In these cases the $ sign is placed in front of the part of the address (column letter or row number) that is to be fixed. So for example when the formula =B5+E$8 is copied, relative referencing will effect all parts of the formula except the row number 8, which is fixed by the $ preceding it. This is known as **mixed referencing**.

Creating applications

The way an application is created depends very much on the program being used. This unit looks at creating applications in spreadsheets using Microsoft Excel. If you decide to create an application in Word, Access or PowerPoint, you will need to check what options are open to you by way of programming tools.

One way of creating a customised application within Excel is to record macros, and then to refine and add to them by editing them like normal programs. Recording a macro involves switching on

377

BTEC National Study Guide: IT Practitioners. See page 293 for order details of individual texts

205

a facility called a **macro recorder**. Then you carry out the actions you want to record (e.g. select cells, choose menu options) and the macro recorder records whatever you do. Once you switch off the macro recorder, you can then replay your recorded actions whenever you want. You need to make sure that you understand the design of the macro and practise the actions you want to record before you actually record it. If you don't do this, you may well end up recording mistakes in your macro; this will mean you have to record it again or edit out the mistakes.

Having recorded a macro, you can then create a button or a shortcut key to make it easy for the spreadsheet user to run the macro. The case study below looks at a simplified version of the spreadsheet application designed earlier. Later, the complete application will be created, but first we need to understand the basics of recording and editing macros.

Case study: Cellphone World

Cellphone World have created a spreadsheet to calculate customers' monthly bills on the different networks (Figure 10.10).

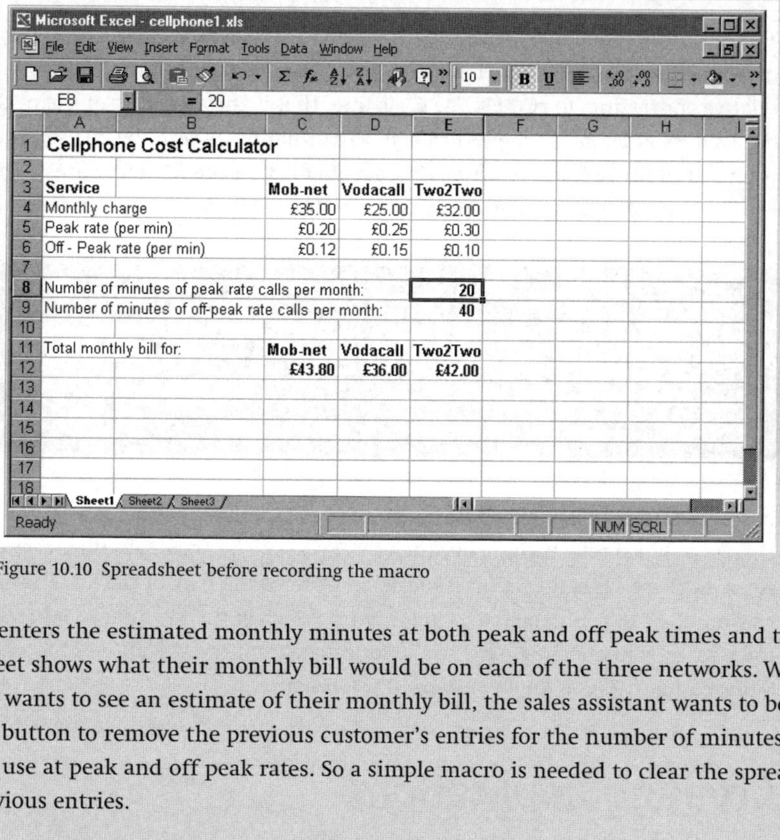

Figure 10.10 Spreadsheet before recording the macro

The user enters the estimated monthly minutes at both peak and off peak times and the spreadsheet shows what their monthly bill would be on each of the three networks. When a customer wants to see an estimate of their monthly bill, the sales assistant wants to be able to click a button to remove the previous customer's entries for the number of minutes they expect to use at peak and off peak rates. So a simple macro is needed to clear the spreadsheet of its previous entries.

1 Make sure your spreadsheet looks like Figure 10.10.
2 Prepare to record a macro:
   - Go to the Tools menu and select the Macro option.
   - A sub menu will pop out and you need to choose the Record New Macro option. You will see a dialogue box asking you for the name of the new macro.
   - Type the name clear_entries into the box.

378

BTEC National Study Guide: IT Practitioners. See page 293 for order details of individual texts

206

3 From now on whatever you do will be recorded in the macro, so be careful to do only the things you want in it:
- Click on Cell E8 (which contains the number of minutes of calls at peak rate) and press the delete key to remove the entry.
- Click on cell E9 and press delete again to remove then entry in that cell.
- Choose the Tools menu again, select the Macro option and from the sub-menu, choose Stop Recording (or click the stop recording button in the macro toolbar, which appears when you start recording a macro).

4 Test the macro by pretending to be a sales assistant at Cellphone World. A customer asks for an estimate of his/her bill, so enter the number of minutes they think they will use at peak time and the number at cheap rate. Then, another customer asks for an estimate. To clear the previous entries, use the macro.

At the moment, to run this macro you need to go the Tools menu, select the Macro option then the Macros sub-option, click on the macro name in the box that appears and then click the Run button. The macro should, if it has been recorded properly, remove the previous entries. At the moment, to run the macro takes more key strokes than deleting the entries yourself! To make the macro easy to run, a button to run the macro is needed or shortcut key must be set up (see page 391).

Further research 10.2

Excel macros are written in a programming language called **Visual Basic for Applications (VBA)**, which is a version of Visual Basic, so as well as recording the macros, you can edit and add to the Visual Basic code yourself. The code for the macro is placed in a procedure, which starts with the word 'Sub' and the name of the procedure (Clear_entries) and an empty set of brackets (indicating that no parameters are passed to the procedure when it starts). The procedure ends with the 'End Sub' statement. Each macro you record is placed in a separate procedure (see Figure 10.12).

Having created the basic macros for an application, they now need to be made easy to run. There are two simple ways to do this:
- by adding a **button** (see page 393)
- by incorporating a **shortcut key** (see page 391)

A button requires a single click of the mouse, but while it is user friendly it does take up space on the screen. A shortcut key is particularly helpful when the spreadsheet operator may be already using the keyboard when they want to run the macro, as they could then run the macro directly from the keyboard rather than having to use the mouse. It requires the user to remember the shortcut key, but also frees up space on the screen.

379

✓ Check your understanding 10.6

1 Look at the code created by the macro recorder for the macro: Select the Tools menu, the Macro option and Macros sub-option and the Macros dialogue box (Figure 10.11) will appear:

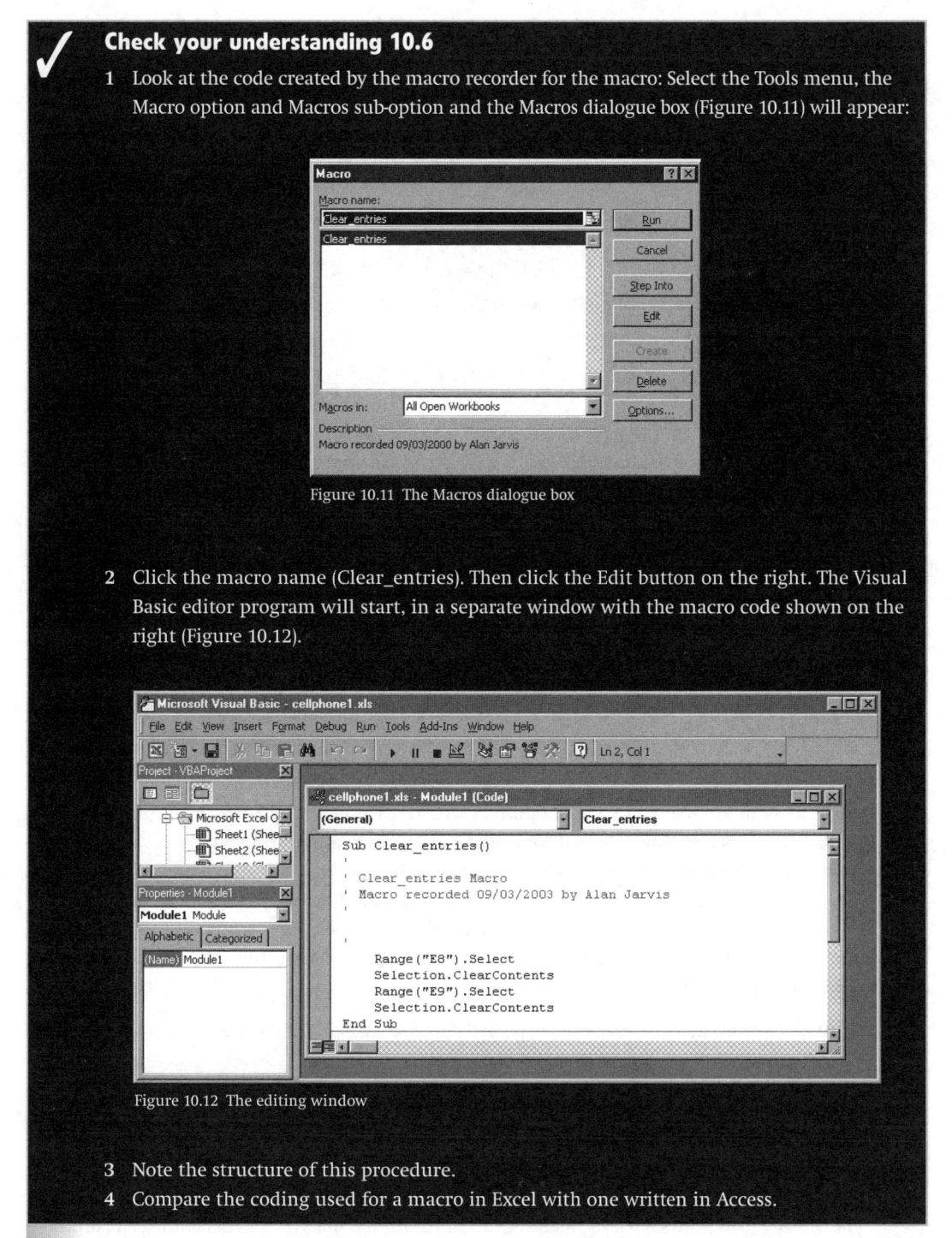

Figure 10.11 The Macros dialogue box

2 Click the macro name (Clear_entries). Then click the Edit button on the right. The Visual Basic editor program will start, in a separate window with the macro code shown on the right (Figure 10.12).

Figure 10.12 The editing window

3 Note the structure of this procedure.
4 Compare the coding used for a macro in Excel with one written in Access.

To create your application, you will need to set up tables and forms (in Access), or worksheets (in Excel), or screens (in PowerPoint), or documents and maybe other formats of material, or templates (in Word). You will need to customise reports and any other outputs that are to come from your system.

380

Once you have created your application, you will need to check your application against the design criteria:

■ Does the application provide all the features required by the user?
■ Do all your controls function as required? You will need to test every button and every short cut to make sure these work as expected.
■ Does your application accept input as expected, and reject invalid data?
■ Does your application produce the expected results?

✓ **Check your understanding 10.7**

Refer back to your design documentation. Check that you have specified exactly what your user requires, so that, when the time comes to evaluate it, you have criteria against which to judge the success, or otherwise, of your finished product.

Adding controls

Controls are used for input and output. For input, there are several options; **buttons**, **text boxes**, **radio buttons**, **list/combo boxes** or **text labels** (Figure 10.2). Similarly, for output there are a variety of controls.

Further research 10.3

2 Investigate the output control options available in Microsoft Access reports.

Adding a button

To add a button to run a macro, the Forms toolbar must be shown on the screen. If the toolbar is not displayed, you can display it by choosing the Toolbars option from the View menu. Once the correct toolbar is displayed, follow these steps:

■ Click on the Create button button.
■ Move to the place on the spreadsheet where the button is required and drag out the button shape.
■ Release the mouse and the button will have been created.
■ A dialogue box will appear asking which macro the button is to run.
■ Click on the clear_entries macro; then click OK.
■ Change the name on the button by clicking inside it and removing the existing name (Button 1) and typing the name 'Clear Entries'.

Every time the button is clicked the macro will run.

✓ **Check your understanding 10.8**

1 Set up a button as described above and compare it to the completed spreadsheet shown in Figure 10.13.
2 Test that the button works.

381

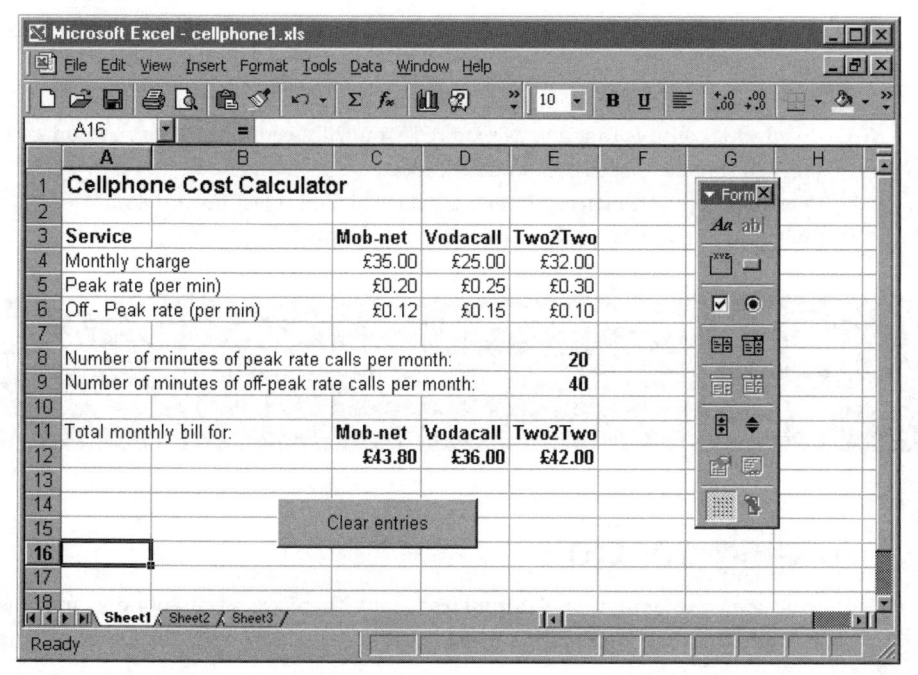

Figure 10.13 Spreadsheet with macro button

Editing a macro

382

BTEC National Study Guide: IT Practitioners. See page 293 for order details of individual texts

210

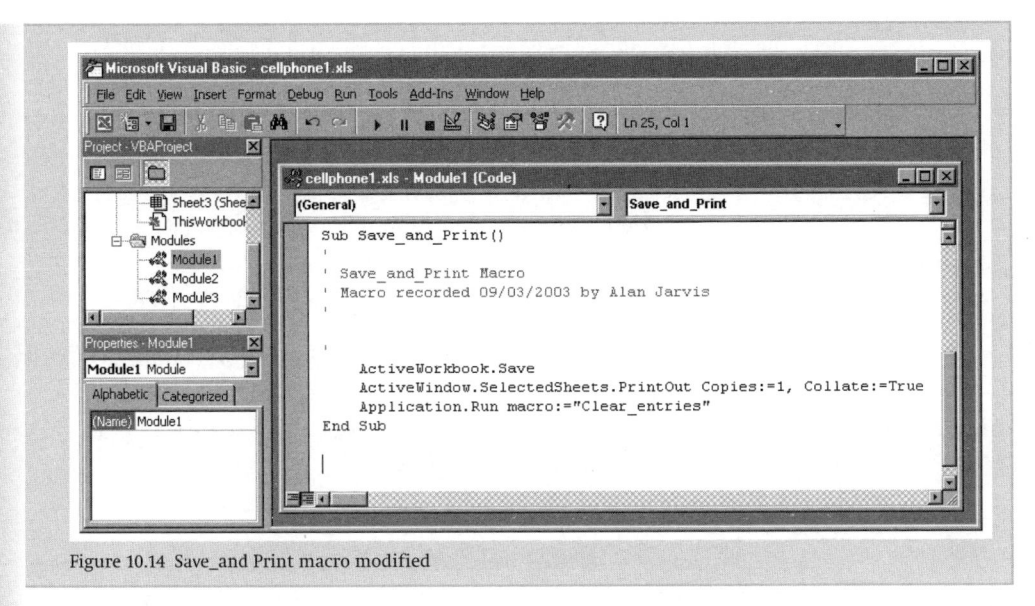

Figure 10.14 Save_and Print macro modified

Using an autofilter

The next case study demonstrates how relevant data within a spreadsheet can be extracted.

Case study: Car–Call

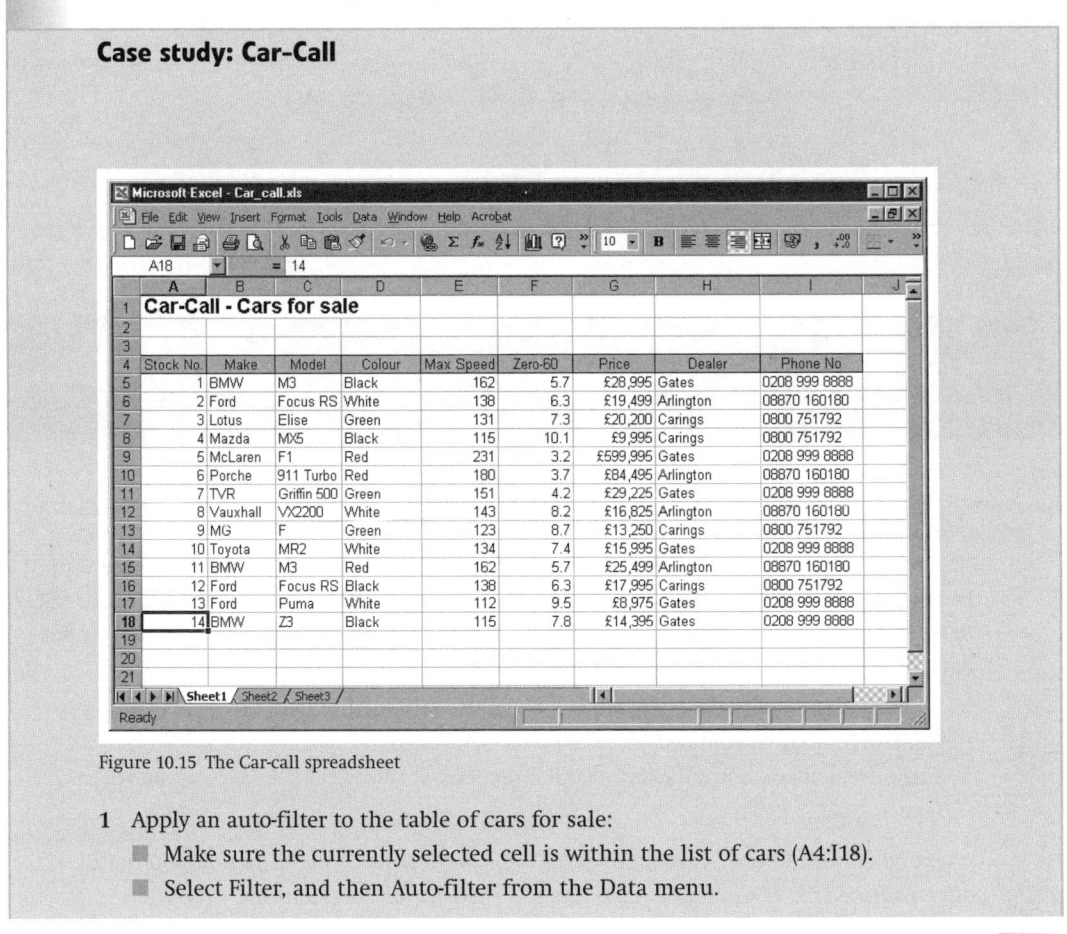

Figure 10.15 The Car-call spreadsheet

1 Apply an auto-filter to the table of cars for sale:
   ▪ Make sure the currently selected cell is within the list of cars (A4:I18).
   ▪ Select Filter, and then Auto-filter from the Data menu.

383

BTEC National Study Guide: IT Practitioners. See page 293 for order details of individual texts

211

■ Check that this has added drop down arrows to the field names at the top of the table of data.

2 Now create the macro for the Find button. This will allow the telesales people to enter the make of car, click a button and see a filtered list of cars with only those of the make they entered showing. Initially, record a simplified macro:

■ Go to the Macro option in the Tools menu and select the Record Macro option from the fly out menu.

■ Enter the macro name as find_make in the dialogue that appears, then click OK to start the macro recorder.

■ Click on the drop-down arrow in the Make field name (B4) and choose (Custom...) from the list that appears. The dialogue shown in Figure 10.16 will then be seen.

■ Enter the name Ford, and click OK. Only Ford cars will now be shown in the list. The word Ford is used as a **parameter** for the filter.

■ Stop the macro recorder.

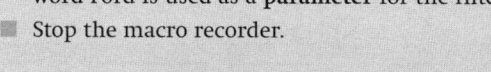

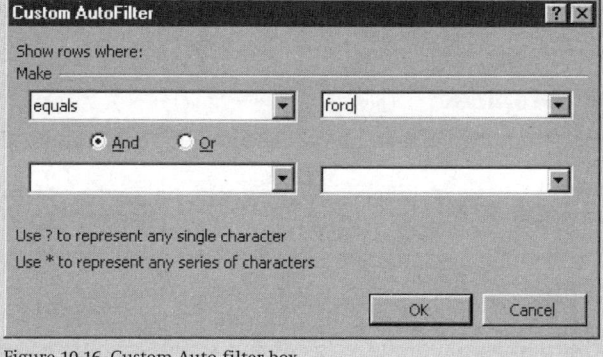

Figure 10.16 Custom Auto filter box

What does it mean?

A **parameter** is a value that is input to a procedure or function that controls how the procedure or function works.

Adding a text box

The macro as it is now will only show Ford cars, but suppose that the telesales people want to be able to list all cars of any given make of car. Adding a text box would allow the make of car to be entered and you would then need to modify the macro just recorded to use this input data. To add a text box, follow these steps:

■ To display the Control toolbox toolbar, go to the View menu, select Toolbars, and the Control toolbox sub-option.

■ Click the text box button and drag out a text box at the top of the sheet, as shown in Figure 10.17.

A text box gives the user freedom to enter whatever text he or she wishes. An alternative is to offer a limited list of options using either a combo box or radio buttons.

384

BTEC National Study Guide: IT Practitioners. See page 293 for order details of individual texts

212

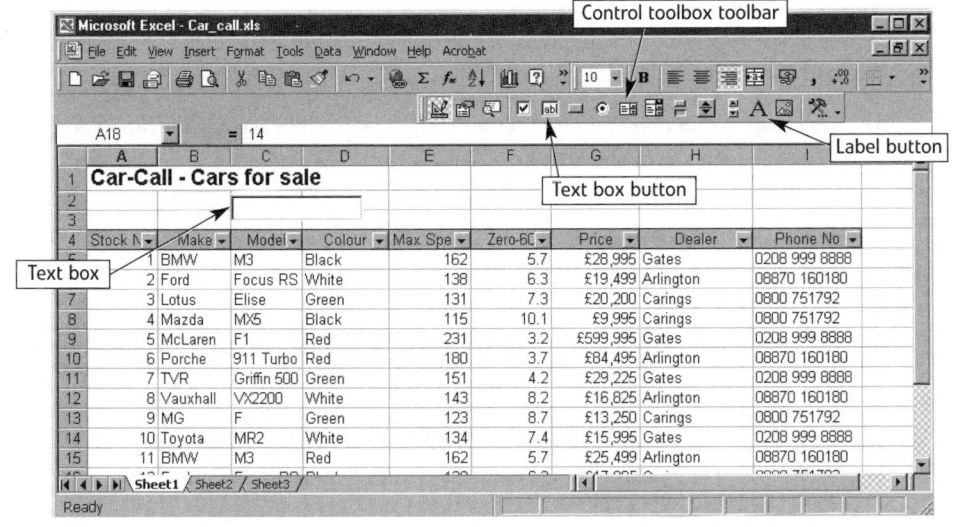

Figure 10.17 The Control toolbox

Further research 10.4

1 Find out how to add radio buttons. Make notes so that you could explain it to someone else.
2 Find out how to create a combo box. Consider how a combo box might suit the needs of your user.

Any text box should have a label so that the user knows what to put in the text box. You can use the Label button in the same was at the Text box button to create an area on the form where the label will appear. Modifying the text in the label is done through the label's properties. To do this, display the Properties window by clicking the Properties button in the Control toolbox (Figure 10.18).

Figure 10.18 Properties window

385

BTEC National Study Guide: IT Practitioners. See page 293 for order details of individual texts

213

The Caption property controls the text displayed in a label. Change its value from 'Label1' to 'Enter make'. Then to activate the controls so they can be used, click the design button to turn off design mode.

Having created a text box named Textbox1, the macro recorded earlier can be modified so it takes the car make from this text box, as follows:

■ Go to the Tools menu, select Macro, and then the Macros sub-option.
■ Click on the find_make macro, and click the Edit button. This will open the Visual Basic editing window, as shown in Figure 10.19.

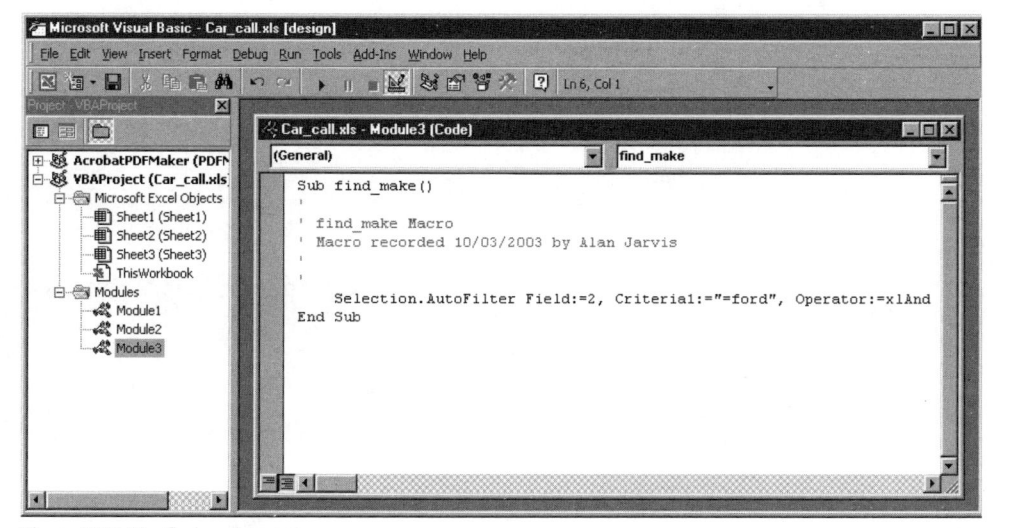

Figure 10.19 The find_make macro

■ The parameter Criteria1:="=ford" must be replaced with the value in Textbox1. This is achieved by placing the value in Textbox1 into a variable (called make), adding an equals sign to it and then using it as the parameter for the autofilter. The modified code is shown in Figure 10.20.

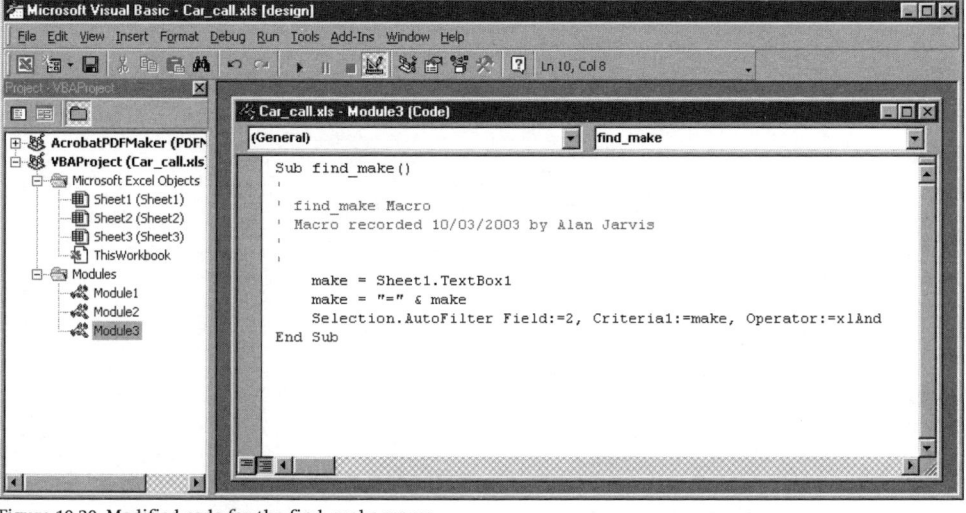

Figure 10.20 Modified code for the find_make macro

386

? **What does it mean?**

A **variable** is like a box allocated to store something in.

■ Finally a button to run the macro is needed and then the edited macro can be tested. To add a macro button, display the Forms toolbar, go to the View menu, choose the Toolbar option and Forms sub-option. Click the **Button** button and drag out a button on the sheet. Select the find_make macro from the dialogue that appears and change the text on the button to read 'Find'.

If the name of a car make is now typed into the text box and the Find button is clicked, the list of cars will only display those made by the maker entered, as shown in Figure 10.21.

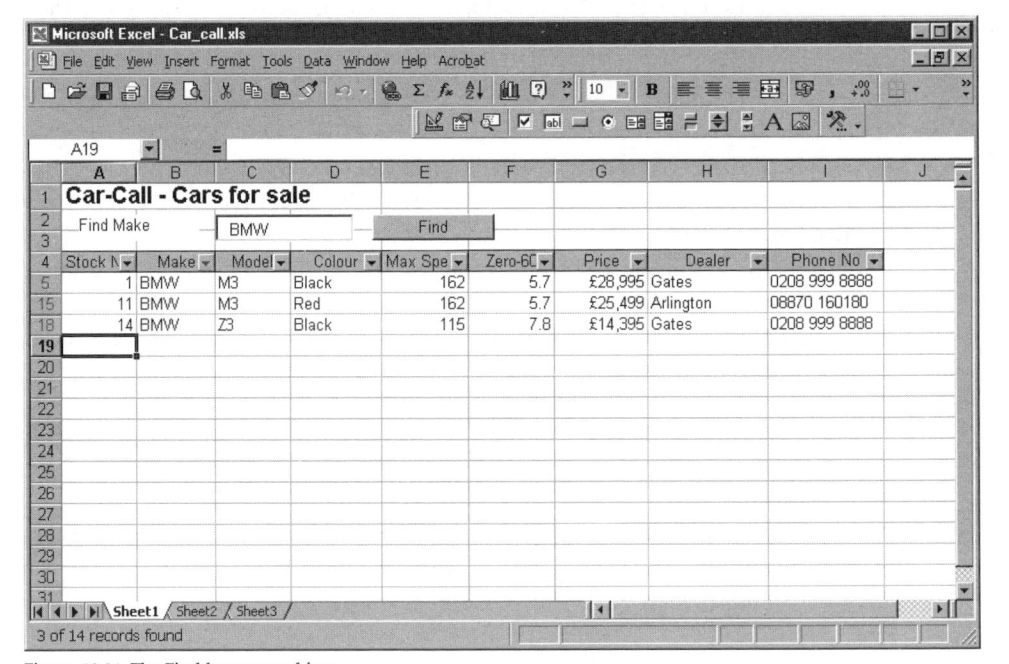

Figure 10.21 The Find button working

Entering text into the text box gives the user more flexibility in the output that can be expected. What would happen if the user entered text incorrectly, e.g. 'Frod' instead of 'Ford'? No matches would be found and the user would soon realise the mistake. You could include all the possible names within a combo box, so that this type of mistake could not happen.

✓ **Check your understanding 10.9**

1 Following the instructions given in the text above, create a text box and a label for it.
2 Modify the macro so that it uses the value entered in the text box.
3 Test the macro to make sure it works.

Further research 10.5

Extend the application to confine the user's entries to selection of an item from a combo box list.

387

BTEC National Study Guide: IT Practitioners. See page 293 for order details of individual texts

215

Three more buttons are needed for your spreadsheet application:

■ the Show all button, needed to remove the filter and display the complete list of cars again.
■ the Sort button
■ the Print button.

For the Show all button, create the macro by recording; there is no need to edit the code.

■ Turn on the macro recorder as before, calling this new macro show_all.
■ Click on the drop down arrow above the make column (if the Find button has previously been used, it will be blue indicating that this column has a filter applied).
■ Select (all) from the list.
■ Stop the macro recorder.
■ Create a button using the Forms toolbar (not the Control toolbar), and assign the show_all macro to it.

The macro for the Sort button is also simple to record:

■ Turn on the macro recorder.
■ Click in the price column (anywhere in the range G5:G18 will do).
■ Select the Data menu and the Sort option. This will display the sort dialogue box, with the Price field selected.
■ Click the OK button on the sort dialogue box and the list will be sorted by price.
■ Stop the macro recorder.
■ Create a button, attach the macro just recorded to the button and change its label to say 'Sort by price'.

Numeric input

When an input is numeric, it is important that it is valid. Input of incorrect data could produce silly results. For example, if the user types 'thirty' instead of '30', the calculation will not work. So some validation is necessary: input from the user needs first to be accepted and then to be validated.

To investigate how to validate numeric entries, we will use the Cellphone World spreadsheet (Figure 10.13) and record and modify a macro to validate the number of minutes used at peak rate (cell E8).

To create a more complex macro, it makes sense first to record a simple version of it, and then to edit the Visual BASIC code to refine the macro. In this example, the end result of the macro will be to insert a number in cell E8, representing the number of peak rate minutes. To start with, record a macro that does just that, insert a number in cell E8:

■ Make sure the cell pointer is not in E8.
■ Start the macro recorder, calling the macro set_peak.
■ Move to cell E8 and type in a value (any value will do).

BTEC National Study Guide: IT Practitioners. See page 293 for order details of individual texts

216

■ Stop the recorder.
■ Click the Edit button on the Macro dialogue box to start the Visual Basic editor to inspect your macro (Figure 10.22).

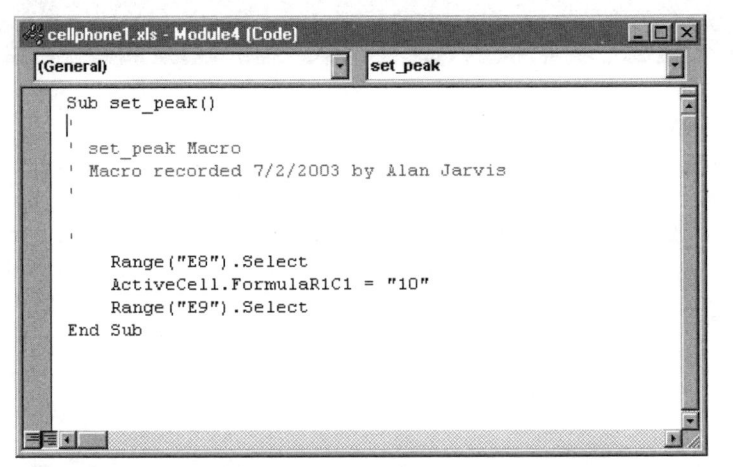

Figure 10.22 The set_peak macro

Using variables

At the moment, this macro will always place a fixed value (in this case 20) in E8. The user

The value stored in the variable will not be known until the macro is run, but the box (or variable) is given a name so that it can be referred to in the macro. The modified macro is shown in Figure 10.23. Notice that the name of the variable is peak_mins, and that an input box is used to collect the real value from the user. The contents of the variable are placed in the cell E8.

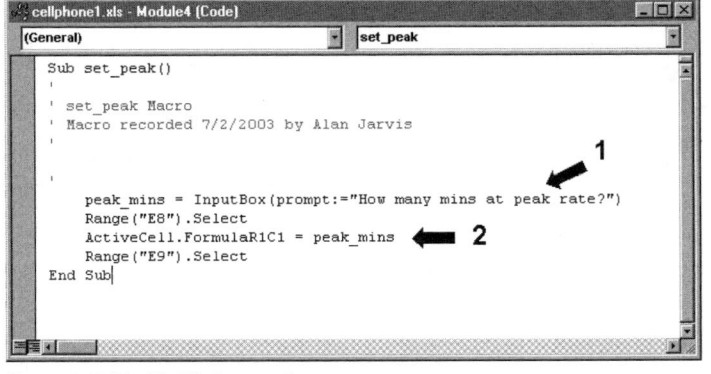

Figure 10.23 The Modified set_peak macro.

Notes:

1 This new line of code uses a variable called peak_mins. The contents of this variable are collected from an input box that appears on the screen with the message (prompt) "How many minutes at peak rate?".

2 In this modified line, rather than having the 'ActiveCell' (E8 here) set to 10, which was the value that was typed in when the macro was recorded, it is set to whatever is contained in the variable peak_mins.

389

BTEC National Study Guide: IT Practitioners. See page 293 for order details of individual texts

217

Validating data

The macro set_peak now allows data to be entered and correctly placed in cell E8. However, it does not validate the entry, so if you leave the input box empty or type text into it, it still accepts this and is happy to put text in E8, although this prevents the formula that calculates the total bill from working correctly and it displays an error. Any entries that are non numeric therefore need to be rejected.

To do this, you not only need to check if the entry made is numeric, you also need to send the macro around in a **loop**.

? What does it mean?

A loop is a type of programming construct known as repetition in which one or more statements are repeated, either a fixed number of times or until some condition is met.

numeric entry is made. The code needs to be modified as shown in Figure 10.24.

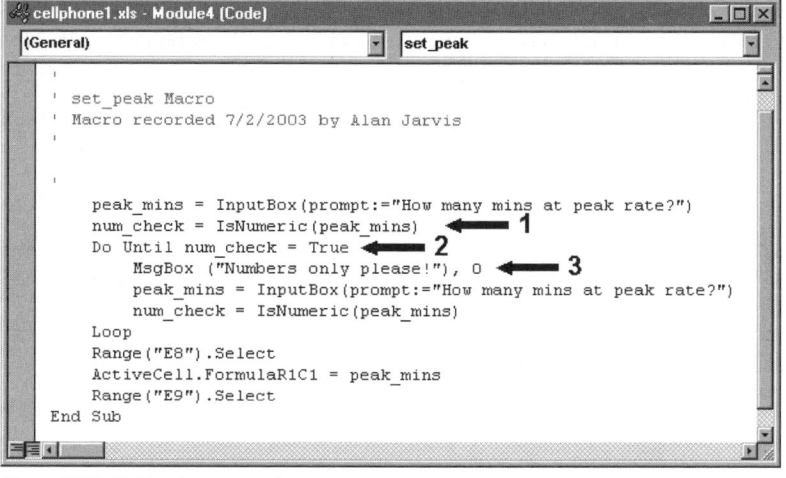

Figure 10.24 Testing for a numeric entry.

Notes:

1 This new line uses a new variable, num_check, which holds the result of testing peak_mins to see if it is numeric. This is done by a function called IsNumeric. If peak_mins is numeric it returns the value True, if is isn't it returns the value False.
2 This is the do until loop. Everything between the do until statement and the loop statement is repeated until num_check is true.
3 This statement displays a message box on the screen, showing the message in quotes. The 0 at the end indicates that the message box contains an OK button to remove it from the screen.

390

BTEC National Study Guide: IT Practitioners. See page 293 for order details of individual texts

218

✓ Check your understanding 10.11

1 Edit your macro to include the do until loop and check that it works. You should find that it will only accept a numeric value. Any other entry (including making no entry at all) results in the appearance of the message box demanding 'Numbers only please'.
2 Check what other looping instructions are available.

Creating a shortcut

Designing a system includes trying to make the system as user friendly as possible for the user, as well as offering the quickest way of achieving what they want to do.

■ Providing buttons attached to macros presents the user with a one-click option for tasks that you know he or she needs to do. The button should be labelled so that it is clear what effect clicking on the button will have.

■ Toolbars also offer a swift route to particular features. The user clicks on an **icon** and any highlighted text or cells or records can be affected, e.g. emboldened, italicised, right aligned and so on.

■ A shortcut is a combination of key depressions, usually involving the ctrl key and/or the alt key and/or the shift key together with a sequence of one or more of the standard QWERTY keys on a keyboard.

What does it mean?

The term 'shortcut' is also used to describe the use of an icon within a toolbar to represent an application. These may be created by the user to speed up the process of opening applications, although usually this involves a double click on the mouse. The same technique is used when icons are used to represent documents or other files; a double click acts as a short cut to opening that file. Here we concentrate on shortcuts involving combinations of key depressions.

Before the mouse was invented, the main shortcut keys were the function keys on a standard keyboard. These can be programmed in much the same ways as macros can be assigned to shortcut keys. Software used to be supplied with a cardboard or plastic strip that could be placed above the function keys and this would explain exactly what each function key could do, if pressed on its own, or with the shift key or with the ctrl key and so on. Much emphasis was placed on keyboarding skills which was fine for clerical staff who were touch typists, but it did not really suit the newer breed of user. Enter the mouse and icons that could be clicked on and the complete **WIMP** environment.

? What does it mean?

WIMP stands for windows, icon, mouse, pointer.

Suddenly everyone was learning how to click, double click, drag and drop. However, history seems to have come full circle, recognising that many users can work more quickly without the mouse! All Microsoft applications offer an extensive list of shortcuts; they have always been there. There are predefined shortcut keys for just about everything that you might do frequently. To discover the full list of shortcuts in Word, for example, including any that you have set up, follow these steps:

- On the Tools menu, point to Macro, and then click Macros.
- In the Macros in box, click Word commands.
- In the Macro name box, click ListCommands.
- Click Run.
- In the List Commands dialogue box, click Current menu and keyboard settings.
- On the File menu, click Print.

Different procedures are necessary in other Microsoft applications.

Further research 10.6

1 In a small group, brainstorm to create a list of shortcut keys that you already use.
2 Check the shortcut keys available in two or three Microsoft applications, and decide to use a few of them in place of the mouse.

To use a shortcut key for a macro in Excel, follow these steps:

- On the Tools menu, select the Macro option Macros sub-option.
- Select the macro that you want to create a shortcut for.
- When the dialogue box appears, choose the Options button.
- In the box marked Shortcut key, type in the key to be used. It will always be used in

✓ Check your understanding 10.12

1 Set up a shortcut key for a macro and test that it works. For example, for the Clear_entries macro, you could enter some values into the relevant cells, and then press the shortcut key combination that you chose and see what happens.
2 Check other Microsoft applications for details of how shortcuts can be created, e.g. for opening applications.

Assessment activity 10.2

Using the design that you created earlier, develop the application, using appropriate features. Include controls such as buttons and shortcuts as appropriate. Check your application against the design criteria.

10.3 Customising the user interface

This section looks at some more options for automating procedures, focusing particularly on the user interface, and considers customising toolbars and menus. So far, the macros created have been run using command buttons and shortcut keys. There are a number of other ways

392

BTEC National Study Guide: IT Practitioners. See page 293 for order details of individual texts

220

that macros can be run, allowing the user interface to be customised to suit different requirements. Two techniques are discussed:

■ adding buttons to the toolbar
■ creating menus.

Adding buttons to a toolbar

Excel has a wide range of toolbars, all of which can be customised by adding and removing standard buttons. Custom buttons can also be added to toolbars to run macros. This example shows how this is done using the first version of the mobile phone call cost calculator created earlier (see Figure 10.13 on page 382).

Suppose that, instead of having a button on the spreadsheet to clear the entries, the user would prefer a button in the standard tool bar. To set this up, follow these steps:

■ Go to the View menu and choose Toolbars.
■ Choose Customise from the bottom of the sub-menu in the dialogue that appears, as shown in Figure 10.25.

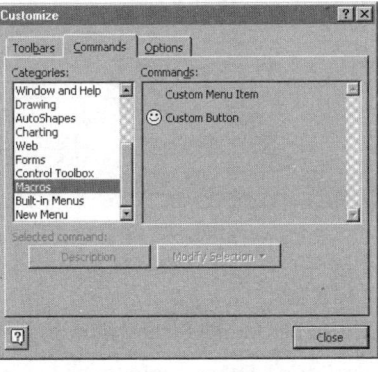

Figure 10.25 The Customise dialogue

■ In the Categories list box, scroll down and select Macros.
■ Click the custom button on the right side of the dialogue (the smiley face) and drag it into the desired place on the standard toolbar (see Figure 10.26).

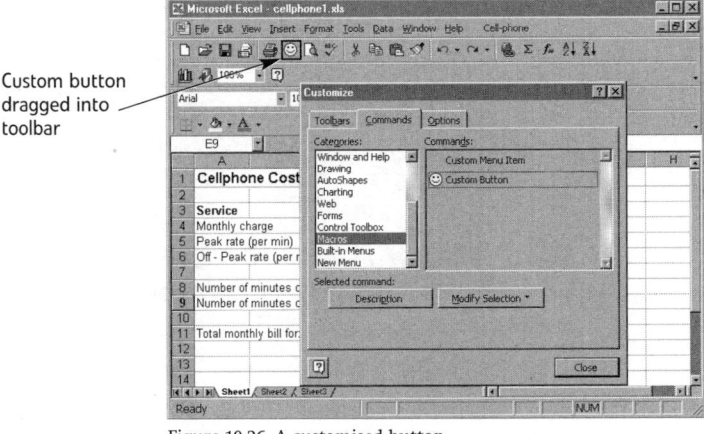

Figure 10.26 A customised button

393

BTEC National Study Guide: IT Practitioners. See page 293 for order details of individual texts

221

Customising a toolbar button

Once a button is in a toolbar, it can be customised and can be given a name, which will appear in the tool tip when the mouse is held over it. For our purposes, it also needs to have a macro assigned to it:

- Right-click on the button and the menu shown in Figure 10.27 will appear.
- Change the name to 'Clear Entries'.
- Click the Assign macro menu item at the bottom of the menu and select the clear_entries macro from the list that appears.

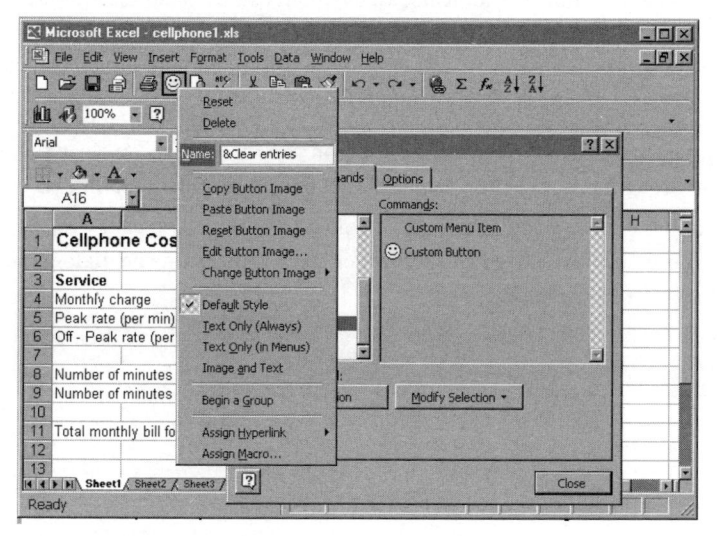

Editing a button image

The button image can also be changed if the smiley face is not appropriate:

- Click on the Change Button Image menu item. A submenu appears with other button images that can be chosen. If none of the button images are suitable then the existing image can be edited.
- Choose the Edit Button Image option from the right click menu. The Button Editor dialogue will appear, as shown in Figure 10.28.
- By selecting the colour required in the Colours area and clicking on the cells in the Picture, the icon can be altered to achieve the required effect.
- Click OK to complete editing the picture and update the icon image in the toolbar.

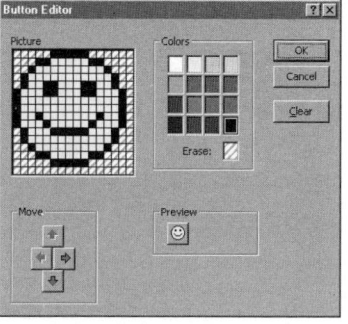

Figure 10.28 The Button Editor

BTEC National Study Guide: IT Practitioners. See page 293 for order details of individual texts

222

Creating a new toolbar

There is a problem with placing buttons like this in the standard toolbar. The button will now be there no matter what spreadsheet file you have open, yet the macro it is associated with only applies to the Cellphone spreadsheet. Running the macro in other spreadsheets may cause important data to be deleted. A better approach to attaching macros to toolbar buttons is to create a special toolbar for that particular spreadsheet. Remove the button from the standard toolbar, by returning to the Customise dialogue box (Commands tab) and dragging the button off the toolbar into the dialogue box. To create a special toolbar, follow these steps:

- From the Customise dialogue box, select the Toolbars tab.
- Click the New button.
- Give the new toolbar a name (e.g. custom1) and then click OK. A new, empty, toolbar will appear.
- Select the Commands tab on the Customise dialogue box, and then, as before, select macro from the list and drag the smiley face icon onto the new toolbar, see Figure 10.29.
- Use the icon's right click menu to change its name and to assign a macro as before.

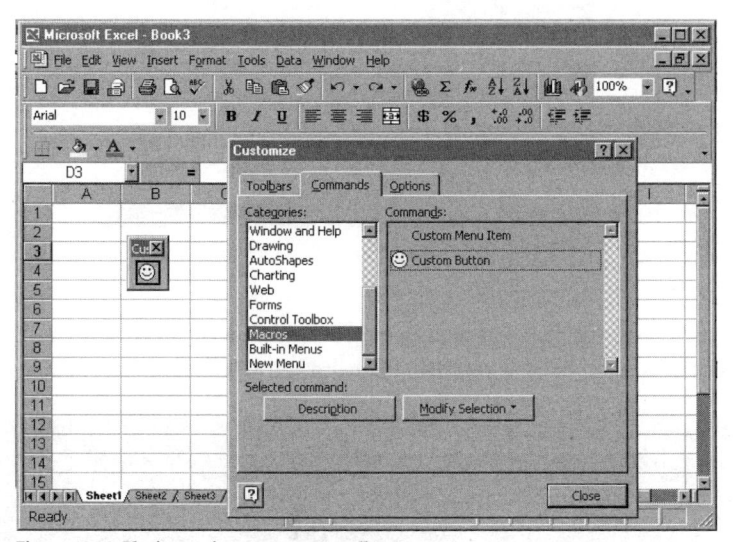

Figure 10.29 Placing an icon on a new toolbar

Assigning a toolbar to a particular spreadsheet

This toolbar still suffers from the same problem as we had before, i.e. once you display a toolbar, it stays on the screen regardless of the spreadsheet file you have open. What is needed is some way of displaying this toolbar when this spreadsheet file is opened, and hiding it when it is closed. To do this, two special macros need to created:

- A macro called auto_open will run automatically when the spreadsheet file in which it is saved opens.
- A macro called auto_close will run when the spreadsheet file is closed.

Recording the auto_close macro is easy:

- Start the macro recorder as before, calling the new macro auto_close.
- Click the close button (with the 'x' in it) on the new custom toolbar so it disappears, then stop the macro recorder.

BTEC National Study Guide: IT Practitioners. See page 293 for order details of individual texts

223

Recording the auto_open macro is almost as simple:

- Run the recorder again, calling this macro auto_open.
- Go to the View menu, and choose Toolbars.
- Select the name of the custom toolbar from the sub-menu (custom1), so the toolbar reappears.
- Stop the recorder.

The new macros can be tested by closing the current file (the custom toolbar should disappear), then opening the file again (the toolbar should re-appear). The code for these two macros in the Visual Basic editor is shown in Figure 10.30.

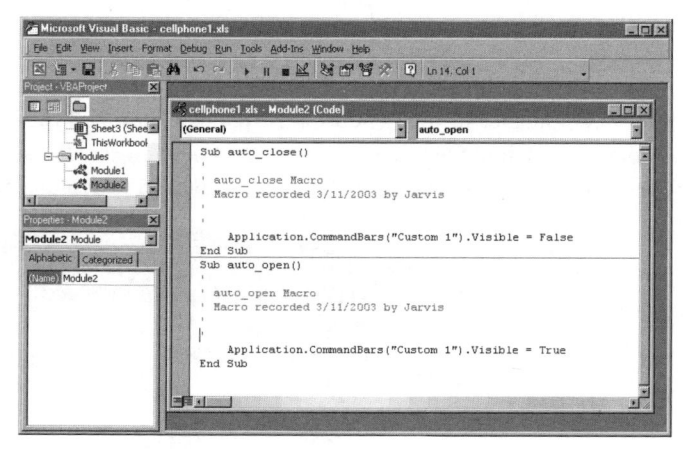

hiding toolbars. Also, because as many buttons as needed can be added to a custom toolbar, it can contain buttons for a number of macros as well as standard spreadsheet functions.

✓ Check your understanding 10.13

1 Add a button to an existing tool bar, and then remove it.
2 Customise a toolbar button and then edit the image.
3 Set up a new toolbar, add some buttons to it and assign it to a particular spreadsheet file by setting up the two macros: auto_open and auto_close. Then, test your toolbar.

It is often a good idea to provide users with some form of help. This should provide instructions on how to use the application and how to deal with common problems. The simplest way to provide a help facility is to add a button (or a toolbar shortcut) which will take the user to another worksheet where help instructions are provided, using a text box. Alternatively, you can add pop-up **comments** to individual cells using the Comment option under the Insert menu.

Creating menus

An alternative to using toolbar buttons to run the macros is to add a custom menu to the menu bar. To add a custom menu to the Cellphone cost calculator, follow these steps:

- Return to the Customise dialogue box, and select the Commands tab.
- In the Categories list, scroll to the bottom and select New Menu.

BTEC National Study Guide: IT Practitioners. See page 293 for order details of individual texts

224

■ Drag the word New menu from the Commands box on the right side of the dialogue box into the menu bar to the left of the Help menu.

■ Right click on the New menu in the menu bar and fill in a name for the menu, Cellphone (Figure 10.31).

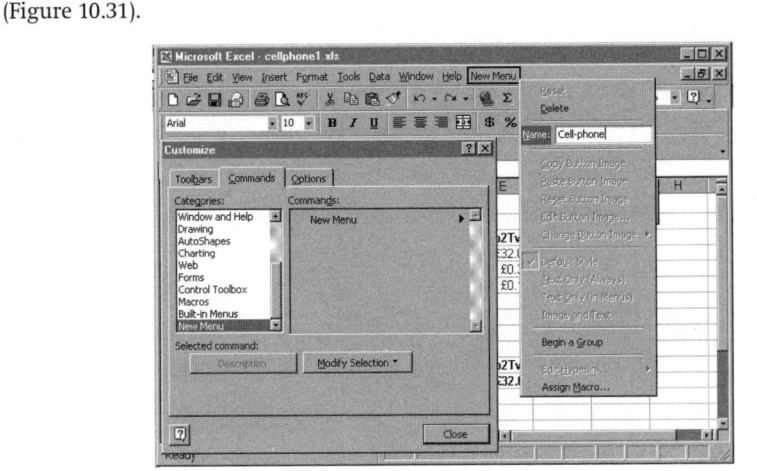

Figure 10.31 Adding a new menu

■ Select Macros in the Categories list on the left side of the Customise dialogue box.

■ Drag the words Custom Menu Item from the Commands box into the Cellphone menu in the menu bar, making sure it is dragged into the empty menu that pops down below the

■ Change the name of the menu item to Clear Entries.

■ Use the Assign macro option to assign the clear_entries macro to this item.

■ Close the Customise dialogue box.

A new Cellphone menu should now be displayed, with a single menu item, Clear entries. If this menu item is selected it will run the clear_entries macro (Figure 10.32).

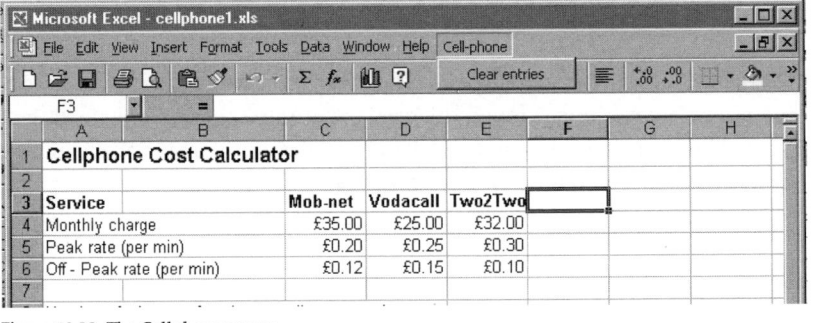

Figure 10.32 The Cellphone menu

However, a menu added in this way will suffer from the same problem as the first attempt to add a button to the toolbar, that is, it will always appear in the menu bar rather than just when the Cellphone spreadsheet is loaded. Just as it is possible to hide and display a toolbar button with auto_open and auto_close macros, so the menu bar can be modified. The changes needed to these two macros are shown in Figure 10.33.

397

BTEC National Study Guide: IT Practitioners. See page 293 for order details of individual texts

225

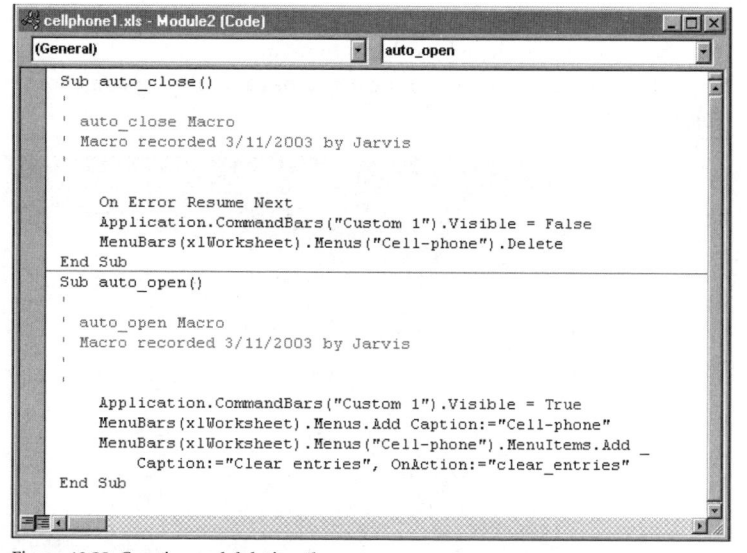

Figure 10.33 Creating and deleting the menu

Assessment activity 10.3

Customise the user interface of the application you have created by adding menus, toolbar buttons and dialogue boxes.

alternative ways of accessing the application's features which give it a professional appearance and make it easy to use.

10.4 Programming facilities

The subject of software development is covered in detail in Unit 4. You need to read that chapter before working through this section because concepts explained there are not repeated here. In this section, we look in more detail at some of the features of Visual Basic for Applications (VBA) programming language.

Defining variables and constants

VBA allows the programmer to be lazy about defining variables. Explicit declaration of variables is not required; any variable can be used and it will automatically be defined and given a data type of **variant**.

? What does it mean?

The **variant datatype** can hold any type of data.

BTEC National Study Guide: IT Practitioners. See page 293 for order details of individual texts

226

There are rules for **variable names**:

- They must begin with a letter.
- They cannot contain a space, full stop, comma or dash.
- They must not exceed 255 characters.
- They must be unique within the procedure.

It is wise to give variables names that give some clue as to what they are used for, so, while x and variable1 are valid variable names, a name such as peak_mins is a better choice for a variable that holds the number of minutes of calls made at peak rate. Descriptive variable names make programs much easier to understand, particularly when problems occur with programs and you need to work out what is happening.

There are four basic data types:

- integer – for whole numbers
- single – for single precision floating point numbers
- double – for double precision floating point numbers (can contain more numbers both before and after the decimal point, and only really necessary for scientific calculations)
- string – for text.

Constants are similar to variables in that they reserve a memory area for a value, but, unlike variables, the values in constants cannot be changed (they are constant, hence the name). Declaring constant is done like this:

```
st my_c st = 3.14
```

While not having to declare variables is convenient, it can lead to subtle errors in your code if you misspell a variable name. When VBA encounters a new name, it cannot determine whether the programmer actually meant to implicitly declare a new variable or it is just a misspelled existing variable name, so it creates a new variable with that name. To avoid the problem of misnaming variables, it can be stipulated that VBA always issues a warning whenever it encounters a name not declared explicitly as a variable:

- From the Tools menu, choose Options.
- Click the Editor tab and check the Require Variable Declaration option.

This automatically inserts the Option Explicit statement in any new modules, but not in modules already created; therefore, Option Explicit must be manually added to any existing modules within a project.

To explicitly declare a variable, the Dim instruction is used, so the instruction

```
Dim my_variable As I teger
```

will declare a variable with the name my_variable and a datatype of integer (whole numbers only).

Scope of a variable

It is important when defining and using variables to understand the issue of the scope of variables. Variables defined in a procedure are local to that procedure, they have no meaning in other procedures, their scope is limited to the procedure they are defined in, and they are known as **local variables**. You can also define **global variables** whose scope extends across all

399

BTEC National Study Guide: IT Practitioners. See page 293 for order details of individual texts

227

the procedures in a module. Global variables are defined in the General Declarations section at the top of the module code window. This can be selected using the objects drop down box at the top of the code window, as shown in Figure 10.34.

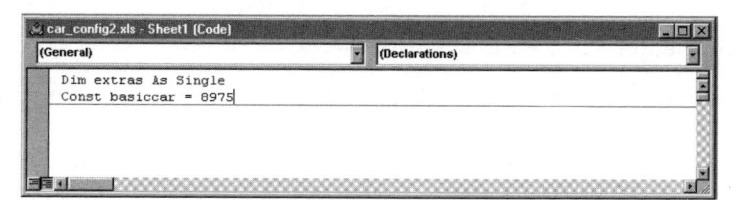

Figure 10.34 Declaring global variables

Naming conventions

It is also important to choose descriptive variable names for objects such as command buttons, text boxes and list boxes. These are automatically given default names when you create them, for example, the first command button you create will be called CommandButton1. You should therefore rename these objects with descriptive names.

However, to be able to tell which objects are command buttons, which are text boxes and so on, you should use a naming convention which adds a prefix to the name which identifies the type of object. So, a text box which holds the total of a calculation might be called Total, but to identify it as a text box the prefix txt is added so it is named

Object	Prefix
Text box	txt
Command button	cmd
List box	lst
Label	lbl

Creating procedures

VBA is an event-driven language, i.e. code procedures are run when certain events occur, such as an object is clicked or a mouse pointer is moved over an object. An example is given below to demonstrate how event procedures can be programmed, and also some of the points made earlier about variables. The spreadsheet shown in Figure 10.35 is used to calculate the cost of

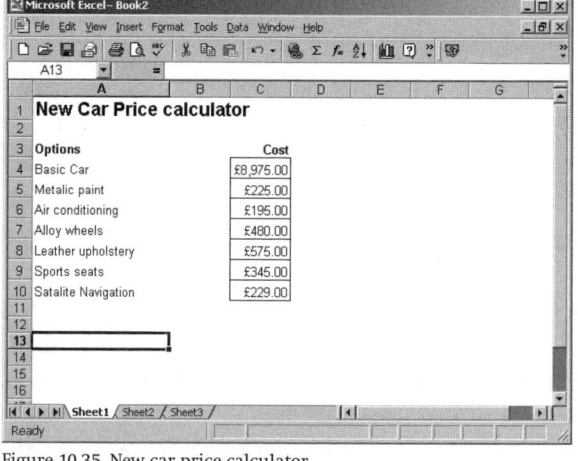

Figure 10.35 New car price calculator

400

BTEC National Study Guide: IT Practitioners. See page 293 for order details of individual texts

228

a new car. Note that the gridlines can be turned off by clicking the Gridlines check box on the View tab of the Option dialogue on the Tools menu.

As well as the cost of the basic car, various extras can be chosen. To allow the customer to see how the cost of various extras affects the total cost, each item needs a **check box**:

■ Clicking a check box puts a tick in the box, indicating the option has been chosen.
■ Clicking the box again removes the tick.

? What does it mean?

Check boxes use a toggle; when you click them, if the tick is in the box it is removed; if it is not then it is added. A check box with the tick in it is known as checked, without the tick it is unchecked.

To add these types of controls, follow these steps:

■ Display the Control toolbar (View menu, toolbars option).
■ Add a check box for each option.
■ Add a text box for the total, with a label so it is clear what it is for, as shown in Figure 10.36.
■ Name each of these objects using the Properties window, as shown.

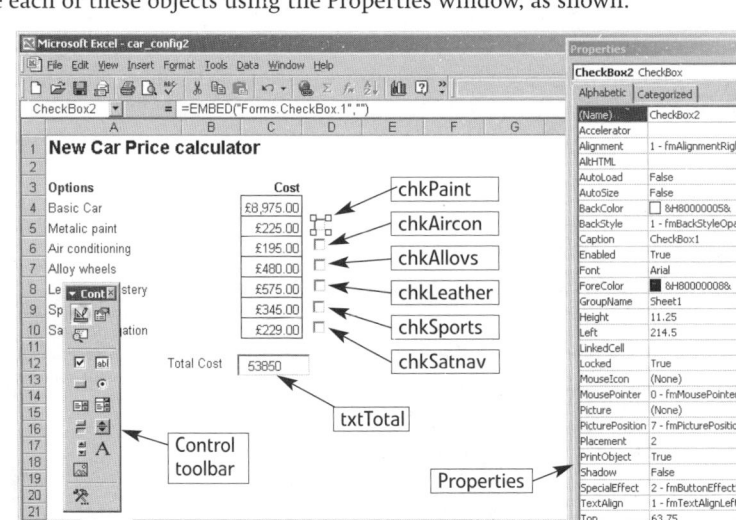

Figure 10.36 Object names

Event procedures are needed for each of the check boxes so when they are clicked they can test to see whether the tick has been added or removed from the box:

■ If the box is checked then the cost of the corresponding extra is added to the total.
■ If it is unchecked then the cost needs to be subtracted.

A variable is needed to hold the total cost of the options, and this variable needs to be available to all the different event procedures that are attached to each of the check boxes, therefore a global variable will be needed rather than a local one:

■ Double-click the first of the check boxes (chkPaint) to open the Visual Basic code window. This will create an empty event procedure for the click event for this check box.

401

BTEC National Study Guide: IT Practitioners. See page 293 for order details of individual texts

229

- To create the global variable, click on the object drop down box at the top of the code window and choose General from the top of the list.
- Use the Dim instruction to create a variable called extras, with a data type of single.

The cost of the basic car is also needed, which, as it does not change, can be held in a constant. The declarations for both the global variable and the constant are shown in Figure 10.37.

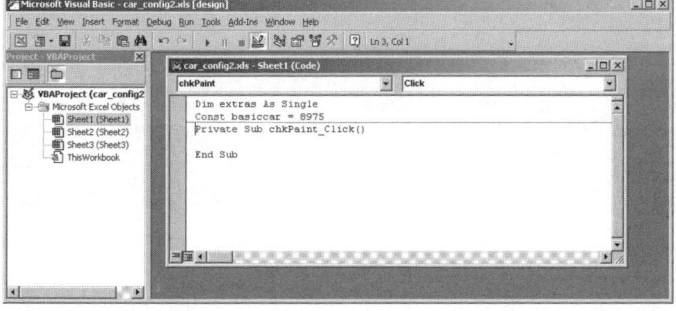

Figure 10.37 Creating a global variable

The code for the event procedure can now be written. As explained earlier, the procedure needs to test whether the check box is checked. Fortunately, this is easily done as the box has a value of true if it is checked and false if it is unchecked. Therefore, the state of the box can be tested with an if statement (objects which can only take the value of true or false are known as **Boolean**). However, before testing the state of the check box, the code needs to

needs to be added to the basic cost of the car and transferred into the total text box. The complete code is shown in Figure 10.38.

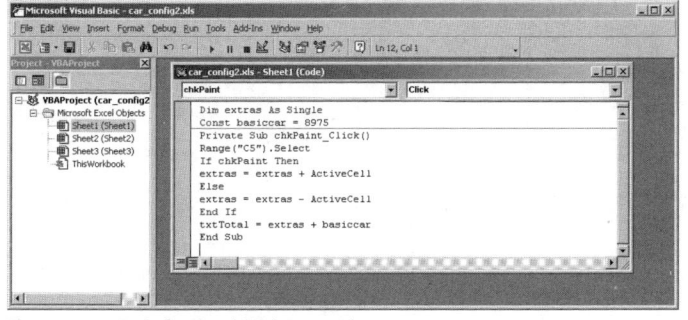

Figure 10.38 Code for the chkPaint procedure

Testing whether this works is straightforward:

- Return to the spreadsheet and click the check box next to the metallic paint option.
- The total cost in the total box will be shown as 9200 (basic cost of the car, £8975 plus the cost of the metallic paint option, £225).
- Click the check box again and the box becomes unchecked, so the total cost of the car becomes 8975.

The only problem is that the total cost of the car in the txtTotal box is not formatted as currency with a pound sign (£) and two digits after the decimal point. To correct this, modify

402

BTEC National Study Guide: IT Practitioners. See page 293 for order details of individual texts

230

the last line of the procedure so that it reads:

TxtT tal = f rmat(extras +basiccar, "curre cy")

The event procedures for the other checkboxes are almost identical to the first one. All that needs to change is the cell that is selected in the first line and the name of the checkbox in the if instruction. It would be possible to simply copy and paste this procedure and make the changes for each of the checkboxes. However, repeating the same code time and time again is a sure sign that a function is needed.

Creating functions

A function is a piece of code which carries out some clearly defined task. Excel and VBA have many built in functions which can carry out a variety of different tasks:

- carry out mathematical calculations such as averages
- convert dates into different formats
- do financial calculations such as calculate the interest payable on a loan.

As well as using the built-in functions, you can also write your own. The example used here tests the status of a checkbox in the car cost calculator program. Functions can be passed values from the procedure that calls them, and, in this case, the procedure needs to pass the function the check box that needs to be tested. The function itself will need a Boolean variable to hold the parameter that the calling procedure passes it. To create a function, follow these steps:

- Go to the Visual Basic window and from the menu bar choose Insert.

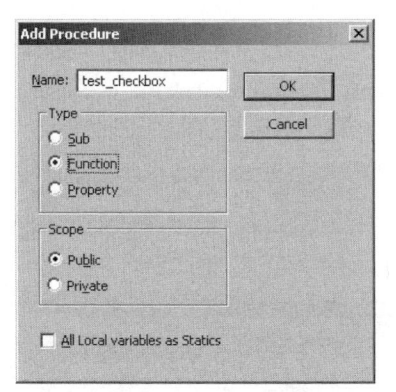

Figure 10.39 The Add Procedure dialogue box

- Give the procedure a meaningful name, such as Test_checkbox, and set the Type to Function, then click OK. This will create an empty function in the code window. The empty set of brackets after the function name is where the variable must be declared that will hold the parameter that is passed to the function by the calling procedure. As already discussed, this must be a Boolean variable; therefore, this first line of the function must be modified so that it reads

  Public Fu cti test_checkb x(checkb x_state as B lea)

  where checkbox_state is the name of the variable used to hold the parameter passed to the function.

The rest of the code for the function can simply be cut from the original chkPaint procedure, leaving behind the first line of the this procedure (Range("C5").Select) as this line will be different for each checkbox click procedure, so it is not worth putting it in the function. The only modification needed to this piece of code is to change the if statement so it uses the checkbox_state variable. The complete code for the function is shown in Figure 10.40.

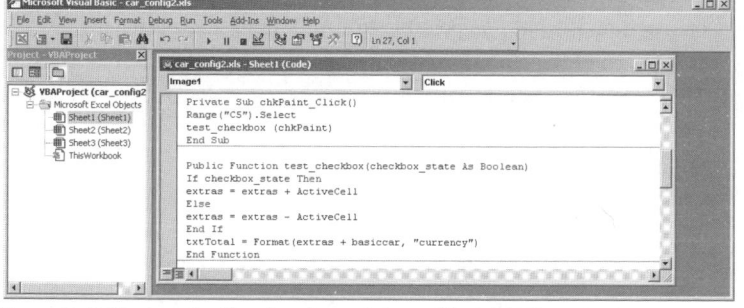

Figure 10.40 The test_checkbox function and the modified chkPaint procedure

The chkPaint procedure now needs to have the function call added to it, passing the function the check box as a parameter (see chkPaint_Click() code shown in Figure 10.40). The click event procedures for the other check boxes can now be created:

■ Double-click on each check box in turn to create the empty event procedure.

■ Copy and paste the procedure code from one of the other checkbox click event procedures.

■ Change the cell that is selected to pick up the price of the particular option and change the name of the checkbox that is passed to the test_checkbox procedure.

of the car to the car cost spreadsheet. When the user clicks the picture the image will change to a different picture of the car:

■ First an image box must be added to the spreadsheet using the image box button on the Control toolbar.

■ Then, using the picture property of the image box, select a suitable picture of a car (see Figure 10.41).

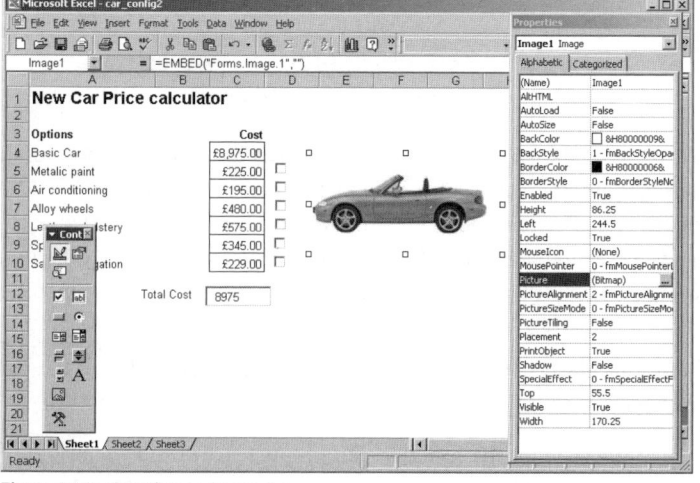

Figure 10.41 Creating an image box

BTEC National Study Guide: IT Practitioners. See page 293 for order details of individual texts

232

- Double-click the image box, and by default a click event procedure is created.
- Use the Procedure drop-down box at the top of the code window to select the mousedown event, and an empty event procedure will be created for that event (the click event procedure can be deleted, although it will not cause any problems if it is not deleted).
- Enter the code to load a different picture into the image box, as shown in Figure 10.42.

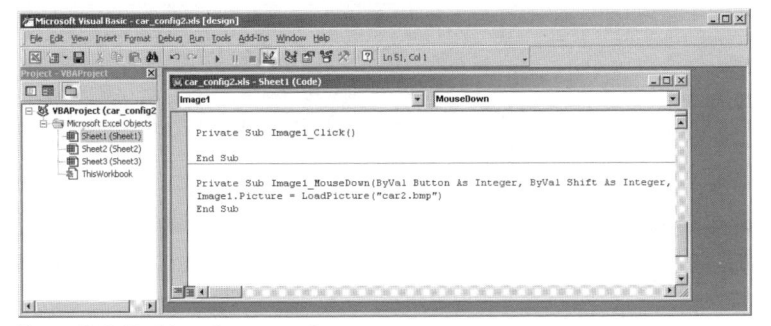

Figure 10.42 The Mousedown procedure

A mouseup procedure is also needed to revert to the original picture when the mouse is moved away form the image box:

- Select the mouseup name from the Procedure drop-down box.
- Enter the same code as in the mousedown procedure, but this time the image file name should be the original one.

such as defining local and global variables, reacting to various events and using functions.

For the distinction grade, you must use both a standard naming convention for objects and make appropriate use of functions to modularise your application.

Debug facilities

Programs can become quite complex and difficult to follow, and when these programs do not work correctly, it can be very hard to work out why. To help you in these situations, Visual Basic has built-in facilities to help you to write correct programs in the first place. Other facilities are then available to identify the bugs in your programs. When writing a program, Visual Basic provides context sensitive help which provides a list of valid options when writing program instructions. An example is shown in Figure 10.43.

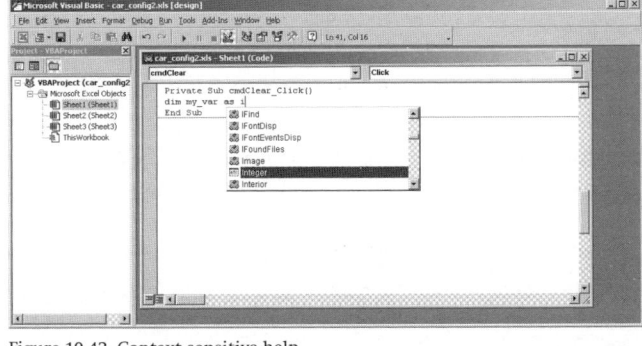

Figure 10.43 Context sensitive help

405

BTEC National Study Guide: IT Practitioners. See page 293 for order details of individual texts

233

Visual Basic also checks the instructions as they are written and will display them in red if they are not valid, along with an error message, as shown in Figure 10.44.

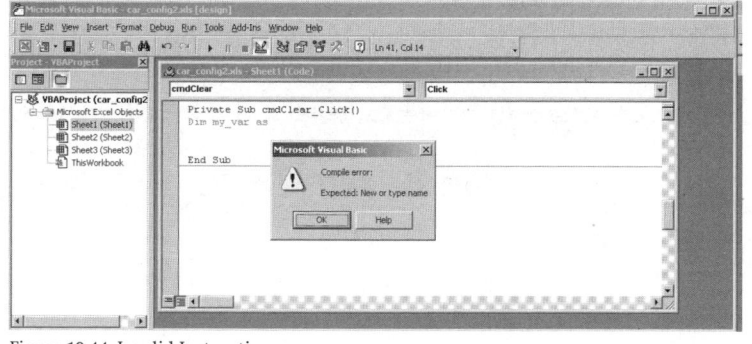

Figure 10.44 Invalid Instructions

However, even if your program statements are valid, when you run your program, it may either not work the way you want it to or it may fail unexpectedly. If the program fails unexpectedly (known as a **run-time error**), you will see a message such as that shown in Figure 10.45.

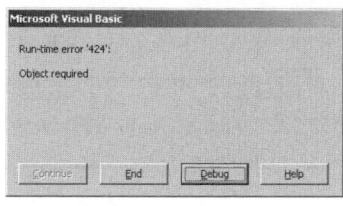

If the Debug button is then clicked, the Visual Basic code window will open with the line that caused the failure highlighted, as shown in Figure 10.46.

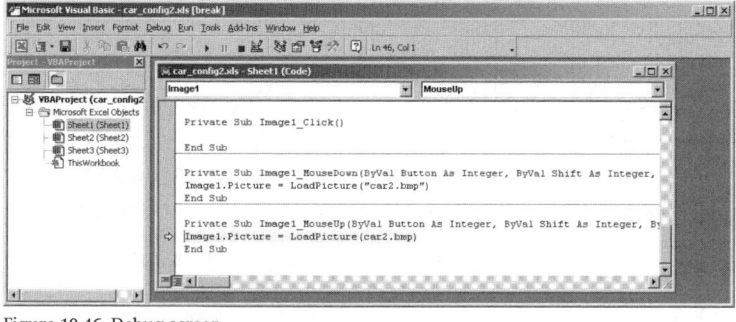

Figure 10.46 Debug screen

It may be that the program does not produce any run-time errors, but it still does not give the expected results. In these cases, it may be helpful to set what is called a **breakpoint**.

 What does it mean?

A **breakpoint** stops the program running at a chosen point so that the user can check the contents of each of the program variables.

406

BTEC National Study Guide: IT Practitioners. See page 293 for order details of individual texts

234

The next example is from the car cost calculator:

The program is not working properly. It does not calculate the cost of the car correctly when the different options are added. A breakpoint is set at the point where the test_check box adds the cost of an option:

■ Click at that point in the Visual Basic code window.

■ From the Debug menu choose toggle breakpoint. This puts a maroon coloured bar though the code, indicating that a breakpoint has been set (Figure 10.47).

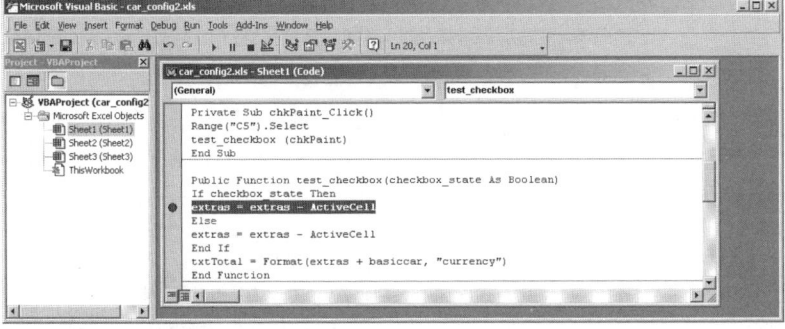

Figure 10.47 Adding a breakpoint

■ Return to the spreadsheet and click one of the unchecked boxes. The code window will reappear with the breakpoint highlighted in yellow.

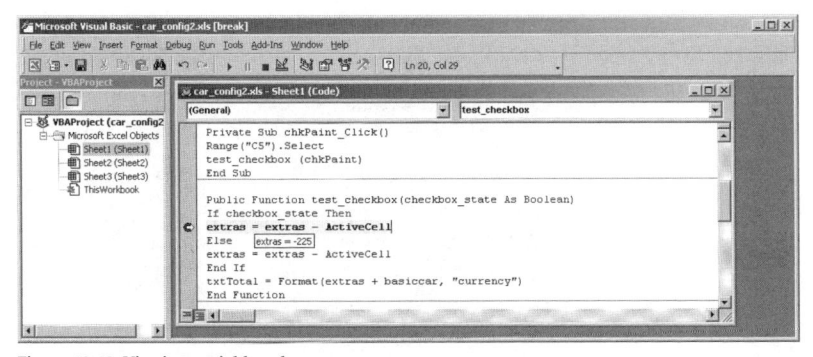

Figure 10.48 Viewing variable values

Being able to view the contents of the variables during the execution of the program can help to identify where things are going wrong. Once you have resolved the problems with the program, you can remove the breakpoint:

■ Go to the Debug menu.

■ Choose Remove all breakpoints.

Assessment activity 10.5

Provide evidence that you have identified and corrected errors in your application. You can do this using the debug facilities explained in this section.

407

BTEC National Study Guide: IT Practitioners. See page 293 for order details of individual texts

235

Portability

Although it is not possible to create a stand-alone executable program with VBA, Excel VBA applications can be distributed to other users that have Excel installed, simply by giving them the .xls spreadsheet file that contains the application. To make applications easier to access, a shortcut to the spreadsheet file can be placed on the desktop and its icon can be changed so it looks like a stand-alone application rather than just an Excel spreadsheet. To create a shortcut, simply right click on the Excel file in Windows Explorer and choose Send to Desktop (Figure 10.49).

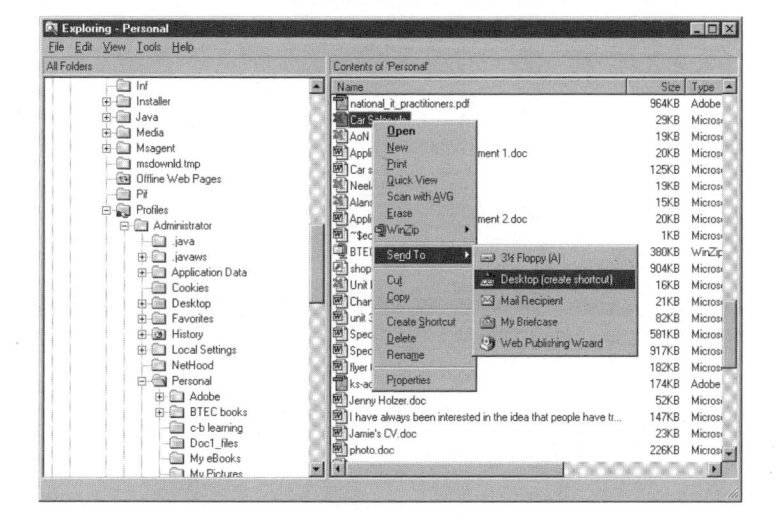

You can change the icon for the shortcut displayed on your desktop by right clicking on it and choosing Properties. Then click the Change icon button and choose the icon you require (Figure 10.50).

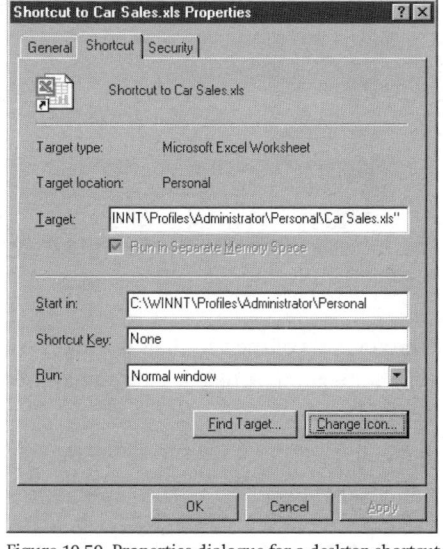

Figure 10.50 Properties dialogue for a desktop shortcut

Alternatively you could add a toolbar button to the standard Excel tool bar which runs a macro that opens the worksheet that contains your application. However, when you record

BTEC National Study Guide: IT Practitioners. See page 293 for order details of individual texts

236

the macro that opens your application you will need to use the *Store this macro in:* drop-down, and select the Personal Macro Workbook option. Macros stored in the Personal Macro Workbook are available to all Excel files, not just the one you save them in. Adding a button to the standard Excel toolbar in this way, users would be provided with an easy way to access the application from within Excel.

Assessment activity 10.6

1 Provide a method of starting the application you have created, either from the desktop or from within Excel.
2 Provide evidence, including screen shots of how to run (execute) you application.
3 Create a document which shows how you developed your application starting with the plan you originally created, through the design stage to the final working application. You should include the diagrams you created during the planning and design stages, printouts of your worksheets and code modules and screen shots showing how the various features of your application, including shortcut keys and menu, work.

Test your knowledge

1 List some of the techniques that can be used to design the data processing in an application.
2 What is the SUM function used for?

6 What is a variable?
7 How can you test that user input is numeric?
8 What is a loop?
9 What name do you give to a macro you want to run when a spreadsheet opens?
10 What sort of data can be held in a variable with a data type of variant?
11 What is the difference between a local and a global variable? How do you create a global variable?
12 What is the meaning of the term Boolean?
13 How can you format a value as currency in VBA?
14 What is a function?
15 What is a breakpoint? What is it used for?

BTEC National Study Guide: IT Practitioners. See page 293 for order details of individual texts

237

UNIT 12: HUMAN COMPUTER INTERFACE

The advance in design of highly interactive computer systems continues at an ever-increasing pace, with new developments in hardware and software being announced more frequently than ever before. The pace of change, which is unlikely to diminish, has placed an increasing burden on the design of the way in which users interact with computer systems.

The way in which computers and people interact is known as the human computer interface (HCI).

The aim of this unit is to provide an understanding of the importance of HCI in the development of user-friendly computer software. You will learn about the currently available HCI technologies and designs, and the appropriateness of each for particular applications and user groups. As a prerequisite, you should have

Learning objectives

- To describe a range of HCI developments and the applications and user groups to which they are suited
- To describe the relationship between the user and the interface, in terms of human motor, sensory and cognitive abilities
- To give examples of specific HCIs which are designed to solve specific problems and produce HCI designs to specification
- To evaluate the effectiveness of HCI models with particular reference to the chosen designs

410

BTEC National Study Guide: IT Practitioners. See page 293 for order details of individual texts

238

12.1 HCI developments and their applications

HCI is a fascinating field of study. It looks at how people and computers communicate with each other, and how their interaction can be improved.

? What does it mean?

HCI stands for **human computer interface**, or sometimes human computer **interaction**.

HCI begins with the premise that computers, and the people who use them, must be seen as a complete unit and that the quality of the work done using a computer depends on four factors:

- the hardware devices that the user is in direct contact with
- the user interface displayed on the screen
- the response of the human user to the computer system
- the environment in which the computer and human are placed.

Organisations invest very heavily in ICT, so they want their computer systems to be used as productively as possible. Many are now aware that to achieve this they need to pay attention to all four factors.

in the home. At work, computer users usually have access to support staff, whereas the home user is largely on his or her own, so the quality of the HCI is of even greater importance.

HCI is also becoming a significant issue in the development of other related technologies. Digital televisions, mobile phones and personal digital assistants (PDAs) have more and more features in common, and we refer to a *convergence* of the technologies. Soon these products, along with desktop computers, will all offer a very similar range of services. The main difference between them will be their size, which will determine the type of input and output devices that can be used with them.

Developments in hardware

You will already be familiar with a number of input and output devices. In this unit, you will not be studying technologies themselves but instead you will be considering the impact that some of these devices have on the way in which people interact with computers. The perspective will always be that of the user, not of the technician.

Input devices

The only way in which a human user can pass information to a computer system is through an input device. The input device carries out two functions: entering information and issuing instructions. Information is in the form of text, numbers, sound and images, all of which

411

BTEC National Study Guide: IT Practitioners. See page 293 for order details of individual texts

239

have to be transferred from the outside world to the inner workings of the computer system. Instructions tell the computer what to do with the information. Of course, the computer system does not make such a distinction, as all signals from input devices are simply treated as data. The user's perception is important though, and has led to the development of different devices for the two functions.

Data entry devices

These are used to enter information into the computer system. They include keyboards, readers, image capture and recognition systems.

Keyboards: These provide the primary method by which a user enters information into a computer. Various types and layouts are produced.

■ The **standard keyboard** uses the QWERTY key layout, which was originally developed for typewriters over a century ago. The arrangement of the keys was designed to prevent the levers from hitting each other and jamming the machine, and to slow down the typist. This layout migrated to the computer keyboard because it was familiar to office workers, even though the original justification was no longer relevant. The standard keyboard includes a calculator-like numeric keypad, which duplicates the keys above the letters, but enables fast entry of numerical data. It also provides a set of control keys and programmable function keys.

■ **Ergonomically designed keyboards** (Figure 12.1) use a similar layout to the standard one,

Figure 12.1 An ergonomic keyboard

■ Experiments with alternative layouts of keys have not proved to be commercially successful for business computers. Some keyboards do use the keys arranged in alphabetical order, and these are found on systems designed to enable people with motor control disabilities to communicate, and also on some children's products. Numerical keypads can be used to enter characters, as any mobile phone user knows, and this makes it possible to use a limited keyboard on a handheld device.

■ A touch-sensitive keyboard which can be programmed and varied in layout is known as a **concept keyboard**. They can be seen in fast food outlets, (Figure 12.2) where an overlay on

412

BTEC National Study Guide: IT Practitioners. See page 293 for order details of individual texts

240

the surface identifies the areas that have been programmed to accept input. A concept keyboard can also be used by children, or by people with disabilities, as the 'keys' can be made as large as necessary.

Figure 12.2 A concept keyboard in a fast food outlet

■ A **touch-sensitive** screen can simulate a keyboard, and a stylus or finger can be used to select keys. These can be seen on PDAs and information kiosks. Either QWERTY or

✓ Check your understanding 12.1

1 Why is the QWERTY key layout widely used on keyboards, and why have manufacturers enjoyed little success in getting the public to switch to other layouts?

2 Describe three or four different keyboards, other than the familiar desktop computer keyboard, that can be used within an HCI. Identify a context where each could be used.

Readers: Sometimes information has already been produced and the user needs a method to transfer this into the computer system. In these cases, a reader device of some kind is used.

■ A **magnetic card reader** inputs the data stored on either a magnetic strip or a chip embedded into a small card. They are widely used by banks (for cash and credit cards), by shops (for loyalty cards), by transport operators (for tickets) and by hotels (for electronic door keys), and are being increasingly used by organisations for ID cards.

■ A **smart card reader** inputs data held on a chip on a plastic card. A complete processor with memory is contained on a single integrated circuit. Their use is expected to grow, especially as travel and entertainment tickets, as cash top-up cards, and to store personal data such as medical records.

Image capture devices: Images are as important as text in HCIs, so methods for inputting and manipulating images are of some significance.

■ A **digital camera** stores a photograph as a bitmap, which can then be uploaded to a computer system.

413

BTEC National Study Guide: IT Practitioners. See page 293 for order details of individual texts

241

■ An **image scanner** is used to digitise existing documents and photos. The output is a bitmap version of the original. The bitmap may then be subjected to further analysis and interpreted as characters or barcodes. Both flat-bed and handheld scanners can be purchased.

Recognition systems: These are complex systems that add sophisticated analytical software to existing hardware technologies.

■ **Character recognition systems** use optical character recognition (OCR) software to analyse the patterns in a bitmap and interpret them as characters. This involves careful matching against standard fonts, and is not entirely error free. The system generates a text or word processing file. Character recognition software usually works in conjunction with a scanner. Specialised systems are used by blind users to input text, which can then be output as speech or in Braille.

■ **Handwriting recognition systems** are mainly used in PDAs and other hand-held devices with touch-sensitive screens. The user writes characters with a stylus one at a time on to the screen and these are then interpreted by the software. Before the system can be used the system has to be given samples of all the characters written by the user. A person's handwriting does vary so this system is not foolproof, and errors do appear.

■ **Speech recognition systems** use a microphone to capture and digitise speech. They then match the phonemes (speech components) against a built-in library of words, and store the text as a text file or word processing document. Just as a handwriting system has to 'learn'

Further research 12.1

1 Switch on the teletext subtitles while you are watching a live broadcast, such as a football match. The television companies use speech recognition systems to analyse and present the commentary. Note down the errors that occur.
2 Are the errors simply amusing or would they cause difficulties for a person who could not hear the spoken words?

In addition to devices for entering information, a number of input devices are used primarily for entering user instructions. These include a range of pointing devices and many of the components of games and virtual reality systems.

Pointing devices

These let the user issue instructions in a natural way and without having to enter words. They can only be used in conjunction with a suitable user interface, which places a pointer icon on the screen that moves in response to inputs from the device.

■ A **mouse** fits neatly into the hand, and its movements across a smooth surface are mirrored by the on-screen pointer. A mouse has two standard types of control: the rollers that touch the ball to register movement, and buttons. The standard mouse has two buttons, which can each be clicked or double-clicked. The use of these buttons is

414

BTEC National Study Guide: IT Practitioners. See page 293 for order details of individual texts

242

determined by the software and, in addition, the user can often configure the buttons to suit his or her speed of movement or handedness.

■ A **light pen** is a pen-like device that is connected to an input port and held close to the screen. It detects the individual pixels of light as they are projected onto the screen and this allows the software to detect the position of the pen. The pen can be used to make on-screen selections.

■ A **tracker ball** (Figure 12.3) is similar to a mouse but with the ball on the top. The user rotates the ball directly, rather than moving it over a surface. Tracker balls are often built in to portable computers as an alternative to a separate mouse.

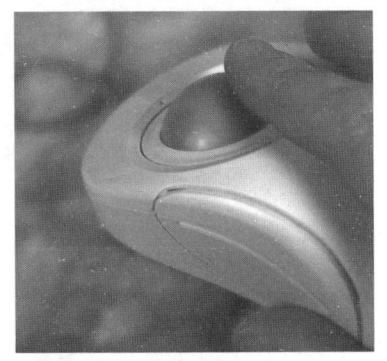

Figure 12.3 A tracker ball

■ An **eye gaze system** requires the user to wear a device that positions a small (safe) laser unit in front of the eye. This records the movement of the eye and can be used as a hands-free method of moving an on-screen pointer. These systems have been mainly used by the military, but are also used increasingly to enable people with very limited movement to control communication devices and computers.

✓ **Check your understanding 12.2**

Why are there so many different types of pointing devices when they seem to carry out very similar functions?

Movement-sensing devices

These are complex devices that allow the user to move around in three-dimensional space and to issue instructions through their position and motion. Virtual reality (VR) systems combine movement-sensing devices with multi-sensory output and these are considered in more detail later.

■ **Data gloves** are worn like ordinary gloves. They have optical fibres built in to the fabric and these detect movement of the finger joints when, for example, the hand makes a grasping movement. Additional sensors measure the position of the hand and the way in which the wrist rotates. Data gloves are used in VR systems.

415

BTEC National Study Guide: IT Practitioners. See page 293 for order details of individual texts

243

■ A **headset** or helmet can track the position and movement of the user's head (Figure 12.4). Sometimes these are combined with eye gaze systems. These can again be used in VR simulations or for hands-free real-life control.

Figure 12.4 A VR head set

■ **Whole-body tracking systems** place movement sensors either directly on the body or on the chair in which the user sits. These systems are in their infancy but will, no doubt, become increasingly important in the entertainment industry.

Humans are traditionally described as having five senses, so computer systems could, in theory, produce output that can be seen, heard, touched, smelt or tasted. In practice, the last two have not yet been exploited by the IT world, largely because no one has yet found a satisfactory method for digitising, and then reproducing, smells and tastes.

Visual output devices

Sight is the dominant sense for humans; so, most research into user interfaces has concentrated on the presentation of visual information.

■ Computer **screens** are also referred to as visual display units (VDUs) or monitors. The most common type is the cathode ray tube (CRT) which fires an electron beam at a coated screen. It fires lines of pixels one after another down the screen, taking around one thirtieth of a second to cover a complete screen. An alternative is the liquid crystal display (LCD) screen, which sends signals to the individual crystals that represent each pixel every time they have to change colour. LCD screens are flat, and are lighter in weight than CRT screens, but are more expensive and can sometimes be more difficult to view. They are widely used in portable machines, such as laptop computers, PDAs and mobile phones.

■ **Printers** are complex systems in their own right. Their large memory buffers enable them to store and process tasks independently of the rest of the computer system. Inkjet and laser printers offer a range of capabilities and print quality.

Sound output devices

These play an important, but under-recognised, role in HCIs.

416

BTEC National Study Guide: IT Practitioners. See page 293 for order details of individual texts

244

■ All desktop computers have a small **speaker** for sound output, and this is often supplemented with a pair of better quality external speakers. Sound is used for playing music and for effects in games, but the HCI also uses sounds to enhance the visual impact on the screen of actions. Many events in both system and application software can be accompanied by a sound, for example, for opening, closing or deleting a file. These sounds catch the user's attention and confirm the action.

■ **Speech synthesis** is a specialised use of sound output facilities, and uses software that generates the voice patterns for text. This is of immediate use to those with visual impairment; for them, a computer can read back word-processed documents, or read text that has been scanned in or viewed on the Internet. Speech synthesis systems can also be used by people who are unable to speak themselves for medical reasons.

Tactile output devices

Touch provides immediate information about the world, but is not as well understood as sight, and is only just beginning to be exploited by computer developers.

■ A **Braille printer** outputs text in Braille, which uses raised dots to represent characters. Blind users who have learned Braille can print and take their documents with them, giving this form of output an advantage over speech output.

■ Tactile feedback can be provided by a **data glove**. It is produced by creating pressure on parts of the hand to give the impression that an object is being touched.

presentation.

■ **Multimedia systems** combine visual and sound outputs. Multimedia is commonly used for reference content (such as encyclopaedias) on CD-ROMs, for games, and for business presentations (using presentation packages such as PowerPoint). The major impact of multimedia, though, has been through the new communications channels that have opened up in the last 20 years. The Internet, 3G mobile networks and digital TV have all exploited visual and sound outputs and have developed new interface standards.

■ **Virtual reality (VR)** systems integrate visual, sound and touch outputs. A complete virtual reality system can include a headset which may have both eye gaze and movement sensors, together with one or more data gloves. The visual output can then be provided through screens placed in the headset and just in front of each eye. 3D vision is created by having a screen for each eye displaying slightly different images.

✔ **Check your understanding 12.3**

You may be familiar with some leisure uses of VR systems. Can you list some, non-leisure applications that currently use VR technologies, or that could use VR in the future?

Processing

Many of the input and output devices we have mentioned are themselves components in complex input or output systems. For example, a printer is normally viewed as an output

417

BTEC National Study Guide: IT Practitioners. See page 293 for order details of individual texts

245

device, but it has all the features of any computer system, in that it receives input from the CPU, it stores data in its memory, it stores configuration data in memory, it processes data using an onboard processor, it sends signals to the CPU, and it sends the main output data to the actual printing components.

Similarly, hand and speech recognition systems include hardware and software components. They take input from the interface, interpret that information with software that draws on artificial intelligence (AI) techniques, and then output the interpreted data to the main system.

Memory and secondary storage

All forms of output and input have data storage requirements, both in main RAM memory and in secondary backing store.

■ **Text** takes up relatively little space in either main memory or backing store. ASCII files use 1 byte per character. This unit has around 100,000 characters, including spaces, so the text alone could be stored in a 100 Kb ASCII file. In practice, much text these days is stored in word-processed files which use considerably more storage space to hold formatting commands. A text-only version of this unit, with no illustrations, could be stored in a word-processed file of around 430 Kb.

■ **Images** can be very memory hungry. An image that is 200 × 300 pixels has 60,000 pixels. Assuming that the image uses colours, the data about each pixel is stored in either 1, 2 or 3 bytes. One byte per pixel gives 256 different colours so is only useful for simple images

provides more colour choices than the human eye can distinguish. So the approximate uncompressed memory requirements for images would be as shown in Table 12.1.

Images are often compressed, using algorithms that avoid the need to keep repeating identical colour values. Compression can bring the size of an image file from megabytes down to a few kilobytes, without any visible loss of quality.

Bytes per pixel	Number of colours	200 × 300	800 × 600	1024 × 768
1	256	60 Kb	480 Kb	768 Kb
2 (High colour)	65,536	120 Kb	960 Kb	1.54 Mb
3 (True colour)	16,777,216	180 Kb	1.44 Mb	2.34 Mb

Table 12.1 Memory requirements of images

■ **Animations** display many images per second, so they use even more memory. Although images that require a substantial amount of memory can usually be stored in today's high capacity hard disks, they can transfer slowly into main memory, and main memory itself may fill up with too many images.

■ **Sound input** is digitised by a process that samples successive moments of sounds, and then gives each sample a set of values representing the pitch and intensity. The quality of the recording depends on the sampling rate (i.e. how often the sound is sampled per second) and the sampling resolution (i.e. the number of bytes used to store each sample). Again, popular sound formats used on computer systems compress the sound with minimal loss of quality.

BTEC National Study Guide: IT Practitioners. See page 293 for order details of individual texts

246

✓ **Check your understanding 12.4**

Calculate the amount of memory required to store these uncompressed bitmap images:

1 An icon 15 pixels square, using 256 colours
2 A small decorative graphic, 120 × 20 pixels, using 2 bytes to store each pixel
3 A 400 × 300 true colour photograph.

Limitations of current and projected developments

There is much imaginative work going on in the HCI field. Future developments will always be constrained by the capabilities of the hardware available at the time, but demands from HCI designers encourage the hardware designers to develop new technologies. The limitations usually revolve around these factors:

- the capacity of and speed of access to internal memory
- the capacity of and speed of access to storage devices
- the speed of processors
- the physical dimensions of devices.

Further research 12.2

Identify a recent development in HCI. It could be a device which has become widely available in the last year or so, it could be the latest generation of mobile phones, or it could be a new use for virtual reality systems. Why was this innovation not available a few years ago? What

Styles of interaction and their development

The term 'user interface' usually denotes the screen display generated by a computer system. As sight is the dominant sense, the design of user interfaces has become a major concern of HCI research. **Graphical user interfaces (GUIs)** have largely, but not entirely, replaced non-graphical ones.

? **What does it mean?**

A **graphical user interface (GUI)** incorporates graphics into the visual display. The graphics are not simply used as decoration but are used to replace text and to convey meaning to the user.

Non-graphical interfaces

It is sometimes difficult to imagine a computer without its familiar GUI, but you will probably be familiar with, or can remember, teletext on television in its original, non-digital form (Figure 12.5). This used only text characters in a simple and limited display. Block images were created by using the IBM extended character set. Input comes from the remote control, which is a simple keyboard.

419

Figure 12.5 A teletext screen

Non-graphical interfaces can also be seen on many point-of-sale terminals in shops. The

and do not use pointing devices, like mice. The user interfaces for many desktop computers in the 1980s were entirely text-based. Although graphical display units were available they were expensive and so they were restricted to specialised users.

Once graphical displays became cheaper and more common, GUIs became the norm. Some of the more useful features of non-graphical user interfaces are still used, especially on small displays.

Command line environment (CLE)

This is a type of non-graphical interface that was widely used in the past. Before GUIs were introduced, all operating systems were controlled using simple text commands. Systems administrators became very adept at using these commands, and some of them today still find that they can work faster in the command line environment than in a GUI.

Further research 12.3

If you are using a version of Microsoft Windows you can switch into the MS-DOS command line environment.

Find the MS-DOS Prompt. Click on this and the window shown in Figure 12.6 will open. As you are still technically in a graphical environment, there are a few icons at the top of the window, but they did not exist on the original DOS-based machines. Once you move into the main black screen you will find yourself in a world in which the mouse does not work, and

420

there are no icons or drop down menus. To make anything happen at all you will have to enter some commands from the keyboard.

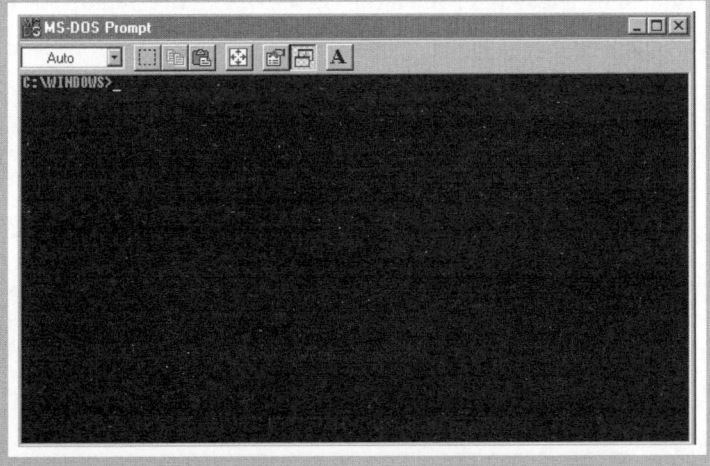

Figure 12.6 The MS-DOS window

You will notice that you are in the Windows directory (folder) on the C drive. Try keying in these commands:

■ **DIR** lists all the files in the current directory (Figure 12.7). The screen will scroll rapidly as the details of all the files and subdirectories are displayed. At the end of the list, the system will state how many files and subdirectories there are in the Windows directory.

Figure 12.7 A directory listing in MS-DOS

■ **DIR /P** pauses the display. This allows you to read the information one screen at a time.
■ **CD <directory name>** changes the directory.
■ **CD HELP** opens a subdirectory called HELP. Use DIR /P to see its contents.
■ **CD..** changes the directory to the root directory, which is the main directory for the C drive itself.
■ **MD <directory name>** makes a directory. For example, MD MYFILES will create a subdirectory called MYFILES in the current directory.
■ **DEL <filename>** deletes a file.
■ **EXIT** leaves MS-DOS.

421

BTEC National Study Guide: IT Practitioners. See page 293 for order details of individual texts

249

Menu-driven systems

Menus can be used in a purely text-based system, without a mouse. The simplest menu system is that offered by teletext, in which the viewer keys in the number of the required option on a key pad. A menu-driven system is a more usable non-graphical alternative to a CLE.

Other menu-driven systems use the cursor keys to move between options and the enter key to select. There are many contexts where it would not be convenient to use a mouse, such as at a point-of-sale terminal.

Form-fill systems

Software applications often require the user to enter data. In a simple user interface the user will be presented with a form to complete. Data will be keyed into small text boxes, known as **response fields**. The user will usually be able to move from one field to another using the tab key, or sometimes the cursor keys. Figure 12.8 shows a form-fill dialogue used in a simple text editor.

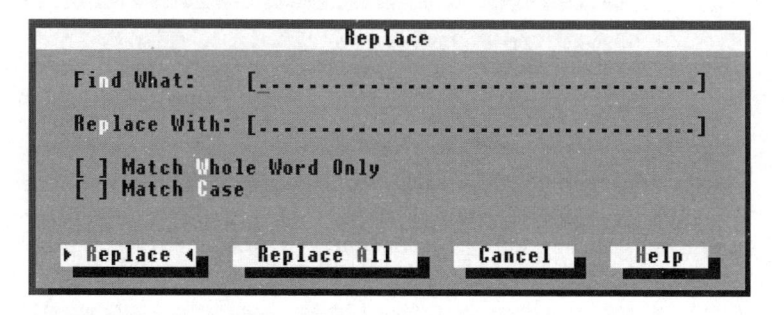

Forms are used in GUIs as well, and they often include extra graphical features such as check boxes and radio buttons.

Hot keys

Selecting from a menu can be a slow process, whether using the cursor keys to sweep through a menu, or a mouse to activate a drop-down menu and then click on an option. A much more direct method is to hit a hot key which will select the option straightaway. The user soon learns the keys or key combinations that are frequently used.

? What does it mean?

A **hot key**, or keyboard shortcut, is a key which initiates an action. Sometimes a key combination of two or more keys have to be pressed together.

Graphical user interfaces

Non-graphical user interfaces served their purpose well while computers were only being used by trained specialists. The rapid expansion of desktop computing forced software and hardware suppliers to consider the needs of ordinary, non-technical users. Software developers started by introducing GUIs for operating systems, so they were able to sell their stand-alone systems to a wider market, including for unsupported home use.

422

BTEC National Study Guide: IT Practitioners. See page 293 for order details of individual texts

250

A working model of a GUI was first developed as long ago as 1973 by Xerox, for its research Alto computer. It was designed to help a non-technical user to work effectively with the operating system. By the early 1980s, the GUI (Figure 12.9) had a three-button mouse and a black and white bit-mapped display with a **WIMP** environment. This was quite remarkable at the time as all other visual display units could only present text and used command line interfaces.

What does it mean?

WIMP stands for Window, Icon, Menu, Pointer. These are the significant components in a GUI.

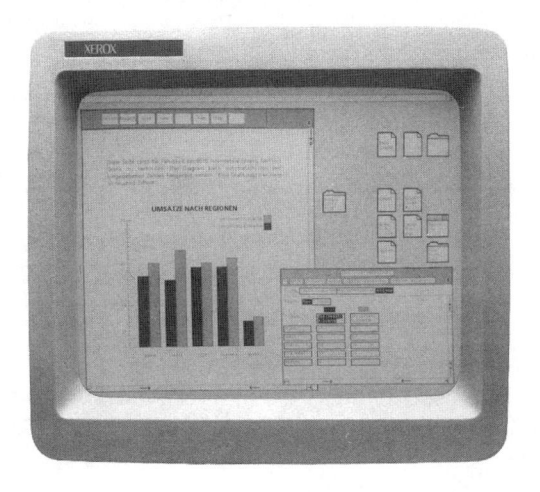

Apple, and then Microsoft, launched their GUI-based systems in the early 1980s. The first version of Microsoft Windows had **windows** that could not be overlapped but introduced the task bar at the bottom of the screen (Figure 12.10).

What does it mean?

A **window** is a rectangular area that displays what a program is doing. It allows the user to interact with one process, for example, to edit a picture, save a document, or change preferences.

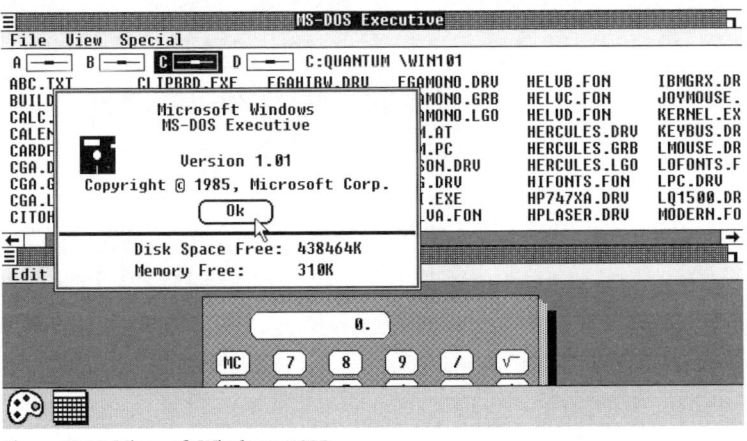

Figure 12.10 Microsoft Windows, 1985

423

BTEC National Study Guide: IT Practitioners. See page 293 for order details of individual texts

251

The standards that were developed for operating systems were gradually adopted by applications developers as well. Most GUIs today make use of one or more of the WIMP elements.

Windows

Windows are widely used in business applications, although they are less commonly used in some multimedia software, especially games. Windows support multi-tasking, as several windows can be open at the same time and the user can often switch between them. At any one time, only one window will be active, that is, ready for the user to input, and this will usually appear to be on top of the other windows. There are two types of window.

■ **Standard windows** carry out the core processes of an application, such as viewing, entering and editing data. They can usually be positioned and sized by the user. In some applications, a standard window can be subdivided into separate mini-windows, known as panes (Figure 12.11). The user can select which panes will appear on screen.

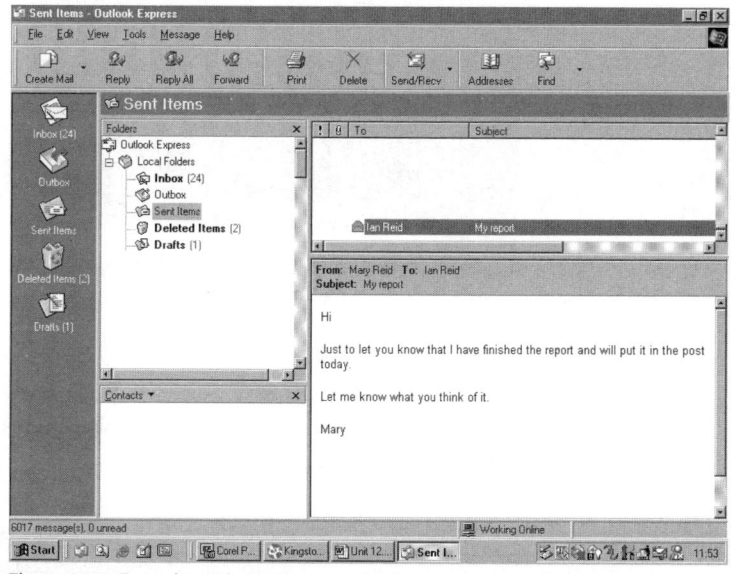

Figure 12.11 Panes in a window

■ **Dialogue windows** enable the user to select options to carry out a specific action (Figure 12.12). They usually appear in response to a selection from a menu. The appearance of a dialogue window depends on the selections that the user makes, and buttons or lists will help the user to choose.

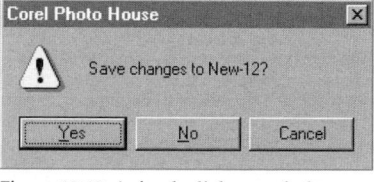

Figure 12.12 A simple dialogue window

Icons

An icon is a graphic which represents an action that the software can carry out, and which the user can select (Figure 12.13). Icons are used instead of words to reduce the space needed on screen and to enhance the user's understanding.

424

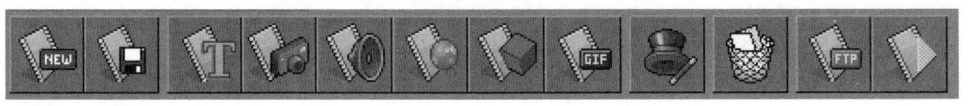

What does it mean?

An **icon** is a small image that represents an action.

Figure 12.13 Some icons

GUI designers try to design icons that convey the same meaning to all users irrespective of the languages they speak, but this can be difficult to achieve. Sometimes words or labels (pop-up screen tips) are added to each icon to explain the meaning.

Menus

While non-graphical menus have been offered to users ever since the first software applications, they have become much more flexible in GUI environments. The main function of a menu is to allow the user to make a selection from a fixed set of options. It also prevents the user from making an invalid selection.

GUIs offer many types of menu.

■ A **static menu** offers a consistent set of choices throughout the application. It is often placed along the top of the screen or down the left-hand side. The main static menus on websites are often referred to as **navigation bars**.

is selected, and it disappears again when not needed.

■ A **pop-up menu** often appears similar to a pull-down menu, except that it can be positioned anywhere on the screen.

■ A **context-sensitive menu** (Figure 12.14) is a type of pop-up menu, which provides the user with a list of options that depend on the context.

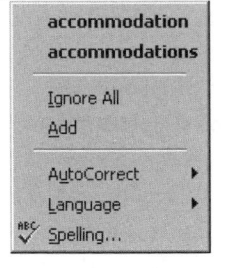

Figure 12.14 A context-sensitive menu

■ **Sub-menus** offer extra choices, which would otherwise overcrowd a menu.

Pointers

The main function of a pointer is to allow the user to make selections on screen, under the control of a pointing device. A pointer is often known as a cursor, especially when editing text.

425

BTEC National Study Guide: IT Practitioners. See page 293 for order details of individual texts

253

> **?** **What does it mean?**
>
> A **pointer** is an icon that is moved around the screen under the control of the mouse or other device.

Pointers are very important in a GUI as the user feels as though he or she is directly carrying out the actions.

Object- and event-driven software

Vector graphics can also be described as **object-oriented** graphics. Each object in a drawing can be manipulated independently of the others; for example you can fill one object, such as a rectangle, with a colour or reposition it, without affecting any other objects on the screen. An object, in this technical sense, possesses properties (such as size, position, colour, transparency) and methods, which are operations that can be applied to the object (such as dragging or rotating).

Object-oriented programming languages, such as Java and C++, let the programmer create objects out of all kinds of things, such as documents, sounds, records, files or even a complete database.

A GUI environment is programmed using an **event-driven** language. An event is an occurrence, like a key press or a click of a mouse, which initiates an action by the operating

sequence, but event-driven software waits for an event to happen before doing anything. Most of the event-driven languages used to create GUIs have object-orientated features. Visual Basic and Delphi are both event-driven languages and are used to build interfaces that conform to the Microsoft Windows standards. Each has some object-oriented elements as well.

Artificial intelligence (AI)

Although the term 'artificial intelligence' is widely used in science fiction, it is important to recognise that it covers a set of advanced software technologies that are already in common use. AI uses rules to analyse problems, much as humans do. As an example, software enables computers to play chess. The simple approach is for the computer system to analyse every single combination of chess moves that could be made from a given position, and then identify those that are more likely to lead to a win. This requires an enormous amount of processing and cannot usually be done in the time allowed. Good chess players do not think in this way. Instead, over time they build up rules for themselves about which moves are likely to be successful; in other words, they learn from their experience. A chess program developed with AI techniques will include the rules that have been developed by a good player. Some chess programs 'learn' by developing further rules from games that they play.

AI is used in HCIs to analyse and interpret inputs. They are able to solve problems in real time that would otherwise take far too long to be useful. An AI application also builds up a database, known as a knowledge base, which contains facts and rules that have been gleaned from experience. Here is a selection of uses of AI in HCIs.

426

BTEC National Study Guide: IT Practitioners. See page 293 for order details of individual texts

254

Interface agents

An interface agent is a software tool, rather like an inbuilt personal assistant, that provides support to the user of an application (Figure 12.15). It learns the user's preferences and habits (by storing them in the knowledge base).

Image analysis

AI techniques are sometimes needed to analyse captured images. For example, in handwriting recognition, the system has to learn the handwriting style of the user and continue to make intelligent guesses about inputs, even though an individual user's handwriting will vary from time to time.

Natural language analysis

Natural language is the ordinary language (in this case, English) that we all use. One of the main aims of AI research is to develop an interface that will allow the user to write or speak in natural language, which will then be interpreted and a response given, also in natural language. With such a system, users would hold conversations with their computers that would appear to be very much like normal human interactions.

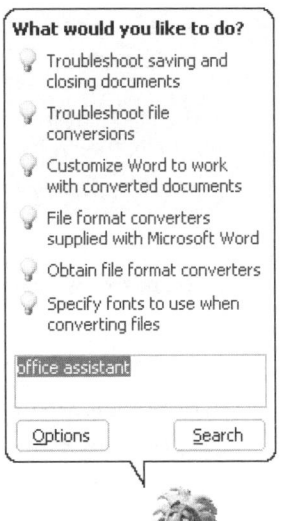

Figure 12.15 An interface agent

means much the same as 'Do you want to go for lunch?'.

■ The meaning of a sentence often depends on the context. 'How's Jim?' will be understood by the hearer who will know who Jim is.

■ In conversation, we express a lot of meaning through non-verbal body language. This may not be so relevant if the user writes the words, but, as speech systems develop, users will tend to treat their computer more and more like a person.

You will have come across the simple natural language interface used by some search engines such as www.ask.co.uk. This takes natural language input from the keyboard, analyses this and converts it into a request for searches.

Further research 12.4

Alan Turing laid down all the foundations of the modern electronic computer when he built machines to decipher German military codes during the Second World War. Even back in 1950, Turing was foreseeing computers playing chess and other aspects of what we now call artificial intelligence.

The Turing Test derived from his thinking about how we judge intelligence. Imagine a user confronted by two computers. The user asks both computers questions (the input method is irrelevant, but a keyboard is the most likely). One of the computers generates its own responses using software; the other one relays the questions to another person sitting in another room, who then sends the answers back. The problem is this: Can the user tell which

427

BTEC National Study Guide: IT Practitioners. See page 293 for order details of individual texts

255

responses come from a human and which come from a computer? If the user cannot distinguish them, then the software can be said to be 'intelligent'.

The Loebner Prize is an annual challenge to produce a software system that is the most human-like in its responses and closest to meeting the conditions of the Turing test. Find out about recent winners of the Loebner Prize, and how convincing their systems were.

Assessment activity 12.1

For this assessment, you should present your findings either in a written report or as a presentation. Your material should cover all these points:

1   Explain what is meant by the human computer interface.
2   Describe a number of different HCIs and the software applications that they support. In each case, explain how the HCI enhances the use of the application.
3   Select at least three specialist environments and describe the hardware and software that is needed to support each. Try to include different types of HCI. For example, you might select a point-of-sale terminal in a particular shop, a games machine in an arcade, and a system used by someone with a disability.

Users

Users can be categorised in several ways.

functions in the software.

- ■ *Familiarity with the system:* A user who is new to a particular system is sometimes referred to as a naïve user.
- ■ *Age:* Children, adults of working age and the elderly respond to systems differently.
- ■ *Usage:* A user of a software package may be using it as a professional, maybe as a business non-specialist, and/or it could be for leisure purposes.

Needs of users

Users' individual needs vary greatly. It is important that an HCI meets the needs of each individual who uses it, but that does pose a problem for HCI designers. How do they design an HCI to meet the individual needs of a wide cross-section of the public?

One approach would be to try to design an interface that will suit everyone. This may seem like a good aim to have, but it can rarely be achieved, except for the simplest of software. A better solution is to design an interface that can be customised to meet individual needs, and this is the solution adopted by most designers. Users can adapt the HCI to suit individual preferences, by, for example, changing the handedness of a mouse, creating a toolbar with their most commonly used buttons, altering the characteristics of the screen display, changing the default font styles, altering the volume and tone of sounds, or altering the sounds themselves.

Some users have special needs, which cannot be catered for so easily using customisable interfaces. They need specially designed HCIs. These users include those with visual impairment, hearing loss, limited motor (movement) control and learning difficulties.

428

BTEC National Study Guide: IT Practitioners. See page 293 for order details of individual texts

256

Applications developments

An HCI designer can draw from many developments in the field of user interaction when assembling an HCI. We will look at some of the key underlying concepts.

Direct manipulation

In many HCIs, the users are given the impression that they are directly controlling the objects on the screen. A user may use the mouse to apparently pick up an object and then move it to somewhere else (also known as 'drag and drop'). Direct manipulation like this makes the interface seem natural and familiar to the user. The techniques are made possible through the use of event-driven programming languages coupled with fast processors and high-resolution screens. Interfaces that use direct manipulation well are sometimes described as **intuitive**.

Metaphors

HCI designers often base their interfaces on real-world situations. Most applications are used in offices, so it does seem sensible to use the familiar language and images of a desktop, such as folder, document and bin. On the other hand, an application created for an artist would be more likely to use terms like palette, canvas, brush and pen.

IT professionals talk of files, directories and programs, but these ideas can be very confusing for a non-technical user. So the GUI designer invents a 'virtual world' that the users understand, employing the images and terms that they use in their work. Icons, often acted

- office desktop
- control panel
- personal organiser
- book
- artist's easel
- workbench
- landscape.

The desktop metaphor is now used widely for operating systems on personal computers. It has also been extended to most office applications. Unfortunately, the metaphor does not always work very well. Programs are referred to as applications, even though the word 'application' would not be used in an office. In addition, terms from other metaphors are often used, such as control panel, task bar and toolbar.

✓ **Check your understanding 12.5**

1 Find examples of each of the types of metaphor listed above.
2 Which ones use the metaphor effectively?
3 Did you find any examples of metaphors that were inappropriate or unhelpful?

Hypertext

The concept of hypertext was developed by Vannevar Bush in 1945, although the actual term was not invented until 20 years later. Scientists across the world were having difficulty in keeping up to date with the rapidly growing body of scientific research. Long before multimedia applications and the **WWW** made use of the concept of hypertext, Bush recognised that individual research papers referred to other papers, which in turn referred to others, linking them all together in a vast information network.

Hypertext was not developed successfully as a technology until the 1980s when it appeared in Help systems and some educational software, using **hyperlinks** on a screen to act as links to other pages of information. Strictly speaking, **hypertext** is a system that uses hyperlinks to link one page of text to another, while **multimedia** or **hypermedia** add images, sounds and other electronic media to the purely textual ones. In practice the three terms are used interchangeably.

What does it mean?

WWW stands for World Wide Web.

A **hyperlink** is a hotspot on a page that links it to other files.

Multimedia

Once hypertext systems had been developed, the way was open for CD-based encyclopaedias

Although the Internet was developed in the 1960s, it was not until Tim Berners-Lee invented the WWW in 1990 that Bush's original vision of a global interconnected system became a reality. The WWW consists of text files written in a hypertext code. A software utility called a browser interprets these files as pages of information with hyperlinks embedded in them. The innovative aspect of the WWW was that these links could link to any other page that uses the same protocol, and this was possible because each page on the Web has its own address, known as its **URL**.

What does it mean?

URL stands for uniform resource locator.

The WWW was always intended to be a multimedia system, and plug-ins can be downloaded today so that any type of file can be shared with any user.

Assessment activity 12.2

Use the Internet, television programmes, books and magazines to research recent developments in the field of HCI. You can also watch out for news about new technologies that are about to emerge.

Present your findings, and make sure you identify the applications and the intended users for whom the HCIs have been designed.

430

BTEC National Study Guide: IT Practitioners. See page 293 for order details of individual texts

258

12.2 HCI and the user

An effective HCI integrates the hardware and software with the humans and with the physical environment. To emphasise the significance of the individual humans in all this, they are sometimes referred to as 'livewire'. Human users have specific skills and needs that must be understood by the designer. The term 'livewire' also suggests that, in some respects at least, humans are a bit like computer systems. In this section, we consider human senses (our input devices), human memory (our storage devices) and human cognition (our processing methods).

Human senses

Human senses are the input methods whereby we capture information about our environment. As mentioned before, humans have five senses, or six if the sense of movement is included. HCI designers work mainly with four of these: vision, hearing, touch and movement. In each case, the sense includes two elements:

■ **Physical reception** – this is how the relevant organs (eye, ear, skin and the movement sensors in the inner ear) receive stimuli from the outside world.
■ **Perception** – this is how the brain interprets the stimulus, so that we interpret it as an image, a sound, an object or motion.

100 million photoreceptors (light sensitive cells). There are two types of photoreceptors: rods, which react to light, even when light levels are low; and cones, which give us colour vision. The rods and cones generate electrical impulses, which travel to the brain along the optic nerve.

Our two eyes are not in the same position, so each receives slightly different stimuli. The images projected on to the back of the eyes are upside down, so, to make any sense of them, the information gathered by the photoreceptors has to be processed by the brain. This processing, called visual perception, also helps us to perceive the size of objects and to work out whether an object is near us or far away. Perception also relates the image to our previous understanding of the world, so we sometimes see what we expect to see, rather than what is actually there.

When designing an HCI, certain aspects of vision have to be considered:

■ The **brightness** of an object is the amount of light it is giving off. Our eyes do not always perceive brightness consistently. The rods and cones in our eyes do compensate for low light levels, so we can perceive the same image as having greater or less brightness depending on the overall level of light.
■ **Contrast** is the comparison of the brightness of two objects.
■ We can distinguish between about 7 million different **colours**. The colour of an object has three components – hue, saturation and brightness (also called intensity). The hue is the actual wavelength of the light which determines whether we see it as blue, red, etc. Saturation is the amount of white in the colour.

431

BTEC National Study Guide: IT Practitioners. See page 293 for order details of individual texts

259

Hearing

Sound waves pass through the canal of the external ear and make the eardrum vibrate. Tiny bones on the other side of the eardrum, in the middle ear, pick up the vibrations and pass them to the inner ear. The inner ear is filled with fluid, and also holds a spiral tube called the cochlea. Tiny hairs called cilia are attached to nerve cells inside the cochlea and these are moved by the vibrations in the fluid. These generate the electrical impulses that go to the brain (Figure 12.16).

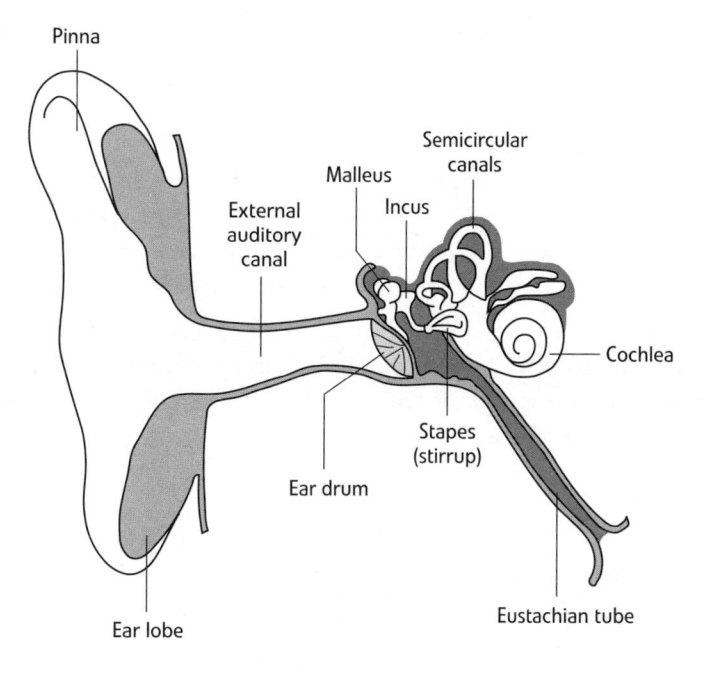

Figure 12.16 The ear

Sound perception processes these signals and interprets them as sounds. We can appreciate a wide variety of sounds, some of which are used with great subtlety in music and speech. Two ears enable us to work out the direction from which a sound originates.

Humans identify the following components of sound:

- **Pitch** is the sound frequency and determines how high or low it sounds. The human ear can hear frequencies in the range 20Hz to 15khz. (One Hz is one cycle, or vibration, per second).
- **Intensity** is the amplitude or loudness of the sound and is measured in decibels. Just as our eyes do not always interpret the brightness of an image consistently, so the way in which we assess the loudness of a sound does depend on the other sounds around it.
- **Quality** (or timbre) depends on how pure the sound is. Most sounds, especially those produced by musical instruments, carry secondary sounds as well, which give them their characteristic tone.

BTEC National Study Guide: IT Practitioners. See page 293 for order details of individual texts

260

Touch

Humans have three types of receptors in the skin which respond to heat, pressure and pain. Some parts of the body, such as the fingers, have a greater concentration of receptors than others and are more sensitive. The nerve endings in the skin send signals to the brain, which are then interpreted as sensations of touching.

Movement

Movement of the body is detected by three semicircular canals, which are also located in the inner ear. The three canals lie in the three perpendicular planes. When the head is moved, the liquid inside the canals moves, and stimulates nerve cells.

Human memory

Human memory is our method for storing information for future recall. Storing and recalling information are not as straightforward as in a computer, because all the information that we hold in our memory is constantly being re-examined and re-interpreted in the light of our experience. We do also genuinely lose memories.

Short-term memory

Short-term (or working) memory stores information for immediate use. When you read from a book, short-term memory holds the previous words so that you are able to make sense of a

of information at any one time.

Some of what we remember in short-term memory is transferred to long-term memory after a few seconds. Information is more likely to be transferred to long-term memory in certain circumstances:

- when it has meaning for the person
- when the person has repeated it out loud (i.e. reframed the information)
- when the person can visualise the information.

Long-term memory

There appears to be no limit to the amount of information that can be stored in long-term memory. It is where we store everything we know. Long-term memory is of two types.

- The memories of events in our lives are held in **episodic memory**. This links together a number of memories that are all associated with the same event, so that when we remember part of the event we also remember the rest.
- The term 'semantic' refers to meaning, and **semantic memory** is our memory of all the facts, rules, concepts and skills that we know. It is our own knowledge base. The concepts that we have are linked to each other and, indeed, we cannot learn a new fact unless we can relate it to something we know already.

How do we retrieve (remember) the right information in memory when we need it? There are two processes.

- We use **recall** when we bring information back from memory.

433

BTEC National Study Guide: IT Practitioners. See page 293 for order details of individual texts

261

- We use **recognition** when some information that we have at present acts as a cue to finding information in long-term memory. The new information is compared with the information that is already known.

Long-term memory is capable of storing memories for a lifetime, so we may wonder how we manage to forget information that we once knew. Sometimes new information seems to interfere with and blot out old information. For example, once you have learned the number of your new mobile phone, you will find it difficult to remember the old one. Sometimes, the emotional content of memories makes them painful and we avoid remembering them. Some researchers believe that we do not forget anything at all, but simply find some information difficult to recall.

Human cognition

Humans process the information that is input through their senses and is stored in their memories. In academic circles, this processing is known as 'cognition', but most of us just refer to it as 'thinking'. Human cognition includes learning, knowing, understanding, reasoning, problem solving, imagining, using language, and planning. We will look at two of these in more detail and then examine why humans make errors.

Reasoning

This is the process of drawing conclusions from information. For example, if you look out of the window and notice that people in the street are putting up umbrellas, you could reason that it has started to rain. You would base this conclusion on your visual perceptions of the

- **Deductive reasoning** takes the facts and rules that we know and moves forward to a conclusion. In the umbrella case, the fact that 'people have put up their umbrellas' together with the rule 'if people put up umbrellas then it must be raining' leads logically to the conclusion that it must be raining.
- You might wonder where the rule about umbrellas has come from, and this is where **inductive reasoning** comes in. Over time, our semantic memories make links and connections between bits of information. If we see two events happening together often enough, we create a rule for ourselves. So, through our lives we will have noted that umbrellas and rain seem to go together and will formulate a rule about them: 'if people put up umbrellas, then it must be raining'. Inductive reasoning is the process of forming a general rule from a number of experiences. The more experiences we have, the more confident we become about our rules.

✓ Check your understanding 12.6

In each of the following scenarios, is deductive or inductive reasoning being used?

1. In other software packages that I have used, a picture of a disk represented saving, so if I click on the disk in this package it will save my work.
2. If I go left at this point I will fall into the dungeon, so I had better go right.
3. In my word processor, some words become underlined with a wavy red line. If I right click on any one of them, up pops an alternative spelling. Therefore, it looks as though the wavy line is telling me that I have made a spelling mistake.
4. Does that ping mean that a new e-mail has arrived in my mailbox?

434

BTEC National Study Guide: IT Practitioners. See page 293 for order details of individual texts

262

Problem solving

This is the process of finding a solution to a problem. We all solve problems every day of our lives, for example, how to travel from A to B, how to pass this unit, or how to avoid speaking to someone we do not like. We may not be aware of the methods we use to solve these problems, but we tend to rely on a few strategies for finding the solutions.

- One strategy is to use trial and error, but in the mind only, and, in this context, it is known as **generate-and-test**. This is the simple approach to playing chess mentioned in relation to artificial intelligence on page 426. You try out all the possible solutions in a systematic way and check whether each works.

- Another approach is to break a problem down into sub-problems and try to solve each one independently. This is the standard approach to writing programs, but it can be used for all kinds of problems.

- Another strategy is to work backwards from the goal. Suppose your problem is choosing which course to take next year. You could start by thinking of the kind of job that you would like to be doing in five years' time. You could then work backwards by finding out what qualifications you would need to enter that profession, and hence what you would need to do to be on the right path.

- If you have met a similar problem before then you can use **reasoning by analogy**. You compare the two problems and check that they are similar enough at the critical points. You then see whether the solution to the previous problem helps you to solve the current

Errors

We are not always successful in finding the solution to a problem, or we arrive at a solution, only to find later that we made a mistake along the way. None of the approaches to reasoning and problem solving is infallible, and any of them can result in errors.

- Some errors arise because we have our facts wrong. This may be due to inaccurate perception. If the 'facts' are then used to make a deduction, then we could find ourselves making an error.

- We may use inductive reasoning to come up with a rule that is simply wrong. This is because each of us only has a limited experience of the world. For example, until you studied this unit you might have believed, based on your own experience, that all HCIs on desktop computers use GUIs.

- The generate-and-test method for solving problems depends on analysing each alternative solution carefully. One simple error at an early stage could mean that no solution is found.

- Breaking a problem down into its sub-problems can lead to error if the sub-problems are not properly defined.

- Reasoning by analogy is fraught with dangers. It assumes that the previous problem and the current one are similar in the respects that matter, but that may not be the case. Analogy is widely used in HCIs, and must be used with care.

435

BTEC National Study Guide: IT Practitioners. See page 293 for order details of individual texts

263

Ergonomics in HCI design

Ergonomics experts look at how humans do their work in their physical environment, so they are interested in office furniture, lighting, heating and the layout of rooms. When they consider people who work with IT, they also study the layout of the computer equipment, the quality of the screen display and the effects that these have on the user's health and well being. As we saw before, HCI includes the physical environment where the computer is used, so ergonomic considerations are a component of HCI.

Sometimes, specialist environments are created for users with special needs, but the vast majority of people share similar work environments. HCI designers have to create environments that would suit potential users whatever their gender, age, height or build. They also have to support many different types of work including rapid data entry, intensive on-screen editing of text and images, information retrieval, e-mail and the use of the telephone. They also have to consider all the other non-IT activities that go on around the computer, such as writing documents, reading books, drinking coffee and talking with colleagues.

The function of a screen display is to enable the user to do work effectively, and the actual layout and appearance of the screen elements can have a significant effect on this.

- **Controls** can be arranged on screen in the sequence in which they should be used. For example, if the user has to key in personal data from a data collection form, then the order of the input boxes should match the order in which the information appears on the document. Data entry errors are easily made when this is not done.
- Some controls, especially buttons that trigger actions, should be grouped with other controls offering similar functions.
- If the same controls appear on several related screens, then they should appear in the same position on each screen.
- Controls that are used more frequently than others should be easy to find.
- Some controls should not be placed next to each other if they have opposing effects. For example, if a 'save' button is placed next to a 'delete' button, then mistakes will inevitably occur.

Text and images should be a suitable size, so that the user can see them without effort. The actual size will depend on the resolution and dimensions of the screen, but should be

436

BTEC National Study Guide: IT Practitioners. See page 293 for order details of individual texts

264

customisable by the user. The brightness and contrast of the display should be comfortable on the eye, and should also be customisable.

Colour should be used carefully. HCI designers have to be aware of the needs of users with achromatic vision (colour blindness) who cannot distinguish between hues. Colour should be used on a screen to enhance the information, but should not usually be used to convey information.

✓ Check your understanding 12.7

Select an application that you use and list all the controls that appear on the screen.

Arrangement of equipment

If users cannot reach the computer equipment easily, or are uncomfortable, then they will not be as productive as they could be.

- **Work surfaces** should be large enough for the tasks to be done, should be clear of obstructions and should have a matt surface. Ideally, it should be possible to raise or lower the work surface to suit the user. There should be sufficient space for a mouse mat.
- **Chairs** should be fully adjustable. The best office chairs can be raised and lowered, the tilt of the seat can be altered and the angle that the back makes with the seat can be changed.
- **Screens** should have brightness controls and be capable of tilt and swivel. They should be

support should be built in to the keyboard or provided separately. The pressure required to depress the keys should be checked; if too much pressure is required then the user's hands will ache, but if too little then the fingers will tend to slip off the keys.

- **Storage** for books, files, manuals, disks, stationery, pens and office equipment should be designed so that items are easy to reach but do not interfere with work.
- **Cabling** should be ducted or fixed in place so that it cannot cause an accident.

Arrangement of users

The seating and work surface, together with the layout of the IT equipment, should allow the user to adopt a comfortable position whilst working (Figure 12.17). The user's feet should be flat on the ground or placed on an angled footrest. Office chairs should be adjusted to give the best position. The top of the screen should be at about the same level as the user's eyes. The screen can be tilted slightly upwards so that the user looks down on to the screen. Looking up for a long period can cause aches in the neck and shoulders. The screen should be placed about an arm's length from the user. The user should try to keep the forearms horizontal. Armrests on a chair can help, but only if they are at the right height.

Figure 12.17 The correct position for a someone using a desk top computer

437

BTEC National Study Guide: IT Practitioners. See page 293 for order details of individual texts

265

Left-handed users should ensure that their equipment is laid out to suit the way they work. Left-handed and ambidextrous mice are available.

Environmental issues

Health and safety regulations cover many aspects of the workplace, such as electrical safety, fire precautions, ventilation, exposure to toxins, and these apply to IT workers as much as anyone else. The HCI designers can take these for granted, but there are some environmental matters that are particularly important for IT workers.

The temperature of the work environment should be controlled. People do not work well if they are too hot or too cold. The ideal temperature is around 21°C. People should not sit close to radiators or doors. Heating and air conditioning systems can also control the humidity. Inappropriate temperatures and humidity can affect the equipment as well as the users.

Background noise can be very distracting, so the workplace should be designed with quiet floor coverings. Open plan offices should have screens to muffle sounds. The equipment itself can sometimes be a problem; whining CPU fans, whirring disk drives and grating printers can all add to stress levels.

The overhead lighting should be satisfactory. Low-frequency fluorescent strip lighting must not be used in rooms that have computer screens because they cause flicker and visual disturbances.

Some years ago, there was concern about the level of electromagnetic radiation that was given off by computer monitors. International recommendations were adopted in the UK and many

Further research 12.5

In 1992, health and safety regulations relating to display screen equipment were introduced in the UK. The regulations require employers to:

- assess and reduce risks
- ensure workstations meet minimum requirements
- plan breaks or changes of activity
- provide eye tests on request (and special spectacles, where the test shows these are necessary for the work)
- provide health and safety information and training.

Find out more about these regulations on www.hse.gov.uk.

Health issues

Computer users can develop physical health problems as a direct result of their work, but these can usually be avoided if care is taken.

Repetitive strain injury (RSI) causes pain in the shoulder, neck, arm, wrist or hand. In some cases, the problem can become permanent. Not surprisingly, some enthusiastic games players develop RSI. Users can avoid RSI by using properly adjustable chairs, by changing position from

438

BTEC National Study Guide: IT Practitioners. See page 293 for order details of individual texts

266

time to time, and by taking frequent breaks, especially from repetitive work at the keyboard. Long periods spent looking at a computer screen can cause eyestrain in the form of headaches and sore eyes. There is no evidence that eyes can actually be damaged by using a computer.

Assessment activity 12.3

1   Select at least three HCIs with which you are familiar. These could be the ones that you looked at in Assessment activity 12.1. In each case, describe how the HCI design meets the needs of the users and helps them to carry out their tasks.

2   Consider other designs that could have been used. In each case, describe these alternative designs and compare them with the design that was used.

Commercial considerations in HCI design and selection

Good HCIs help people to work more effectively. It might seem surprising that some well-run companies still use applications with poor quality interfaces. The reason they do so, is that the decision to upgrade software must be taken on business grounds. A business organisation has to weigh up the costs of upgrading against the benefits that it might bring. The costs will be measured in financial terms. The benefits may also be measured in terms of the money

- **Software upgrades** can be developed in-house or bought as off-the-shelf software applications. If the software already in use carries out all the functions needed by the organisation, then it may be possible to build a new user interface on to the existing system. This is a common approach for upgrading database systems, because the underlying structure of the database (tables and relationships) is developed and stored independently of the user interface (screen forms).

- **Hardware upgrades** may be necessary if the input and output devices are inadequate to support new software. For example, a good GUI should be viewed on a high-resolution screen. Extra memory and backing storage may be needed to support the additional processing.

- **Environmental improvements** can be expensive. New furniture, heating systems, lighting, and flooring may be needed, and complete remodelling of offices may be required.

- **Training** is always necessary when software is changed. An organisation can either send employees to outside training agencies, or provide it in-house. In both cases, the employees will not be doing their normal work while they are being trained, so temporary staff may have to be hired. A good HCI should minimise the amount of training that is needed.

Improved HCIs could bring one or more of the following benefits to an organisation.

- The main reason for investing in new systems is to increase productivity. Employees will be more productive if they can do more work during the day, or if their work is more accurate and requires less correction. These are exactly the aims of HCI designers.

439

BTEC National Study Guide: IT Practitioners. See page 293 for order details of individual texts

267

> **? What does it mean?**
>
> **Productivity** measures the amount of goods or services produced by workers in a given time.

- An effective HCI will give the organisation more control over the quality of output. If users are clear about what they should do when using an application, they are less likely to make mistakes, and more likely to do work that matches the standards laid down.

- Changes happen all the time within organisations; employees are promoted and new staff take on their work, new business develops so the nature of the work may change for some staff, new premises are acquired, and equipment is updated. Through all these changes, it is important that the business systems have resilience to outside pressures, so that the work can carry on uninterrupted. Good HCI designs across an organisation will ensure that old and new employees will continue to use software applications effectively, and will adapt quickly to new ones. This is because the skills learned using an effective HCI can be transferred to other contexts.

Assessment activity 12.4

Write a short report in which you assess the importance of HCI design in society.

12.3 Examples of HCIs

In this section, you will examine the process of creating an HCI and develop some examples yourself.

Project development

All projects go through a number of phases:

- analysis, leading to a requirements specification
- design
- implementation
- testing and evaluation.

This approach does not just apply to ICT projects, but can be used for any project that has to be planned and managed from start to finish. HCI development is always part of a larger project, the end result of which will be an IT application. Indeed, any application should have two main facets, functionality and HCI. The functionality of an application is the tasks that it can perform, while the HCI is the means by which the user can interact with the application to perform those tasks. It is a mistake to design functionality first and then to add the HCI as an afterthought; the two facets should be designed and implemented in conjunction with each other.

The stages in a project are given different names and varying degrees of significance depending on the context. When this process is applied to software projects it is known as the **software life cycle**.

440

BTEC National Study Guide: IT Practitioners. See page 293 for order details of individual texts

268

Traditionally, software projects were developed in a strict sequence. The complete design had to be approved and checked against the specification, before the programmers were allowed to start on the implementation. No changes to the design were allowed once implementation had begun. This disciplined process, known as the **waterfall approach**, ensured that the final product matched the specification exactly.

HCI model design

User-centred design

The traditional waterfall approach to software development is very successful if all the requirements of the system can be established before the design begins. Today, software engineers recognise that this is not usually the case when producing interactive systems, and it is interactive systems that need effective HCIs. The alternative approach to software development for interactive systems is known as user-centred design.

What does it mean?

An **interactive system** is one in which the user and the system communicate with each other throughout a process.

User-centred design is user-centred in two senses:

User-centred analysis

The analysis stage for user-centred design includes four main elements:

- task analysis
- user analysis
- environment analysis
- usability requirements.

The HCI designer will be fully involved throughout the analysis stage.

Task analysis

This studies the way people perform tasks. It can include tasks that are done on the computer as well as related tasks that are purely manual. The description of task is known as a **model** of the task. HCI designers need to know what tasks people want to do when using an IT system, and the sequence in which they carry out those tasks. They can investigate this by reading manuals, observing users at work and interviewing users.

Tasks can usually be decomposed (broken down) into subtasks. Below is an example of task decomposition.

To write a report:

- carry out research
- write the report using word processing software
- check the report

441

BTEC National Study Guide: IT Practitioners. See page 293 for order details of individual texts

269

■ edit the report
■ distribute the report.

The task of writing a report has been decomposed into five subtasks. Each of these can now be broken down further. We usually number the subtasks to show the hierarchy.

To write a report:

1 carry out research
2 write the report using word processing software
    2.1 create a new document
    2.2 write an introduction
    2.3 create the main headings
    2.4 write the text for each section
    2.5 write the conclusion or recommendations
3 check the report
4 edit the report
5 distribute the report.

Subtasks 1, 3, 4 and 5 can also be decomposed (and so could each of the subtasks within subtask 2).

Planning is used to decide the sequence in which the task should be done. So the plan for carrying out the whole task could look like this:

Plan 0:   Do 1, 2, 3 in that order.

Subtask 2 can also be planned. Although the subtasks 2.1–2.5 appear to be in a logical sequence, most people write the introduction last of all. So the plan for this subtask could be:

Plan 2:   Do 2.1, 2.3, 2.4, 2.5, 2.2 in that order.

More decomposition can be done on the task of writing a report, and plans can be drawn up for each subtask. The final version of tasks and plans is known as the **task model**. The task model for an HCI includes all the tasks that should be carried out using the HCI. Once a task model is ready, the HCI can be designed to match the way in which users work.

User analysis

This establishes the needs of the intended user. There is hardly any software that has been designed for the specific needs of a single person, the main exception being systems designed for individuals with complex disabilities. Most software is used by a variety of users, so the problem for the HCI designer is to create, on paper, a user model. This would describe how the typical user would normally be expected to work with the software, but would also cover some variations to allow for human differences.

User analysis identifies all the people who are affected by the application, known as stakeholders. Stakeholders fall into four groups:

■ **Primary users** are people who use the application directly.
■ **Secondary users** use the application indirectly, by receiving output from it or preparing input for it (e.g. the manager who reads a computer-generated report, or a market surveyor who collects data for input).

442

BTEC National Study Guide: IT Practitioners. See page 293 for order details of individual texts

270

■ **Tertiary users** do not use the application but are affected by the system (e.g. the directors of a company, or the general public).

■ **Facilitators** are the technical specialists who design and maintain the system.

Several questions have to be answered about each stakeholder. The following questions would be asked to the primary and secondary users:

■ What role does the person play in the organisation?

■ What task (from the task analysis list) does each person do?

■ What knowledge and skills does each person have?

■ What **work groups** does the person belong to?

■ Does the person have to abide by privacy or security procedures?

What does it mean?

A **work group** is a group of people who work together on a task.

At the end of this process, the designer should have a clear picture of the typical primary and secondary users of the application.

Environmental analysis

This investigates the physical environment where the system will be used:

■ the physical environment, i.e. location, temperature, etc.

using it.

Usability requirements

The concept of usability is central to HCI design. It assesses the extent to which a system supports interactivity. We commonly refer to the 'user friendliness' of interactive interfaces, but that term is used very loosely. Usability is a much more precise technical term, covering similar ideas. The usability requirements are effectively those HCI requirements that can be measured. Usability is defined by an internationally agreed standard as 'the extent to which a product can be used by specified users to achieve specified goals with effectiveness, efficiency and satisfaction in a specified context of use' (ISO 9241).

User analysis will identify the 'specified users', task analysis will identify the 'specified goals', and environmental analysis will identify the 'specified context'. The usability requirements then lay down some rules about what would count as **effectiveness**, **efficiency** and **user satisfaction**. These can then be checked, along with all the other requirements, at the testing stage.

What does it mean?

The **effectiveness** of an HCI (or any other IT development) is the extent to which the user can carry out tasks accurately and completely.

The **efficiency** of an HCI is the amount of resources (especially time) needed to carry out tasks.

User satisfaction is the acceptability of the HCI to the users.

443

BTEC National Study Guide: IT Practitioners. See page 293 for order details of individual texts

271

Below are some possible ways of measuring the usability of an HCI:

Effectiveness:

- percentage of a task completed by a new user
- number of software features used
- ratio of successes to failed attempts to complete a task
- number of times the users seek help.

Efficiency:

- time taken to complete a task
- time taken for a new user to learn to do a task
- number of errors made when carrying out a task.

Satisfaction:

- number of users who prefer the new system
- ratings (e.g. on a scale of 1 to 5) given to the new system by users.

✓ Check your understanding 12.8

1   Describe the components of user-centred analysis.
2   Why is each important in the development of an HCI?

User-centred design and implementation

HCI. The outcomes of the analysis, with the detailed usability specification, enable the designer to produce a design for the HCI. At this stage, it will be a preliminary design and, as we shall see, the design may go through several versions before being finalised.

The designer should answer the following questions:

- What input and output devices should be used in the HCI?
- If non-standard equipment is needed, what should it do and how should it be laid out?
- What style of interaction is needed?
- What should the screen interface look like?
- Are there any environmental design issues?

The aim of all HCI design is to maximise usability. There are a number of techniques that can help the designer to create a good design rather than a mediocre one.

Standards and guidelines

These are rules that can be followed by the designer, although none is, strictly speaking, obligatory.

- Standards are set by national or international bodies, such as the British Standards Institution (BSI) and the International Organisation for Standardisation (ISO). You have already met ISO 9241 which lays down the standards for developing usability (page 443). It also deals with a number of ergonomic issues for people using computers in the office. Another relevant standard is ISO 13407: *Human-centred design processes for interactive systems,*

BTEC National Study Guide: IT Practitioners. See page 293 for order details of individual texts

272

which describes many of the procedures that are mentioned in this section. This states that user-centred design should involve the user at all the stages in the project, from analysis to testing.

The BSI standards that are relevant to HCI are mainly concerned with general health and safety issues, such as BS 1335-2, which deals with the safety requirements of office chairs. There are also several that relate to broader IT issues such as data protection, security, document management and the physical environment, such as BS 7083: *Guide to the accommodation and operating environment for information technology (IT) equipment.*

- Guidelines are not as widely adopted as standards and are produced by individual suppliers or organisations. Both Apple and Microsoft produce HCI guidelines for developers who want to produce software for their platforms. There are several guidelines for producing user interfaces for people with special needs; for example, the World Wide Web Consortium (W3C) publishes its *Web Content Accessibility Guidelines*, which give advice on making a web-style user interface accessible to people with a variety of disabilities.

Iterative design

? What does it mean?

Iterative design is a method for developing software in which a design is implemented and tested with users. In the light of their reactions, the design may be amended, and checked again. In some cases, the specification may also be changed in response to the testing.

before anything is produced, yet it is often difficult to describe the final application so that the client can visualise it in action. HCIs have to be experienced before users can be sure that they meet their needs.

It would clearly be wasteful to develop a full working application first time through and then go back and change the design in response to tests with users. So a cut-down version of the HCI, known as a **prototype**, is developed and checked with users. There are two main methods for developing prototypes, and both can be used at different points in the same project:

- **Storyboards** are created on paper, and are simply drawings of the HCI designs. A series of pictures show how the HCI changes as the result of actions by a user. Storyboards can be produced quickly and cheaply and give the user a good idea of what the final application will look like.
- **Computer-based simulations** are generated using software tools, plus mock-ups of any new hardware devices. The prototype will represent the look and feel of the interface, but will not carry out the functions of the applications. A developer can develop the prototype with any suitable software tool, and is not forced to work with the software that will be used to build the final application.

✔ Check your understanding 12.9

1 What is a prototype?
2 Why do software developers use prototypes when designing HCIs?

445

BTEC National Study Guide: IT Practitioners. See page 293 for order details of individual texts

273

General design issues

There are a number of design issues that the HCI designer may need to consider.

■ Professional users will have different expectations of systems than general users. In the first place, they will be very familiar with their field of work so will need support that relates to their level of knowledge and does not start from the beginning. Second, they will be **power users**, in other words, people who use their systems very efficiently, so prefer to use hot keys instead of mouse-driven menu selections. Third, they will want systems with a high level of functionality, and which match any industry standards.

■ **System navigation** refers to how the user moves from one subtask to another. In a GUI, menus and submenus are commonly used, menu bars display the most commonly used options, and hot key alternatives are provided for the power user. Context-sensitive menus will display only those options that are directly relevant to the action being taken. Normal menus can be made more sensitive to context by greying out options that are not accessible at the time.

■ **Simulators, virtual reality** and **games** all develop their own virtual worlds, and do not have to match the accepted standards for office software. Indeed, they lie at the cutting edge of developments, so can be as innovative as the designers choose.

Design issues for special needs

The 'typical user' envisaged for many HCIs is a healthy, normal sized adult, with no disabilities or learning difficulties. They do not always cater for children, for elderly users, for general public. Some HCIs are designed to meet the specific needs of individuals or groups of users, and particularly for those with special needs.

■ HCIs can be designed for users with **visual impairment**, which may vary from partial to complete blindness. Outputs include screen readers, speech synthesis and Braille printing.

■ Users with **hearing loss** need interfaces that do not rely on sound clues.

■ Speech loss can be overcome with an HCI that incorporates **speech synthesis**.

■ Input devices can be adapted or developed for users with **limited motor control**. A concept keyboard can be programmed so that the touch-sensitive areas are large, and easily used variations on the mouse can be produced. Speech input suits some users. Devices can also be attached to the user's foot or head, exploiting whatever movement is possible. Eye gaze systems have been used successfully by users with very limited movement.

■ People with learning difficulties often benefit from a well-designed HCI. Users with dyslexia work well with GUIs with a high graphical content, and they can use intelligent correction software (built-in to some word processors) to produce text output.

■ Children have needs that are very different from those of adult users, and HCIs for children must take account of these.

User-centred testing

In any kind of IT project, all designs should be subjected to two processes, known as **validation** and **verification**. These are the testing techniques that are used throughout the iterative design process.

BTEC National Study Guide: IT Practitioners. See page 293 for order details of individual texts

274

In this unit, we are only thinking about the HCI, not about the functionality of the application but, of course, validation and verification tests have to be carried out on all aspects of the software.

- **Validation** tests check that the application meets the client's expectations. All aspects of an application can be submitted to the user for testing at the validation stage, but it is a particularly important method for assessing the HCI.

- **Verification** tests check that the application matches the full requirements specification. In traditional software development, this covered the functionality only. Formal program testing is carried out to show that the application performs all the functions accurately, and that it handles normal, extreme and erroneous data.

Case study: Automatic Teller Machine (ATM)

ATMs (or bank cash machines) are terminals that link directly to a bank's main networks.

Figure 12.18 An ATM

The features of the HCI of a typical ATM, like the one in Figure 12.18, include:

- input devices, e.g. card reader, numeric keypad, up to eight additional keys alongside the screen
- output devices, e.g. screen, printer, cash dispenser
- user interface, e.g. a simple GUI (although some non-graphical interfaces can still be found)
- devices laid out so that card, printout and cash are handled on the right
- robust physical design for outdoor public use and to resist theft
- shaped for maximum privacy and readability
- usable by a naïve adult user

447

BTEC National Study Guide: IT Practitioners. See page 293 for order details of individual texts

275

■ not (usually) accessible to wheelchair users, very short people, or users with visual impairment.

The original developers of the ATMs had to work to a specification provided by the bank. This would have detailed the functionality required, e.g. to check the ID and status of the user, to dispense cash up to a limit specified by the account, to display details of the account and to provide printouts of transactions and information. The HCI designers would have worked closely with the application developers to create an environment that would allow the user to carry out transactions quickly and with as few errors as possible. They would have suggested several alternative HCIs, from which they would have chosen the final one.

Look at the ATMs for various banks and building societies and note the variations in HCI design.

1   What alternative input devices are used?
2   Are there variations in the positioning of the devices?
3   How do the screen interfaces differ?
4   Can you suggest why some of these choices were made by the designers?

Assessment activity 12.5

Find three examples of HCIs that meet the needs of different types of user. Imagine that you were the designer who developed each HCI.

requirements in any measurable detail, but you should be able to deduce the intentions in general terms.
2   Do the HCIs match up with the usability requirements?

Development of HCIs

This section explores some of the practical issues around designing an HCI. You will be expected to design your own HCIs for assessment.

An HCI is a window on to an application. For assessment purposes, you are not expected to develop a full application, so you have two options:

1   Design the HCI for an application that you are developing, or have already developed, for another unit. This is the most straightforward option.
2   Design the HCI for a new application. In this case, you should specify the application, but you will not be expected to implement any of the functionality of the application.

In each case, you are expected to go as far as producing a final prototype. You are not expected to implement a fully working HCI.

Selection of correct interface

Before you design an interface, you should carry out a full analysis (task analysis, user analysis and environmental analysis) and then write the usability specification. On the basis

BTEC National Study Guide: IT Practitioners. See page 293 for order details of individual texts

276

of this, you should then make some initial decisions. See page 444 for advice on the choices you need to make.

Selection of correct tools

Prototypes can be demonstrated on paper (storyboards) or on a computer (computer-based simulations).

Some designers like to use graphical design software to draw the screens for a storyboard. Vector drawing packages are usually more suitable than bitmap painting packages, because individual objects, such as pictures of buttons, can be repositioned easily.

Computer-based simulations can be generated using any suitable software. They do not have to be created in the same software that will be used to generate the final application. Computer-based simulations should have clickable buttons and menus that appear to work, in the sense that they jump to another screen or produce a message. However, they do not have to carry out the functionality of the application.

You can create prototypes using any of the following:

■ form design tools in database management systems such as Microsoft Access
■ form design tools in standard office software such as Microsoft Excel or Word
■ customisable toolbars, menus and other components in standard office software
■ web design editors such as Macromedia Dreamweaver
■ event-driven programming languages such as Visual Basic.

Development of working model

You then need to go through a period of evaluation of your prototype. For more details on how to carry out an evaluation see page 450. You may go back and change the design as the result of the evaluation.

Carry on until you are satisfied with the prototype. For assessment purposes, you are not required to create a working application, but if you are developing the application for another unit, you may like to implement it fully.

Assessment activity 12.6

1 Design HCIs for one or more applications. Page 441 describes the steps you should take when preparing a design, and page 444 gives you some practical advice for this activity. Note that you do not have to implement the application (although you can design an HCI for an application that you have developed for another unit). You should take the design to the point where an on-screen prototype of screen interactions responds to events, even if it does not process any data. Designs for non-standard input and output devices should be drawn on paper and, if appropriate, simple mock-ups can be built.

Your designs should, between them, cover at least three different input methods and at least three different output methods. Keep detailed notes of all stages of the projects and provide full evidence of the analysis, design, prototyping and evaluations that you carried out.

2 Write a short report analysing your HCI designs, picking out any unusual or non-standard features. Compare them with other solutions to the same problems.

449

12.4 Evaluate the effectiveness of HCI models

Evaluation is an alternative term for the validation processes that are part of the testing stages. It is not simply an informal assessment of what worked and what did not work. Instead, it is a structured process for comparing the design with the usability requirements. User-centred design involves the user at all stages. It also uses iterative design methods, which means that designs are prototyped then evaluated, and this process is repeated until the final design is agreed.

Evaluation of an HCI

Usability is 'the extent to which a product can be used by specified users to achieve specified goals with effectiveness, efficiency and satisfaction in a specified context of use', and usability requirements lay down some rules about what counts as effectiveness, efficiency and user satisfaction. Therefore, evaluation of an HCI focuses on effectiveness, efficiency and user satisfaction.

■ **Walkthroughs**. An evaluator presents a user with a prototype of the HCI and asks the user to carry out some tasks. The user has to explore the prototype and learn to use it. There are two ways of managing a walkthrough. In the first, the evaluator observes the user, but does not give any help. In the second, known as co-operative evaluation, the evaluator prompts the user by asking 'what-if?' questions and can help if necessary.

■ **Interviews**. Any formal discussion between two people can be described as an interview. For HCI evaluation purposes, the evaluator prepares questions in advance about the tasks that the user has to do.

■ **Questionnaires**. Questions can be general, open or closed. General questions ask for simple factual information (e.g. When did you join the company?). Open questions simply leave space for the users to say whatever they like in response (e.g. What improvements could be made to the interface?). Closed questions allow the users to select from a fixed number of options. Closed questions can be posed as multiple-choice questions, where the users can select from several possible options, with tick boxes for the responses.

Evaluating effectiveness

Effectiveness is best evaluated through walkthroughs, although some useful additional information can be gained from interviews and questionnaires. The evaluator is trying to discover whether the HCI enables the users to do their tasks accurately, using the correct

450

BTEC National Study Guide: IT Practitioners. See page 293 for order details of individual texts

278

functions and without making mistakes. An evaluation of effectiveness should provide answers to these questions:

■ What percentage of each task did each new user manage to complete?
■ If several users tried the same task, what was the ratio of success to failure?
■ How many options (buttons, menu choices, etc.) did the user try before discovering the 'right' way of carrying out a task?
■ How many errors (e.g. incorrect key presses) were made by a user for each task?
■ How many software features were used by each user?

Evaluating efficiency

Efficiency can be measured by carefully analysing walkthroughs. The evaluator needs to know whether the user is carrying out the task in the shortest possible time and with the least effort. An efficient user will be more productive – he or she will be able to do more work for the same amount of effort.

An efficiency evaluation will answer questions like these:

■ How long did it take for a user to learn how to do a task?
■ How long did it take for a user to complete each task, having learned how to do it?
■ What percentage of the time taken to do a task was spent making errors?
■ What percentage of the time taken to do each task was spent finding out what to do next?

The users might also provide some ideas in their interviews and questionnaires about how tasks could be simplified.

User satisfaction is best evaluated through a questionnaire with closed questions. It could ask users to rate various aspects of the HCI on a scale from 1 to 5. For example, they could be asked questions like those shown in Table 12.2.

	5 Strongly agree	4 Agree	3 Neither agree nor disagree	2 Disagree	1 Strongly disagree
I found it easy to carry out the task.					
I was able to find help when I needed it.					
I could find my way around all the screens.					
It was easy to see what each button was for.					
The colours used on the screen did not distract me from the task.					
The messages that the system gave me were easy to understand.					
Overall, I found the system easy to use.					

Table 12.2 Example questionnaire to evaluate user satisfaction

451

BTEC National Study Guide: IT Practitioners. See page 293 for order details of individual texts

279

The responses to these questions are often known as **satisfaction ratings**, especially to general questions like the last one. The responses can be analysed by comparing the numerical values and calculating the mean for a group of users. The HCI designer should certainly take action if satisfaction ratings are 3 or less.

Alternative techniques for evaluation

So far, we have been thinking about how to evaluate HCIs that are aimed at the general user, but some HCIs are developed to meet the needs of users with specific disabilities, or even for individual users. In these cases, walkthroughs, interviews and questionnaires should still be used, but they can be augmented by other methods of evaluation.

For such projects, the usability requirements must be developed with great care. The HCI designers will have worked with the user (or a group of typical users) to establish the specific needs, but will also have talked to experts. The usability requirements will themselves be thoroughly discussed with both users and experts. Evaluation will be carried out at all stages of the project. So we can see that systems designed to meet special needs should be subjected to even more rigorous evaluation than systems for the general user. Two alternative evaluation techniques can also be used for general systems but are particularly valuable for systems developed for specific needs.

- **Heuristic evaluation.** Several evaluators work independently with an early prototype. They should all be experts in the type of needs that the HCI addresses. Each evaluator applies

  can be used to identify usability problems. The evaluators then compare their findings. In practice, it has been found that five evaluators will between them uncover 75 per cent of usability problems.

- **Review-based evaluation.** There has been a great deal of research into HCIs and also into the needs of users with a variety of special needs. The designer should research all the relevant expertise and academic knowledge, and find out whether similar systems have been built before and how successful they were.

Further research 12.6

1 Use the Internet or books to find Jakob Neilson's ten usability heuristics.
2 Use the ten heuristics to analyse your own HCI designs.

Assessment activity 12.7

1 Refer back to one of the HCIs that you designed. Carry out a full evaluation of it.
2 Describe the role of verification and validation in the development of an HCI and explain why it is important that they are done.

452

BTEC National Study Guide: IT Practitioners. See page 293 for order details of individual texts

280

Test your knowledge

1   What are the main factors that must be considered when designing an HCI?
2   What are the advantages of ergonomically designed keyboards over standard ones?
3   What is a smart card? Describe three different uses for a smart card.
4   Where can you find a handwriting recognition system, and why is it used in that context?
5   What are the main features of a data glove?
6   What is the difference between speech recognition and speech synthesis?
7   What is virtual reality?
8   Why do images and sound files take up so much memory? What techniques can be used to reduce their size?
9   Identify at least three non-graphical user interfaces that are still in use today.
10   What is the difference between a pointer and a pointing device?
11   Some programming languages are object-orientated and event-driven. Explain the two terms.
12   Outline some uses for artificial intelligence in HCIs.
13   Outline the hardware and software that would be needed for a system that could hold a conversation in spoken natural language with a user.
14   What are the main components of colour and sound?
15   What is the difference between long-term and short-term memory in humans?
16   Describe how a workstation in an office should be laid out.
17   What are the possible costs and benefits to an organisation of upgrading a system to one

user-centred approach?
19   What is usability?
20   Distinguish between verification and validation in the context of testing software.

BTEC National Study Guide: IT Practitioners. See page 293 for order details of individual texts

281

BTEC National Study Guide: IT Practitioners. See page 293 for order details of individual texts

282

TEN STEPS TO A GREAT IVA

What is the IVA?

IVA stands for **Integrated Vocational Assignment**. This is a specific piece of work you will do for your BTEC National qualification.

The IVA is set by Edexcel, marked by your tutors and the assessment is checked by Edexcel. The IVA is **compulsory**. You cannot gain the complete award unless you attempt it. Obviously, though, you should do a lot more than just attempt it! Indeed, it is sensible to aim as high as you can. You might even surprise yourself.

This guide gives you hints and tips on researching and completing your IVA so that you will target all your efforts productively. In other words, you won't waste time doing things that aren't needed or you weren't intended to do! This doesn't mean that you can get by without doing any work at all. It does mean that you will get the maximum benefit for the work that you do.

Step 1: Understanding the basics

The IVA is a set of tasks you have to do. The tasks only relate to one or two specific units. These are identified on the front cover of the IVA. You will only be expected to complete tasks after you have learned about the unit(s) in class.

The IVA *must* be all your own work. If you have to do part of the work as a member of a group then the conclusions you write must be your own. If any part of the work has been done with someone else this must be clearly stated. This also means that you should not share your ideas or your researched information with anyone or copy anyone else's work

The IVA is not an examination. It is a series of tasks that you have to do to check that you understand the information you have learned. If you can demonstrate that you can apply and use this information in more than one situation and make informed judgements then you will gain a higher grade. You will be expected to research your own information to add to the work you have done in class. However, you must always list and identify your sources and never try to pass them off as you own work. How to do this is shown under Step 4.

You can produce your IVA over a period of time. Your tutor will tell you how long you have to complete it when it is issued. Make sure you know your deadlines for each stage and for any reviews that you have with your tutor. These will be included on a **Centre IVA Issue Sheet** that your tutor will give you. It also includes information about the resources you can use and support that is available to you. Keep this sheet safely and enter all the dates into your diary or onto your wall planner immediately. It is also sensible to enter a 'warning' a week before each important date, to remind yourself that it is looming!

Always remember that if you have any worries or concerns about your IVA then you should talk to your tutor. Don't wait for the next review date to do this – especially if the problem is serious.

1

BTEC National Study Guide: IT Practitioners. See page 293 for order details of individual texts

283

> **Help yourself . . .**
>
> . . . by making sure you possess a diary or wall planner on which you can write deadline dates when you receive your Centre IVA issue sheet.

Step 2: Obtaining your IVA

You are unlikely to be expected to start your IVA until you have completed most, if not all, of the unit(s) to which it relates. However, you might be given it sooner so that you know what to expect and you can see the actual tasks you will have to answer.

You can see the IVA at any time, yourself, by logging onto the Edexcel website at www.edexcel.org.uk . Click on to 'qualifications', then select 'BTEC National' then click on the subject you are studying. The document you want is entitled *IVA – Learner Instructions*. It is normally quite short, between 8 and 10 pages, and contains the following information.

- The title page, which gives you

    - the level and title of your BTEC National qualification
    - the subject
    - the unit(s) to which the IVA relates
    - the date of issue and specification to which it relates. Ask your tutor if you are not sure whether this matches your course.

- Full instructions for completing and presenting the IVA. This is on page 2. It is very important that you read this carefully.

- Your assignment tasks and a copy of the assessment criteria grid(s). You will find out more about these under Step 3.

> **Help yourself . . .**
>
> . . . by starting a special IVA file that includes the IVA, the Centre IVA issue sheet and any specific notes your tutor gives you relating to the IVA.

Step 3: Understanding the tasks

This is the most important step of all. If you don't understand what you have to do to answer a question then you are very unlikely to get a good grade. You may do a lot of work but much of it may be irrelevant or – more likely – you will miss out important information.

It is quite normal for students to panic when they first read a set of assignment tasks! For this reason you are likely to be introduced to your IVA in a special session held by your tutor. Although your tutor cannot do the work for you (obviously!) you are allowed to receive guidance and can discuss general ideas, just like you would for an internal assessment. Your tutor can also answer any queries you have and give you ongoing advice and support in your review sessions to help you to do your best.

All IVAs are written in a certain format, or design.

- They start with a scenario or context to 'set the scene'. This may be quite short – just a few lines – or take up most of a page.

BTEC National Study Guide: IT Practitioners. See page 293 for order details of individual texts

284

- Below this are several tasks. Each task usually starts with some introductory or background information and is then divided into lettered sub-sections.

- You are often expected to provide your answer in a specific document, such as a report, a letter, a leaflet, a table or a summary.

- At the end of each task you will see the unit number and assessment criteria covered by that task, eg Unit 2, P1, M1, D1. In this case it would mean that particular task related to Unit 2 and your answer must focus on providing evidence against the first assessment criterion under each of the pass, merit and distinction columns. You can match up this information in the assessment criteria grid(s). Your tutor will show you how to do this if you are not sure.

You will not be expected to do all the tasks at once. Let's assume you have been told to start with Task 1. There are two things you can do to make sure you understand *exactly* what you have to do.

1 Break the task down into chunks and analyse it.

2 Complete a task checklist before you start work.

You will read how to do this in Steps 4 and 5.

Help yourself . . .

. . . by first reading all the tasks you will have to do to get the overall picture and then reading – far more carefully – the first task you have to do. Then note down anything that puzzles you or that you do not understand.

Step 4: Analyse the task

Although IVAs aren't meant to be daunting or difficult to understand, it can be useful to know what to do if you do experience any problems. If a scenario or a task is short it is normally easier to understand. If it is long it may be more difficult. This is because there is more 'additional' information and if you miss any of this, it may affect your grade.

If there is a lot of information don't expect to understand it fully the first time you read it. Just read it to get a general impression. Then read it again, more slowly, to get the meaning. It is often helpful to go through it again, much more thoroughly, to identify the important words. This is called **task analysis**. The aim is to identify:

- the **background information** – which sets the scene or the context. You need to understand this for the task to make sense

- the **command words**, such as 'describe' or 'explain' – which tell you what you have to do. You *must* obey these when you answer the questions. If you are unsure what any of these words mean, check back to the explanation in *The Smart Way to Achieve Your BTEC National* at the start of this book

- other **specific instructions** which tell you what you have to do – such as 'provide three examples' or 'write a report'

- any important **topic words** which give you the subject of the task.

Finally, make sure you now understand the purpose of the task you have to do and the audience you are preparing it for. Both these factors affect the way you will structure and present your answer.

BTEC National Study Guide: IT Practitioners. See page 293 for order details of individual texts

285

Task 1: Prove your understanding of the IVA

Edexcel issues an assessment called an IVA that covers the whole of either one or two units of a BTEC National programme. This tests all learners nationally on the same set of tasks. <u>Produce a short report</u> *which identifies* <u>your own tasks in relation to your IVA.</u> <u>Your report should include:</u>

a A <u>brief</u> **description** <u>of the IVA.</u>

b An **explanation** <u>of the main instructions given to learners.</u> This <u>must include</u> the **identification** <u>of</u> <u>three</u> <u>requirements which ensure that each IVA is the student's own original work.</u>

c <u>Your own plan</u> <u>for producing your IVA which shows how you have</u> **analysed** <u>your options and provides</u> **justifications** <u>for the decisions you have made.</u>

Background information which sets the scene.

To produce a short report, and what the report should include are both <u>instructions</u>. <u>Your own tasks in relation to the IVA</u> are topic words

'Brief' is an instruction, 'of the IVA' is the topic. 'Description' and 'explanation' are both **command words**. 'Must include' is an instruction but 'identification' is a command word. The remaining words are topic words except for 'three' which is an instruction.

'Your own plan' is an instruction. The remaining words give you the topic. This must involve 'analysis' and 'justification', so these are both **command words**.

Help yourself . . .

. . . by practising task analysis yourself.

In agreement with your tutor, select **one** task in the IVA you have been issued and carry out the following tasks.

a Identify the background information, command words, instructions and topic words that it contains. You can use any combination of colour or highlighting (such as bold or underscore) that you find easiest to understand.

b Explain the purpose of that task and identify your audience. Then say how these two factors will influence your answer.

c Compare your ideas with those of other members of your group.

Step 5: Completing a task checklist

This will confirm if you really do understand what you have to do. Simply read the following list. If you can complete the column on the right with ticks then you understand the task. If you can't then you must resolve the problem before you start work.

BTEC National Study Guide: IT Practitioners. See page 293 for order details of individual texts

286

Checklist for understanding your IVA task		✓ or x
Read the scenario or context that 'sets the scene'	Does it make sense? Do you understand all the words used? Can you identify the key words? Would it help you to highlight these? Could you accurately explain the scenario or context to someone else, using your own words?	
Read the task you have to do and then analyse it	Have you carried out task analysis? Can you identify the background information? Can you identify *all* the command words? Can you identify *all* the instructions? Do you understand the topics? Can you clearly state what you have to do, using your own words? Do you know how to set out the document(s) you have to produce?	
Do you know the purpose of the task and have you identified your audience?	Can you explain the reason for doing this task? Who is your audience? How will these two factors affect your answer?	
Check the evidence statement at the bottom of the task and check this against the assessment criteria grid	Do you know the grades you can get for this task? Can you see how the command words differ within the task to cover merit and distinction questions? Are you *certain* that you know what is meant by each command word?	

- If you don't understand a word that is used then look in a dictionary or check the list of command words and their meanings given in *The Smart Way to Achieve your BTEC National*.

- If there is any instruction that you do not understand, such as how to set out a document that is required, talk to your tutor.

- If there is any aspect of the topic that you missed when it was covered in class then talk to your tutor about obtaining the information you need.

Help yourself . . .

. . . copy the checklist and complete it for the first task on your list. Remember that you *must* obtain help if you still cannot understand anything about the task you have to do.

Step 6: Planning your work

Completing any task(s) will take some time. You have to allow enough time for obtaining the information, deciding what to use, getting it into the right order and writing it up. You also need to bear in mind the review date(s) agreed with your tutor – as well as all the other college and personal commitments you have! It is therefore sensible to make a plan.

- The IVA is designed to cover the unit content and each task covers different parts of the unit. You can check which parts of a unit are covered by a particular task by looking at the key words. These will relate to the assessment criteria for the unit and the unit specification, which gives detailed information on the content.

BTEC National Study Guide: IT Practitioners. See page 293 for order details of individual texts

287

- Next estimate how long it will take you to find the information you need. You will do this more accurately if you identify your information sources. Although this will obviously depend on the format of your IVA and the task you are doing you will probably want to refer to

  - notes you have been given in class
  - your course textbook
  - two or three library books or journals
  - some online resources.

  If you are researching for a project or need to use evidence from a particular event then you may need to arrange to talk to people to get their views. You must therefore allow enough time to obtain your information.

- Decide how long it is likely to take to sort through your information before you can start to write your first draft answer.

- Allow time for rereading and revising your answer and then for checking the way you have presented the information.

- Decide how many hours a week you will need to spend on your IVA to stay on schedule.

- Split these up into sensible sessions. Longer than two or three hours is too much – you won't work well when you're tired. Shorter than half an hour isn't much good unless you've a specific small job to do.

- Identify times during the week when you will do the work and mark these in your diary or on your wall planner, eg Tuesday 5 pm – 7 pm. Then stick to them! If an emergency means you can't work at that time remember that you then need to reschedule these hours at another time to keep on target!

Help yourself . . .

. . . by always allowing more time than you think you will need, never less. You should also find a quiet place to work, where you can concentrate. Now make out your plan for the first task you have to do. Aim to finish a week early to allow time for slippage.

Step 7: Researching, storing and selecting your information

Problems with researching are always linked to the quality and quantity of information. For information to be good quality it needs to relate directly to the topic. You also need to understand it! Quantity is also important. If you only rely on your course notes then you are unlikely to produce original work and this will affect your grade, but too much information is very confusing and you are likely to get bogged down trying to decide what to use.

Start by listing all the potential sources of information you can use. These will depend largely upon the type of task you are doing and the information you need.

- If you are looking for books you are best to aim for two or three that specifically cover the topic. Check this by looking in the index when you are in the library, then skim the text to make sure it is written at the right level and that you find the style 'user-friendly'. You are wise to schedule in a prompt visit to your college library – particularly if there are many students doing the same IVA as you!

- If you are searching online you will have far more success if you learn how to do advanced searches on websites such as Google. It is also important to keep focused and not get distracted by interesting but irrelevant information you come across as you search! If you need help searching on line, talk to the IT resource staff at college.

- If you need to visit organisations or interview someone then prepare well in advance. Make the arrangement and then draft a list of questions. If you want to take a tape recorder, first check this is acceptable.

BTEC National Study Guide: IT Practitioners. See page 293 for order details of individual texts

288

- If you are preparing a presentation that involves other people in your group arrange a first meeting to decide your roles and responsibilities. Check in your library for useful guidelines on preparing and giving a presentation.

- Buy a box file and label it. If you are broke use an empty cardboard box! Put in every scrap of information that might be helpful for your IVA. If your IVA covers two units then you might find it helpful to keep the information that relates to each one in separate folders.

- Make sure that all the information you put into your box file is dated and labelled with its source (see below). This includes any photocopies you have taken or print-outs you have made.

- Have a cut-off date when you stop collecting information and start to write. If you don't, you can easily find yourself running out of time to complete the task.

- Only select the most relevant information after re-reading the task *and* your task analysis. It's often easiest to start by spreading out all your information on a large table (or the floor!). Then select everything you think you might need and put the rest away.

- Read through your information and make draft notes to answer the question. *Don't* copy out reams of information – note down the source of the information instead. Remember that most of your IVA must be in your own words.

- Make sure you only include relevant information and that you re-word or adapt information to match the task you are doing. It is very tempting to 'cut and paste' lots of information, particularly from the Internet, just because you found it! A good trick is to keep looking back to the question at regular intervals to keep yourself focused and *never* include everything 'just 'cos it's there'! Remember that marks are always awarded for quality of work, not quantity!

> ## *Help yourself . . .*
>
> . . . by being self-disciplined when you are looking for information. This means not getting distracted, *always* noting down the source of information you print out or photocopy and *always* storing it safely so you can find it again!

Step 8: Identifying your sources

You must do this if you quote from any source. If you forget then you could be guilty of plagiarism. This is a serious academic crime as it is assumed that you were trying to pass off someone else's work as your own. It is so serious that some colleges and universities have installed special software to catch plagiarists!

Your tutor or your college library will be able to give you detailed information on citing references. If not, use the following as your guide.

In the text:

- Always put quoted information in quotation marks. Mark Twain said 'There are lies, damned lies and statistics.'

- If you refer to an author put their name and then the date and/or page number in brackets. Chaffey (2002) argues that . . . .

At the end of the task, in your bibliography, list your references in alphabetical order of author. Put the title in bold or in italics so that it stands out.

- If your source is a newspaper or magazine, state the name of the author(s), year of publication in brackets, title of the article, the title of the publication, volume or date, pages of the article eg Gascoigne, C (2005) **Leading from the front**, Sunday Times Smarter Business, 6 February 2005, page 7.

- If your source is a book, give the author(s), date of publication in brackets, title and the publisher eg Chaffey, D (2002) **E-Business and E-Commerce Management**, Prentice Hall, page 25.

- If your source is from the Internet then you should give enough information for your tutor to be able to find the article online. However, you are also wise to keep your print-out as Internet sites are regularly updated and you may need proof of your information. It is recommended that you give the name of the person or organisation responsible for the article or site, the title of the document, the word Internet in square brackets, the URL and the date you accessed the information. This is the address line that shows on screen and is normally printed at the bottom of the page eg Sport England, **What the 2012 Olympics would do for the UK**, [Internet], http://www.sportengland.org/index/news_and_media/olympics_2012/2012_uk.htm [Accessed 7 February 2005]

Help yourself . . .

. . . by checking if there is a course or college guide to citing references. Ask your tutor or librarian if you are not sure. Alternatively you can test your research skills by finding information online. Type 'Harvard referencing' into any search engine. This is the most usual method used by students at university.

Step 9: Writing and presenting your IVA

The first thing to do is to plan your answer. Re-read your task analysis to refresh your memory. Check carefully the command words, the instructions and the topic words. Make sure you know what type of document you have to produce and how to set it out.

There are two ways in which you can plan your answer. Use the one that is most natural for you:

1 Write a list of all the information you want to include. Then put it into the correct order. Decide what will go in the introduction, what in the middle of the answer and what your conclusion will be.

2 Write the question in the middle of the page and write your information around it. Link the information with arrows so you end up with different themes. Decide the best order to introduce each theme and how these will be reflected in your paragraphs.

If you find that you are missing any information write this on a 'to do' list. You can still plan and draft your answer. Your 'to do' list is to make certain you don't forget to find out the remaining details.

Decide the approach you want to use. For example, if you have to contrast and compare two things then you could write all about one and then the other; alternatively you could describe each one and then analyse the similarities and differences afterwards. *Neither is right or wrong* – do the one you find easier. If you find that it then doesn't work very well when you start to draft your answer, be prepared to change it.

Don't think that you need to write in a more flowery or grandiose style than you normally do. In fact, there are lots of pitfalls if you do this – such as using the wrong word or writing a complex sentence that no-one can understand! Instead, keep your writing style simple and only use words you understand. If you also keep your sentences relatively short but vary the length a little then your answer will also be more interesting and easier to read.

Don't expect to write the answers to merit and distinction level questions quickly. These are deliberately written to make you think! Look back at the command words information and examples in *The Smart Way to Achieve your BTEC National* if you are struggling. Then draft your answer as best you can and discuss your ideas with your tutor at your next review meeting. This might help to put you on the right track again.

The type of task and your audience will determine your writing style. If you are asked to prepare a formal business document such as a report it is better to use a quite formal writing style. In this case try to write using the third person. This means you don't say 'I think that ' but 'it is considered that' or 'it would appear that'. Equally you wouldn't say 'You can do this by . . .' but 'This could be done by . . .'. The situation is different, though, if you are preparing an informal account, such as an article for a staff newsletter. In every document, though, you should avoid using slang or contracted words (eg can't or hasn't) and *never* use the abbreviated words or jargon that you would use in a text message or if you were talking to your friends.

BTEC National Study Guide: IT Practitioners. See page 293 for order details of individual texts

290

Leave your work alone for a day or two before you make a final check. This way you are more likely to spot errors. You may also find this easier to do if you take a print-out rather than read it on screen. Check it against the question. Have you obeyed all the command words? Have you included everything that was asked for? Is the information given in a logical order?

Now check the presentation and your writing style. Have you set out the document correctly? Is it in the right style? For example a letter or report must be set out in the right format and not written as an essay style answer. Is the grammar correct? Is every word spelt properly? Don't rely on your spellchecker here. It cannot tell the difference between 'hear' and 'here' or 'there' and 'their'! Word processing packages are also very limited in their ability to correct grammatical errors, so never assume that you don't need to check your work carefully yourself. If you are preparing a draft print-out to discuss with your tutor it is useful to use wide margins and double spacing then you have plenty of room to note down comments.

Make sure you have included a sheet with all your references on it. It is usually easier to compile this as you go – rather than create these at the end when some notes will be buried under a mountain of paper.

Finally check that the presentation of your IVA matches *all* the requirements set out on page 2 of your *Instructions for Learners completing IVAs*. For example, you must not put your work into plastic pockets or into a box file or a lever arch file. You also need to put a cover sheet on the front and sign a declaration that all the work you are submitting is your own.

Help yourself . . .

. . . by asking someone you trust to read through your work and make comments. This can be a close friend or a family member but shouldn't be a fellow student who is doing the same IVA as you. If your friend or relative can't understand what you are trying to say then it is probably true that your tutor will have the same problem!

Step 10: Is this the best you can do?

It always seems a tragedy when students just miss a better grade because of carelessness or silly mistakes. As a final check, before you give in your work, run through the following list. Only hand in your work when, hand on heart, you know you honestly couldn't do any more.

- You have incorporated all the suggestions and ideas that you discussed with your tutor at your review meetings.
- You have answered every part of every task and there are no gaps or omissions.
- You have addressed all the command words correctly and taken account of all the instructions.
- You have checked the spelling, punctuation and layout.
- You have checked and double-checked that all the references are included.
- All your pages are numbered and your name is on every sheet.
- You have followed every other instruction for completing and presenting your work. Do a final check of page 2 of your *Instructions for Learners completing IVAs* before you hand in your work. For example, are all your pages in the right order and are they securely fastened together?

Help yourself . . .

. . . by handing in your work before the deadline and then relaxing! Once you have done your best and submitted your work you cannot then alter the grade for that particular piece of work. Remember, though, that the grade you achieve is very important feedback for future work you will do. Learn from your mistakes and build on your successes – and your work will always continue to improve.

BTEC National Study Guide: IT Practitioners. See page 293 for order details of individual texts

291

BTEC National Study Guide: IT Practitioners. See page 293 for order details of individual texts

292

BTEC National Study Guide

IT PRACTITIONERS

The Units in this Study Guide are taken from a variety of books. If you found any to be of help, then follow the instructions to purchase a copy.

Unit 2 Computer Systems comes from

BTEC National IT Practitioners
by Sharon Yull and Howard Anderson, published by Newnes

If you liked this book, and would like to order a full copy, either go to your local bookshop and quote the ISBN number: 0 7506 5684 0 or order online at www.newnespress.com

Unit 4 Introduction to Software Development comes from

BTEC National IT Practitioners
by Geoff Knott and Nick Waites, published by Brancepeth Computer Publications Ltd

If you liked this book, and would like to order a full copy, either go to your local bookshop and quote the ISBN number: 0 9538848 2 1 or order online at www.bcpublications.co.uk

Unit 10 Applications Software Development and Unit 12 Human Computer Interface both come from

BTEC National IT Practitioners
Edited by Jenny Lawson and published by Heinemann Educational Publishers

If you liked these units and would like to order a full copy of one of the Heinemann *BTEC Nationals: IT Practitioners* texts (select the book that matches the Certificate or Diploma you are studying – see p vi for details) either go to your local bookshop or order online at www.heinemann.co.uk